Sephardic and Mizrahi Jewry

Sephardic and Mizrahi Jewry

From the Golden Age of Spain to Modern Times

EDITED BY

Zion Zohar

New York University Press

NEW YORK AND LONDON

*This book is dedicated to our beloved parents
Rosa and Shim'on Saraf, z"l
Marsela-Chaviva and Shlomo Ezra, z"l
May their memory be blessing for us all
With love, Rina and Yoel Saraf*

NEW YORK UNIVERSITY PRESS
New York and London
www.nyupress.org

© 2005 by New York University
All rights reserved

Library of Congress Cataloging-in-Publication Data
Sephardic and Mizrahi Jewry : from the Golden Age of Spain to modern times / edited by Zion Zohar.
p. cm.
Includes bibliographical references and index.
ISBN 0-8147-9705-9 (cloth : alk. paper)
ISBN 0-8147-9706-7 (pbk. : alk. paper)
1. Jews—Spain—History. 2. Sephardim. 3. Jews, Oriental.
I. Zohar, Zion.
DS135.S7S4525   2005
909'.04924046—dc22   2005001776

New York University Press books are printed on acid-free paper, and their binding materials are chosen for strength and durability.

Manufactured in the United States of America

10 9 8 7 6 5 4 3 2 1

Contents

Acknowledgments   *vii*

PART 1: Sephardic Jewry in the Middle Ages: Origins, Development, and Flowering

1. A Global Perspective on Sephardic and Mizrahi Jewry: An Introductory Essay   3
   Zion Zohar

2. The Origins of Sephardic Jewry in the Medieval Arab World   23
   Mark R. Cohen

3. The Judeo-Arabic Heritage   40
   Norman A. Stillman

4. Judeo-Spanish Culture in Medieval and Modern Times   55
   David M. Bunis

5. Literatures of Medieval Sepharad   77
   Jonathan P. Decter

6. Medieval Sephardic-Oriental Jewish Bible Exegesis: The Contributions of Saadia Gaon and Abraham ibn Ezra   101
   Isaac Kalimi

7. Jewish Philosophy and Kabbalah in Spain   120
   Moshe Idel

PART II: From Expulsion to the Modern Era: Exile, Decline, and Revival

8 Hispanic Culture in Exile: Sephardic Life in the Ottoman Balkans 145
   Annette B. Fromm

9 Sephardic Jurisprudence in the Recent Half-Millennium 167
   Zvi Zohar

10 Safed Kabbalah and the Sephardic Heritage 196
   Morris M. Faierstein

11 Jewish Women in the Ottoman Empire 216
   Paméla Dorn Sezgin

PART III: Sephardic Jewry in the Modern Era and Special Topics

12 Early Modern Sephardim and Blacks: Contact and Conflict between Two Minorities 239
   Jonathan Schorsch

13 Diversity and Uniqueness: An Introduction to Sephardic Liturgical Music 259
   Mark Kligman

14 A Double Occlusion: Sephardim and the Holocaust 285
   Henry Abramson

15 Sephardim and Oriental Jews in Israel: Rethinking the Sociopolitical Paradigm 300
   Zion Zohar

About the Contributors 329
Index 333

Acknowledgments

The editor of this book wishes first to thank all the contributors to this volume, since, if not for their work and dedication, the publication of this volume would not be possible.

It is with great pleasure and gratitude that I thank the Yovel Foundation for its generous donation for the endowment of the President Yitzhak Navon Program for the Study of Sephardic and Oriental Jewry. The Yovel Foundation's generosity allowed me, as the chair of this program, to be involved in the composition and editorial work of this and other academic projects in Judaic and Sephardic Studies. Specifically, I would like to thank Dorothy and Rafael Elkayam, Sheila and David Kadoch, Rina and Yoel Saraf, and Shoshi and Carmel Shashua who are the founding donors and members of the board of Yovel.

Many thanks also to the partners in excellence concerning this endeavor: the provost of Florida International University (FIU), Professor Mark Rosenberg; FIU's vice provost, Professor Raul Moncarz; the previous dean of the College of Arts and Sciences, Professor Arthur Herriot; as well as the present dean, Professor Bruce Dunlap, who granted me for the past three years a summer research grant that allowed me to dedicate the needed time to complete this project. My thanks also go to my colleagues in the Department of Religious Studies; its past chair, Professor Nathan Katz; and the current chair, Professor Christine Gudorf, for their support and encouragement.

I'm greatly indebted to my assistant, Lee Spalter, for her very valuable help in all aspects of this project and beyond.

Special thanks go to Jennifer Hammer, the religion editor of New York University Press, and Despina Papazoglou Gimbel, managing editor of NYU Press, and all their staff in the editorial office. Ms. Hammer was extremely helpful throughout the process and remarkably patient with me and the other contributors to this work. Her skills and professionalism were of enormous assistance in helping me to navigate this project and seeing it through to completion.

I would like to thank my friend Richard Ashenoff for his rare friendship, love, and support. Last but certainly not least, I would like to thank my family. My wife, Efrat Zarren-Zohar, has encouraged and supported me in my academic pursuits for the past many years and has specifically contributed many hours—days as well as nights—to this project. To my wonderful son, Matan, who numerous times offered to help me in completing this proj-ect so that I finally would have the time to play with him again. He gave me tremendous strength and energy during the low times as well as the high ones.

To my mother, Zohara Zohar, for her incredible capacity for giving endless love, for her support, and, most importantly, for instilling in her children the importance of maintaining hope, no matter what. And to my father, Haim Zohar, for his persistent focus on his children's education, even in times of economic distress. This book is dedicated to my parents and the past generations of my family, who passed down the great Sephardic and Oriental heritage to me. Also to the generation of my son, Matan, the conduit of this legacy for future generations.

May God bless us with a vision to see the potential of the future generation fulfilled, since "where there is no vision, the people become unruly: But he that keepeth the heritage, happy is he" (Proverbs 29:18).

Part I

Sephardic Jewry in the Middle Ages
Origins, Development, and Flowering

Chapter 1

A Global Perspective on Sephardic and Mizrahi Jewry
An Introductory Essay

Zion Zohar

Sephardic and Mizrahi Jewry: From the Golden Age of Spain to Modern Times seeks to introduce readers to some of the most important aspects of the history, culture, and thought of Sephardic and Mizrahi Jews. The significance of Sephardic/Mizrahi studies lies not only internally—for Jews in Israel and the Diaspora—but is also of great value to the world at large, given the contributions of Sephardic and Mizrahi Jewry throughout history.

The idea for this book was born from a realization by the editor that no published work exists that simultaneously meets all of the following goals: a) including the latest findings by scholars regarding key topics in the study of Sephardic and Mizrahi Jewry in English; b) being written in language accessible to undergraduate students and lay people, yet presenting material at a superior academic level in the field; and c) exposing the reader to the thinking of many of the most prominent scholars in the field regarding their area of expertise. I hope that this book will become a companion work to the many excellent textbooks of Sephardic Jewish history used by anyone teaching in the field of Sephardic studies or seeking knowledge of this fascinating area of the history of Jewish civilization. Each chapter of this book seeks to summarize the author's and other scholars' findings so as to present a wide spectrum of topics in the most comprehensive way.

The history of Sephardic and Mizrahi civilization may be divided into three major parts. The first part covers the period from the origin of Sephardic culture to the expulsion from Spain in 1492. The second part covers the period between 1492 and the beginning of the modern age, a time in which the Sephardic Diaspora became a distinct phenomenon in Jewish history. The third period covers the modern era and contemporary accounts of Sephardic existence in the State of Israel and abroad. This book is structured according to these three historical and chronological stages.

At the outset, we must of course address two key questions: What constitutes Sephardic and Mizrahi Jewry? And what differentiates these groups from Ashkenazi Jews?

Oriental Jews, Ashkenazim, and Sephardim

The question of precisely when each of these three groups originated is not entirely clear and is one that I leave to social historians to settle. However, generally speaking, Mizrahi Jewry can trace its origins back the farthest—to the forced exile from the Land of Israel to Babylonia (modern Iraq) in the year 586 BCE.[1] Thus, Iraqi Jewry can claim to be among the oldest Diaspora communities in the Jewish world. With the mass exodus of the majority of Jews from Iraq in the modern era (1950s) and continued emigration thereafter, that community no longer exists apart from a few individuals numbering fewer than a hundred souls.

Around that same time in the sixth century BCE, Jews also fled to Egypt where they established themselves as well.[2] Following the assassination of the military governor Gedaliah, the Jewish leadership that remained behind after the initial exile fled to Egypt with the prophet Jeremiah, who reports these events in detail. In the ensuing centuries, Egyptian Jewry too would grow, founding communities in such diverse locales as Elephantine, near the modern city of Aswan, and in the multi-ethnic port city of Alexandria. Additionally, during the five centuries preceding the Common Era, other Oriental Jewish communities grew in stature in the Diaspora, such as Greece,[3] Syria, Asia Minor (modern Turkey), Cyprus and Crete, among other islands in the Mediterranean, as well as Cyrenaica (modern Libya).[4]

During the period stretching from the destruction of the Second Temple in 70 CE until the rise of Islam (early seventh century CE), a great many developments took place in Oriental Jewish history. For example, at the start of the period, the majority of Jews lived within the Roman Empire, though a significant minority still resided in Babylonia and its environs under the Parthian regime and its successors. By the end of this era, most of the Jewish population worldwide and all of its important centers had come under Muslim rule.[5] Culturally, Jews who lived under Rome were naturally shaped by the prevailing Hellenistic-Roman civilization of their surroundings, whereas those dwelling in the area of Babylonia formed their own distinct patterns of life outside the sphere of Hellenistic and Roman influence.[6] These developments, as will become apparent below, affected the creation of the Ashkenazim and Sephardim as separate Jewish subgroups later on.

Following the Great Revolt (66–70 CE) as well as other subsequent Jewish insurrections, the situation of Jews in the Roman Empire began to decline. Upon Emperor Constantine's conversion from paganism to Christianity in 313 CE, the decline intensified, such that the community in the Land of Israel soon lost its place of prominence among world Jewry. As a result, from approximately the fourth through the tenth centuries, a new leading center of Jewish life emerged in Babylonia along the Tigris and Euphrates Rivers. It was here that the Babylonian Talmud—the holiest and most authoritative Jewish text second to the Bible—reached completion by the end of the sixth century, representing the culmination of Babylonian Jewry's productivity over more than a thousand years.

From the Muslim conquest onward, the vast majority of Oriental Jews lived under Islam, establishing themselves at one time or another in almost all the known Muslim and Arab countries throughout the world. Thus, while the Sephardi and Ashkenazi subgroups originated and lived to a greater or lesser extent under Christian regimes, Oriental Jewry, though older than Islam itself, reached maturity and developed its own particular character under Islam, with the exception of most of the Jews of India and the Far East.[7]

Ashkenazim are the descendants of Jews who first settled in the Rhine River valley (Germany) and northern France during the era of Roman rule and over subsequent centuries.[8] Many of them later migrated eastward to Poland-Lithuania and other Eastern European areas because of the forced expulsions[9] decreed by Western European monarchs and the persecutions accompanying the Crusades (eleventh through thirteenth centuries). In the seventeenth and eighteenth centuries, the Ashkenazim's inexorable march eastward reversed course as some Ashkenazi Jews returned to Western Europe to escape pogroms and poverty in the East. Despite the twisted path Ashkenazi Jewry took from one country and region to another, their movement always occurred within Christendom. Thus, Ashkenazi Jewry developed and matured solely within the context of Christian majority culture.

Mark R. Cohen, in chapter 2 of this book, following the views of Bernard Lewis,[10] will suggest that world Jewry can be divided into two main groupings—those Jews who lived "under the crescent" (under Islam) and those who lived "under the cross" (under Christianity). Oriental Jewry, as we have pointed out, lived almost exclusively under the crescent. Cohen argues that the Sephardim constitute a third entity, bearing similarities to both Jews under the crescent and Jews under the cross, and suggests that their real origins lie under the crescent in the medieval Arab world.

Sephardim are the descendents of Jews who had at one time lived on the Iberian Peninsula (Spain and Portugal). Jews initially settled in Spain during Roman times and endured life there during Christian rule, though legends tell of Jews living there as early as King Solomon's time. However, as will be explored at length in several chapters, Sephardic culture reached its full flowering following the Muslim conquest in 711 and for the next several centuries, under Islam. The Christian reconquest of Spain, conducted in earnest during the twelfth century, gradually brought most Jews under Christian rule once again until they were forcibly expelled from the peninsula at the close of the fifteenth century, though some chose the path of remaining and conducting Jewish practice in secret.[11] Those who elected to leave migrated to the Ottoman Empire[12] in large numbers as well as to the Maghreb (North Africa), parts of Italy, and the city of Amsterdam in Holland. In time, many secret Jews, known as "Marranos" or crypto-Jews, also journeyed overseas to the Spanish and Portuguese colonies in North and South America.

Distinctions between Sephardim and Ashkenazim

One of the main distinctions between Sephardim and Ashkenazim[13] historically has been the Sephardic exposure to a relatively more tolerant and often welcoming culture under Muslim rule. During the Golden Age of Spain (in the tenth through the twelfth centuries), Muslim rulers encouraged a sophisticated cultural legacy that was distinctive from Islam, thus allowing Jews and other minorities to partake in this cultural legacy without feeling any pressure to convert. Consequently, Sephardim are historically distinguished by several features: a) their desire for and attainment of secular political positions; b) their ability to appreciate and harmonize religion and secular aspects of culture; c) their skill at mastering both religious works (like the study of the Bible and Talmud) and more secular subjects (such as poetry and philosophy); and d) their multicultural proficiency, which enabled them to converse and publish in both Hebrew and Arabic. Because of their acceptance into Muslim society and culture, Sephardim were more open to external influences and more tolerant of differences.

By contrast, Ashkenazi Jewry originated first in a Hellenistic-Roman culture and subsequently under Catholic hegemony, both of which were far less tolerant than either the Babylonian culture that nurtured Oriental Jewry or the Islamic one that gave birth to the Sephardic Golden Age. After centuries of living under oppressive conditions in Catholic countries where the high culture was defined and dictated primarily by the Church, Ashkenazi Jews intentionally closed themselves to any outside cultural and intellectual influences. Instead, they immersed themselves almost solely in internal Jewish sources, ideas, and customs, fearing that a deeper exposure to Christian culture might shake the foundations of their faith. As a result, the average Ashkenazi rabbi's sphere of interest was generally circumscribed by study of the Bible and Talmud to the nearly total exclusion of other sources of wisdom. In addition, Ashkenazi rabbis were far stricter in matters of "halakha." For example, Rabbi Asher ben Jehiel, born and educated in Germany, wrote, after settling in Toledo, Spain: "Although I know nothing of their secular wisdom," referring to those who held rationalistic views among the Sephardic political and rabbinic leadership, "blessed be the Merciful God who spared me from it. For examples and evidences come along for the purpose of diverting man from the fear of God and His Torah."[14]

There were times when Sephardim also turned inward, debating whether the exposure to and assimilation of other cultures was indeed a positive development, especially when exposed to Christian persecution before the expulsion from Spain in 1492. However, once the trauma of Christian persecution had worn off, many Sephardim settled in lands where they again enjoyed a fair measure of security and were relatively free to practice Judaism. This may be the reason why, even after the trauma of the expulsion from Spain, many Sephardim still displayed a more sympathetic attitude toward outside culture than Ashkenazim and were, on the whole, more inclined to seek knowledge beyond the "four cubits of the law."

While Sephardim do not differ from Ashkenazim regarding the basic tenets of Judaism (for example, both groups view the Talmud as their ultimate authority in belief and practice), there are many differences in matters of custom and outlook. Sephardim follow the rulings of Rabbi Joseph Caro, a Spanish Jew, in his work, the *Shulhan Arukh*, the accepted code of Jewish law, whereas Ashkenazim adhere to the particular traditions outlined in the same work by Rabbi Moses Isserles, a Polish Jew. In general, Rabbi Caro's perspective represents a more liberal and permissive tendency than that approved by Ashkenazi authorities such as Isserles. Developing as they did under such different conditions, the Ashkenazi and Sephardi communities gradually established separate customs, norms, and characteristics, which led to differences in ritual, pronunciation of Hebrew, and the liturgical rite, among many other factors.

A Brief History of the Sephardim

The history of Jews living on the Iberian Peninsula stretches back, according to some legends, as early as the exile from Judea in 586 BCE.[15] At any rate, Jewish presence in Spain is very old, dating at least as far back as Roman times.[16] The great historian of Spanish Jewry Eliyahu Ashtor described the life of the Jews during Roman times and subsequently under Visigoth rulers in the following manner:

> The Jewish settlement on the Iberian Peninsula was a very ancient one and in its early stages had prospered. Even after the Visigoths had established their rule over the land, the condition of the Jewish communities remained favorable for a long time. They earned their livelihood with dignity, and they fulfilled the laws of the Torah and observed its commandments without hindrance.[17]

Shortly after the Visigothic regime adopted Roman Catholicism in the late sixth century, Catholic clergy assembled at synods where they passed anti-Jewish legislation that made the life of Spanish Jewry intolerable.[18]

After a time, the government legitimized forced baptisms, creating the first cases of "anusim," namely, Jews who were forced to profess Catholicism publicly while practicing Judaism in secret. Thus, when Muslims crossed the Straits of Gibraltar from North Africa in 711 CE and invaded the Iberian Peninsula, Jews welcomed them as liberators from Christian persecution.[19] The relatively small band of Muslim conquerors, in turn, entrusted Jews to watch over the cities as they continued their march through Spain. They were also naturally more wary of Christians, against whom they were fighting. Later, they awarded Jews positions of prominence in civic life and in some rare cases, high positions in the military as well. The relatively tolerant Muslim rulers welcomed and esteemed Sephardic Jews who were adept political advisers, skilled financial managers, gifted writers, learned scholars, and pioneering scientists.

The Muslim invasion and conquest of the Iberian Peninsula also enabled the creation of a closer political and linguistic link between the Jews of Spain, situated at the heart of a newly formed Muslim land, and the Jews of Babylonia, the dwelling place of many of the foremost Jewish spiritual authorities at that time. This association gave the Babylonian community the opportunity to pass on their traditions to Iberian Jewry and assisted the Sephardim in assuming leadership of the majority of the world Jewish community shortly after the turn of the millennium.[20]

Born during this era of Islamic rule, the famous Golden Age of Spanish Jewry (circa 900–1200) produced such luminaries as: statesman and diplomat Hasdai ibn Shaprut, vizier and army commander Shmuel ha-Nagid, poet-philosophers Solomon Ibn Gabirol and Judah Halevi, and at the apex of them all, Moses Ben Maimon, also known among the Spaniards as Maimonides. A physician, philosopher, and religious legal scholar ("halakhist"), Maimonides was born and, during his early years, educated in Spain. Although he and his family were forced to flee the Iberian Peninsula due to Muslim persecutions, he continued to refer to himself as "HaSepharadi" or "the Spaniard" even though he eventually lived most of his life in Egypt. Such was the prestige and the heritage of Sephardim.

The Contents of the Book

Mark R. Cohen, in chapter 2, outlines the beginning and early history of the Sephardim. Noting their similarities to both the Jews living under the crescent and the Jews under the cross, he traces their real origins to the medieval Arab world. Cohen goes on to carefully examine the political and cultural features of Jewish existence under Islam to better comprehend the special character of Sephardic Jewry. He notes its many distinctive features: "its sense of noble descent; tradition of service to gentile rulers; experience of high cultural achievement in philosophy and poetry;

feeling of superiority to Ashkenazic Jewry; and history of crypto-Judaism, the practice of Judaism in secret after conversion to Christianity under duress."

While rejecting the "myth of the interfaith utopia" and "the myth of Sephardic supremacy" proposed by some nineteenth-century Jewish historiographers, he nonetheless notes that medieval Jewish life in the Arab world, especially in contrast to Jewish life under Christendom during that same time, was far more favorable and secure. Cohen's essay provides the reader with a clear, concise comparison between Jewish life under the cross and Jewish life under the crescent, delineating the various advantages and disadvantages Jews experienced in both circumstances and attempting to explain why.

Cohen also addresses in his essay the persistence of the term "Sephardic" to encapsulate all non-Ashkenazi Jews, even those who clearly lived in lands where Sephardim never dwelt in any numbers. He asserts that in part, this misnomer reflects the overwhelming historical influence that Jews from Spain had on other Jewries, particularly those living within the Ottoman Empire (which at its height encompassed all of the territories around the eastern Mediterranean). Overall, Cohen provides great insight into the link between Sephardic civilization as a whole and its roots in the medieval Arab world.

The authors of chapters 2 through 5 of this book examine, in one way or another, a wide spectrum of Jewish creativity during the Muslim era and beyond. In chapter 3, Norman A. Stillman surveys the development and utilization of Judeo-Arabic through early, medieval, and modern times. He claims that amongst all the many Diaspora languages of post-Talmudic times, including Yiddish and Ladino, Judeo-Arabic is the premier Diaspora language. Over the last 1400 years, it was spoken by more Jews than any other language and was used by Jews across a greater geographical expanse (in the Middle Ages, from Spain to India) than any other Jewish language. Moreover, after Hebrew and Aramaic, it enjoys the longest history (from the ninth century to the present).

Stillman indicates that "Judeo-Arabic was the literary medium for some of the greatest works of the Jewish spirit" and sets out to enumerate the vast and varied literature written in it. He notes that medieval Judeo-Arabic literary culture reached its apex in Muslim Iberia, where Jewish scholars and men of letters produced works in Judeo-Arabic on Hebrew grammar, lexicography, prose, and philosophy. While Spain's Judeo-Arabic tradition continued even after Sephardic Jews fled Muslim persecutions—most notably in Maimonides' major works, with the exception of the halachic code *Mishnah Torah*—its usage changed in the centuries following the Golden Age. Like Yiddish and Ladino, Stillman acknowledges that today Judeo-Arabic is a dying language. However, he maintains, "it lives on in a myriad of ways through the maintenance of traditional practices, the ever-increasing scholarly study of Judeo-Arabic language, literature, and history, particularly in Israel and France, but also in North America, and through the popular interpretations and translations of Judeo-Arabic wit and wisdom."

In chapter 4, David M. Bunis examines how and when Judeo-Spanish culture was born in medieval Spain and grew to prominence as Judeo-Arabic lost its foothold during the Christian Reconquista. As Arabic cultural influence declined, Jewish contact with speakers of Castilian and other Romance languages led to a re-Hispanization and a return to Ibero-Romance. Bunis notes that Sephardic Jews embraced the traditions of Hispanic oral folk literature, including proverbs, ballads, popular songs, stories, and legends. After the expulsion from Spain, Sephardim then carried Jewish Ibero-Romance languages and cultures to the lands that offered them shelter: the Ottoman Empire, North Africa and the Middle East, and parts of Western Europe, especially Italy. In time, among the many varieties of dialects that had been spoken in Spain, only Castilian remained, becoming the predominant Jewish language of all Jews in much of the Mediterranean region, thus attesting to the influence and authority of the Spanish exiles in their new lands.

Bunis outlines how over the centuries the language received many names such as Ladino, Judezmo, and in Morocco, Hakitia. In addition, he traces the changes Judeo-Spanish went through as it evolved in lands beyond Spain. Through his assessment of the language, written literature, and numerous oral traditions of the Sephardim following their expulsion from Spain, Bunis demonstrates the rich contribution made in this language as well as the impact of other societies on Sephardic Jewish culture. In the modern period, the spread of education in western languages, the rise of local nationalism, pressure to conform linguistically and culturally, emigration from the Mediterranean postexpulsion home regions, and the devastating effects of World War II on the Sephardic communities of Europe, all contributed to a decline in Judeo-Spanish culture. Despite the negative impact of these factors, the culture continues to be maintained today as the modern heir to a noble, centuries-old, East-West Jewish heritage due to the efforts of writers, scholars, performers, and other activists in the surviving speech communities.

In chapter 5, Jonathan P. Decter's essay surveys the belletristic writing of medieval Sephardim, first focusing on their literary production in Andalusia under Muslim rule and then under Christian hegemony. He begins by tracing the development and revolutionary changes that took place in the sphere of Hebrew poetry in the tenth century. One may see that Hebrew retained premier status as the language of literature, which demonstrates the impulse to maintain community and fortify identity, even as Jewish writings in other languages testified to a high degree of Jewish acculturation within Islamic and Christian cultures. The author indicates that the choice of Hebrew as a poetic language can be viewed as one of the greatest expressions of Jewish self-assertion, even nationalist aspiration, during this period.

In time, Jews either moved from Islamic al-Andalus[21] to Christian Spain due to persecutions or fell under Christian rule as the Reconquista progressed. Decter seeks to show how the Hebrew literature of Christian Spain is understood to be both a continuation of the tradition of al-Andalus and an innovative corpus of its own. He provides examples to illustrate this contention from the field of Hebrew poetry and prose, particularly investigating the influence of the Arabic "maqama" (a rhymed prose fictional narrative derived from an eastern Arabic form in which rhymed metered poems were interspersed in a loose rhyming prose). Finally, he notes the beginnings of literary works in Judeo-Spanish, which include translations of previous works in Hebrew and Judeo-Arabic as well as ballads, proverbs, and love songs. Throughout his essay, Decter allows us glimpses into the lives of several poets and authors such as Solomon Ibn Gabirol and Judah al-Harizi, providing the reader with insight into the concerns and issues prevalent during this era. Overall, the author helps us to appreciate the multifaceted position Jews occupied within the complex cultural environment of medieval Iberia and to assess the degree of porousness between Jewish and non-Jewish culture.

The centrality of the Hebrew language was celebrated and honored by medieval Sephardim in another form of literature known as biblical exegesis. In chapter 6, Isaac Kalimi examines how Jewish biblical commentary flourished among such Diaspora communities in Northern France, Provence, Spain, and parts of the Middle East. Within the Sephardic community as a whole, the two main groups that engaged in biblical interpretation were the Karaites[22] and the Rabbinites,[23] who often engaged in intense polemical disagreements regarding each other's perspectives. In his essay, Kalimi focuses particularly on two extraordinary biblical commentators, philologists, and philosophers—Rav Saadia Gaon and Rabbi Abraham ibn Ezra. Though they lived in entirely different eras and countries, these prolific exegetes shared several common methodological approaches to biblical interpretation, and each disputed repeatedly with commentators from the Karaite community. By examining their attempts at defending the rabbinic tradition against the Karaite challenge, the reader begins to comprehend some of the religious, cultural, and political elements operative in their respective eras as well as the vital connection between the Jewish people and the "Book of Books."

Indeed, socially and politically, with the transition from the Islamic regime to the Christian one, the seeds of the destruction of the Jewish community in Spain had been planted. However, it is important to note that according to Gerber,

> for a while, the Sephardim were able to sustain their new forms of creativity in the Christian North. Removed from the special atmosphere and human alchemy of al-Andalus, however, the unique symbiosis of Jewish and Muslim culture did not survive long, and a new era in the Sephardic life began to unfold in Christian Spain. There, the intellectual heirs of the Golden age, whether philosophers or translators in Southern-France, or poets, mathematicians and scientists in Castile and Aragon, were forced to contend with unfamiliar forces of reaction and repression. No longer would their heritage of synthesizing secular and religious learning be considered appropriate or acceptable.[24]

One of the more distinctive forms of Sephardic spiritual and intellectual creativity during the Christian era was Kabbalah, which embodied a mixture of continuity and innovation in the subject of Jewish mysticism.

The first section of the book concludes with Moshe Idel's thought-provoking chapter on a topic that is so distinctive to Sephardic creativity, Jewish Philosophy and Kabbalah. In an attempt to gain a better understanding of the emergence and influence of philosophy and Kabbalah throughout the Sephardic world, Idel examines the surrounding non-Jewish cultures that hosted these two forms of religious and intellectual expression. In the case of Jewish philosophy, the Islamic world was instrumental in its materialization and development; whereas earlier phases of

Kabbalah (the most important form of Jewish medieval mysticism), evolved under Christian rule.[25] Furthermore, the phenomenon of continuity and change regarding intellectual Sephardic life is also evidenced in Idel's essay.

Toward the end of the fourteenth century, a radical change for the worse took place in the political and religious life of the Jews living on the Iberian Peninsula. In 1391, severe persecutions broke out, this time provoked by the preaching of Dominican monks. This led many Jews to convert to Christianity in order to save their lives. Many of these "New Christians," or "conversos" (who were known derogatively as "Marranos," meaning "swine," but called themselves "anusim," meaning "ones who were forced") accepted Christianity but practiced Judaism underground and taught their children to do the same. The Inquisition was consequently established by the Church to uncover these secret (or "crypto-") Jews and prevent them from relapsing back to Judaism. However, the existence of outwardly practicing Jews, often supportive of the conversos, many of whom were family members, was a constant thorn in the side of the Church.[26] Finally, under strong pressure from the Dominicans, Queen Isabella and King Ferdinand issued an edict in March 1492, permanently expelling from Spain all Jews who refused to accept Christianity. This edict was not officially repealed until 1968.

Thousands of Jews accepted conversion; thousands more left the country. Those who emigrated eastward primarily settled in areas already or soon to be contained in the Ottoman Empire,[27] where the Jews were openly welcomed. The rest settled in Morocco to the south or in Holland (Amsterdam) to the north. With the expulsion from Spain, a new era in the history of the Sephardim began.

From Expulsion to the Modern Era: Exile, Decline, and Revival

The Edict of Expulsion in 1492 by no means brought an end to Spanish or Sephardic Jewry. The actions leading to the actual expulsion, however, brought to a close an important era in Jewish history. In medieval Spain, a rich secular and sacred creativity influenced by the unique interactions of Jews, Christians, and Muslims had flourished. This tradition, though it had developed there, continued to live throughout the centuries, in one form or another, all the way to the present day.

In very general terms, the Sephardic emigration from Spain proceeded in two general geographical directions, either north and west to Europe and the Americas or east and south to the Mediterranean basin and North Africa. The sagas, traditions, and languages, as well as the modes of religious and cultural expression of the exiles and their descendants represent great diversity, reflecting both the Spanish heritage they carried with them and the cultures of the lands in which they established residence. In northwestern Europe—Holland, France, England, and, ultimately by extension, the Americas—the Sephardic Jews, in time, assimilated to the prevailing Jewish (and later secular) cultural milieu far more than those who migrated east and south did. Due to their large numbers in various communities of the Ottoman Empire and North Africa, the Sephardim established major communities where Iberian Jewish culture not only was preserved, but also thrived. Despite the economic and intellectual decline that took place in the eighteenth and part of the nineteenth centuries, Ottoman Sephardic culture survived until the eve of the Holocaust.[28] Largely due to twentieth-century settlement in North America and Israel, Sephardic and Mizrahi Jewish identity and culture are enjoying a revival.

In the second part of the book, Annette B. Fromm examines one of the most creative communities in the Sephardic Diaspora. In chapter 8, Fromm traces the experiences of the Jews from the Iberian Peninsula to the Ottoman Balkans as they encounter their new multicultural context. She lends insight into how the Sephardim preserved and augmented their culture and traditions during the four centuries following exile. Her analysis focuses on the cultural diversity in which they flourished while residing in Spain, the character of the communities that preceded them in the Ottoman Empire, and how the Hispanic culture they transported came to influence the native populations they encountered in their new lands.

While Fromm's essay in large part covered the sociohistorical aspects of the Sephardic Diaspora in the Ottoman Empire, the next two essays, by Zvi Zohar and Morris M. Faierstein, delve into the religious and intellectual history of the Sephardic Diaspora. Zvi Zohar, in chapter 9, explores the development of Sephardic halakha, from the Spanish expulsion to the present. It traces the renewal of Sephardic scholarship in the exilic communities of the sixteenth century as well as the creative currents of Sephardic halakha during the seventeenth and eighteenth centuries. While limitations on communal autonomy, emancipation, increasing Westernization, and other changes radically transformed the conditions of

Sephardic Jewish existence and led to some dwindling of first-rate talent in the rabbinate, Sephardic halakhic activity continued vigorously during the nineteenth and twentieth centuries, without falling into the schisms that characterized European Jewry. The two major figures of Sephardic juris-prudence in the second half of the twentieth century were Hayyim David HaLevi (1924–1998) and Ovadia Joseph (b. 1924). Ovadia's vision of "return" to an earlier "state of grace" within halakha differed from the ethos and vision articulated by HaLevi and earlier great figures in the Sephardic classic halakhic tradition. HaLevi and others championed the tradition of halakha as a forward-looking, innovative religious phenomenon transforming itself organically through the dynamic response of halakhic masters to changes in social history and culture. Intriguingly, the very same rabbis who were great legalists, making bold attempts to establish halakhic conditions they hoped were appropriate to Messianic times, also engaged in mystical speculation and were involved in the well-known Kabbalistic revolution that took place in sixteenth-century Safed.

In chapter 10, Morris Faierstein examines the impact of the sixteenth-century spiritual revolution in Safed on the beliefs and traditions of Judaism as it is practiced throughout the world. He asserts that the exiled Jews of Spain and their descendants played a central role in the development of the esoteric and exoteric teachings and rituals that first began as the practices of mystical brotherhoods in Safed in 1492. Kabbalistic opinions concerning the development of Sephardic Judaism during this time ranged from a quietist approach to a more apocalyptic reaction. While some Jews hoped for a hurried recovery, others sought signs of the forthcoming redemption. Many saw the expulsion from Spain as perhaps *the* sign of tribulation that would herald the beginning of the Messianic Age as foretold in Rabbinic literature.

As with the first section of this book, part II also concludes fittingly with the lesser-known history of the vital role that women have played in the Ottoman Empire, the Sephardic Diaspora's most populous region. In chapter 11, Paméla Dorn Sezgin studies the lives of Sephardic women as compared to those of men, looking at historiography, Judeo-Spanish culture, and social organization and decline. First, the author focuses on the general, sociocultural, and historical milieu in which women of different social classes lived. She compares the lives of women from minority groups with those of their Muslim counterparts.

Second, she identifies elements that are unique to Jewish women, such as their adaptation to the historical events and culture particular to Sephardic Jewry. Her commentary serves as a bridge to help the reader make the transition from one era to the next. Sezgin demonstrates how traditional Judeo-Spanish culture, which was preserved by almost 450 years under Ottoman rule, has given way in modern times under the onslaught of increasing societal changes, particularly those that have altered long-standing patterns in women's lives. She notes how practices such as mandatory schooling for women, women's emancipation at the ballot box, increasing options to work outside of the home and become self-supporting, and greater fluency in national languages, have all enabled greater participation in the majority culture and served to transform the everyday life of Sephardic women.

Sephardic Jewry in the Modern Era and Special Topics

From the seventeenth century onward, the prior prominence of Sephardic Jewry within world Jewry began to diminish as Ashkenazi Jewry grew in significance and size. The Sephardim continued their predominance among many of the communities of North Africa, the Middle East, Italy, and Asia Minor.[29] However, throughout the Jewish Diaspora, Ashkenazim quickly outnumbered Sephardim and Oriental Jews.

Toward the end of the nineteenth century, persecutions and extreme poverty within Russia's pale of settlement caused a massive Ashkenazi emigration from eastern to western Europe and on toward South Africa, Australia, and the United States. Ashkenazi Jewry rapidly swelled to 90 percent or more of the population in these diverse but increasingly prominent Jewish communities. However, the population decline of Sephardic and Oriental Jews is by no means the last word on their relevance in the modern era. In Israel, Sephardic and Oriental Jews constitute approximately half of the Jewish population. Their role in shaping Israeli society and politics continues to be a vital one, and by extension, they have affected the identity of world Jewry as a whole.

Chapters 12 through 14 engage in a discourse regarding three aspects of Sephardic and Oriental Jewry in the modern era outside of the Land of Israel—Diaspora identities and attitudes toward the "Other," the development of Sephardic and Oriental modes of music, and the impact of the Holocaust.

In transition to the modern era, part III of this book opens with the essay by Jonathan Schorsch, chapter 12. The perceived importance of being

Iberian is reflected in Sephardic discourse regarding race and blackness in the Atlantic world from the fifteenth to the eighteenth centuries. Schorsch asserts that this self-perception as Iberians helped Spanish and Portuguese Jews as well as (ex-)conversos navigate their ambiguous status as both religious outsiders and racial and cultural insiders (as whites).

Schorsch explores the relations and mutual imagining of Sephardic Jews and black Africans under the pressures of Iberian anti-Jewish hysteria and the incipient racism generated by European overseas expansion. The behavior of Sephardim in the Atlantic world toward blacks in general and their own slaves in particular so closely resembled that of their host populations, and often is so lacking in Jewish particularities, that one can forget at times that this slave-owning minority was a severely ostracized and persecuted one.

Schorsch attempts to describe this facet of the Sephardic cultural history by turning to a wide variety of sources, many hitherto ignored, such as Sephardic biblical exegesis, halakhic writings, quasiscientific literature, sermons, poetry, letters, notarial records, and archival sources. The essay undoubtedly adds another layer of distinctiveness to this volume.

In chapter 13, Mark Kligman studies the variability and distinctiveness of Sephardic liturgical music beginning with the Ottoman Empire. Sephardic liturgical music is a true reflection of the cultural diversity of Sephardic Jews, reflecting a wide range of musical styles—cantillation, liturgical song, and "piyyutim"—that have absorbed, adapted, and reacted to a variety of influences over the ages. By focusing on the liturgical traditions of European and Middle Eastern Jewish communities, Kligman demonstrates the similarities and differences among the various Sephardic practices. He notes how the Spanish and Portuguese tradition is Western in its approach to liturgical music, using melodies that are stylistically Western. In contrast, the Middle Eastern Jewish tradition, known as "Yerushalmi Sephardim," displays a considerable amount of Arab influence. Other communities display a more blended style. The Moroccan or North African Tradition contains some Western musical elements but is mixed with the Andalusian Spanish style, producing ornate melodic patterns. The Turkish or Ottoman Jewish tradition reflects a mixed musical tradition that contains elements of Arab, Spanish, and Balkan styles.

According to Kligman, the uniqueness of Sephardic and Oriental Jewish music is exemplified by the manner in which it is integrated into Jewish life. As traditions evolve, so does Sephardic music, inspiring both religious and secular musical composition. Sephardic music's connection to Jewish culture has persisted despite the greater Ashkenazi religious influences and institutions both in the Americas and in Israel today.

In focusing on modern Jewish life, the Shoah, the decimation of European Judaism, is clearly a seminal event that must be addressed. What is largely overlooked and unknown is its enormous effect upon Sephardic Jewry. Henry Abramson addresses this lacuna in chapter 14. By contrasting Sephardic experiences in Greece, Yugoslavia, Serbia, Croatia, Algeria, Tunisia, Morocco, and Libya before and during the Holocaust, Abramson gives insight into the technical as well as intellectual factors that create this double occlusion of being ignored by the public and academia alike.

While world Jewry was involved in assessing the damage of the Holocaust and contemplating ways of recovery, the establishment of the future Jewish state was under way. In the closing chapter of this volume, I explore the life of the Sephardic and Oriental Jewry in Israel. The majority of Ashkenazi Jews who moved to Palestine in the beginning of the twentieth century were Western, secular, and socialist in orientation. These immigrants became both the political leaders and cultural architects of the emerging State of Israel. When Sephardi Jews immigrated to Israel mainly between 1948 and the mid-1960s, they found a very different culture and society from the one to which they had grown accustomed in their countries of origin. Under Ashkenazi leadership, to be a "good Israeli" meant subscribing to socialist ideals, living out Western values, and rejecting all but the most modern adaptations of religious identity.[30] Naturally, this paradigm presented a serious problem for Sephardi immigrants and their children. To accept it, meant to reject their past, their traditions, and their very sense of self. Yet, to reject the Ashkenazi-defined ideal meant to reject becoming fully "Israeli." Caught in this paradox, many Sephardic youth were not wholly able to integrate their Sephardic heritage with their sense of Israeli identity, consequently suffering a loss of pride and self-esteem. Even within the Orthodox world, Ashkenazi Jews dominated the yeshivoth and academies of learning, compelling Sephardim to model themselves after an Ashkenazi-defined religious model.

Today, Sephardic culture and leadership have reached a critical point. After years of modeling themselves after Ashkenazi Jews, Sephardi and Oriental Jews have come perilously close to losing their sense of self and their rich cultural heritage. In spite of the pressures arrayed against them in recent years, Sephardic and Oriental Jews, among the observant and even more so among the secular population, are rebelling, as they seek to return to their roots and from them create an old-new Sephardi paradigm.

NOTES

I wish to thank two very helpful colleagues, Professors Henry Abramson of Florida Atlantic University and Norman Stillman from the University of Oklahoma, who kindly gave of their valuable time to look over the preliminary draft of this introductory essay and offered their excellent suggestions.

1. BCE (Before the Common Era) and CE (Common Era) are the scholarly alternatives to BC and AD, which have religious connotations.

2. Jeremiah 40–44.

3. In Greece, an inscription from the third century BCE refers to a Jewish slave. See Haim Hillel Ben-Sasson, *The History of the Jewish People* (Cambridge: Harvard University Press, 1976), 278.

4. Ibid., 277–78.

5. Ibid., 307.

6. Ibid., 277.

7. The Jews of India and China lived under Hinduism, Buddhism, and other religions of the area. However, these Jews' origins were often traced to Oriental Jewish communities further west, such as Yemen, Syria, and Iraq, where they lived under Islam.

8. For a graphic representation of the periods of settlement and migration, see Martin Gilbert, *The Atlas of Jewish History* (New York: William Morrow, 1992), 17, which shows a Jewish presence already by 100 CE.

9. See ibid., 47, for a map of expulsions from 1000 to 1500. Also Ben-Sasson, *History*, 465, 486–87.

10. Bernard Lewis, *The Jews of Islam* (Princeton, NJ: Princeton University Press, 1984).

11. There had been several instances, most notably in 1391 in many cities in Castile, where Jews were given the choice to convert to Christianity or die, and so fled before 1492.

12. The Ottoman Empire then encompassed the Balkans, Greece, Asia Minor, Lebanon, Syria, Palestine, and Egypt.

13. Mark Cohen will address these distinctions in much more detail in Chapter 2.

14. Yitzhak Baer, *A History of the Jews in Christian Spain*, vol. 1 (Philadelphia: Jewish Publication Society, 1961), 319, in which the author takes the statement from *She'eloth u'Teshuboth ha-ROSH*, kelal 55, no. 9.

15. Hasdai ibn Shaprut, in his letter to Joseph, the king of the Khazar kingdom, describes himself as "belonging to the exiled Jews of Jerusalem, in Spain." See Franz Kobler, *Letters of Jews through the Ages*, vol. 1, *From Biblical Times to the Renaissance*, East and West Library (New York: Hebrew Publishing, 1978), 98. See also chapter 1 in this volume.

16. See Esther Benbassa and Aron Rodrigue, *Sephardi Jewry: A History of the Judeo-Spanish Community, Fourteenth through Twentieth Centuries* (Berkeley and Los Angeles: University of California Press, 2000), xxvi.

17. Eliyahu Ashtor, *The Jews of Muslim Spain* (Philadelphia: Jewish Publication Society, 1992), vol. 1, 11.

18. Ibid., 11.

19. Ibid., 11–16.

20. Though Ashkenazi Jewry would continue to follow its own rabbinic leadership, Sephardic and Oriental Jewry, who were the vast majority of world Jewry at this time, largely looked to Spanish-born rabbis for spiritual guidance.

21. Al-Andalus is known in English as Andalusia.

22. Karaites (literally "scripturalists") are an offshoot of Judaism thought to have been founded in eighth-century Babylonia. They flourished between the late ninth century and the eleventh century and are distinguished from Rabbanites by their rejection of the Talmud and rabbinical tradition. Their liturgy, calendar, and many rituals differ markedly from rabbinic Judaism. For more about Karaites, see Nathan Schur, *History of the Karaites* (Frankfurt: Peter Lang, 1992); Leon Nemoy, *Karaite Anthology* (New Haven: Yale University Press, 1987); and Daniel J. Lasker, "Rabbinism and Karaism: The Contest for Supremacy," in *Great Schisms in Jewish History*, ed. Raphael Jospe and Stanley M. Wagner (New York: Ktav, 1994).

23. Rabbinites are followers of the rabbinical tradition detailed in the Talmud and other works of oral law. The name was coined by the Karaites to characterize their opponents.

24. Jane Gerber, *The Jews of Spain: A History of the Sephardic Experience* (New York: Free Press, 1992), 89.

25. In chapter 7, Idel also asserts that although the Jewish exile from Spain was traumatic, ironically, it provided the refugees with a sense of liberty, by releasing them from the pressures of Spanish authorities and the Inquisition. Though a comprehensive survey of the postexpulsion Kabbalah will be treated in chapter 10 of this book, it is important to note that according to Idel, the creativity exhibited by sixteenth-century Sephardi Kabbalists may be related more to a sense of urgency and responsibility toward rebuilding the Sephardic communities in new places, than to lamenting the loss of "Sepharad" and the tribulations created by the expulsion. In contrast, Gershom Scholem saw the emergence of Lurianic Kabbalah in sixteenth-century Safed primarily as a response to the expulsion of the Jewish community from Spain in 1492. In asserting this viewpoint, Scholem was following a trend that goes back to nineteenth-century German Jewish historiography, in which mystical movements were viewed as responses to historical events. Moshe Idel and others have recently challenged this explanation of the relationship between the Spanish expulsion and the rise of Lurianic Kabbalah. See Gershom Scholem, *Major Trends in Jewish Mysticism* (New York: Schocken, 1961),

244–51; idem, *The Messianic Idea in Judaism* (New York: Schocken, 1995), 41; idem, *Kabbalah* (New York: Dorset, 1987), 68. For a different perspective, see Moshe Idel, *Messianic Mystics* (New Haven: Yale University Press, 1998), 152–53.

26. Moreover, the Inquisition was authorized to prosecute only self-professed Catholics, not Jews, who still had a legal right to practice their religion.

27. These areas were Greece, Bulgaria, Yugoslavia, Turkey, the Levant, Egypt, Libya, Tunisia, and Algeria.

28. A detailed discussion of the effects of the Holocaust on Sephardic Jews can be found in chapter 14 in this book.

29. Howard M. Sachar, *Farewell España: The World of the Sephardim Remembered* (New York: Random House, 1998), 193–95 (on their influence in Asia Minor and the Balkans), 76–90 (in Morocco), 211–13 (in Italy), 257–58 (in Bulgaria).

30. See Amnon Rubenstein, "The End of the Sabra Myth," in *The Zionist Dream Revisited: From Herzl to Gush Emunim and Back* (New York: Schocken, 1984), 138–39. He specifically addresses the Sabra image, stating: "The typical Sabra has always been depicted as an Ashkenazi son of European parents. . . . To the new arrivals from North Africa and other Moslem countries, the Sabra image was so remote that even attempts at assimilation were inconceivable."

Chapter 2

The Origins of Sephardic Jewry in the Medieval Arab World

Mark R. Cohen

World Jewry can be divided into two parts, "the Jews of Islam" and "the Jews of Christendom,"[1] or, as I have referred to them, as Jews living "under the crescent" and Jews living "under the cross."[2] The Jews "under the crescent" comprise those who formed their traditions in the Islamic world and encompass populations stretching from Persia in the East to North Africa and Muslim Spain in the West. The Jews "under the cross" are those of the Christian-Roman Empire and the predominantly Greek Byzantium who survived in the eastern Mediterranean into the Middle Ages. This group also includes the Jews of Latin Europe: England, France, Germany, and Italy, and, from the thirteenth century on, the Kingdom of Poland and its affiliated states in eastern Europe. Collectively, the Jews of northern and eastern Europe are referred to as Ashkenazic Jewry.

The Ashkenazim are commonly contrasted with the Sephardim, the Jews of Spain or of Spanish descent.[3] However, a problem exists as to whether or not Sephardic Jews comprise a third group of Jewry, distinct from the two groups I mentioned at the outset. The difficulty stems from the fact that the Sephardim are historically a part of the Jews of Christendom, since they descend from those expelled from Catholic Spain in 1492, while the term "Sephardim" has also been employed in recent times to designate those Jews in Israel who emigrated from Muslim-Arab lands.

Originally, "Sepharad" was a place mentioned in the Bible. In the Book of the Prophet Obadiah, which is only one chapter long, Israel's enemy, Edom, is threatened with destruction. An oracle indicates there will come the "day of the Lord," when all of Israel's enemies will be defeated, and the entire Israelite dispersion will return to Zion. Among other Diaspora communities, the oracle prophesies that "the Jerusalemite exile community of Sepharad shall possess the towns of the Negev."[4]

In other words, Sepharad was a place in the ancient Jewish Diaspora. It was thought to be Sardis in Asia Minor. The Aramaic translator of the Bible rendered "Sepharad" by the word "Aspamia," presumably thinking of Apamea, a city in Mesopotamia. But the word sounded similar to "Hispania," an ancient name for the Iberian Peninsula. The Jews who lived in Muslim Spain in the Middle Ages believed they were descendants of the Jewish nobility of Jerusalem who were captured by the Romans and later deported to Rome and Spain after the destruction of Jerusalem in the first century CE. These medieval Spanish Jews concluded that "Sepharad" in the oracle of the Prophet Obadiah meant "Spain," and therefore, they called themselves Sephardim.

In terms of the crescent-cross scheme, the Sephardim constitute a third entity, bearing similarities to both the Jews under the crescent and the Jews under the cross. Jews were found in Spain after the fall of the Roman Empire, where they experienced considerable persecution under the Christian Visigothic regime.[5] In 711, these Jews came under the rule of the crescent, when the Arabs conquered the peninsula.[6] The dominion of the cross then returned to Spain's Jews when the Christians reconquered the Peninsula from the Muslims.[7] The Reconquista was mostly completed by the end of the thirteenth century. It was final two hundred years later, in 1492, when the army of the Catholic monarchs, Queen Isabella and King Ferdinand, captured the principality of Granada, the last Muslim kingdom in Spain. Self-professed Muslims were forced into exile the same year that the Jews were expelled from Spain.

Sephardic civilization began long before the Reconquista,[8] in a time when the peninsula was ruled by the Muslims and when Arabic culture surrounded and influenced the Jews. Sephardic society in the medieval Arab world was characterized by several features: its sense of noble descent; its tradition of service to gentile rulers; its high cultural achievement in philosophy and poetry; and its history of crypto-Judaism, the secret continued practice of Judaism after apparent conversion under duress.

Conventional wisdom has traditionally held that medieval Jews living in the Arab world enjoyed substantially greater security and a higher level of political and cultural integration than Jews living under the cross did. The suffering of the Jews of Christendom was first recorded by Ashkenazim who memorialized persecution in medieval Hebrew narrative accounts of martyrdom and in liturgical elegies to be recited in the synagogue.[9] The theme of persecution was picked up in the sixteenth century by Spanish exiles in several long "chronicles." These accounts, by both Ashkenazic and Sephardic Jews, enumerated and described links in a long chain of Jewish suffering, mainly under the cross and culminating with the expulsion from Spain.[10] The chronicles reflected a distinctly gloomy vision of Jewish-gentile relations in medieval times.

During the nineteenth century, in the wake of the French Revolution, Jews in Western Europe, predominantly Ashkenazim, began to emerge from their past of Christian oppression and exclusion. They slowly moved into the light of emancipation, freedom, and supposed equality. But old Christian hatreds did not dissolve with the disappearance of the "old regimes." Many Jews discovered that the only road to true equality was through conversion to Christianity. Others tried, through religious reform, to gain approval by ridding Judaism of the medieval attributes that Christians loathed.

Toward the end of the nineteenth century, the religious anti-Semitism of the Middle Ages reappeared with new virulence—as a political weapon. The so-called evil and conspiratorial Jews were blamed for the ills of society. Old, theologically based Christian doctrines about the Jews were remolded into a new political and racial anti-Semitism. The most devastating outcome of this transformation would be the Holocaust.[11]

The nineteenth-century fathers of modern Jewish historiography, mainly in Germany, followed medieval Ashkenazic and postexpulsion Sephardic writers, finding very little cause for optimism from the past experience of Jews living under the cross. Salo W. Baron, the greatest Jewish historian of the twentieth century, disparaged this gloom-and-doom approach to the Jewish past, calling it the "lachrymose conception of Jewish history."[12]

The standard-bearers of the "lachrymose conception" found the experience of Jews living under the crescent in the Arab-Muslim world, notably in Muslim Spain, strikingly different from that of the Jews under the cross. In the Arab-Muslim world of the Middle Ages, German-Jewish historians found tolerance, acceptance of Jews as peers, and Jewish participation—without abandoning Judaism—in the political and cultural life of the majority society. During this period, which they called the Golden Age, Jews suffered relatively little persecution, certainly nothing comparable to the mistreatment inflicted under the cross. Life under Islam seemed to be an interfaith utopia. The Ashkenazic Jews of central Europe yearned for similar acceptance by so-called liberal, post-Enlightenment European Christians.[13]

The "myth of the interfaith utopia" under the crescent ("myth" because it overlooked episodes of hardship and periodic persecution) was accompanied by a "myth of Sephardic supremacy."[14] According to this view, the most admirable Jews in history were those living first in Arab, then in Christian Spain. Rational and cultured, these Jews were integrated into gentile society. They were superior to the irrational, ultrareligious, insular Ashkenazic Jews, who were represented by the Yiddish-speaking Jews of eastern Europe. This historiographical construct corresponds with the self-perception of some Sephardic Jews even today.[15]

Despite several serious instances of persecution, the Jews of Arab lands enjoyed much greater security than Jews living under the cross. In this comfortable atmosphere, they openly adopted Arab culture. They early on shed Aramaic for Arabic, not only as their spoken tongue, which was natural, but also as the language of almost everything they wrote.

Jews normally brought legal cases before the Jewish *bet din*, but they did not shrink from Muslim courts. They felt secure before the Muslim *qadi* and trusted the due process of Islamic law. Halakhic writings in Arabic even absorbed principles of Islamic jurisprudence.[16] Jews read Islamic literature, even the Qur'an—pages of the Qur'an transcribed into Hebrew letters were found in the Cairo Geniza. Jewish intellectuals studied philosophy in a neutral setting with Muslim colleagues. Medicine, widely open to the Jews, provided another means of access to high Arab society. Jews attained prestigious posts in the courts of Arab rulers as physicians, clerks in the bureaucracy, or, on rare occasion, as close advisers to the caliph or sultan. The most famous Jewish courtier, Samuel ibn Nagrela, in the eleventh century, served the Berber-Muslim sultan of Granada as his vizier. He also played an unspecified military role in battles against neighboring Muslim states.

In their own communities, the Jewish elite formed illustrious courts similar to those of Muslim rulers. There they discussed Jewish topics and listened to readings (sometimes sung) by Hebrew poets. Themes ranged from love, wine, nature, and women, to, in the unique case of the Samuel ibn Nagrela, war. Courtier-rabbis, like Samuel, thought of themselves as Jewish nobility. "I am the David of my generation," wrote Samuel in one of his most famous war poems. In this context, the Jews of Muslim Spain proudly traced their roots back to the noble elite of Jerusalem, exiled by the Romans after the suppression of the Jewish revolt of 68–73 CE and the destruction of the Second Temple. Arab poets considered Arabic, the language of the Qur'an, the most beautiful of all languages and Arabic verse the highest form of poetry. Thinking similarly about their own holy scriptures, Jewish poets composed poems in classical Hebrew, the Hebrew of the Bible.[17]

How can we account for the comfortable atmosphere that made Jews open themselves up so enthusiastically to the influence of Arab cultural forms? First of all, in contrast to Christianity, Islam started off with a less confrontational attitude toward Judaism. During the long, uphill process of achieving legitimacy in the Roman Empire, Christianity elaborated a hostile ideology about Jews and Judaism. The Jews were said to have been punished by God because they rejected Christ, the Messiah. God turned away from the "Old Israel" in favor of the "New Israel" of pagan-Roman converts to Christianity and their descendants. Alleged killers of Christ, the Jews had to be suppressed because they supposedly continued to harbor evil intentions toward Christians. At the same time, God wanted the Jews to be preserved within Christendom. As St. Augustine wrote, the Jews served as "witnesses": bearers of the Old Testament that prefigured the New; witnesses by their abject, degraded state to the triumph of Christianity; and future witnesses to the truth of Christianity upon their conversion at the Second Coming of Christ.[18]

In contrast, Muhammad, the founder of Islam, claimed neither messiahship nor divinity. Though openly ridiculed during his lifetime by the Jews, the Prophet of Islam died a natural death. Thus, unlike Christians, Muslims had no grounds for holding the Jews responsible for the demise of their founder. They lacked a "propheticide." They also lacked, as Christians did not, a religious iconographic tradition that might have provided the illiterate Muslim masses with a graphic depiction of Jewish enmity toward Muhammad in Medina. Therefore, the Islamic-Jewish conflict could not generate the tension and hatred that so inflamed the conflict between the Christians and the Jews.

In addition, Islam did not have to struggle for recognition against a hostile and powerful enemy like Rome. Tensions similar to those experienced by early Christians with Jews, pagans, and Roman authorities dissipated rapidly following the relatively swift Islamic victory, first in Arabia, then in the former Byzantine and Sassanian-Persian empires.

Theologically, Islam did not represent itself as the divine fulfillment of Judaism. Rather, Muslims traced their origins back to Abraham, the first monotheist. They claimed that Islam represented a restoration of his pristine, original belief in and "surrender" (which is the meaning of the word "Islam") to the one God. Arabs did not portray themselves as a "New Israel." They traced their descent from Abraham through Ishmael, Abraham's first-born son, the brother of Isaac.

Unlike Christianity, Islam felt no need to establish its identity at the expense of the Jews and no need to deny, to either the Jews or the Christians, their continued history alongside Islam. Muslims viewed Christians and Jews as "people of the book" (*ahl al-kitab*) or "protected people" (*ahl al-dhimma*, or *dhimmis*), but still as "people" living out their own histories scattered among the Muslims.

Islam exhibited a less confrontational attitude than Christianity toward Jewish scripture. Christians accepted the Jewish Bible as their own—the "Old Testament" which prefigured the "New." Shared claim to scripture laid the foundation for continued tension over the interpretation of the message of Jewish holy writ. This fueled, at times, a belligerent polemical literature and often aggressive attempts to convert the Jews. Islam, however, dismissed the existing texts of the scriptures of the Jews (and Christians) as a corruption of their original, divinely inspired teaching. This, among the other factors mentioned before, helped moderate Muslim polemics against Judaism. True to a Qur'anic dictum ("There is no compulsion in religion," Sura 2:256), Muslims spent relatively little energy trying to force Jews into their religion. A small number of persecutions in which Jews and Christians were given the choice of Islam or the sword were exceptions proving the general rule.[19]

Other mitigating factors reinforced Islam's less confrontational relationship with the Jews. One of these was legal status. In the Christian world, the Jews were affected by different, often conflicting, laws including the canon law of the church, feudal custom, the law of the state, and the law of the city. The mixture of laws sometimes worked to Jews' advantage. But, for the most part, the legal situation of the Jews expressed itself in a certain arbitrariness and irksome unpredictability.

The Jews were unique in that they were the only infidels living within Christian society after the last pagans in Eastern Europe were converted. As they became more vulnerable to Christian violence beginning with the Crusades, secular rulers tightened their jurisdiction. The Jews turned into monarchical "property," "serfs of the royal chamber," as they were called in Latin, subject to a special and oppressively restrictive legal status. The unmediated legal relationship between the monarch and the Jews continued to provide some measure of badly needed protection in an increasingly hostile atmosphere. But it further underscored their alien status, their "otherness." It gave rulers license to place limits on the Jews' freedom of movement and exploit them through heavy taxation and extraordinary exactions. The "enserfment" of the Jews to secular rulers had its most severe consequence in the widespread expulsions of the thirteenth to fifteenth centuries.[20]

In the Islamic world, the Jews did not have a unique legal status.[21] They were not the only infidels on the scene. There were many Christians in the former Byzantine domains, many more than Jews, while Persia contained a significant Zoroastrian population. Islamic law subsumed these groups under the same legal umbrella. They were all *dhimmis,* protected by the Islamic state in return for an annual poll tax payment and adherence to restrictions that suited their lowly position vis-à-vis Islam. Jews were not singled out for special treatment. With the exception of the annual poll tax paid by all non-Muslims, the restrictive laws were often ignored by the *dhimmis* with the tacit approval of the authorities.

Moreover, *dhimmi* law resided in a unitary corpus: the *shariᵓa,* or Islamic holy law. It was essentially consistent, predictable, and hardly subject to arbitrary interpretation and application. The relative stability over time of the basic law regarding the treatment of non-Muslims thus assured the Jews a considerable degree of security.

In economic life—especially during the first six centuries of Islam, the period known as the Golden Age—Jews exhibited substantial occupational differentiation. They participated in nearly every walk of life characteristic of society at large. This contrasted sharply with those parts of Christian Europe, mainly the northern Latin lands, where Jews were almost always economic pariahs. They were long-distance merchants in early medieval Europe, where a predominantly rural society frowned upon the alien merchant and his profit-seeking acquisitiveness. Later, they were predominantly moneylenders, when usury was vigorously combated by the church and bitterly hated by debtors who resented Jewish power over their economic well-being.

There was nothing in Islamic economic history comparable to the feared Jewish merchant or the despised Jewish moneylender. From its outset, Islam was favorably disposed toward profit seeking. Compared to their coreligionists in Christendom, the Jews of Islam were well integrated into the economic life of society at large. Letters and documents from everyday life found in the Cairo Geniza (the famous cache of discarded writings discovered in a medieval synagogue in Old Cairo more than a century ago) show Jews active not only in commerce, but also in scores of different skilled and unskilled occupations. Measured against the European standard, the relative absence of economic discrimination against Jews in the Muslim world during the tenth to thirteenth centuries makes a vivid impression.

As in Europe, Jews under Islam also engaged in money lending. However, the main arena for Jewish credit transactions in the Islamic world during the so-called Golden Age was within the Jewish community. Judaism found ways to accommodate the new commercial economy while allowing Jews—despite the biblical prohibition—to invest with their coreligionists and realize a return. There was some lending with interest to the non-Jew, which biblical law expressly permitted. Jews also regularly borrowed with interest from Muslim moneylenders. Jewish money lending activities among Muslims were diverse and not concentrated in consumption loans to strapped clients—the kind of credit that dominated Jewish money lending in the West and engendered resentment and, frequently, violence.[22]

In the Muslim world, Jews had a fixed and assured place in the social and religious hierarchy and so were never expelled in the way they were from most of western Europe by the end of the fifteenth century. Ethnic and religious diversity formed an essential ingredient in the long-lasting pluralism of Islamic society. The fluid and noncorporate nature of Islamic urbanism and other institutions attenuated the "otherness" of the Jew. Restrictive Islamic laws, such as the ones concerning distinctive dress—seen as the ancestor of the infamous "yellow Jewish badge" in Europe—were geared not simply to discriminate. They unambiguously distinguished between the rulers and the ruled, delineated boundaries, and facilitated the proper functioning of an interethnic etiquette in an inherently hierarchical society.

Living mostly in cities, Jews did not suffer the infamy of townsmen that they, along with Christian merchants, experienced in the early period of urban revival in the West. This was due to the fact that the city in the Islamic world had a longer and more organic history than in medieval Europe. Within the Muslim town, residential separation of ethnic and religious groups was normal, voluntary, and generalized. There was no stigma attached to neighborhoods housing predominantly Jews. This was in contrast with the northern Christian town. There, a geographical segregation of Jews into separate streets, or "Jewries," existed. The Jewish quarter in the Christian city, home of the "diabolical" Jew, instilled suspicion and dread in the popular imagination. Finally, socialization between Jews and Muslims was more extensive and conducted with far less tension than the socialization between Jews and Christians in the Christian world was.[23]

Persecutions marred the historical record of Muslim-Jewish relations. From time to time, a zealous sect, a conscientious reformist ruler, or a pious cleric campaigned to clamp down on the letter of the law and enforce its restrictions. With one exception, in 1066 in Granada, these episodes could not be called anti-Semitic or anti-Jewish. They were almost always directed against the non-Muslims as a class, not at the Jews per se, and erupted when the non-Muslims were seen to be flouting the law and failing to respect the superiority of Islam. Most importantly, compared to the devastation experienced by European Jewry (especially from the time of the First Crusade, in 1096, onward), Islamic persecutions were fewer in number. With some exceptions, they also had less serious short- and long-range consequences.

Forced conversion to Islam was extremely rare. On the few occasions that it did happen, Jews and Christians were allowed to return to their former religion after Muslim fanaticism calmed down. Jews did not suffer the anguish of expulsion under Islamic rule in the tenth to thirteenth centuries. The few instances, recorded in the late Middle Ages, were temporary and typically under more intolerant Shiite regimes.

The Jews under Islam transmitted no real collective memory of Jewish persecution—nothing comparable to the Ashkenazic collective memory of persecution in the Christian Middle Ages. The relative absence of literary commemoration, whether in prose or in poetry, of even the major persecutions of the Jews under Islam during the tenth to thirteenth centuries is telling. It is symptomatic of a fundamentally different experience of life under gentile domination, marked by discrimination, to be sure, but less violent and less exclusionary.[24]

The cultural efflorescence of the Jews living under the crescent (ancestors of the Sephardic Jewry of today) can thus be better understood as a by-product of their relative lack of experience with violent persecution and their relative tolerance by majority society. These Jews imitated the cultural forms of the society around them in ways unparalleled by the medieval Ashkenazic Jewish community living under the cross. A deeply oppressed, persecuted, and excluded minority does not normally admire, embrace, and emulate the culture that is its source of misery. Relatively secure, Jews living under the crescent were open to the influences of Arabic-Islamic civilization for many centuries. Though not an interfaith utopia, lands under the crescent were a considerably more tolerant environment than were lands under the cross.

If the historical experience that defined the Sephardim of Christian Spain was, in general, that of the Jews of the Arab world of an earlier period of time, this had much to do with the military consequences of the Christian Reconquista. The advance of Christianity weakened the kingdoms of Muslim Spain. In the late eleventh century, therefore, a Berber force in North Africa (known as the Almoravids) was invited into Spain to help stave off the Catholic advance.[25] For a time, the Jewish community lost its favored position. Many Jews decided to emigrate to the north, where they were welcomed by the advancing Christians and treated with a large measure of tolerance, which was not unlike their treatment in Muslim Spain up to the arrival of the Almoravids. In the 1140s, another North African Berber group, the fanatic Islamic sect of the Almohads, invaded and conquered Muslim Spain. The Almohads did not stem the tide of the Reconquista, but they did impose their own stringent form of Islam on the Muslim sector. This included violent oppression of those who, in their eyes, had weakened Islam, especially Jews and Christians living under Muslim rule. Those thought to be libertine Muslims were also oppressed. The Sephardim of Muslim Andalusia who were not massacred either converted to Islam or fled abroad. Thousands escaped to southern France, where they established a Sephardic community alongside the already present Ashkenazim. Others fled a shorter route across the ever-advancing border of the Christian kingdoms of Spain and settled in reconquered territory in the bosom of Jewish communities formed earlier by the exiles who had fled from the Almoravids.[26]

Jewish law prescribed that one must accept martyrdom rather than succumb to idolatry. Ashkenazic Jewry generally chose death over conversion to Christianity during the First Crusade, in 1096, and after. Sephardim during the Almohad terror responded in circumvention of the letter of Jewish law. The reasons for this included their belief that Islam was truly monotheistic, the example of dissimulation by heretics in Muslim society (known as *taqiya*), and religious doubts about the uniqueness and superiority of Judaism that had been instilled by philosophical study.[27]

Incidentally, the mass Sephardic apostasy in Muslim Andalusia during the Almohad period was not the first in the Muslim world. In Egypt and Palestine at the beginning of the eleventh century, the caliph al-Hakim persecuted the Christians and Jews. He ordered the destruction of many houses of worship, including the Church of the Holy Sepulcher in Jerusalem. He also forced upon Jews and Christians the choice between Islam and the sword, in violation of the Qur'anic prohibition against compelling non-Muslims to accept Islam. Few Jews in Egypt and Palestine embraced martyrdom. Instead, thousands openly converted to Islam, attended the mosque prayer services, and practiced Judaism in secret.

At the end of the persecution, the Egyptian caliph and his son and successor permitted Jews and Christians to return to their former religions, and pay arrears in their poll tax. Synagogues were rebuilt, and, in the following years, Jews resumed their place as a tolerated minority with an upper crust of courtiers and a large class of successful merchants.[28] One explanation for Jewish apostasy in the face of Islamic oppression in Almohad Spain was the memory of the restoration to Judaism in Egypt at the beginning of the eleventh century.[29]

The Jews who fled from Almoravid rule in Spain and then from Almohad terror to the then-more-secure, steadily expanding Christian sector of northern Spain pursued the same diversified economic life that mitigated their "otherness" and attenuated their persecution in the Muslim world.[30] Their upbringing in Muslim society also played to their advantage during the Reconquista. Catholic kings sent many as colonists to newly conquered Muslim towns in the south. Some Jews were even assigned important political posts as administrators. They had the advantage of knowing Arabic and being intimately familiar with Muslim ways. Furthermore, Christian rulers could trust them because they were refugees from recent persecution by the Almohads.

Thanks to the Reconquista the Sephardim of Arab Spain brought the superior Arab culture of the Muslim world to Castile and Aragon. In Christian Sepharad, they translated Arabic works into Latin. The Sephardim were honored with elite positions in the courts of Spanish Christian kings, just as they had served caliphs and sultans in the Muslim domain. Jewish physicians, learned in Greco-Arabic medicine, flourished in Christian circles because of their superior medical knowledge. The Jewish intelligentsia from Andalusia (which included the physicians) also imported Greco-Arabic philosophy to a society that did not know its traditions. The Sephardim of Christian Spain continued to pursue the philosophical study of Judaism, notably the Aristotelian approach known as Averroism. Two Arabic-speaking Sephardim of the twelfth century, Moses Maimonides and Abraham ibn Daud, paved the way in Jewish Aristotelianism. Maimonides left Spain and wrote in Muslim Egypt. Ibn Daud wrote in reconquered Christian Toledo.

Many Jews in Christian Spain and others in southern France feared that the Aristotelianism imported by the Sephardim would weaken traditional Judaism. They opposed the teaching of Maimonides' philosophical works. A huge controversy over his writings erupted in the thirteenth century on both sides of the Pyrenees. This escalated until heresy-hunting Dominican friars burned Maimonides' writings, even as they were hunting down Catholic heretics in southern France.[31]

The literary culture of the Sephardim of Christian Spain drew inspiration from its Arabic roots. Hebrew poetry in the Arabic mode continued to be cultivated in Christian Spain. It soon, however, came under the influence of local verse, including that of the troubadours. Jewish courtiers served Christian rulers in Spain, just as their ancestors had served rulers in Muslim Andalusia and elsewhere in the medieval Arab world. Jews in Christian Spain also established Jewish courts, where poetry formed one of the centerpieces of cultural expression.

In short, the political status, economic position, and literary traditions of the Sephardim of Christian Spain during, and to a large extent after, the period of the Reconquista had their antecedents in the Arab-Muslim world.

It should not be implied that Sephardic civilization in Christian Spain lacked originality or mimicked entirely the culture of Jewry of Arab lands. Transformations included—in addition to the developments in poetry previously mentioned—a new Talmudism of commentaries. These largely replaced the codificatory tradition and Bible-centricism of the Jews of Muslim Spain and other parts of the medieval Arab world. It also embraced a new pietism, influenced by the Jewish pietistic movement in Germany in the twelfth and thirteenth centuries (*hasidut ashkenaz*).

The Spanish Kabbalah first appeared in twelfth-century Provence. It spread across the Pyrenees to Spain, where the Zohar was written at the end of the thirteenth century. And Sephardic culture in the Christian phase evolved new and creative forms of interreligious debate with Christianity, as well as within the Jewish community between professing Jews and Jewish converts to Catholicism.[32]

In the late thirteenth and early fourteenth centuries, with the Reconquista mostly completed, the attitude toward the Jews changed in Christian Spain. As their political utility as administrators and colonists of newly annexed territories waned, Christian anti-Semitism came to the fore, especially among the nobility. A turning point occurred in 1391 when anti-Jewish pogroms broke out in various cities in the kingdoms of Spain.

The violence was sudden and terrifying. But there, too, the surviving Sephardim reacted in the tradition of their ancestors in Muslim Spain and Muslim Egypt. Instead of suffering martyrdom, thousands fled to then-more-tolerant Muslim North Africa, while thousands of others converted to Christianity. A major disputation against Judaism in Barcelona in 1412 to 1414, followed by severe anti-Jewish legislation, inflated the numbers of converts. Unlike the victims of the Almohad and al-Hakim persecutions, these Sephardic conversos, as they were known in Spanish, were not permitted to return to Judaism. Rather, they formed a new class in Spain of former Jews, known pejoratively as "Marranos" (a word probably meaning "swine"). These Jews observed Christianity outwardly and followed Jewish practices in the secrecy of their homes. This was nothing more than the *taqiya* of Islamic society. Like other cultural characteristics of the Sephardim, the Marrano phenomenon had its antecedent during the Muslim period and underscored the Arab-world origins of Sephardic Jewry.

In 1492, after their exile from Spain, Jews had limited options for migration. They were not able to resettle in most of the lands of Christendom. Jews had been expelled from England in 1290, from France in 1394, and from dozens of duchies and cities in Germany throughout the fifteenth century. Parts of Italy that fell under Spanish control were similarly uninviting. Consequently, the bulk of Sephardic émigrés fled to Muslim territory, stretching from nearby Morocco and Algeria, to Egypt, Palestine, and Syria, as well as to the Muslim Ottoman Empire in Anatolia, Turkey, and the Balkans.

Because the two groups had an enemy in common, the Habsburg Empire (which from the beginning of the sixteenth century included Catholic Spain), the Ottomans were particularly happy to receive the Jews. As the Sephardic courtiers of Christian Spain had done for their rulers, the Jewish immigrants now applied their political and economic talents toward Ottoman interests. When the Ottomans conquered Syria, Palestine, Egypt, and North Africa (up to the Moroccan border) at the beginning of the sixteenth century, Sephardim who settled there in 1492 (alongside the descendants of those who had come as early as 1391) gained economic and political advantages. In the sixteenth century, many Marranos—that is Sephardim who had claimed to convert to Catholicism and their descendants—left Spain and Portugal to escape indictment by the Inquisition for practicing Judaism in secret. As nominal Catholics, they could resettle in Christian lands. But many of them also ended up in the Ottoman Empire. There, they easily reverted to Judaism and joined the already flourishing communities of Sephardic victims of the expulsion of 1492 and descendants of exiles from the Spanish pogroms of 1391.[33]

In the Ottoman Empire, Sephardim rapidly rose to a position of dominance over other Jewish communities. The older, Greek-speaking communities of Byzantium (the Romaniotes) and the more recently arrived Ashkenazic refugees from Christian persecution and expulsions (especially in Germany) were heavily impacted by the Sephardic presence. The same was true of the indigenous Arabic-speaking Jews living in North Africa, Palestine, and Syria. Sephardim, including former Marranos, rose to positions of power in the Ottoman central and provincial governments. Ladino, the Castilian dialect that the Sephardim carried with them from Spain, achieved a permanent foothold, especially in present-day Bulgaria, Greece, Israel, Rhodes, Romania, Turkey, and Yugoslavia. Sephardic synagogue customs infiltrated the Ashkenazic rite.

One of the most telling signs of the Sephardic ascendance in the Muslim lands of the Ottoman Empire is that in Israel all Jews from Arab and even non-Arab Muslim countries are lumped together, imprecisely, under the unified rubric "Sephardim." The Jews of Iraq, Yemen, Persia, Afghanistan, and the central Asian Muslim republics of the former Soviet Union never experienced a significant Iberian influence. The Hebrew term *"edot ha-mizrah"* (Jewish communities of the Orient) better encompasses the non-Ashkenazic portion of the Israeli population. The persistence of the nomenclature "Sephardic" in part reflects the overwhelming historical influence that Jews from Spain had on Jewry in the Ottoman Empire and in Morocco. At the same time, as a term of belittlement, it betrays an Ashkenazic "Orientalism," meaning a reassertion of European Jewry's own superiority. It is an answer to the "myth of Sephardic supremacy" that, paradoxically, Ashkenazic Jews themselves invented in the nineteenth century as a stick to beat both European Christians and their own eastern European Jewish brethren.

The Sephardic influence on the Arab world has an ironic and somewhat amusing connection as well. The so-called Sephardic pronunciation of Hebrew was adopted by Ashkenazic Zionists immigrating from Russia to Palestine at the end of the nineteenth century. This was the pronunciation in use by the indigenous Jewish communities, as well as among the descendants of Sephardic immigrants living in the Ottoman Empire since the late fifteenth century. Originally, this pronunciation came from Babylonia in the early Islamic period and was disseminated to regions as far away as Spain by Babylonian Jews who migrated to the western Mediterranean.

The Russian Zionists, among them Eliezer ben Yehuda (the founder of modern Hebrew), eagerly shed the trappings of their Ashkenazic, Yiddishized Judaism. They, too, were enamored by the "myth of Sephardic superiority" and its correlative, the "myth of the interfaith utopia" in Muslim Spain. Thus, they enthusiastically embraced the Hebrew accent of the indigenous Jews of Arab Palestine. They surmised that this accent preserved the original pronunciation of biblical times. They were unaware that the oldest pronunciation of Hebrew would later be shown to be closer, in many ways, in its features to Ashkenazic than to Sephardic phonology.

NOTES

1. Bernard Lewis, *The Jews of Islam* (Princeton, NJ: Princeton University Press, 1984).

2. See my book, *Under Crescent and Cross: The Jews of the Middle Ages* (Princeton, NJ: Princeton University Press, 1994), some of whose argument is reproduced in parts of the present essay

3. H. J. Zimmels, *Ashkenazim and Sephardim: Their Relations, Differences, and Problems as Reflected in the Rabbinical Responsa* (reprint, Hoboken, NJ: Ktav, 1996), for instance.

4. Obadiah 1:20.

5. Solomon Katz, *The Jews in the Visigothic and Frankish Kingdoms of Spain and Gaul* (Cambridge, MA: The Medieval Academy of America, 1937).

6. Eliyahu Ashtor, *The Jews of Moslem Spain*, trans. Aaron Klein and Jenny Machlowitz Klein, 3 vols. (Philadelphia: Jewish Publication Society, 1973–1984).

7. Yitzhak Baer, *A History of the Jews in Christian Spain*, trans. Louis Schoffman, 2 vols. (1961–1966; reprint, Philadelphia: Jewish Publication Society, 1992).

8. Jane S. Gerber, *The Jews of Spain: A History of the Sephardic Experience* (New York: Free Press, 1992).

9. *Sefer gezerot Ashkenaz ve-Tzarfat*, ed. A. M. Habermann (Jerusalem: Tarshish, 1945); and Susan Einbinder, *Beautiful Death: Jewish Poetry and Martyrdom in Medieval France* (Princeton, NJ: Princeton University Press, 2002), for instance.

10. Yosef Hayim Yerushalmi, *Zakhor: Jewish History and Jewish Memory* (Seattle: University of Washington Press, 1982), chap. 3.

11. Robert S. Wistrich, *Antisemitism: The Longest Hatred* (London: Thames Methuen, 1991). From the vast library of books on the subject, this work is a useful and accessible overview.

12. Salo W. Baron, "Ghetto and Emancipation," *Menorah Journal* 14, no. 6 (June 1928): 515–26, at the end. The essay was reprinted in *The Menorah Treasury*, ed. Leo W. Schwarz (Philadelphia: Jewish Publication Society, 1964), 50–63.

13. Heinrich Graetz, *A History of the Jews* (Philadelphia: Jewish Publication Society, 1894), vol. 3, 53, 326, for example.

14. Ismar Schorsch, "The Myth of Sephardic Supremacy," *Leo Baeck Institute Year Book* 34 (1989): 47–66; and Graetz, *A History of the Jews*, vol. 3, 326.

15. For more elaboration of the discussion in the previous paragraphs see Cohen, *Under Crescent and Cross*, introduction, chap. 1.

16. Gideon Libson, *Jewish and Islamic Law: A Comparative Study of Custom during the Geonic Period* (Cambridge: Harvard University Press, 2003).

17. Maria Rosa Menocal, Raymond P. Scheindlin, Michael Sells, eds., *The Literature of Al-Andalus* (New York: Cambridge University Press, 2000); Peter Cole, *Selected Poems of Shemuel HaNagid* (Princeton, NJ: Princeton University Press, 1995); Raymond P. Scheindlin, *Wine, Women, and Death: Medieval Hebrew Poems on the Good Life* (Philadelphia: Jewish Publication Society, 1986); and idem, *The Gazelle: Medieval Hebrew Poems on God, Israel, and the Soul* (Philadelphia: Jewish Publication Society, 1991).

18. Marcel Simon, *Versus Israel: A Study of the Relations between Christians and Jews in the Roman Empire* (New York: Littman Library, 1986), 92–94; Cohen, *Under Crescent and Cross*, 17–22.

19. Cohen, *Under Crescent and Cross*, 22–29, 145–51.

20. Kenneth R. Stow, *Alien Minority: The Jews of Medieval Latin Europe* (Cambridge: Harvard University Press, 1992), overview; Jeremy Cohen, *The Friars and the Jews: The Evolution of Medieval Anti-Judaism* (Ithaca, NY: Cornell University Press, 1982); and the collection of sources Robert Chazan, *Church, State, and the Jew in the Middle Ages* (New York: Behrman House, 1980). These works are among the vast literature on the status of the Jews in medieval Europe.

21. Antoine Fattal, *Le statut légal des non-Musulmans en pays d'Islam* (1958; reprint, Beirut: Dar El-Machreq, 1995); Cohen, *Under Crescent and Cross*, 52–74; Mark R. Cohen, "What Was the Pact of 'Umar? A Literary-Historical Study," *Jerusalem Studies in Arabic and Islam* 23 (1999): 100–157. Fattal's work is the standard.

22. S. D. Goitein, *A Mediterranean Society: The Jewish Communities of the Arab World as Portrayed in the Documents of the Cairo Geniza*, vol. 1, *Economic Foundations* (Berkeley and Los Angeles: University of California Press, 1967); Cohen, *Under Crescent and Cross*, chap. 5, for the comparison with Christian Europe.

23. The ideas compacted into the previous two paragraphs are discussed at much greater length in Cohen, *Under Crescent and Cross*, chaps. 6–8, which approach the issue of Jewish life under Islam from some new angles.

24. Cohen, *Under Crescent and Cross*, chap. 10.

25. On the Almohads and the Jews, see H. Z. Hirschberg, *A History of the Jews in North Africa*, vol. 1 (Leiden, the Netherlands: Brill, 1974), 123–39.

26. Gerson D. Cohen's edition of Abraham ibn Daud, *Sefer ha-Qabbalah* (Philadelphia: Jewish Publication Society, 1967), introduction; David Corcos, "The Attitude of the Almohad Rulers towards the Jews" (Hebrew), *Zion* 32 (1967): 137–60, reprinted in his *Studies in the History of the Jews of Morocco* (Jerusalem: Rubin Mass, 1976), 319–42; and Menahem Ben-Sasson, "On the Jewish Identity of Forced Converts: A Study of Forced Conversion in the Almohad Period" (Hebrew), *Pe^camim* 42 (1990): 16–37. The effect the Almoravid and Almohad conquests had on Andalusian Jewry are discussed in the introduction to Gerson D. Cohen's work.

27. Gerson D. Cohen, "Messianic Postures of Ashkenazim and Sephardim (Prior to Sabbethai Zevi)," in *Studies of the Leo Baeck Institute,* ed. Max Kreutzberger (New York: F. Ungar, 1967), 115–56, reprinted in Gerson Cohen, *Studies in the Variety of Rabbinic Cultures* (Philadelphia: Jewish Publication Society, 1991), especially 289ff.; Haym Soloveitchik, "Between Islam and Christendom" (Hebrew), in *Qedushat ha-hayyim ve-heruf ha-nefesh* (Sanctity of Life and Martyrdom: Studies in Memory of Amir Yekutiel), ed. Isaiah M. Gafni and Aviezer Ravitzky (Jerusalem: Merkaz Zalman Shazar, 1992), 149–52; Lewis, *The Jews of Islam,* 82–84; Hava Lazarus-Yafeh, "Queen Esther: A Forced Convert?" (Hebrew), *Tarbiz* 57 (1988): 121–22; Ben-Sasson, "On the Jewish Identity of Forced Converts," 20.

28. Yaakov Lev, "Conversion and Converts in Medieval Egypt" (Hebrew), *Pe^camim* 42 (1990): 79; and idem, "Persecutions and Conversions to Islam in Eleventh-Century Egypt," *Asian and African Studies* 22 (1988): 87.

29. Goitein, *A Mediterranean Society,* vol. 2, *The Community* (Berkeley and Los Angeles: University of California Press, 1971), 299–300.

30. On the Jews in Reconquest Spain, see again Baer, *A History of the Jews in Christian Spain*; and Gerber, *The Jews of Spain*.

31. Joseph Sarachek, *Faith and Reason: The Conflict over the Rationalism of Maimonides* (Williamsport, PA: Bayard, 1935); and Daniel Jeremy Silver, *Maimonidean Criticism and the Maimonidean Controversy, 1180–1240* (Leiden, the Netherlands: Brill, 1965).

32. Benjamin Gampel, "A Letter to a Wayward Teacher: The Transformations of Sephardic Culture in Christian Iberia," in *Cultures of the Jews: A New History,* ed. David Biale (New York: Schocken, 2002), 389–447. A good recent survey of Sephardic culture in Christian Spain is to be found in Gampel's work.

33. Avigdor Levy, *Sephardim in the Ottoman Empire* (Princeton, NJ: Darwin, 1992); and idem, ed., *The Jews of the Ottoman Empire* (Princeton, NJ: Darwin, 1994).

Chapter 3

The Judeo-Arabic Heritage

Norman A. Stillman

Introductory Reflections

Nearly forty years ago, I brought my fiancée, who had been born in Morocco and raised in Israel, home to meet my family. I shall never forget the moment when she met my grandmother. My grandmother, whose English, even after fifty years in the United States, was still heavily accented, asked my fiancée, "Does your family speak Jewish?" Not understanding what she meant, my bride-to-be replied, "Of course, we all speak Hebrew. That is the language in Israel." "No, no," my grandmother insisted, "Not *ivres*. Does your family speak Yiddish?" "Ah," exclaimed my fiancée. "No, not Yiddish. We have our own 'Jewish'—Jewish Arabic." My poor grandmother was bewildered. For her, Yiddish (literally "Jewish," but short for *yiddish taytsh*, Judeo-German, or better Judeo-Germanic) was *mameloshn* (mother tongue). It was thought of by Eastern European Jews as essentially "Jewish." In the nineteenth and early twentieth centuries, there were those who actively opposed the revival of Hebrew as a living language for a modern national movement. Although Hebrew was *leshon qodesh* (the holy tongue), it was not the people's language—at least not the language of the Eastern European Jewish masses.[1]

Another personal experience of mine occurred at a bus stop in the Baqʿa quarter of Jerusalem in the early 1970s, where my wife and I encountered a friend of her mother's. She was an elderly, traditional Moroccan woman. She was easily recognizable even before she spoke by her headscarf, jewelry, and various other cultural cues. My wife introduced me to her, and we chatted in the Judeo-Arabic of Sefrou, their hometown in Morocco. I had, at that time, begun a study of this particular vernacular both in Morocco and Israel.[2] I was delighted by the opportunity to practice my speaking skills, and my wife was clearly delighted to show off her Ashkenazi American husband who could speak their native tongue. A short while later, after the woman departed, I noticed that my wife had tears in her eyes. When I asked her why, she told me that she suddenly remembered how years earlier, when she was a schoolgirl, that if she saw that same woman from a distance, she would walk blocks out of her way to avoid her. This was to avoid embarrassment from having to speak Moroccan Arabic in public because of the strong prejudice against Jews from Muslim countries (so-called *mizrahim*, or Oriental Jews) and especially Moroccan Jews. In the 1950s and early 1960s, it was not at all chic to speak Arabic of any kind in Israel—and certainly not to be Moroccan.

The great irony in these two personal anecdotes is that, amongst all the many Jewish Diaspora languages of post-Talmudic times (Yiddish, Ladino, Shuadit (Judeo-Provençal), Judeo-Persian, Judeo-Greek, Judeo-French, Judeo-Tat, Judeo-Berber, and still others less well known), Judeo-Arabic held a place of special distinction. It had the longest recorded history after Hebrew and Aramaic (from the ninth century to the present).[3] It had the widest geographical diffusion, extending across three continents during the Middle Ages. Furthermore, and even more significantly, it was the medium of expression for one of the foremost periods of Jewish cultural and intellectual creativity.

Judeo-Arabic and Jewish Languages

The existence of Jewish languages was a function of Jewish history. For more than two millennia, Jews lived scattered throughout many lands and cultures. But the transformational effects of their dispersion were mitigated or tempered by their own group cohesion within the far-flung lands in which they lived. They perceived these lands as *galut*, or exile, both spiritually and politically. Wherever they lived, Jews created their own distinct vernaculars that were usually written in Hebrew script and contained considerable amounts of Hebrew/Aramaic vocabulary. These Jewish idioms differed also from their non-Jewish cognates in their pronunciation, grammar, syntax, and lexical choices within the non-Hebrew root vocabulary. The Jews, subconsciously, created and preserved a unique linguistic identity.[4]

Judeo-Arabic may be considered the premier Diaspora language. For most of the last 1400 years, Arabic, in its Jewish form, was spoken by more

Jews than any other language. From the seventh until the end of the seventeenth centuries, the majority of the world's Jews lived in the *Dār al-Islām* (Domain of Islam). Furthermore, Arabic was spoken or used as a cultural language by Jews across a greater geographical expanse than any other language was. In the Middle Ages, Arabic was the Jewish language from Spain (and even to some extent from Provence) all the way to India. Although Yiddish spread to the ends of the earth in the late nineteenth and early twentieth centuries as Ashkenazi Jews poured out of eastern Europe to the New World, South Africa, and Australia, it did not sink long-lasting roots and was quickly abandoned by the second and third generations.

Some forms of Judeo-Arabic also spread beyond their original heartlands in the nineteenth and twentieth centuries, to Iraqi Jewish trading colonies in India, Southeast Asia, Hong Kong, and Shanghai; to Aleppan Jewish enclaves in France, England, and the Americas; and to Yemenite Jewish communities in India and elsewhere.[5] Most importantly, however, Judeo-Arabic was the literary medium for some of the greatest works of the Jewish spirit. This did not include Mizrahi, Sephardi, regional, or temporal works, but contributions that belonged to the common heritage of Judaism and the Jewish people. In the Judeo-Arabic world, many of the key elements of Judaism, as a religious civilization under the constitutional framework of the Talmud, were crystallized, formulated, and systematized. These elements included law, liturgy, philosophy and theology, scriptural exegesis, Hebrew grammar and lexicography, and Hebrew poetry and belles lettres.

Historical Survey of Judeo-Arabic

Early Judeo-Arabic

Before the spread of Islam, the only Jews speaking Arabic were those of the Jewish tribes in Arabia. Their everyday language was apparently similar to that of their Arab neighbors, except for the Hebrew and Aramaic words they used to express specifically Jewish religious and cultural concepts. The Arabs referred to this Judeo-Arabic dialect as *yahūdiyya* (Jewish speech). Some of the Hebrew and Aramaic vocabulary of this early Judeo-Arabic, as well as a number of religious concepts, passed into the speech of the pagan Arabs and, thereafter, into Muslim Arabic.[6] Although the Jews of sixth- and seventh-century Arabia most likely wrote letters and documents in Hebrew characters, they left behind no Judeo-Arabic literature. The only literary art at the time was oral poetry. The poems preserved in later Arabic tradition by Jewish bards from this period, such as al-Samaw'al, were completely devoid of any Jewish content. There seemed to be no continuation between this early Judeo-Arabic and the great Jewish language of the Middle Ages.

Medieval Judeo-Arabic

The Islamic conquests of the seventh and eighth centuries established a domain that stretched from the borders of India and China in the East, to the Atlantic Ocean and the Pyrenees in the West. The majority of Jews living in the world during this time came under Arab rule. The Arabic language became the lingua franca of this vast empire, taking the place of Aramaic and Greek, which served as the international languages of culture and administration throughout much of the Middle East and North Africa previously. As the conquered people adopted Arabic, it underwent a variety of metamorphoses, evolving into Middle Arabic (or rather, Middle Arabic dialects). This simplified form of the language dropped the case endings of the old Arabian dialects, transformed the syntax from a synthetic to an analytical structure, and greatly enriched the vocabulary.[7]

The Jews also adopted the new international language of culture. By the tenth century, it became not only their daily vernacular, but also the language used for most of their written expression. Arabic was used for day-to-day correspondence—as we know from the rich treasure trove of documents called the Cairo Geniza—as well as for religious queries and responsa (Heb., *she'elot u-teshuvot*), documents, biblical exegesis and other textual commentaries, philosophy and theology, and works on Hebrew grammar and lexicography.[8]

For linguistic and psychological reasons, the transition to Arabic for the majority of Jews in the caliphate was presumably not very difficult. Arabic was a Semitic language with many affinities to Hebrew and Aramaic. Furthermore, Islam was a strictly monotheistic religious civilization based on the notion of a divine law that was partially written and partially oral. This was similar, in many respects, to Judaism. Islam, like Judaism, eschewed religious iconography, and did not manifest the kind of hostility toward Judaism that Christianity did. In the Arabic world, in contrast to the Christian world, Jews were not the only subjects not belonging to the ruling faith. They shared their status with the far more numerous Christians and Zoroastrians. Medieval Islamic civilization was not a totally clerical or feudal one, as medieval Latin Christendom was.

The ninth through twelfth centuries witnessed the Commercial Revolution, the rise of the bourgeoisie, and a revival of Hellenistic science and humanism in the Muslim world. There was a high degree of interconfessional cooperation in the fields of science, philosophy, and commerce, which Islam—like Judaism—held in high esteem. Consequently, there were many aspects of the general emerging Islamic secular culture that Jews found attractive and unthreatening. They could participate in a symbiotic way with cultural commensalism.[9]

Jews normally wrote Arabic in Hebrew characters that were already familiar to them, as they were taught Hebrew from early childhood for religious purposes. Members of the intelligentsia could read Arabic script with at least some degree of proficiency. Some even produced works for a broader audience in the standard Arabic script as well. However, it was not uncommon for Jews to have books by Muslim writers transcribed into Hebrew letters for more convenient reading, according to the Geniza. Although Hebrew and Arabic both belonged to the Semitic family of languages, Arabic has several consonants not found in Hebrew. Judeo-Arabic made up for this by adopting a system of diacritical points in imitation of the Muslim Arabic writing system (for example, the Arabic consonant *dād* was indicated by a dotted *sadī,* and *zā'* by a dotted *tet*). The system was somewhat haphazard, and there were minor deviations among different writers in the transcription of uniquely Arabic sounds into Hebrew (for example, both the Hebrew *gimel* and ʿ*ayin* with a mark were used to indicate the Arabic *ghayn*).

The Jews in the medieval Islamic world did not write in the vernacular language they spoke on a daily basis. Instead, they used a literary Middle Arabic—a form of the language between Classical Arabic (the only acceptable medium of expression in Islamic culture) and the local dialects. The medieval Judeo-Arabic literary language varied in style. One style was a Classical Arabic with some Middle Arabic elements (as for example, in works of philosophy, theology, biblical translation, and commentary). Another was a slightly classicized Middle Arabic, bristling with colloquialisms, depending upon the education of the writer and formal or informal nature of the written material (seen, for example, in the personal correspondence by people from all walks of life preserved in the Cairo Geniza).

The rich literary output in medieval Judeo-Arabic was stimulated by the intellectual and spiritual ferment that occurred in the caliphate, beginning in the second half of the eighth century and continuing throughout the ninth and tenth. The first Jewish thinker to take up the challenges posed by the rise of rationalism, free-thinking, and sectarian movements (such as Karaism) was Saʿadya Gaon (882–942). Saʿadya was the leading rabbinic scholar of his day. He responded in the language best understood by his fellow Jews—Arabic. Born in Egypt, he became the gaon, or head, of the Sura Academy in Baghdad, and was recognized as one of the highest religious authorities in the Jewish world. He produced a massive body of writings, not only for other scholars, but for educated laymen as well. To resolve the spiritual confusion caused by conflicting claims to truth by different religions, sects, and philosophical schools, he wrote the first exposition of Jewish theology, *The Book of Doctrines and Beliefs* (Ar., *Kitāb al-Amānāt wa 'l-Iʿtiqādāt*).

To meet the challenges posed by the Karaites' emphasis on the study of the Bible, Saʿadya translated the Scriptures into Arabic (*al-Tafsār*) and wrote a rational commentary (*al-Taʾwīl*). His translation was more than a pioneer work. It was a literary milestone that influenced many later Jewish and Christian Arabic Bible translations. His commentary affected many later works of exegesis, including Abraham Ibn Ezra's Hebrew commentary. To facilitate the study of the Bible, Saʿadya composed the first Hebrew dictionary (Heb., *ha-Agron*), which followed the models of Arabic lexicography and used Arabic as the language of explanation. He also produced the first real siddur, or prayerbook, with accompanying notes and instructions in Arabic (*Jāmiʿ al-Salawāt*). Saʿadya was the first scholar to write legal tracts (e.g., *The Book of Inheritance Law*—Ar., *Kitāb al-Mawārith*) and responsa in Arabic.[10]

During this time, a major center of Jewish scholarly activity developed far to the west of Iraq in the North African city of Qayrawan (modern-day Tunisia). The "sages of Qayrawan" were noted in Hebrew literature for their religious and secular learning. The earliest and most famous of these sages was the physician and Neoplatonic philosopher Isaac Israeli (ca. 850–950). Israeli's Arabic works were translated into Hebrew and Latin and studied for centuries in medieval and Renaissance Europe. He was named "the distinguished monarch of medicine." His disciple, Dunash ben Tamim (d. ca. 960), in addition to being a physician and philosopher, was a Hebrew grammarian and philologist. He authored a commentary on the popular mystical treatise, *The Book of Creation* (Heb., *Sefer ha-Yesira*).

In the realm of religious scholarship, many figures were produced. Of these, the most outstanding writer in Judeo-Arabic was Nissim ben Jacob Ibn Shahin (d. 1062). He wrote an important commentary on the Talmud, entitled *The Key to the Locks of the Talmud* (Ar., *Kitāb Miftāḥ Maghāliq al-Talmūd*). He also produced a book of didactic and entertaining tales, *The Book of Comfort* (Ar., *Kitāb al-Faraj baʿd al-Shidda*), the first work of its kind in medieval Jewish literature.[11]

In Muslim Iberia ("al-Andalus" in Arabic and "Sepharad" in Hebrew) medieval Judeo-Arabic literary culture reached its apogee. Under the patronage of Jewish courtiers, such as Ḥasday Ibn Shaprut (905–75) and Samuel ha-Nagid Ibn Naghrela (993–1056), Jewish scholars and men of letters produced works on Hebrew grammar, lexicography, prosody, and philosophy in Judeo-Arabic. Jonah Ibn Janaḥ (fl. first half of the eleventh century), for example, wrote what became the most influential grammar of the Hebrew language for centuries to come, *The Book of Variegated Flower-Beds* (Ar., *Kitāb al-Lumaʿ*). He also completed a dictionary of biblical Hebrew, *The Book of Roots* (Ar., *Kitāb al-Uṣūl*). Moses Ibn Ezra (ca. 1055–after 1135) produced the first and most comprehensive study on the art of Hebrew rhetoric and poetry from the Middle Ages, *The Book of Conversation and Discussion* (Ar., *Kitāb al-Muḥādara wa'l- Mudhākara*).[12] Solomon Ibn Gabirol (ca. 1027–57), who was known to the schoolmen of Christian Europe as Avicebron, wrote a widely read Neoplatonic treatise, *The Source of Life*. Though the Arabic original was lost, it lived on in its Latin translation as *Fons vitae*. One of the most popular works of mystical and ethical devotion in later Judaism, *The Duties of the Heart* (Ar., *Kitāb al-Hidāya ilā Fara'id al-Qulūb*), was originally written in Arabic in Spain by Baḥya Ibn Paquda (fl. second half of the eleventh century).[13] Also written in Judeo-Arabic was the classic apologetic for traditional faith against philosophical rationalism, Judah ha-Levi's *The Kuzari* (Ar., *Kitāb al-Khazarī*). This dramatic dialogue, together with ha-Levi's cycle of poems known as the "Songs of Zion," became a chief inspirational work of proto-Zionism.[14]

The Arabic-speaking Jews of Sepharad produced a rich, new Hebrew poetry that used the rhymes, meters, and many of the themes of Classical Arabic poetry. In addition to sublime religious poetry, Jewish poets such as Dunash ben Labrat, Moses Ibn Ezra, Solomon Ibn Gabirol, and Judah ha-Levi, wrote panegyrics to Jewish courtiers and poems celebrating such traditionally un-Jewish subjects as carousing, nature, and love, including poems with homoerotic themes.[15] Poetry was the one genre that was almost exclusively in Hebrew. Contrary to the suggestions of some scholars, this was not due to the fact that the Jewish poets did not have a sufficient command of Classical Arabic or that they were not sufficiently imbued with the Arabic cultural ideal of *al-ᶜarabiyya* (there were some Jewish poets such as Samuel and Joseph Ibn Naghrela and Ibn Sahl al-Isrā'īlī who wrote elegant Arabic verse). Instead, it was because they had so thoroughly absorbed the values of Arab society. Poetry in Islamic civilization was the ultimate national art form. Hence, Jews cultivated Hebrew poetry as a national response to prove that the language of their scripture and national heritage was in no way inferior to the language of the Koran and the Arab poets.[16]

Although the Hebrew poetry of medieval Iberia was written according to Arabic stylistic models, one ought not to consider it merely to be an epigone literature. The Sephardi poets wrote inspired liturgical poems as an ornament to synagogue worship and other religious occasions. This was a genre that had no parallel in the Arabic poetic canon.

Sepharad's Judeo-Arabic tradition continued outside of Iberia after the Almohads snuffed out open Jewish life in the Muslim parts of Spain. In Egypt, Moses Maimonides (1135–1204), who saw himself as an Andalusian and upholder of its intellectual heritage, wrote all his works, with the exception of his law code, in Arabic. His medical and scientific treatises, which were aimed at a general audience, were composed in the standard form of the language. But his voluminous responsa, commentary to the Mishna, and great philosophical oeuvre, *The Guide of the Perplexed* (Ar., *Dalālat al-Hā'irīn*), were all in Judeo-Arabic. His son and successor as Nagid of the Egyptian Jewish community, Abraham Maimonides (1186–1237), continued the intellectual tradition, composing his great work of mystical pietism *The Complete Guide for Servants of God* (Ar., *Kifāyat al-ᶜĀbidīn*) in Judeo-Arabic. The next generations of the Maimonides family also continued to write in the Judeo-Arabic tradition.[17]

Modern Judeo-Arabic

Around the late fifteenth century, medieval Judeo-Arabic began to give way to modern Judeo-Arabic, or rather, to modern varieties of Judeo-Arabic. The main universal characteristic of the many heterogeneous forms of these modern varieties was their colloquial nature. Arabic society was always a diglossic one, with very different written and spoken forms of the language. This was true for Jews in the Middle Ages as well. However,

Jews began writing in a language that was much closer to the vernaculars they spoke.

The shift from Middle Arabic to modern communal dialect forms resulted, in part, from the increased social isolation of the Jews of the Arab world. At the end of the Middle Ages, they lived within restrictive ghetto-like quarters, such as the *mellāh* and the *hārat al-Yahūd*.[18] This isolation was never hermetic. Jews interacted with Muslims on many levels in the economic and commercial sphere, buying, selling, and providing various services to each other. However, socially, intellectually, and psychologically, Jewish isolation was almost total. The shift from the literary medieval written language to more vernacular forms of Judeo-Arabic also represented an overall decline in the general level of education throughout the Islamic world. The ability to write in Classical Arabic, for example, seriously deteriorated among Muslims during this period. It was only revived with the *Nahda* (Awakening) movement led by Syrian and Lebanese Christians during the second half of the nineteenth century. The *Nahda*, however, held little appeal for the vast majority of Arabic-speaking Jews in modern times who at that point did not identify with Arab culture, much less with Arab nationalism.[19]

A third factor that might have contributed to the decline of the universal medieval literary form of Judeo-Arabic was the mass influx of Sephardi refugees to the major population centers of the Islamic world. The Iberian exiles came from Christian Spain and Portugal. Their forefathers had given up the Arabic culture of al-Andalus centuries earlier. The Sephardi rabbinical elite that became dominant in many of the Arabic-speaking lands used Hebrew as their primary language of literary expression.

Until a generation ago, most surveys of the Judeo-Arabic cultural heritage ended here. This was due to a classicist bias that viewed the intellectual, spiritual, and artistic work of the late Middle Ages and early modern times in the Islamic world as essentially decadent. Not untypical was the judgment expressed by a distinguished scholar in his article in the *Encyclopaedia Judaica* surveying Judeo-Arabic literature. He concluded by dismissing everything written after the fifteenth century as follows: "[I]t must be admitted that there is little value in these works, most of which are liturgical, exegetic, or translations of Hebrew pietistic works."[20] This dismissive judgment was grossly subjective and untrue. Modern Judeo-Arabic continued to be the medium of a rich and varied cultural heritage, some of whose roots went well back into the Middle Ages.

There always existed, alongside the Arabic high culture, a vibrant popular culture. During the Middle Ages, very little "vulgar" literature, such as folk poetry and prose for mass entertainment, was preserved in writing. The *Thousand and One Nights* was perhaps the best-known exception and is now widely considered a classic of world literature. The Jews of the Middle East and North Africa continued to create and consume a popular literature in Judeo-Arabic that was not merely of ethnographic or linguistic interest, but could be truly appreciated for its own sake and judged on its own terms. Both men and women from Morocco in the West to Yemen in the East composed a variety of poetic genres (ranging from the literary *qasīda* to the folk *muwwāl* and ᶜ*arobī*) in Judeo-Arabic. Some of this poetry was written, and some was entirely oral. Even illiterate women could compose sophisticated Judeo-Arabic poetry and compete in singing duels comparable to such contests as the medieval Arab *naqā'id* or the Provençal troubadour *tensons*.[21]

Most works of rabbinical high culture were written in Hebrew. However, throughout the Arabic-speaking world and all Diaspora Jewish societies, a living tradition of highly literal calque translations of religious texts, such as the Bible, the Mishna, and the Haggada existed. They were translated into the local vernacular used both for teaching young students and for the edification of adults with limited knowledge of Hebrew. These translations were known most commonly as *sharh*, but also as *tafsīr* and *maqshiyya*. There were also scriptural commentaries written in Arabic in the style of the *sharh*. Rabbi Raphael Berdugo (1747–1821) of Meknes, Morocco, known as "The Angel Raphael" (Heb., *ha-mal'akh Refa'el*), authored one such commentary, *Leshon Limmudim*.[22]

In the late nineteenth and early twentieth centuries, Judeo-Arabic newspapers and periodicals began to appear in the Middle East and North Africa. They even appeared outside of the region in Bombay and Calcutta, where there were substantial colonies of Iraqi Jewish merchants. These works were never as numerous as the thousands of such journals in Yiddish in Europe or the hundreds in Ladino in Turkey and the Balkans. However, the Judeo-Arabic newspapers and magazines served a similar function to their Yiddish and Ladino counterparts as vectors of modernization. They not only conveyed local and world news, but also discussed specifically Jewish issues such as Zionism, secularism, westernization, and anti-Semitism. They serialized and adapted modern European novels and short stories, such as Defoe's *Robinson Crusoe* and Dumas's *The Count of*

Monte Cristo. Tunisia had, by far, the largest number and the greatest variety of Judeo-Arabic periodicals of any country.

After World War I, Judeo-Arabic journals increasingly gave way to French publications from Morocco to Egypt due to the tremendous educational influence of the Alliance Israélite Universelle schools and the impact of French colonial rule in the Maghrebi countries. In Iraq and Lebanon, where modern Arabic culture made its strongest impression upon Jews, Jewish newspapers were published in Modern Standard Arabic beginning in the 1920s. A few Judeo-Arabic periodicals, however, continued to be published in Morocco, Tunisia, and Libya until the mass exodus from these countries following the establishment of the State of Israel. Several Judeo-Arabic periodicals were published in the new homeland to serve the new immigrants in the early years following their arrival.[23]

Modern Judeo-Arabic never became a major medium for original belletristic expression. Most world-class Middle Eastern and North African Jewish novelists, such as Naïm Kattan from Iraq and Albert Memmi from Tunisia, wrote their books in French. A number of important Jewish writers in Iraq, such as Anwar Sha'ul, Murad Michael, and Shalom Darwish, wrote in Modern Standard Arabic. One or two continued writing in Arabic even after immigrating to Israel.[24] There were a few Judeo-Arabic plays and novels published, mainly in Tunisia, by intellectuals such as Eliezer Farhi and Jacob Chemla. However, Modern Judeo-Arabic did serve to introduce Arabic-speaking Jews to western literary genres in translation. In addition to French and English novels, plays, and short stories, some of the new Hebrew fiction of the Haskala movement in Europe was translated into Judeo-Arabic. For example, Avraham Mapu's Zionist novel *Ahavat Siyyon* (*The Love of Zion*) appeared in Judeo-Arabic in Tunis in 1890 as *al-Hubb wa'l-Watan* (*Love and Homeland*).

Only a handful of Jews remain in the Arab world today. The overwhelming majority of Jews from Arab lands and their descendants live in Israel and France, while others reside in large communities in Canada, the United States, and elsewhere. Like Yiddish and Ladino, Judeo-Arabic is a dying language. But the Judeo-Arabic cultural heritage is anything but moribund. Judeo-Arabic words and expressions entered into modern Israeli Hebrew to no less—and perhaps to a greater extent—than Yiddishisms penetrated into American English. More importantly, Judeo-Arabic lives on in a myriad of ways through the maintenance of traditional practices, the ever-increasing scholarly study of Judeo-Arabic language, literature, and history, particularly in Israel and France, but also in

North America, and through the popular interpretations and translations of Judeo-Arabic wit and wisdom.

NOTES

1. On the competition between proponents of Hebrew and Yiddish, see Max Weinreich, *History of the Yiddish Language,* trans. Shlomo Noble (Chicago: University of Chicago Press, 1980), 286–99.

2. Norman A. Stillman, *The Language and Culture of the Jews of Sefrou, Morocco: An Ethnolinguistic Study.* Journal of Semitic Studies Monograph, no. 11 (Manchester, England: University of Manchester Press, 1988).

3. See Joshua Blau, *The Emergence and Linguistic Background of Judaeo-Arabic: A Study in the Origins of Middle Arabic* (Oxford: Oxford University Press, 1965).

4. As Haim Hillel Ben-Sasson has observed, "once an initially alien language gained acceptance, it became not only a vehicle of Jewish cultural and religious creativity, but also gradually became converted into a specifically Jewish idiom and a mark of Jewish identity that even formed barriers to later assimilation." See Haim Hillel Ben-Sasson, "Assimilation: Antiquity and the Middle Ages," *Encyclopaedia Judaica,* vol. 3, cols. 771–72.

5. Concerning the Iraqi Diaspora, see Abraham Ben-Jacob, *Babylonian Jewry in Diaspora* (in Hebrew) (Jerusalem: Kiriath-Sepher, 1985). On the Aleppan Diaspora, see Walter P. Zenner, *A Global Community: The Jews from Aleppo, Syria* (Detroit: Wayne State University Press, 2000); also Joseph A. D. Sutton, *Magic Carpet: Aleppo-in-Flatbush: The Story of a Unique Ethnic Jewish Community* (New York: Thayer-Jacoby, 1979).

6. Concerning *yahūdiyya,* which I would designate as proto-Judeo-Arabic, see Gordon D. Newby, "Observations about an Early Judaeo-Arabic," in *Jewish Quarterly Review,* n.s. 61 (1970): 212–21; also Charles Torrey, *The Jewish Foundation of Islam* (New York: Jewish Institute of Religion Press, 1933), 47–53. The two major studies on loanwords in old Arabic are Siegmund Fraenkel, *Die aramäischen Fremdwörter im Arabischen* (Leiden, the Netherlands: Brill, 1886); and A. Jeffrey, *The Foreign Vocabulary of the Qur'ān* (Baroda, India: Oriental Institute, 1938).

7. The standard work on the evolution of Middle Arabic is Johann Fück, *ᶜArabīya: Recherches sur l'histoire de la langue et du style arabe,* trans. Claude Denizeau (Paris: Marcel Didier, 1955); and for Judeo-Arabic, Joshua Blau, *The Emergence and Linguistic Background of Judaeo-Arabic: A Study in the Origins of Middle Arabic* (Oxford: Oxford University Press, 1965).

8. The Cairo Geniza is the name given to a unique cache of nearly a quarter of a million discarded papers and documents dating from the Middle Ages to early modern times, primarily in Hebrew script, that were deposited according to Jewish practice in a storage room attached to the Ben Ezra Synagogue in Fustat (Old

Cairo). The Geniza is the most important single source for medieval Judeo-Arabic literary and nonliterary materials as well as the most important primary source for Jewish life in the Islamic High Middle Ages. For the story of the discovery of this treasure trove and a general description of its contents, see Stefan C. Reif, *A Jewish Archive from Old Cairo: The History of Cambridge University's Genizah Collection* (Richmond, England: Curzon, 2000).

9. This notion is developed in Norman A. Stillman, "The Commensality of Islamic and Jewish Civilizations," in *Middle Eastern Lectures*, vol. 2 (Tel Aviv: Moshe Dayan Center for Middle Eastern and African Studies and Tel-Aviv University, 1997), 81–94.

10. The standard biographical and bibliographical study on Saʿadya which is now woefully outdated is Henry Malter, *Saadia Gaon: His Life and Works* (Philadelphia: Jewish Publication Society, 1921; reprint, New York: Hermon, 1969). For a bibliography—also not up to date—of additional scholarship on Saʿadya, see Aron Freimann, "Saadia Bibliography: 1920–1942," in *Saadia Anniversary Volume: Texts and Studies*, vol. 2 (New York: American Academy for Jewish Research, 1943), 327–38. Most of Saʿadya's surviving writings, both complete and in fragments, were published in the nineteenth and twentieth centuries. His great theological work has been translated twice into English: a complete translation by Samuel Rosenblatt, *The Book of Beliefs and Opinions* (New Haven: Yale University Press, 1948); and an abridged, but better annotated translation by Alexander Altmann, *The Book of Doctrines and Beliefs* (Oxford, England: East and West Library, 1946).

11. The best work on Qayrawan and its sages is Menahem Ben Sasson, *The Emergence of the Local Jewish Community in the Muslim World: Qayrawan, 800–1057* (in Hebrew) (Jerusalem: Magnes, 1996). Readers of English must still have recourse to H. Z. [J. W.] Hirschberg, *A History of the Jews in North Africa*, vol. 1 (Leiden, the Netherlands: Brill, 1974), 298–361. For Isaac Israeli, see Alexander Altmann and S. M. Stern, *Isaac Israeli: A Neo-Platonic Philosopher of the Early Tenth Century* (London: Oxford University Press, 1958). For Ibn Shahin, see Nissim Ben Jacob Ibn Shahin, *An Elegant Composition Concerning Relief after Adversity*, trans. William M. Brinner (New Haven: Yale University Press, 1977).

12. Regrettably, this important work has never been translated into English. However, there is a very good Spanish translation Moše Ibn ʿEzra, *Kitab al-Muhadara wal-Mudakara*, vol. 2, *Traducción*, trans. Montserrat Abumalham Mas (Madrid: Consejo Superior de Investigaciones Científicas, 1986).

13. This work came to have great popularity among Jews north of the Pyrenees after its translation into Hebrew, and there have been numerous translations into western languages in modern times. The best English translation from the original Arabic is *The Book of Direction to the Duties of the Heart*, trans. Menahem Mansoor (London: Routledge & Kegan Paul, 1973).

14. This work too has enjoyed numerous editions in its Hebrew translation and has also been translated several times into English. See, e.g., *Judah Hallevi's*

Kitab al Khazari, trans. Hartwig Hirschfeld (London: Routledge; and New York: Dutton, 1905).

15. For important studies of medieval Andalusian poetry, see Ross Brann, *The Compunctious Poet: Cultural Ambiguity and Hebrew Poetry in Muslim Spain* (Baltimore: Johns Hopkins University Press, 1991); and Raymond P. Scheindlin, *Wine, Women, and Death: Medieval Hebrew Poems of the Good Life* (Philadelphia: Jewish Publication Society, 1986); and idem, *The Gazelle: Medieval Hebrew Poems on God, Israel, and the Soul* (Philadelphia: Jewish Publication Society, 1991). How to interpret the subject of homoeroticism in this poetry has been the subject of fierce debate. Some scholars, such as Nehemia Allony have argued the theme is merely an artistic exercise in imitation of Arab models, whereas others, such as Jefim Schirmann, have taken the position that it reflects a social reality. See Nehemia Allony, "The 'Zevi' (Nasib) in the Hebrew Poetry in Spain," *Sefarad* 23, fascicle 2 (1963): 311–21; and Jefim Schirmann, "The Ephebe in Medieval Hebrew Poetry," *Sefarad* 15, fascicle 1 (1955): 55–68. For a good survey of some of the corroborating literature on pederasty, see Norman Roth, "Deal Gently with the Young Man: Love of Boys in Medieval Hebrew Poetry of Spain," *Speculum* 57, no. 1 (1982): 20–51.

16. The position that the Jews possessed neither the cultural enthusiasm nor educational formation to write Arabic poetry is taken by Joshua Blau, "Medieval Judeo-Arabic," in *Jewish Languages: Theme and Variations,* ed. Herbert H. Paper (Cambridge, MA: Association for Jewish Studies, 1978), 123–24. I counter this argument in my "Response," in ibid., 138–39; and in more detail in Norman A. Stillman, "Aspects of Jewish Life in Islamic Spain," in *Aspects of Jewish Culture in the Middle Ages,* ed. Paul E. Szarmach (Albany: State University of New York Press, 1979), 62–66. For Jewish poets who wrote Classical Arabic verse, see S. M. Stern, "Arabic Poems by Spanish-Hebrew Poets," in *Romanica et Occidentalia: Études dédiées à la mémoire de Hiram Peri (Pflaum),* ed. Moshé Lazar (Jerusalem: Magnes, 1963), 254–63.

17. Although Maimonides lived in Spain only in his youth, he always saw himself as an Andalusian and a follower of the Sephardi tradition. He frequently uses such phrases as "among us in Sepharad" (Ar., ᶜ*indanā fi 'l-Andalus*). See Joshua Blau, "Maimonides, Al-Andalus, and the Influence of the Spanish-Arabic Dialect on His Language," in *New Horizons in Sephardic Studies,* ed. Yedida K. Stillman and George K. Zucker (Albany: State University of New York Press, 1993), 203–10. Though written initially in Judeo-Arabic, Maimonides' philosophical magnum opus was probably transcribed also into standard Arabic. It was also translated into Hebrew and Latin and became known to Christian theologians such as Aquinas. See Moses Maimonides, *The Guide of the Perplexed,* trans. Shlomo Pines, with an introductory essay by Leo Strauss (Chicago: University of Chicago Press, 1963); and for a partial translation of *Highways to Perfection,* see Abraham Maimonides, *The Highways to Perfection of Abraham Maimonides,* trans. Samuel

Rosenblatt, vol. 1 (New York: Columbia University Press, 1927), vol. 2 (Baltimore: Johns Hopkins University Press, 1938).

18. Concerning this social decline and stress, see Norman A. Stillman, *The Jews of Arab Lands: A History and Source Book* (Philadelphia: Jewish Publication Society, 1979), 64–94, 255–323.

19. For some exceptional Jews who were attracted to modern Arabic language and literature, see Sasson Somekh, "Lost Voices: Jewish Authors in Modern Arabic Literature," in *Jews among Arabs: Contacts and Boundaries,* ed. Mark R. Cohen and Abraham L. Udovitch (Darwin, 1989), 9–20; also Norman A. Stillman, *The Jews of Arab Lands in Modern Times* (Philadelphia: Jewish Publication Society, 1991), 32–34, 228–30.

20. Abraham S. Halkin, "Judeo-Arabic Literature," in *Encyclopaedia Judaica* (Jerusalem: Keter, 1972), cols. 410–23 (quote is from the final paragraph).

21. For women's Judeo-Arabic poetry from Morocco, including an example of a poetic duel, see Norman A. Stillman and Yedida K. Stillman, "The Art of a Moroccan Folk Poetess," *Zeitschrift der Deutschen Morgenländischen Gesellschaft* 128, no. 1 (1978): 65–89.

22. For the *sharh* tradition in Morocco, see Stillman, *The Language and Culture of the Jews of Sefrou*, 137–39; for Egypt, see Benjamin Hary, "Egyptian Judeo-Arabic Sharh—Bridging the Cultures of Hebrew and Arabic," in *Judaism and Islam: Boundaries, Communication, and Interaction: Essays in Honor of William M. Brinner*, ed. Benjamin H. Hary, Fred Astren, and John L. Hayes (Boston: Brill, 2000), 395–407.

23. A history of Judeo-Arabic journalism remains a major desideratum, and the few short surveys are primarily in Hebrew and French. Some of these journals are discussed in Stillman, *The Jews of Arab Lands in Modern Times,* 69, 77, 86–87, 104, 318–19 and passim. For a catalogue of North African Jewish periodicals, many in Judeo-Arabic, see Robert Attal, *Periodiques juifs d'Afrique du Nord* (Jerusalem: Institut Ben-Zvi, 1980). For an excellent sociohistorical study on Yiddish and Ladino journalism, see Sarah Abrevaya Stein, *Making Jews Modern: The Yiddish and Ladino Press in the Russian and Ottoman Empires* (Bloomington: Indiana University Press, 2003).

24. Nancy Berg, *Exile from Exile: Israeli Writers from Iraq* (Albany: State University of New York Press, 1996). Some of these writers were pioneers in the development of modern Iraqi literature.

Chapter 4

Judeo-Spanish Culture in Medieval and Modern Times

David M. Bunis

Before the Expulsion of 1492

Throughout the Diaspora, new Jewish "subcultures" have arisen in response to changes in the social and cultural interaction of Jewish groups and their non-Jewish neighbors. Sometimes this occurred when Jews migrated to a new land, as in the case of Jews from Italy and France who settled in medieval Germany where they created the foundations of the Yiddish culture of Ashkenazi Jewry. Later, when Ashkenazim migrated from Germany to Slavic lands, the unique subculture they created through the syncretism of elements of ancient Hebrew and medieval Romance and German origins was further enriched through contact with the cultures of Slavic peoples, and still later, with the cultures of western Europe. At other times, new Jewish cultures were created when Jews residing in a particular area became highly influenced by the arrival of a group foreign to the area.

Of the Jewish people's diverse subculture groups—Yiddish, Judeo-Aramaic, Judeo-Persian, Judeo-Arabic, Judeo-Italian, and others—the Spanish or Sephardic Jews were especially interesting. Much of Yiddish culture in Europe is connected with Jewish migration and resettlement, all of it within the Christian world. This led to interaction with neighbors who all spoke Indo-European languages and shared certain basic elements of culture and belief. The traditional Judeo-Arabic culture of North African Jews developed essentially through interaction with the culture and belief system introduced there in the late seventh century by Arabic-speaking Muslim conquerors. Thus, the elements of Yiddish culture, which may be linked to the interaction between the Ashkenazim and their non-Jewish neighbors, had a European character. The cultural elements of North African Judeo-Arabic speakers deriving from contact with their non-Jewish neighbors had a primarily North African/Middle Eastern character. The development of traditional Sephardic culture was distinctive. It reflected an intimate encounter over centuries with local and imported non-Jewish cultures of European and Eastern character, in the land of its earliest origins as well as other regions.

Sephardic or "Judeo-Spanish" culture first arose through migration, as Jewish speakers of varieties of Greek and Latin from the Roman Empire reached Iberia. They came into contact with its indigenous populations, of European stock, most of whom—under Roman influence—came to speak Romance and other Indo-European languages. They accepted Christianity. It was through interaction with these groups that Iberian Jews developed their earliest varieties of Jewish Ibero-Romance—Jewish Castilian, Aragonese, Catalan, and others—and created Jewish variants of the local cultures in those languages.

From 711, the culture of much of Iberian Jewry took quite a different turn: with the conquest of most of Iberia by Muslims from North Africa, the Arabic language began to predominate throughout the territory which came under Muslim domination. Jews in the extremities of Iberia, such as the far north and west (which remained free of Muslim occupation) continued to use Jewish Ibero-Romance. But Iberian Jews under Islam adopted the newly introduced Arabic and evolved unique Judeo-Arabic variants of their own. Besides its elements of North-African Arabic origin, which the Jews sometimes used in innovative ways, their language contained a Hebrew and Aramaic component, comprised mostly of elements referring to Judaism. The Jews wrote Judeo-Arabic in a distinctive Hebrew cursive script.

During the centuries of contact with Moorish culture, the Jews of Muslim Spain, using Judeo-Arabic and Hebrew, produced liturgical and secular poetry, composed legal and scientific tracts, and delved deeply into the fields of mysticism, philosophy, and ethics. The Jews shared aspects of material culture (e.g., costume, cuisine, and religious artifacts) and fine arts (e.g., music and calligraphy) with their Muslim neighbors.[1] But with the increasing success over the centuries of the Reconquista, the Jews residing in newly re-Christianized areas began substituting their Judeo-Arabic language and culture with Jewish Hispano-Romance replacements. As an independent entity, the Judeo-Arabic culture of the Iberian Jews came to an end in 1492. In that year, the final military triumph of the Spaniards over the remaining Muslim leaders in Andalusia was followed by the Arab retreat from Spain, and the end of Arabic cultural dominance in the country.

In Christian Spain, Jewish contact with speakers of Castilian and other Romance languages led to incipient Jewish Ibero-Romance languages. Like Judeo-Arabic, these languages were written in the Hebrew alphabet. Their linguistic raw material consisted of elements of local Romance origin, elements of Hebrew-Aramaic origin,[2] and preservations from the Diaspora languages formerly spoken by their ancestors. Preservations from Jewish Greek (e.g., *meldar*[3] "to read, study" [especially a Jewish text], cf. Greek *meletáo*)[4] memorialized the Judeo-Greek roots of the community. Following the Muslim conquest of much of Spain, the Jews in the conquered territories adopted Arabic, while those in free areas continued to use Ibero-Romance. The gradual Christian reconquest and re-Hispanization of Islamized Spain led to a return to Ibero-Romance by the formerly Arabicized Jews.[5]

Nevertheless, in their re-adopted Ibero-Romance speech and culture, they continued to preserve certain elements of Arabic origin to which they had grown accustomed. For example, in their Ibero-Romance, the Jews continued to call Sunday *alhad,* from the North African Arabic form *al-ḥadd,* literally meaning "first (day)." This was to avoid using Castilian *domingo* (from Latin *[dies] dominicus*) meaning "[day of the] Lord," which they understood as a reference to Jesus.

Among the speakers of Jewish Romance in Spain, the traditions of Hispanic oral folk literature—proverbs, ballads and popular songs, stories, and legends—as well as the dramatic arts were beloved. Scholarly works were composed mostly in Hebrew, although some serious writing was in Jewish Romance. The latter consisted mostly of collections of communal regulations, poetry having a Jewish motif, and translations of sacred texts. Like their language and literature, the material culture of the Jews of Christian Spain displayed some features reminiscent of those found among their Christian neighbors, as well as preservations from the earlier Iberian Judeo-Arabic culture.

After the Expulsion of 1492

Those Jews who insisted on maintaining their ancestral religion in fifteenth-century Spain were forced to leave the country with the Edict of Expulsion. But unlike the case of the Iberian Judeo-Arabic culture, which had sung its swan song even before the Expulsion, the forced emigration from Spain did not put an end to the Jewish Ibero-Romance languages and cultures that had characterized most of Iberian Jewry. Along with whatever material possessions they could manage, the refugees took with them several varieties of these languages and cultures. They carried them to the lands that offered them shelter: the Ottoman Empire, North Africa and the Middle East, and parts of western Europe, especially Italy. With time, all of the Ibero-Romance varieties that had exited Spain with the Jew exiles ceased to exist except the most predominant variety, Castilian—just as Castilian became the predominant variety of Ibero-Romance in Spain itself.

In "Sepharad II," as the linguist Max Weinreich called the lands which received and sheltered the Sephardic refugees, the "Jewish Castilian" of the Sephardim did not merely survive the Expulsion and linger on uncultivated. The break with Iberian Castilian enabled the language of the Jews to develop more independently of Castilian influence than it had in Spain. The internal tendencies and trends of its speakers took their natural course without pressure from the host community to conform to its linguistic rules. In time, among the Sephardim and their new Gentile neighbors, the maturing "Jewish Castilian" was identified as the distinctive group language of the Levantine Sephardim. Because of their preponderance in the area and tendency to absorb smaller Jewish groups speaking other languages (e.g., Yiddish, Judeo-Italian, and Judeo-Arabic), the language of the Spanish exiles became the language of all Jews in much of the Mediterranean region.

Over the centuries, the language received many names among its speakers. Names alluding to the "Latin" and "Spanish" origins of the language's principle Romance component were "Ladino," and "Spanyol." "Djudezmo" and "Djudyó/Djidyó" emphasized the perception of the language as "Jewish" or "the language of the Jews," especially in the context of the linguistically heterogeneous Ottoman Empire. In Morocco, a distinctive name was "Hakitia," possibly deriving from Arabic *ḥaka*, *ḥikaya* "to tell a story," *ḥikaya(t)* "story," an allusion to the popular variety of language used by the Sephardim of Morocco in reciting stories and folktales.[6] In the modern period, the pseudo-scientific hybrid name "Djudeo-Espanyol" (Judeo-Spanish) was borrowed from philologists who began to take an interest in what they classified as a "Jewish variety of Spanish."

The forced emigration of the Sephardim from Spain did not put an end to their use of the distinctive Ibero-Jewish language and the culture they had created in it. Neither did their resettlement throughout the Mediterranean basin result in their loss of contact with either Christians or Muslims. The migrations following the Expulsion brought the Sephardim into contact with new and distinctive Christian and Muslim languages and cultures: those of the Turks and diversified Balkan peoples of the Ottoman Empire, of the variegated nationalities of the Austro-Hungarian Empire, of western European nations such as Italy, Holland, France, and England, and numerous Islamic peoples of the Middle East and North Africa.

From the late eighteenth century, intensive western European incursions into the Ottoman Empire and other Islamic lands increasingly brought the Sephardim in those regions into contact with modern European culture, reawakened them to their medieval ties to the West, and led to profound changes in their language and culture.

The Language of the Sephardim Following the Expulsion

The Judeo-Romance and Judeo-Arabic languages of the Jews in Spain arose as fusions of local varieties of Romance and Arabic with ancient elements such as Hebrew and Aramaic. Following the Expulsion, "Jewish Castilian," or Judezmo, grew further distant from the varieties of Spanish used in Spain and Latin America. This happened mostly as a result of three tendencies:

(a) The Sephardim preserved some elements of medieval Ibero-Romance with greater conservatism than the Spaniards in Spain itself. Judezmo preserved certain medieval sounds which gave way to other sounds in later Spanish: in Judezmo, the "j" in *mujer* "woman" continued to be pronounced as in Old Spanish (i.e., as "j" was sounded in French), whereas in later Spanish it came to sound like "ch" in German *ach*. Some Judezmo words appeared archaic when compared with their contemporary Spanish counterparts, too. For instance, for "shade" the Sephardim used *solombra*, as in Old Spanish, rather than *sombra*, which is used in Spanish today. Judezmo also preferred certain popular or regional Castilian forms of words to the forms that became standard in Spanish. For example, "much" was *muncho*, as also heard in the popular Spanish of Andalusia, Mexico and Puerto Rico, rather than *mucho*.

(b) Judezmo grew apart from Spanish through the introduction of innovations, changing parts of the Hispanic component of the language in ways unknown among Spanish speakers. Many speakers in Istanbul pronounced the word for "Thursday" as *djugeves* or *djugweves*, as opposed to

Spanish *jueves* (which was pronounced *djweves* in the Middle Ages, *hweves* today). The verbal ending marking the second person plural of all verbs in Judezmo was *-sh*, as opposed to Castilian *-is*. For example, "you (familiar plural) look" was *mirash* in Judezmo, *miráis* in Castilian.

(c) Sephardim also borrowed from the languages of the people with whom they came into contact following the Expulsion. Until the middle of the nineteenth century, the most important of these contact languages were Turkish in the Ottoman Empire, and Arabic in North Africa and the Middle East.[7] Other local languages of the Ottoman Empire such as Greek[8] and South Slavic[9] (Bulgarian, Macedonian, and Serbian) also contributed. Thereafter, a profound impact was also made by prestigious languages of western Europe such as French,[10] Italian, German—and in North Africa, Spanish.

The historical development of the language of the Sephardim was illustrated in the terminology used during the past centuries in the context of formal education. Until modernization, the primary components of Judezmo and Hakitia in this field were of Ibero-Romance, Hebrew-Aramaic, and Turkish, in the Ottoman regions, or Arabic, in North Africa and the Middle East.

For example, from the sixteenth century to the nineteenth century, young pupils (boys) were called *talmidim*[11] (from Hebrew). They studied in a religious primary school known variously as a *havrá* (from Hebrew *hevra* "society"), *meldar* (from Greek *meletáo*) or *kutab* (from Arabic *kuttab*) under the direction of a teacher addressed as *sinyor haham* (compare Spanish *señor* "sir," Hebrew *hakham* "scholar, rabbi"). The pupils' main concerns included: (a) learning "to pray" (*[f]azer tefilá*, compare Old Spanish *f-/hazer* "to do," Hebrew *tefila* "prayer"); (b) developing a fine Hebrew-letter calligraphic style written with a *péndola* (from Old Spanish "pen"; (c) translating (*enladinar*) and explicating (*deklarar*) the weekly *perashá* "portion of the Bible" (from Hebrew *parasha*) from the original *lashón* (compare Hebrew *lashon* "language," *leshon haqodesh* "Hebrew") into *Ladino*; and (d) acquiring the basics of *dikduk* "(Hebrew) grammar" and *hejbón* "mathematics" (Hebrew *diqduq, heshbon*).

Before the modern period, lessons were conducted while both pupils and teacher sat in Oriental fashion on mats or low benches. Reading and translation exercises were often sung by rote, using melodies founded upon the modes (*makames*, compare Turkish *makam* from Arabic *maqam*) of Ottoman or Arabic classical music. The *bokadikos*[12] or "little snacks" (compare Spanish *bocado* "mouthful," the usual Castilian diminutive forms of which are *bocaditos, bocadillos*) which pupils brought from home, such as *panezikos* "rolls" (Spanish *pan* "bread," diminutizing *-esico*; Castilian diminutive *panecillo*), illustrated the fusion of Hispanic and Eastern culinary traditions that characterized the traditional Sephardic diet.[13] The traditional games (*djugos*, compare Spanish *juegos*), songs (*kantikas*, compare Spanish *cantigas*), riddles (*endivina[nsa]s, hidod*; compare Spanish *adivinanzas*, Hebrew *hidot*) and other pastimes the pupils engaged in also derived partly from pre-Expulsion Spanish and Arabic as well as post-Expulsion Ottoman or North African sources.[14]

After completing their elementary education, those students whose families could afford it might go on to study at a higher level *yeshivá* "yeshivah" (from Hebrew) or the *midrash* "study hall" of a local rabbi. An especially talented rabbinical student (*talmid haham* from Hebrew "wise student") might contribute to the local religious literature—in the prestigious Hebrew language or in rabbinical Judezmo. On the other hand, an unsuccessful student (*pudrebankos*, literally "bench rotter" from Spanish) or a student from a poor family (*aniyento*, compare Hebrew *ani* "poor," Spanish adjective-forming *-ento*), had to leave his studies and try business. If he failed, he might end up a *sedakadji* "charity collector, beggar" (Turkish agent suffix *-ci*).

Like other groups in the Mediterranean region, the eastern Sephardim were affected by the European Enlightenment of the late eighteenth century. The Sephardic communities of the Mediterranean region underwent modernization and westernization.[15] They were aided by the Alliance Israélite Universelle, founded in 1860 by French Jews in Paris.[16] From the 1870s the schools they opened throughout the Levant offered young Sephardim—both boys and girls—a French education.

The vocabulary, grammar, and syntax of Judezmo underwent profound changes, as did the culture of its speakers in general, as linguistic and cultural elements of Eastern origin (Hebrew, Turkish, and Arabic) began to be supplanted by those originating in western Europe, considered to be more prestigious and "civilized."

Although Jewish studies were not neglected entirely, the stress in the *eskola*, or "European-style school" (from Italian *scuola*), was more on an intellectual, at times critical, examination of Jewish history, holidays, and customs than on the recitation and translation of sacred texts. At the core of the program were secular subjects such as the grammar and literature —*gramer* and *literature*—of prestigious Western languages such as French and Italian, as well as *estorya* "history" and *matematik* "mathematics"

(French *grammaire, littérature, histoire,* and *mathématiques*). Lessons were written with a *kreyón* "pencil" (French *crayon*) or *penino* "pen" (Italian *pennino*), in careful Roman rather than Hebrew script. Those who could read the *Rashí* Hebrew characters traditionally used to write Judezmo were fewer. Those who wrote the language at all did so in romanizations derived from French, Italian, or Modern Turkish romanizations, and in North Africa, from Castilian.

Teachers and pupils—now called *maestros* and *elevos* (from Italian *maestro,* French *élève*)—sat at desks, in Western-style classrooms. They dressed in European clothes and learned songs according to European musical scales and melodies. They were often warned by their teachers to speak French, Italian, and later Turkish, Greek or other local national languages, or Castilian (in Morocco), and not their family "*jargón*" (which they were told was a corrupt form of Spanish).

Although traditional foods continued to be eaten, European dishes were also introduced in some families. Those who could afford to moved out of the old "Jewish" *malás* "neighborhoods" (from Turkish *mahalle* from Arabic *mahalla*) into more modern, mixed *kwartyeres* "quarters" (Italian *quartieri,* French *quartiers*). Synagogue attendance and religious observance among the *frankeados* "Westernized" declined. Some who continued their studies beyond the elementary level, did so in non-Jewish schools, believed to be at a higher level. Some were even sent to a European *universitá* "university" (Italian *università*), where they pursued professional careers.

From the early twentieth century, significant numbers of Judezmo/Hakitia speakers seeking better economic and social conditions began leaving the lands in which their families had resided for centuries following the Expulsion. Most went to North and South America, or Western Europe. Their earlier Mediterranean locales had been characterized by linguistic and cultural heterogeneity. In their new, Western homes, people tended to emphasize linguistic and cultural homogeneity. So too did the new nation states that arose out of the crumbling Ottoman and Austro-Hungarian Empires, in which the Sephardim who had not emigrated now found themselves. In an attempt to acclimate themselves to these new conditions, most Judezmo/Hakitia speakers made little effort to maintain their centuries-old group language. Instead, they sought to master the local language. Judezmo/Hakitia became an "endangered species" with a greatly reduced speech community.

The Literature of the Sephardim following the Expulsion

Oral Traditions

Part of the cultural heritage faithfully maintained and expanded upon by the Sephardim during the centuries following their exile from Spain was a rich oral literature. It included representatives of all the oral literary genres—both sung and spoken—that were enjoyed by Ibero-Romance speakers in medieval Spain. After the Expulsion, the repertoire was augmented through independent creativity, often in the form of pieces reflecting Jewish life and traditions, and through the adaptation of material from the oral traditions of local peoples, selected and modified with an eye toward Jewish tastes and values.

SUNG REPERTOIRE

The Sephardic song repertoire was rich and varied.[17] In their earliest years children grew familiar with it through songs designed to impart the hopes and dreams of Jewish parents. Included in this repertoire of children's songs were ditties traditionally sung to, and by, boys attending the *meldar* or religious elementary school.

One of the more ancient sung genres cultivated by the Sephardim was the ballad (*romansa*), composed by anonymous authors and once belonging to the repertoire of wandering minstrels. Some examples assumed epic proportions.[18] Combining motifs and language from the world of medieval chivalry with images drawn from the Bible and Midrashim, the Judezmo ballad had a strophic structure, used various rhyme schemes, and was sung to a plaintive tune. Generally belonging to the repertoire of women, *romansas* were sung during celebrations of the life cycle such as births, circumcisions, weddings, and funerals.

More contemporary in language than the ballad, and of freer structure, were types of paraliturgical hymns (*komplas, piyutim, pizmonim*). The *komplas* were generally characterized by their Jewish themes and various repetitive rhyme schemes, often spread over four-line stanzas.[19] Many of them were traditionally sung as vernacular complements to the older, more formal men's Hebrew-language repertoire. They were often connected with weekly- and annual-cycle religious celebrations such as the Sabbath, Purim, and Passover, or as edifying summaries of Jewish ethics and beliefs.

Over the centuries, Judezmo and Hakitia speakers developed a large repertoire of popular songs (*kantikas*) in contemporary language, some in rhymed stanzas, others lacking rhyme patterns, and sometimes including a refrain. The *kantikas* may be subclassified according to numerous thematic categories and in relation to the diverse contexts in which they were sung.

Many songs of the popular type celebrated significant events in the life cycle. During circumcision ceremonies, for instance, custom required the singing of birth songs (*kantikas de parida*), including praises in honor of Abraham the Forefather, the first Jew to practice circumcision. Other songs focused—often with a touch of irony—on mundane, everyday living. Among these were work songs. Some of the Judezmo song repertoire, including the love songs, evidenced the influence of local non-Jewish musical traditions or were adaptations or translations of popular songs in languages such as Turkish, Greek, and Arabic.

The growing Westernization and modernization of the Mediterranean Sephardic communities were not without effect on their repertoire of oral literature. The popular songs of Italy and France, the urban *sarki* of Turkey and *rebetika* of Greece, even the fox-trot, and the Argentine tango had their reflections in the modern Sephardic song repertoire. So too did the music of the nascent social and political ideologies: socialism, communism, Ottomanism, Turkish republicanism, and other forms of local nationalism. One theme among these songs was the deep Jewish yearning for Jerusalem and the Land of Israel.

SPOKEN GENRES

Over the centuries since the Expulsion, Judezmo speakers cultivated and extended their repertoire of storied and other nonsung oral genres: folktales and legends (*konsejas, maasiyod*), parables and fables (*meshalim*), jokes (*shakás*), riddles (*endivinansas, hidod*), proverbs and sayings (*riflanes i dichas*), and others. While sometimes used as forms of entertainment, these genres were often employed didactically, to transmit to younger and less experienced members of the community religious, ethnic, moral, and other values considered significant.

Many stories and anecdotes (*kwentos*, diminutive *kwentezikos*) revolved around the foolish/clever heroes known as Djohá, Bohoriko, and Moshiko, who were similar in character and behavior to folk heroes of neighboring cultures such as the Turkish Nasreddin Hodja. Some of the stories were completely original, while others were adaptations of local non-Jewish tales.[20]

Jokes (*shakás* from Turkish *saka*) told by the Mediterranean Sephardim were often tinged with irony. Many exhibited a characteristic scorn for authority and impatience with fastidiousness, combined with an admiration for the quick thinking man-of-the-people. Many Judezmo jokes and anecdotes acquired a distinctive Jewish flavor through references to biblical and other heroes rooted in Jewish tradition.

Children and adults enjoyed challenging one another with riddles (*endivina[nsa]s, hidod*) and other "brain twisters." They were often introduced with a seductive phrase such as *Una koza, koza muy maravyoza* "It's something, something just marvelous," presenting a contradiction that the hearer was dared to resolve.

Today Westerners tend to shy away from the use of proverbs (*riflanes*) and sayings (*dichas*), seeing them as being trite or passé. Judezmo speakers, on the other hand, used them generously in both speech and writing.[21] Just as "a picture is worth a thousand words," a proverb was felt to express succinctly what might otherwise require whole paragraphs of ordinary prose.

The Sephardic appreciation for economy in speech was summarized in a proverb adopted from a Talmudic expression in Aramaic (*Mila besela⁽ mishetuqa bishnayim*, Megilla 18): *El avlar vale un grosh, el kayar vale dos* "Speech is worth one piaster; silence is worth two." Some Judezmo proverbs and sayings echoed the oral traditions of Medieval Spain, such as the question and retort *Ken es tu enemigo? El de tu ofisyo!* "Who is your enemy? He who practices your profession."

Other Judezmo proverbs corresponded to sayings used in other cultures of the region, e.g., *De la kavesa fyede el pishkado* "The fish stinks from the head" (i.e., where there is corruption, it inevitably starts at the top), variants of which are used among the Turks, Arabs, and other Mediterranean peoples. A belief in the absolute "truth value" of the proverb would seem to be conveyed, although perhaps with a certain Sephardic sarcasm, by means of a proverb: *Riflán mentirozo no ay* "There is no such thing as a proverb that lies."

Constituting a bridge between the oral traditions of the Eastern Sephardim and the written literature were the highly literal Ladino calque translations of the Bible and other sacred Jewish texts which, taught and recited orally, comprised a core component in the syllabus of elementary religious schools in all Judezmo and Hakitia speech communities.[22] According to tradition, the Ladino version of the Bible began with the following literal translation of Genesis 1:1:

> *En prisipyo kreó el Dyo a los syelos i a la tyerra.*
> (Literally: "In beginning created the God to the heavens and to the earth," corresponding to Hebrew *Bereshit bara Elohim et hashamayim veet haares.*)
> "In the beginning God created the heavens and the earth."

Written Literature

A continuous Judeo-Spanish literary tradition in writing made it possible to trace the historical development of Judezmo literature from the period before the Expulsion, through the Ottoman sojourn, and into modern times in Europe, Asia, and the Americas.[23] North Africa was more problematic since, although a rich Hakitia oral tradition was maintained there, very few written sources were known.

BEFORE THE EXPULSION (OLD JUDEZMO PERIOD)

The relatively few surviving Ibero-Romance texts by Jewish writers from medieval Spain consisted mostly of material intended for a Jewish readership[24] and thus were written in the Hebrew alphabet.[25] These included: translations of daily and holiday prayers,[26] instructions for holiday observances such as the Passover seder service, communal regulations,[27] and various other rabbinical, communal, and medical writings, among others.[28] Jewish writers also wrote works in the Latin alphabet, dedicated to or commissioned by non-Jews, for example, the rhymed *Proverbios morales* of Santob de Carrión, composed for King Pedro the Cruel.[29]

AFTER THE EXPULSION

Following their exile from Spain, the Sephardim who continued to use distinctive forms of Ibero-Romance written in the Hebrew alphabet settled mostly in the Ottoman Empire (first in Istanbul, the capital of the empire, and Salonika) and in North Africa.[30] They gradually established communities in many of the smaller cities and towns of the empire. At various stages in the history of their residence, Jewish presses that printed material in Judezmo were founded in Izmir, Edirne, Sofia, Plovdiv, Ruse, Bucharest, Sarajevo, Belgrade, Jerusalem, and Cairo. In the sixteenth century and later, Sephardic immigrants from the Ottoman regions migrated to Italian cities such as Venice and Livorno; in the eighteenth century, a Levantine Sephardic community was established in Vienna, the capital of the Austro-Hungarian Empire. In the late nineteenth and twentieth centuries, some Ottoman Sephardim resettled in Paris, New York, and other major cities of the United States. Judezmo works were printed in all of these places.

SIXTEENTH TO EIGHTEENTH CENTURIES
(MIDDLE JUDEZMO PERIOD)

A glimpse at the premodern language of the Sephardic exiles who migrated to North Africa following the Expulsion was possible thanks to rare texts published in nineteenth-century Italy, such as the regulations of Fez, set down in 1494. They were included, along with later regulations, in Abraham Ankawa's *Kerem hemer*. Brief illustrative passages also appeared in rabbinical works such as *Vayomer Yishaq* by Isaac Ben Walid, and in some manuscript documents.

A richer literary picture emerged from the Ottoman Empire and from the Ottoman Sephardic immigrant communities in Italy, Austria, France, and the United States. Within two decades after the Expulsion, the Ottoman Sephardic rabbis began creating publications in diverse varieties of the Jewish Castilian vernacular to help facilitate the maintenance of traditional Jewish institutions such as the ritual slaughter of cattle (e.g., *Dinim de shehitá i bediká* "Laws of Ritual Slaughter and Inspection of Cattle," which did not survive); other facets of Jewish law (e.g., *Shulhan hapanim* "Shew Table"); and diverse fields of Jewish study such as the Bible,[31] Jewish morals and philosophy (e.g., *Hanhagat hahayim* "Conduct in Life"), ethics (e.g., a translation by Sadik ben Joseph Formón of Bahye ibn Paquda's *Hovot halevavot* "Duties of the Hearts"), and others.[32]

Not much was known about Sephardic literary creativity in Judezmo in the seventeenth century. Many works may have been lost. In the eighteenth century, the Ottoman Sephardic communities experienced a veritable flowering of Judezmo rabbinical literature, meant to strengthen Jewish knowledge and observance among the less learned. Perhaps the use of Judezmo for this purpose was partly inspired by the temporary success which had been enjoyed in the preceding century by Sabbatai Zevi, the false messiah of Izmir, part of whose attraction among the Ottoman Jewish masses seemed to have been his practice of singing Judezmo love songs.

The Ottoman rabbis may also have been encouraged to write in Judezmo when they heard about the success of Yiddish works of a religious nature published in eastern Europe. Whatever their sources of inspiration, the eighteenth century saw the publication of rhymed couplets (*komplas*) by rabbis of Istanbul, Salonika, and other parts of the empire, such as Abraham ben Isaac Asa, Abraham Toledo, Judah ben Leon Kalai, Ḥayim ben Yom Tov Magula, Jacob Uziel, and Jacob Berav II. The singing of these *komplas*, at communal feasts and at home, was meant to enrich the celebration of religious festivals and other facets of Jewish life.

Numerous Judezmo prose works on religious themes appeared in the eighteenth century. Abraham Asa was a prolific translator of Hebrew works, including *Letras de Rabi Akiva* "Letters of Rabbi Akiva," as well as moralistic, mystical, philosophical, and historical works. He published collections of Jewish law both in prose and rhymed verse. He also published an edition of the entire Bible in Ladino, based on texts published in the sixteenth century.

Isaac ben Makhir Hulí initiated a monumental series of Bible commentaries known as *Me^cam Lo^cez* "From a Foreign People" in Istanbul 1730. After his death, the series was continued by rabbis in the Ottoman Empire into the nineteenth century.[33] Other original Judezmo rabbinical works included *Meshivat Nefesh* "Restoring the Soul" by Shabbetai ben Jacob Vitas, and *Tiqune hanefesh* "Corrections of the Soul" by Reuben ben Abraham of Shtip.

As in the popular Judezmo sermons delivered orally by religious lecturers in Sephardic synagogues, the authors of Judezmo rabbinical works often studded their serious learned treatises with samples of folk genres such as the tale and legend, parable and fable, dream interpretation, and personal anecdote. This made the moral and legal lessons of their works more palatable to the average reader.

Until the late eighteenth century, almost all works published in Judezmo were religious. A sign of the changing times was the book *La gwerta de oro* "Garden of Gold," published by David ben Moses Athias. It was a general educational manual, with no religious content, offering basic instruction in Italian and Greek and their alphabets, and provided advice of interest to Eastern Sephardim planning to travel to the West.

NINETEENTH TO TWENTIETH CENTURIES
(MODERN JUDEZMO PERIOD)

The waves of secular "enlightenment," which began emanating from western Europe, did not put an immediate end to rabbinical literature in Judezmo. Rather, popular religious literature continued to flourish until the end of the nineteenth century. One of its leading nineteenth-century proponents was Belgrade-born Israel Ben Ḥayim, the "father of Modern Judezmo literature,"[34] who settled in Vienna in the early nineteenth century. His contributions were essentially religious in orientation—mostly translations or retranslations of sacred and rabbinical works (e.g., the entire Bible with Ladino translation). He also published a broader-focused educational manual entitled *Osar hahayim* "Treasury of Life" which acquainted readers with the Arabic script used to write Ottoman Turkish, provided basic lessons in German, and introduced biblical and rabbinical Hebrew. His language had many of the traces of the modern idiom.

Among other noteworthy Judezmo works of rabbinical orientation published during this period were translations of Hebrew texts such as Sevi Hirsch Koidanover's *Qav hayashar* "Circle of the Righteous." There were also original treatises, such as those published in Belgrade by scholars from Sarajevo, including *Darke Noam* "Paths of Pleasantness," an introduction to Hebrew grammar by Judah Alkalay; *Leqet hazohar* "A Gathering from the Zohar," by Abraham Finzi; and *Dameseq Eliezer* "Eliezer of Damascus," by Eliezer Papo. Significant volumes published elsewhere, included *Hanokh lanaar* "Train Up a Child," by Abraham Pontremoli; *Asat HaShem* "Counsel of the Lord," by N. R. H. Perahya; and *Vehokhiah Avraham* "And Abraham Reproved," by Abraham Palachi. Other rabbinical scholars contributed volumes of Jewish history, biography, ethics, and mysticism, collections of stories and legends, and calendars and almanacs.

Judezmo rabbinical literature had a rival from the middle of the nineteenth century. The growing presence and importance of Westerners in the regions of the Mediterranean and Near East, and a desire to increase trade with commercial agents in the West, led local businessmen to acquire a practical familiarity with French, Italian, and other Western languages, primarily through self-instruction. From the 1870s, Sephardic young people began to study Western languages formally and grew acquainted with their literatures.

Toward the middle of the nineteenth century, the European Jewish periodical press inspired Westernized Sephardic intellectuals to found Judezmo newspapers in the Ottoman regions.[35] One of the first was *Shaare Mizrah* "Gates of the East," published by Refael Uziel in Izmir in 1845 to 1846 at the press of the Christian missionary G. Griffith.[36] It was followed by over three hundred periodicals, almost all of which were printed in the Hebrew alphabet until World War I, after which some appeared in romanization. Among the earliest papers were *Djornal Yisreelit* of Istanbul, *El Lunar* of Salonika, and a Judezmo edition of the Hebrew periodical *Ḥavaṣ elet*, founded in Jerusalem in 1870.[37] Most of the early efforts were short-lived. However, some later periodicals sustained themselves for decades, including *El Tyempo* of Istanbul,[38] *La (Bwena) Esperansa* of Izmir, and *La Epoka* of Salonika.

As some Judezmo speakers emigrated westward, Judezmo periodicals and books began to be published in centers of immigration such as New York and Paris. The Jews who remained in Turkey began publishing Judezmo books and periodicals in Turkish romanization.[39] In Salonika, Judezmo periodicals and books continued to be published, in the Hebrew alphabet, until the Nazis entered the city in 1941 and began the systematic destruction of its Jewish community. Judezmo speakers, who after 1948, immigrated to the new State of Israel, also published Judezmo newspapers and books in romanization.

The success of the Judezmo press reflected a growing desire on the part of the public to be kept abreast of domestic and foreign news and of world trade conditions likely to effect local business. The Judezmo press also served as a means of inexpensive native-language entertainment. Judezmo periodicals of a literary bent featured plays,[40] poetry, satire, short stories, historical writings, and serialized novels, many of which were later published as separate volumes.

The Judezmo press provided a forum for the exchange of ideas about the diverse social and political ideologies that were gradually taking root in the community, such as Western humanism, local nationalism, socialism, and Zionism. An especially controversial subject was the "language question."[41] Journalists pondered the linguistic future of their community. They considered questions such as, Should their centuries-old group vernacular continue to serve as their everyday language? If so, how should it develop—in emulation of French, Spanish, or some other language, or for the most part along independent lines? And if Judezmo was to be abandoned, which language should replace it—Hebrew, French, or a local language?

Of the numerous journalists who addressed the "language problem," Hizkiya Franco, editor of the periodical *El Komersyal*, perhaps offered the most unequivocal defense of "Judeo-Espanyol" as the unique, independent language of the descendants of Spanish Jewry. In an essay on the "Judeo-Spanish Question," phrased in the variety of Judezmo that characterized the highly Westernized sector of the community, Franco argued that the language should be maintained by the Eastern Sephardim and allowed to follow its own natural course of development. The essay was published in *El Tyempo* of Istanbul in 1923 and addressed to its editor David Fresco, who had urged that the community abandon its separate group "jargon" in order to facilitate the integration of the Sephardic community within the larger society.[42]

Following World War II, the practical necessities of everyday living proved to outweigh the romantic arguments for language loyalty. In their home communities and in the new centers to which many immigrated, the Sephardim felt an increasing pressure to assimilate linguistically to their surroundings. From the rich language of thriving Sephardic communities throughout the Mediterranean region, Judezmo and Hakitia began to deteriorate into "endangered species" spoken mostly by elderly people. By the 1960s and 1970s, very few speakers used them for creative writing.

In the 1980s, however, several members of the speech community, in middle age, became possessed by a sense of nostalgia and concern for their endangered communal language and culture. This prompted them to use "Judeo-Spanish" as a literary language of ethnic self-expression. Its main outlet was the periodical *Aki Yerushalayim*, edited by Moshe Shaul and published entirely in "Djudeo-Espanyol." Among others, the periodical published regular notices of the books and articles published in Judezmo and Hakitia by writers in Israel, Turkey, Western Europe, and the Americas.

As we have seen, the culture of the Sephardic Jews was born in medieval Spain, and later cultivated outside it, through the interaction of Sephardic communities with their Christian and Muslim neighbors. Throughout the ages, in certain fundamental ways—the main one of course being religion—the Jews remained distinct from either of these groups of neighbors. But characterized by an exceptional openness to their linguistic surroundings, and to what they perceived as the most positive elements of Christian and Muslim culture in Spain and in the lands of their later exile, the Sephardim selectively assimilated elements from them. In doing so, the Spanish Jews created two uniquely rich and supple Jewish subcultures, Judeo-Arabic and Judeo-Spanish, which were both extraordinary syntheses of Eastern and Western traditions.

The cultural heights reached by members of Iberian Jewry's two subcultures placed them at the forefront of the medieval Jewish cultural world. Despite the hardships suffered by the Sephardim after the Expulsion from Spain in 1492, Judeo-Spanish culture continued to flourish. Despite the greatly decreased number of its bearers, traditional Judeo-

Spanish culture continues to be maintained today as the modern heir to a noble, centuries-old, East-West Jewish heritage.

NOTES

1. On Judeo-Arabic culture in general, see chapter 3, by N. Stillman, in the present volume.

2. For a comprehensive inventory of the Hebraisms in Modern Judezmo, with a historical introduction, see D M. Bunis, *A Lexicon of the Hebrew and Aramaic Elements in Modern Judezmo* (Jerusalem: Magnes and Misgav Yerushalayim, 1993). On the Hebraisms used in Hakitia, see Y. Bentolila, "Le composant hébraïque dans le judéo-espagnol marocain," *Judeo-Romance Languages*, ed. I. Benabu and J. Sermoneta (Jerusalem: Misgav Yerushalayim and Hebrew University, 1985), 27–40.

3. The spelling of "Judeo-Spanish" or Judezmo material used in the present article is, with slight variations that adopted for the modern language by the Israel Authority for Ladino Culture. Note the phonetic values of the following symbols: "a," "e," "i," "o," "u" are essentially as in Spanish; "b" = "b" in English "about"; "ch" = "ch" in Spanish *chico*, "d" = "d" in Spanish *grande* or *nada* (depending on the word); "dj" = "dj" in English "adjust"; "g" = "g" in Spanish *sangre* or *agua* (depending on the word); "h" = "ch" in German *ach*; "j" = "j" in French *jamais*; "k" = "k" in English "kayak"; "ny" = "ñ" in Spanish *año*; "r" and "rr" = "r" and "rr" in Spanish *caro* and *carro*, respectively; "s" = "s" in Spanish *casa*; "sh" = "sh" in English "shore"; "v" = "v" in English "volley"; "w" = "w" in English "warrant"; "y" = "y" in English "yard"; "z" = "z" in English "zoo." Unless otherwise indicated by an accent mark, the stress is on the next to last syllable in words ending in a vowel or "n" or "s" (e.g., *kaza* "house"), and on the last syllable in words ending in a consonant other than "n" or "s" (e.g., *kazal* "village").

4. For treatment of (Old Jewish) Greek elements in Jewish languages of Romance stock, see D. S. Blondheim, *Les parlers judéo-romans et la Vetus Latina* (Paris: Champion, 1925).

5. The "Jewish Castilian" used by the Jews of Spain is treated in S. Marcus, "A-t-il existé en Espagne un dialecte judéo-espagnol?" *Sefarad* 22 (Madrid, 1962): 129–49; P. Wexler, *The Non-Jewish Origins of the Sephardic Jews* (Albany: State University of New York Press, 1996).

6. English-language introductions to the traditional languages of the Ibero-Romance–speaking Sephardim include D. M. Bunis, "The Language of the Sephardim: A Historical Overview," in H. Beinart, *The Sephardi Legacy*, vol. 23 (Jerusalem: Magnes, 1992), 399–422; P. Díaz-Mas, *Sephardim: The Jews from Spain*, trans. G. Zucker (Chicago: University of Chicago Press, 1992); T. K. Harris, *Death of a Language: The History of Judeo-Spanish* (Newark: University of Delaware Press, 1994). For a classified if outdated bibliography of research on the sub-

ject, see D. M. Bunis, *Sephardic Studies: A Research Bibliography* (New York: Garland, 1981).

7. A general review of the Turkish contribution to Judezmo is M.-C. Varol, "Influencia del turco en el judeoespañol de Turquía," in *Sephardica 1: Hommage à Haïm Vidal Sephiha*, ed. W. Busse, H. Kohring, and M. Shaul (Berne, Switzerland: P. Lang, 1996), 213–37. The most comprehensive inventory and study of the Arabisms in Hakitia is found in J. Benoliel, *Dialecto judeo-hispano-marroquí o hakitía*, 2d ed. (Barcelona: n.p., 1977).

8. On Greek elements in post-expulsion Judezmo, see A. Danon, "Les éléments grecs dans le judéo-espagnol," *Revue des Études Juives* 75 (1922): 211–16. For numerous Greek elements used in the Judezmo of modern Salonika see J. Nehama, *Dictionnaire du judéo-espagnol* (Madrid: Consejo Superior de Investigaciones Científicas, 1975).

9. On Slavisms in the Judezmo of the former Yugoslavia, see E. Stankiewicz, "Balkan and Slavic Elements in the Judeo-Spanish of Yugoslavia," in *For Max Weinreich on His Seventieth Birthday* ed. Lucy S. Davidowicz, Alexander Erlich, Rachel Erlich, and Joshua A. Fishman (New York: Walter De Gruyter, 1964), 229–36; D. M. Bunis, "On the incorporation of Slavisms in the grammatical system of Yugoslavian Judezmo," *Jews and Slavs* 9 (Jerusalem: Hebrew University, 2003), 325–37.

10. The impact of French on Modern Judezmo is analyzed in H. V. Sephiha, "Le judéo-fragnol," *Ethno-Psychologie* 2–3 (1973): 239–49.

11. On Judezmo plurals, see D. M. Bunis, "Plural formation in Modern Eastern Judezmo," in *Judeo-Romances Languages*, ed. I. Benabu and J. Sermoneta (Jerusalem: Misgav Yerushalayim and Hebrew University, 1985), 41–68.

12. For diminutive formation in Judezmo, see D. M. Bunis, "Ottoman Judezmo Diminutives and Other Hypocoristics," in *Linguistique des langues juives et linguistique générale*, ed. F. Alvarez-Pereyre and J. Baumgarten (Paris: CNRS, 2004), 193–246.

13. The culinary traditions of the Eastern Sephardim are portrayed in many cookbooks, among them V. Alchech Miner, with L. Krinn, *From My Grandmother's Kitchen* (Gainesville, FL: Triad, 1984).

14. A recent collection of children's oral folklore is S. Weich-Shahak, *Repertorio tradicional infantil sefardí* (Madrid: Compañía Literaria, 2001).

15. On the modernization of the Eastern Sephardic communities and its impact on their language, see D. M. Bunis, "Modernization of Judezmo and Hakitia (Judeo-Spanish)," in *The Jews of the Middle East and North Africa in modern times*, ed. R. S. Simon, M. M. Laskier, and S. Reguer (New York: Columbia University Press, 2003), 116–28.

16. The impact of the Alliance Israélite Universelle on Eastern Sephardic communities is analyzed in A. Rodrigue, *French Jews, Turkish Jews* (Bloomington: Indiana University Press, 1990), and in idem, *Images of Sephardi and Eastern Jewries in Transition* (Seattle: University of Washington Press, 1993).

17. For a recent collection of Judezmo songs with analysis, see E. Seroussi, ed., *Alberto Hemsi: Cancionero sefardí* (Jerusalem: Jewish Music Research Center, Hebrew University of Jerusalem, 1995).

18. The Judezmo ballad has been investigated extensively. Some of the finest work is by S. G. Armistead and J. H. Silverman. For example, see their *The Judeo-Spanish Ballad Chapbooks of Yacob Abraham Yoná* (Berkeley and Los Angeles: University of California Press, 1971).

19. For a comprehensive bibliography of Judezmo *kompla* collections, see E. Romero, *Bibliografía analítica de ediciones de coplas sefardíes*, with an introduction by I. M. Hassán (Madrid: Consejo Superior de Investigaciones Científicas, 1992).

20. For an extensive inventory and analysis of Judezmo folktales, see R. Haboucha, *Types and Motifs of the Judeo-Spanish Folktale* (New York: Garland, 1991). See also T. Alexander, "The Sephardic Folktale as an Expression of Ethnic Group Identity," *Cahiers de Littérature Orale* 20 (1986): 131–52.

21. On Judezmo proverbs see I. J. Levy, *Prolegomena to the Study of the Refranero Sefardí* (New York: Las Americas, 1969); D. M. Bunis, *Voices from Jewish Salonika* (Jerusalem: Misgav Yerushalayim-Ets Ahaim, 1999), 158–62.

22. See D. M. Bunis, "Translating from the Head and from the Heart: The Essentially Oral Nature of the Ladino Bible-Translation Tradition," in *Sephardica 1: Hommage à Haïm Vidal Sephiha*, ed. Busse, Kohring, and Shaul, 337–57.

23. For full-length overviews of Judezmo literature, see M. Molho, *Literatura sefardita de Oriente* (Madrid: Consejo Superior de Investigaciones Científicas, 1960); E. Romero, *La creación literaria en lengua sefardí* (Madrid: Consejo Superior de Investigaciones Científicas, 1992); for an English summary of the latter, see E. Romero, "Literary Creation in the Sephardi Diaspora," in *The Sephardi Legacy*, ed. H. Beinart, vol. 2 (Jerusalem: Magnes, 1992), 438–60.

24. For a selection of texts with analysis, see L. Minervini, *Testi giudeospagnoli medievali*, 2 vols. (Naples: Liguori, 1992).

25. For an English-language treatment of traditional Judezmo orthography, see D. M. Bunis, "The Historical Development of Judezmo Orthography: A Brief Sketch," *Working Papers in Yiddish and East European Jewish Studies* 2 (1974): 1–54.

26. See M. Lazar, ed., *Siddur Tefilot: A Woman's Ladino Prayer Book*, The Sephardic Classical Library, vol. 10 (Lancaster, CA: Labyrinthos, 1995).

27. For a photographic reproduction of the original manuscript as well as a transcription and transliteration, see Y. Moreno-Koch, "The Taqqanot of Valladolid of 1432," *American Sephardi* 9 (1978): 58–145.

28. The earliest examples are the *hardjas*, or final stanzas, in Romance, adapted from popular medieval Ibero-Romance songs, appended to samples of the Hebrew and Judeo-Arabic poetry genre known as *muwashshaḥ at*. For an example of a later text, see L. Minervini, "An Aljamiado Version of 'Orlando Furioso': A Judeo-Spanish Transcription of Jerónimo de Urrea's Translation," in *Hispano-*

Jewish Civilization after 1492, ed. M. Abitbol, Y.-T. Assis, and G. Hasan-Rokem (Jerusalem: Misgav Yerushalayim, 1997), 191–201.

29. See I. González Llubera, ed., *Santob de Carrión: Proverbios morales* (Cambridge, England: Hispanic Seminary of Medieval Studies, 1947).

30. The present article does not deal with the cultural heights reached by former crypto-Jews, the descendants of Spanish and Portuguese Jews who had ostensibly converted to Christianity, practiced Jewish rites in secret, and returned to the open observance of Judaism in Western European cities such as Amsterdam, Ferrara, London, and Bordeaux, as well as in the Americas. Of necessity having assimilated linguistically to the varieties of Ibero-Romance used by their non-Jewish neighbors, this group did not use a distinctive "Judeo-Spanish" per se following their return to Judaism but rather judaized varieties of Spanish and Portuguese.

31. A detailed study of two sixteenth-century Ladino Bible translations is provided in H. V. Sephiha, *Le ladino, Judéo-espagnol calque, Deutéronome*, 2 vols. (Paris: Institut d'Études Hispaniques, 1973, 1979). See also O. Schwarzwald, "Linguistic Variations among Ladino Translations as Determined by Geographical, Temporal and Textual Factors," *Folia Linguistica Historica* 17 (1996): 57–72.

32. For a description of Istanbul and its population, see P. Romeu, ed., *Moisés Almosnino: Crónica de los reyes Otomanos* (Barcelona: Tirocinio, 1998).

33. For an English adaptation of the *Meam Loez* series, see A. Kaplan, trans., *The Torah Anthology, Yalkut Meam Loez*, 19 vols. (Brooklyn: Moznaim, 1977–1991).

34. On him see D. M. Bunis, "Yisrael Haim of Belgrade and the history of Judezmo Linguistics," *Histoire, Épistomologie, Langage* 18, no. 1 and in *La linguistique de l'hébreu et des langues juives*, ed. J. Baumgarten and S. Kessler-Mesguich (Paris: Société d'Histoire et d'Épistemologie des Sciences du Langage and Presses Universitaires de Vincennes, 1996), 151–66.

35. For an attempt at a comprehensive bibliography of the Judezmo press, see M. D. Gaon, *The Judeo-Spanish Press: A Bibliography* (in Hebrew) (Jerusalem: Ben-Zvi Institute and Jewish National and University Library, 1965).

36. For an analysis of the language used in this periodical see D. M. Bunis, "The Earliest Judezmo Newspapers: Sociolinguistic Reflections," *Mediterranean Language Review* 6–7 (1993): 5–66.

37. On Judezmo in the Land of Israel, see D. M. Bunis, "The Dialect of the Old *Yishuv* Sephardic Community in Jerusalem," in *Studies in Jewish Languages*, ed. M. Bar-Asher (Jerusalem: Misgav Yerushalayim and Hebrew University of Jerusalem, 1988), 1–40.

38. On *El Tyempo* as a modernizing force, see S. Abrevaya Stein, *Making Jews Modern: Yiddish and Ladino Press of the Russian and Ottoman Empires* (Bloomington: Indiana University Press, 2003).

39. On Judezmo in romanization, see the articles in W. Busse, ed., *Judenspanisch*, vol. 7 (also titled *Neue Romania*, vol. 28) (Berlin: Institut für Romanische Philologie der Freien Universität Berlin, 2003).

40. The language used in what appears to be the first play in Modern Judezmo is analyzed in D. M. Bunis, "Pyesa di Yaakov Avinu kun sus ijus (Bucharest, 1862): The First Judezmo Play?" *Revue des Études Juives* 154, nos. 3–4 (1995): 387–428.

41. For various views on this "question," see D. M. Bunis, "Modernization and the 'Language Question' among the Judezmo-Speaking Sephardim of the Ottoman Empire," in *Sephardi and Middle Eastern Jewries: History and Culture in the Modern Era*, ed. H. E. Goldberg (Bloomington: University of Indiana, 1996), 226–39.

42. Most of Franco's essay is reproduced in D. M. Bunis, *The Judezmo Language* (in Hebrew) (Jerusalem: Magnes, and Hebrew University of Jerusalem, 1999), 377–81.

Chapter 5

Literatures of Medieval Sepharad

Jonathan P. Decter

During the first half of the eleventh century, the Jewish poet and philosopher Solomon Ibn Gabirol (c. 1020–c. 1057) decried the decline of Sephardic Jews' knowledge of Hebrew: "Half of them speak Edomese and half of them the language of Qedar that darkens."[1] Ibn Gabirol meant that Jews had neglected Hebrew and knew only the other languages of the Iberian Peninsula: Hispano-Romance, the language of Christians (descendants of the biblical Esau, whose nickname was Edom [Genesis 25:30]), and Arabic, the language of Muslims (descendants of Ishmael, father of Qedar [Genesis 25:13]). Like Muslims and Christians in al-Andalus (Islamic Spain), Jews spoke mainly Arabic and a form of Hispano-Romance.[2] When Ibn Gabirol identified Arabic as the language of Muslims and Romance as the language of Christians, he was probably referring to the communities in which each language originated, since Muslims, Christians, and Jews all spoke Arabic and Romance in eleventh-century al-Andalus.

In their literary writing, the Jews of al-Andalus used Hebrew, Arabic, and Hispano-Romance to varying degrees. Some authors wrote in more than one language, sometimes even within the same work. During the twelfth century, the centers of Jewish life in the Iberian Peninsula moved from the Islamic south to the kingdoms of the Christian north. In Christian Spain, the dialects of Spanish (descendants of the Romance dialect) gradually emerged as the Jewish vernacular, though Arabic continued to be respected as a language of learning and sophistication for the educated class. Jewish literary works in the dialects of Spanish were rare but significant.

For nearly fifty years, scholars have hailed medieval Iberia as a unique *convivencia* through which Muslims, Christians, and Jews interacted to produce the single entity of Spanish culture.[3] Medieval Sephardic writing testified to the profound influence of non-Jewish culture upon its forms, themes, aesthetics, and worldview. At the same time, the culture of medieval Spain could not have taken form but for the active participation of Jews, Muslims, and Christians.

Al-Andalus

In al-Andalus, as in the rest of the Arabic-speaking world, Arabic was the typical language of Jewish writing for anything but belles lettres. Virtually all Jewish expositions on philosophy, theology, mathematics, and so on, were written in Arabic, usually in Hebrew characters. Such writing was called Judeo-Arabic, though there was often little to distinguish it from the contemporary language of non-Jews.[4] Letter writing was executed almost exclusively in Judeo-Arabic, though sophisticated letters often included Hebrew or Aramaic quotations from canonical Jewish texts and salutations in a florid Hebrew style.

Hebrew Poetry in al-Andalus

Late tenth-century al-Andalus witnessed a revolution in the composition of Hebrew poetry.[5] Yet, in order to understand the development and role of Hebrew poetry in medieval Spain, a brief historical review is in order.

The Hebrew Bible contains many poetic sections, including songs such as the Song of the Sea (Exodus 15) and the Song of Deborah (Judges 5), as well as poetic books such as Psalms and Job. Between the fifth and seventh centuries, liturgical poetry (called *piyyut*) for the synagogue service flourished in Byzantine Palestine. Since the poetics of the ancient *piyyut* were complex and opaque, digesting it entailed the recognition of rare vocabulary, foreign words, complex grammatical forms, and a vast repertoire of allusions from Jewish sources.[6] The Talmud also includes numerous poetic sections.[7]

In tenth-century Islamic Baghdad, a poetic trend was initiated by the head of the Babylonian academy, Saʿadia Gaon. This trend tended toward a more transparent style, relying mainly on biblical vocabulary and diction. Saʿadia composed the first Bible commentary, the first complete prayer book, the first theological treatise, and the first monographs dedicated to discrete legal subjects.[8] In the field of poetry, Saʿadia may be credited with composing the first nonliturgical Hebrew poems since the Bible and with introducing medieval philosophical and theological concepts into Hebrew verse. He wrote the *Agron* (Gatherer), also known as *Kitab Usul al-Shi'r al-'Ibrani* (The Book of the Principles of Hebrew Poetry), which was the first book designed as a manual of Hebrew poetics. Saʿadia's verse may be seen as a link between the ancient *piyyut* and the Arabized poetry of the Sephardic school.[9]

Toward the end of the tenth century, a North African student of Saʿadia's named Dunash Ibn Labrat revolutionized Hebrew poetry in al-Andalus. By the time of Dunash's arrival, the province had grown to a cosmopolitan intellectual center with a grand capitol at Cordoba. It was around the so-called courtier Jews that the Hebrew literary culture of al-Andalus took form. The composition of poetry by and for men of power was one of the hallmarks of the medieval Sephardic literary tradition.

Dunash invented a system that made Hebrew poetry sound like Arabic poetry. The Arabic language naturally consisted of vowels of short and long duration, which lent themselves to meters whose rhythms were distinct and memorable. To the medieval Jewish sophisticate, the Hebrew poetry of the Palestinian and Iraqi schools felt arrhythmic. Dunash synthetically imposed a system of long and short vowels on the Hebrew language so that it could mimic the rollicking meters of Arabic. By adding monorhyme, another prosodic requirement of classical Arabic poetry, Dunash's innovation allowed Jews to participate through the medium of their own historical language. The famous scholar, S. D. Goitein, called the Hebrew poetry of the Sephardic School the "acme of Jewish-Arab symbiosis."[10]

Virtually all medieval Sephardic poets adopted Dunash's innovation. Moses Ibn Ezra maintained that the finest form of Hebrew poetry was that composed after the Arabic model.[11] However, Judah Halevi, Ibn Ezra's younger contemporary, expressed much ambivalence toward the metrical innovation, at times condemning it as the ultimate cultural sell-out.[12]

The choice of Hebrew as a poetic language may be the greatest expression of Jewish self-assertion, even nationalist aspiration, during this period. The Hebrew poems of al-Andalus utilized a high register of the language that sought to emulate the diction and style of biblical Hebrew while suppressing elements that had crept into the language following the Bible's canonization. The composition of literary texts in a refined biblical style was greatly facilitated by concurrent achievements in the study of Hebrew grammar and biblical exegesis.[13]

By adhering to the biblical style, Jewish authors were able to compete with ʿArabiyya (Arabism), which asserted the superiority of the Arabic language over other tongues, and the Islamic doctrine Iʾjaz al-Qurʾan (The Inimitability of the Qurʾan),[14] which affirmed the rhetorical perfection of the Qur'an as the revealed word of God. As Ross Brann put it, the Bible came to be regarded as a "Jewish Qur'an," a literary model whose emulation signified an assertion of Jewish nationalism even as it testified to the Arabized cultural values of Andalusian Jews.[15] It may be because of the near-obsession with biblical Hebrew as a rhetorical model that examples of belletristic texts by Jewish authors in other languages are relatively rare.

Beyond prosodic features, the Hebrew poetry of al-Andalus was deeply indebted to the Arabic tradition for its thematic material. By the tenth century, Arabic developed a rich and varied poetic tradition, ranging from the desert poetry of the pre-Islamic period (the Jahiliya period) to the urban poetry of the Abbasid and Andalusian periods. Arabic poems on wine and garden description were imitated extensively in secular Hebrew verse. Themes of Arabic love poetry, recast in the language of the Bible (especially the Song of Songs), penetrated secular as well as sacred Hebrew poetry.[16]

The most famous theme of Jahiliya poetry was al-bukaʾ ʿala al-atlal (Arabic, "weeping over the ruins"). According to the topos, the poet arrived at the remnants of an abandoned campsite, and began to weep. The sight of the ruins triggered a series of memories that whisked the reader back in time to the idyllic days of the tribe's presence.[17] Hebrew poets exploited the nostalgic tone of this theme in national and personal poems of exile. The following poem by Moses Ibn Ezra (c. 1055–after 1138) on the subject of Israel's exile fused the themes of al-buka ʿala al-atlal and love poetry,

> Hurry to the lover's camp,
>   Dispersed by Time, a ruin now;
> Once the haunt of love's gazelles,
>   Wolves' and lions' lair today.
>
> From far away I hear Gazelle,
>   From Edom's keep and Arab's cell,
> Mourning the lover of her youth,
>   Sounding lovely, ancient words:
> "Fortify me with lovers' flasks,
>   Strengthen me with sweets of love."[18]

The Hebrew poet recalls the effacement of the Jewish encampment *par excellence*, the Temple in Jerusalem, where God and Israel once met as "lovers." Once home to gracious gazelles, the abandoned camp became inhabited with carnivorous animals. In the second part of the poem, the lovesick Gazelle (Israel), caught in the fetters of Edom (Christendom) and amongst the Arabs (indicating Islam), calls out to her lover (God). In the final verse, Israel muses nostalgically through the language of the Song of Songs (2:5), long understood in the Jewish tradition as an allegory of the love between Israel and God.

The Hebrew poetry of al-Andalus also carried the imprint of contemporary philosophical culture. Neoplatonic philosophy was of great interest to the Andalusian poets.[19] Many poems on the soul originated as introductions to the prayer beginning, "The soul of All praises God." Solomon Ibn Gabirol captured numerous aspects of Neoplatonic soul theory:

> For you, like God, have everlasting life,
>   And He is hidden just as you are hid;
> And is your God immaculate and pure?
>   You too are pure, you too are innocent.
> The Mighty One bears the heavens in His arm,
>   Just as you bear the mortal, speechless clay.
> My soul, greet God, your Rock, with gifts of praise,
>   For nothing has He put on earth like you.
> My body, bless your Rock for evermore,
>   To whom the soul of All sings ever praise.[20]

The subject of this poem is the soul, taken from her celestial home, now confined within the prison of the body. The soul is bound to the lowly body. The path toward reunification with her celestial abode lies with the sublime soul contemplating her bond with her Creator.

Hebrew poets of al-Andalus also composed "secular poetry" or the "poetry of entertainment"[21] that reflected the lifestyle of an aristocratic class whose values approximated those of their Muslim contemporaries. The following poem by Samuel ha-Nagid (993–c. 1055) describes a garden:

> We went out to the flowerbeds of the garden,
>   Arranged in it like lines in a scroll . . .
> The wine pourer filled a cup with rubies,
>   And set it on a boat of variegated papyrus.

> He sent the cup like a bride in her palanquin
>   Over to the drinker, her groom,
> Who drank and returned his cup,
>   And addressed the servant as at the start...
>
> Like the activity of friends drinking
>   In a round garden along a canal,
>   There is no activity.[22]

This scene was typical of a medieval Arab wine party. The poem strikingly resembled contemporary Arabic garden poetry.[23] Drinking companions consumed wine served by a professional wine pourer. Everything about this garden was round. The canal was round like the heavens that encompassed the sphere of the earth. The flowerbeds were lines in the scroll of the garden. Likewise, the activity in the scene was cyclical. The wine pourer sent the cup over a pool to the drinker who drank and returned the cup to be refilled, a cycle that could continue indefinitely. The feeling of circularity was captured even in the syntax of the concluding verse, which began and ended with the same word ("Like the activity ... There is no activity"). The overall sense of delight and ease was reinforced by the circularity of poetic space and time.[24]

The wine pourer, who is rather nondescript in the poem above, frequently played a coquettish and erotic function for the pleasure of the aristocratic drinkers. For example, in a short poem by Samuel ha-Nagid, the (male)[25] wine pourer, seeing the wine cup in the drinker's hand, demands, "Drink the blood of grapes from between my lips!"[26] Medieval Hebrew (and Arabic) verse treating the erotic may be described best as "poetry of desire" or "poetry of passion" rather than "love poetry." The poems generally did not recount episodes of actual experience, but rather, feelings of unconsummated longing. The following excerpts from a poem by Moses Ibn Ezra illustrated this type of eroticism well,

> The wine pourer speaks languidly,
>   Though he fells mighty men
>   With his soft words.
> His eyes are wide with magic,
>   They are beautiful,
>   They are sorcerers.

The beloved was almost always unattainable. Even in poems wherein the poetic speaker recounted a seemingly nonfictitious experience, it is debatable whether the poem should be understood as the author's personal experience or as a kind of literary fashion.

Samuel ha-Nagid, vizier of the Berber prince of Granada, Badis Ibn Habbus, was the only Jewish poet to write poems recounting experiences in battle. He boastfully pronounced himself the "David of the Age," for David was known both as a mighty conqueror and as a delicate poet who wrote the Psalms. Solomon Ibn Gabirol emerged as an introspective poet consumed with the philosophical quest, his own genius, and misfortune. He presented himself as a social misfit, shunned by contemporaries for his incendiary personality and sickly appearance. Moses Ibn Ezra, who was forced to flee Muslim Spain after the Almoravid conquest from North Africa (1090), portrayed himself as an isolated prisoner trapped in the culturally barren environment of Christian Spain, the land of his refuge. Judah Halevi composed a series of poems during his famous journey to the Land of Israel that portrayed him as a devout pilgrim imbued with a prophetic spirit.[27]

Abraham Ibn Ezra (1089–1164) was the last poet of the "Golden Age" of al-Andalus and a conduit of Judeo-Arabic culture to the Christian world.[28] Ibn Ezra commemorated the destruction of cities in al-Andalus in a moving poem,

> Woe for calamity has descended upon Spain from the heavens!
> My eyes, my eyes flow with water.
> My eye weeps like an ostrich's for the city of Lucena!
> Without guilt, the Exile dwelled there untroubled,
> Undisturbed for one thousand and seventy years.
> She became like a widow when the day arrived and her people departed. . . .
> For this I weep and strike my hand; lamentation is constantly in my mouth.
> I cannot be silent so I exclaim, "Would that my heart were water!"[29]

The strophic form of the poem was sustained by concluding each stanza with the word "water." The poet lamented through rituals mentioned in the Bible (weeping like an ostrich, striking the hand, shaving the head) and, referred to the cities of al-Andalus by name, a practice seldom found in earlier poetry.[30] The act of naming in this poem served as a means of commemoration, a way of setting the period of al-Andalus firmly in the past. After Ibn Ezra, Hebrew poetry lay dormant for a generation until it regenerated on the soil of Christian Spain.

Arabic and Romance in Poems by Jews in al-Andalus

Arabic poems by at least eleven Iberian Jewish authors were preserved in Arabic sources such as biographical dictionaries and poetry collections compiled by Muslims.[31] For example, Ibn Saʾid al-Andalusi contained an entry in his *Banners of the Champions and Standards of the Elite* on the Jewish poet Abu Ayyub Suleiman Ibn al-Muʿallim,

> Abu Ayyub the Jew. My father told me that he was employed in the private service of the Commander of the Muslims ʿAli son of Yusuf son of Tashufin. My father also recited to me some verses, which Abu Ayyub had composed about a knife sent by him to his beloved who subsequently abandoned him:
>> When I sent you that knife, I thought its name was an omen, and indeed the augury and presage came true: the knife signifies that you are inhabiting[32] my heart, its cutting signifies rupture and distance. [33]

The same author was praised by Moses Ibn Ezra as one "who [performed] sorcery in both the Hebrew and Arabic tongues."[34] Arabic poems by Judah al-Harizi and by the poetess Qasmuna also survive.[35]

A number of Hebrew poems included Arabic in their concluding verses. These poems adhered to a poetic form adopted from Andalusian Arabic literature called the *muwashshah* (Arabic, "girdle poem"),[36] a strophic form that utilized variations on the classical scheme of meter and rhyme. Within the corpus of Andalusian Arabic poetry, the concluding verse (called the *kharja*) of the *muwashshah* often switched from classical Arabic to vernacular Arabic. Rather than merely changing registers within a single language, the Hebrew poems actually changed languages. The *kharja* was frequently a quotation placed in the mouth of a character within the poem. For example, in a poem of desire by Judah Halevi, the lovesick suitor pined away as the hard-to-get beloved flirted in a mixture of Hebrew and Arabic,

> His song splits my heart,
> He sings to ignite my flames of desire,

"Kiss my mouth, love! Let that be enough for you!
*Kiss me, kiss me, kiss me on the mouth
And forget, my love, all about your sadness!*" (Arabic in italics)[37]

In 1948, the Arabist S. M. Stern discovered that a number of Hebrew *muwashshahs* concluded not with a *kharja* in Arabic but, rather, in Hispano-Romance.[38] These *kharjas* were the earliest traces of Hispano-Romance ever documented. While scholars debated whether or not the Romance *kharjas* represented the surviving remnants of a full-fledged tradition of Romance song,[39] the *muwashshah* was an undisputed testimony to the bilingual (or in the case of Jews, trilingual) literary climate of al-Andalus.

Mention should also be made of a highly unconventional bilingual poem by Solomon Ibn Gabirol that opened with an address to the soul, urging her to return to her celestial abode with her Maker,[40]

What is the matter, my soul,[41] that you sit silent like a king in captivity,
Gathering ostrich wings and dragging the hem of sorrow?
How long will your heart mourn, how many tears will you shed?
You have cleaved to sorrow so much that you have hewn out a grave within it!
Wait quietly, my soul, for God! Wait quietly and do not despair!
Stand and keep watch until the Enthroned One looks and beholds you.

Toward the end of the lengthy poem, the poet lamented his fate as a social outcast, yearning to depart from his boorish contemporaries. In a fury of self-pity, the language of the poem switched mid-verse from Hebrew to Arabic while maintaining the same meter and rhyme:

Alas to you, O land of my enemies, now you are forsaken!
I have no portion in you whether you are welcoming or hostile.
It is my heart's desire to depart; when will you, my soul, fulfill your task?
Lo, I am caught among cattle, *Woe for what has befallen me!*
Woe for the people of good fortune who did not understand my purpose!
Woe for I dwell among them and am bound to them!
Woe for the time of my rejection that left me utterly bewildered!
Woe for my home, my desire for it has grown short!
I have remained there alone so that I wish only to depart!
Incivility has replaced my speech! Only God knows my path!
(Arabic in italics)

The shocking switch to Arabic in the final verses offers the reader a rare glimpse of raw emotion. Even Ibn Gabirol, who lamented the Jews' neglect of Hebrew in favor of foreign tongues, found the language of Qedar appropriate for expressing his most personal feelings.

Christian Spain

Beginning with the Reconquista's capture of Islamic Toledo (1085), the Christian North emerged as the new center of Sephardic life.[42] Abraham Ibn Daud, author of the Hebrew historical narrative *The Book of Tradition* (1161) explained that the transfer of the Jewish population from south to north was divinely ordained,

> The rebels (the Almohads) against the Philistine Kingdom (the Almoravids) had crossed the sea to Spain after having spared no remnant of Jews from Tangiers to al-Mahdiya. . . . Some [Jews] were taken captive by the Christians, to whom they willingly indentured themselves. . . . Others fled on foot, naked and barefoot, their feet stumbling upon the mountains of twilight.[43]

Like many of his contemporaries, Ibn Daud believed that Christian Spain could serve as surrogate soil for replanting Andalusian Jewish leadership and culture.

Christian Spain provided a viable site for Andalusian culture to survive and flourish. Jews played an essential role in the enterprise of translating Arabic texts into Latin (usually translating the Arabic into Castilian orally in the presence of a Christian, who would then translate it into Latin). In Christian Spain and in Provence, Arabic and Judeo-Arabic philosophical and scientific works were translated into Hebrew. New works on these subjects were also written in Hebrew.

Naturally, the reemergence of Hebrew belletristic writing was central to the Jewish cultural renaissance in Christian Spain. The revival of Hebrew belles lettres had been seen by some as an epigonic "Silver Age," a dim reflection of the Golden Age of al-Andalus. In truth, the Hebrew literature of Christian Spain can be merited as a continuation of the tradition of al-Andalus and as an innovative corpus. Hebrew authors wrote volumes of rhymed, metered poetry and many fictional narratives in rhymed prose, a form represented in al-Andalus by only a single text.

Hebrew Poetry

In Christian Spain, the ability to compose poetry continued to be one of the prerequisites of the learned man. Famous Talmudists such as Meir Abulafia and Moses Ben Nahman were skilled in poetic composition. The Hebrew poetics of Christian Spain largely followed those of al-Andalus with respect to genre, theme, and prosody. However, the literary output did not merely ape the conventions of the former era. Todros Halevi Abulafia (1247–after 1298) breathed new vitality into poetry while adhering to the prosodic features of the Andalusian school.[44] In love poetry, Todros spoke of the frustrated love of the Islamic period, love consummated, and of spiritual love,

> Daily she afflicts me with her wandering and gives my eyelids no sleep,
> Though I do not think of touching her ever—what is my life worth that I might touch her?
> I know that her mouth holds a honeycomb sea while I die of thirst!
> It would be enough for me to hear sweet words and behold her lovely form!
> If I could hear or behold her, no trouble would remain with me.
> With her appearance she revives the dead, with her word she lifts the fallen.
> My desire for her is not to delight in the body but only to delight in the soul.[45]

The speaker's desire is spiritual rather than sensual, even if the beloved is unattainable, like the wine pourer in the poem by Moses Ibn Ezra. This poem testifies to the spirit of a new age.[46]

The composition of poetry in the style of the Andalusian school continued into the fifteenth century.[47] In fact, Hebrew poems survived that were exchanged between members of the so-called Saragossa School (including Don Vidal Benveniste, Solomon da Piera, Solomon Bonafed, and Joseph Ben Lavi) even after some of its members had converted to Christianity.[48] One dominant structural feature of the poetry of Christian Spain was the use of a "return verse"—the practice of beginning and ending a poem with the same sentence or phrase. The work of critically editing and analyzing this poetic corpus is still incomplete.

Hebrew Fiction

The most conspicuous difference between the Hebrew literary environments of al-Andalus and Christian Spain was the dominance of the rhymed prose fictional narrative in the latter. The prosodic features of these texts—a loose rhyming prose with rhymed, metered poems interspersed—derived from an eastern Arabic form called the *maqama*. The Arabic *maqama* was invented in tenth-century Nishapur (modern Iran) by Badi^c al-Zaman (the "Wonder of the Age") al-Hamadhani (d. 1008). He fashioned existing genres into lively fictional narratives revolving around the travels and encounters of two main characters, a narrator and a protagonist rogue. Although plot structure varied from episode to episode, a few elements prevailed in the classical *maqama*: fine rhetoric, the mendacity of the protagonist, the gullibility of the narrator, and the narrator's ultimate recognition of the protagonist.

Al-Hamadhani's form was not imitated until the arrival of a collection of *maqamat* by the more rhetorically sophisticated author al-Qasim Ibn ^cAli al-Hariri of Basra (d. 1122). By the twelfth century, al-Hariri's *maqamat* achieved a canonical status, meriting memorization, public recitation, copious commentaries, and a translation into Hebrew. In al-Andalus, the Arabic *maqama* developed in ways that departed from the Eastern tradition. Some examples abandoned normative elements such as the narrator/protagonist dichotomy, the ruse, or the concluding recognition scene.[49]

Even after the Islamic context faded, the Arabic influence on Jewish culture persisted. However, Hebrew *maqamat* (sometimes called *mahbarot*, compositions in Hebrew) cannot be seen as a curious revival of the Arabic literary form only. Their production is best understood as an outcome of the complex interaction of Hebrew, Arabic, and European literatures in the Iberian Peninsula.

The earliest Hebrew *maqama*, Solomon Ibn Saqbel's *Asher Son of Judah Spoke*[50] (first half of twelfth century), was composed in al-Andalus according to the prosodic features of the Arabic *maqama*. It owed much of its thematic content to European notions of courtly love.[51] In the story, Asher was humiliated when he was led to a veiled woman who he believed was his beloved. He lifted the veil and found "a long beard, a face like death and a mouth open wide as a steaming cauldron."[52] The bearded man turned out to be a "friend" of Asher's, a trickster called the "Adulamite" who ensnared Asher in a ruse.[53] The story fused the theme of courtly love as emerging in the European tradition and the *maqama*'s penchants for trickery and denouement through recognition.

Joseph Ibn Zabara's (c. 1150–1209) *Book of Delights* was a cornucopia of tales, proverbs, and scientific teachings set within the frame narrative of an imaginative journey.[54] The story began when a mysterious stranger,

"Enan Hanatas son of Ornan Hadesh," and Ibn Zabara began a journey together in which they exchanged knowledge and lodged in various cities, among other activities.[55] The travelers ultimately alighted in Enan's city, rife with sin and mischief, where Enan revealed that he was actually a demon. The letters in his name could be reversed to expose his true self: Enan Ha*satan* son of Ornan Ha*shed*, meaning Enan the Satan son of Ornan the Demon!

Judah Ibn Shabbetai's (1168–c. 1225) *Gift of Judah the Misogynist*[56] was a Hebrew parody in which the youth Zerah swore off women to devote himself to the pursuit of wisdom. Central to the group's identity was the belief in the wanton and nefarious nature of women. Zerah learned misogyny from his father, who was granted a prophetic experience in which an angel spoke,

> If (men's) sins and debts are grave, it is because their wives incline their hearts. . . . Were it not for (the women's) earrings, the golden calf would not have been made! . . . Abraham, on account of his upright deeds, never had a daughter. . . . Because of whom did Samson's strength falter? . . .
>
> Behold Pharaoh's wisdom and consider his insight when he gave wondrous counsel for persecuting the Israelites:
>
> He afflicted them and increased their grief by killing the boys but sparing the girls![57]

Zerah preached the misogynist cult of celibacy abroad, eliciting a venomous response from women everywhere. The women devised to trick Zerah by exposing him to a beautiful and eloquent maiden and pressing him into marriage before he knew what hit him. Using the ruse of the veil, the beauty Zerah had beheld was switched with a hideous and quarrelsome hag.

A debate immediately ensued among the throng of bystanders as to whether Zerah should be allowed to divorce his wife. The author himself stepped into the narrative and declared the whole thing fiction. Thus, the narrative progresses from a scenario of fictional characters, to one in which fictional and real characters intermingle. Although some have linked the story's misogynist strains to the "wiles of women" motif of Arabic literature, its inspiration might be located in misogynist European literature and debates over celibacy within the Catholic Church.[58]

Thus, the earliest Hebrew rhymed prose narratives exhibited great innovation with respect to plot development and fictional devices.[59] Their variety was striking, considering that the classical *maqama* genre was so conventional and predictable.⁶⁰ However, the tides soon turned in favor of classicism.

Judah al-Harizi's (1165–1225) *Tahkemoni*⁶¹ was the collection of Hebrew *maqamat* most faithful to the Arabic parent literature.⁶² Born in Toledo, al-Harizi began his career as a translator of Arabic and Judeo-Arabic legal, philosophical, and belletristic works into Hebrew.⁶³ Famously, al-Harizi composed a fluid translation of Maimonides' *Guide of the Perplexed* commissioned by notables in Provence who had requested a translation in "simple and clear words."⁶⁴

Before undertaking the *Tahkemoni*, al-Harizi composed a rhymed prose Hebrew translation of al-Hariri's Arabic *maqamat*, probably in response to a challenge that their perfection could not be imitated.⁶⁵ In his translation, titled *Mahbarot ʾIttiʾel*,⁶⁶ al-Harizi strived to capture the sense of the original while creating a new work that was belletristic in its own right. Arabic names were changed to biblical names, cities around the Islamic world were replaced with biblical place names, and ironic biblical allusions were used.⁶⁷

Unlike *Mahbarot ʾIttiʾel*, the *Tahkemoni* was the work of an author who left his homeland. Following the classical *maqama* collection of al-Hariri, the *Tahkemoni* was comprised of 50 narratives. The constant movement of characters from place to place imbues the text with the ideal of wanderlust common in *maqama* literature.

Like the Arabic *maqama*, the *Tahkemoni* used profound language and humorous scenarios. Al-Harizi stated that he wrote the book in order to ennoble the Hebrew language, which had "declined appallingly"⁶⁸ in his day, and to "demonstrate the power of the Holy Tongue to the Holy Nation."⁶⁹ Al-Harizi claimed that his book was entirely original, "I took nothing from the book of the Ishmaelite (al-Hariri)."⁷⁰ However, it is well known among modern scholars that the author borrowed liberally from al-Hamadhani, al-Hariri, and other Arabic sources.⁷¹

Throughout the *Tahkemoni*, al-Harizi undertook many literary feats: the inclusion of an epistle that when read forward was panegyric but when read backward was invective,⁷² a trilingual poem (Hebrew, Aramaic, and Arabic) in a single rhyme and meter,⁷³ and a *maqama* with two speeches structured so that every word in the first speech included the letter *"resh"* but every word in the second omitted the same letter.⁷⁴

The *Tahkemoni* was remarkable for its ironic exploitation of traditional texts. David Segal translated one episode:

Lo, the cantor entered and took his honoured seat, and in tones dulcet sweet began the daily blessings, as is meet. According to the practice of our nation, he begged God's lumination, thundering, *Make the words of Thy Torah pheasant in our mouth,* rather than *pleasant in our mouth;* and *May the Lord flavour you and grant you peas,* instead of *May the Lord favour you and grant you peace.* In the next section of the service, his zeal mounting, he made errors beyond counting. For *It is our duty to bless and hallow Thy name* he said *It is our duty to blast and hollow Thy name;* for *Exalt the Lord our God,* he said, *Assault the Lord our God;* for *Praise the Lord O my soul,* he said *Prize the Lard, O my soul;* for *Thine, O Lord is the greatness and the power,* he said *Thine, O Lord, is the gratings and the flour;* for *Thou rulest over all,* he said *Thou droolest over all.*[75]

Although the scene was intended to be humorous, its setting in a real city of the Islamic East, Mosul of Iraq, suggested that al-Harizi, the wanderer, may have found Jewish learning lacking in the lands of his journey. Al-Harizi spent his final years composing Arabic poetry in honor of Muslim patrons[76] and left an account of his Eastern journeys in Arabic rhymed prose.[77]

Al-Harizi's attempt to restore luster to the Hebrew language was well received in the thirteenth century. In Christian Spain, the *Tahkemoni* was followed by several original works in rhymed prose. Even more than the Hebrew *maqamat* that predate the *Tahkemoni*, these narratives reveal affinities for the burgeoning literary traditions of Europe.[78] Hebrew authors in Italy, Egypt, Yemen, Turkey, and Greece continued to utilize rhymed prose for centuries to come.[79]

Spanish

Neither Latin nor the dialects of vernacular Spanish played a role in the Jewish culture of Christian Spain comparable to the role of Arabic in al-Andalus. There were no Latin literary compositions by medieval Spanish Jews.[80] Only rarely did Jewish authors compose works in the dialects of Spanish. An example of a Catalan text of Jewish authorship was the *Refutation of Christian Dogmas*[81] by Hasdai Crescas (1340–c. 1410). This non-belletristic work was intended to challenge the abundant polemical literature aimed at the conversion of Jews to Catholicism by persuasion. The only example of a belletristic work by a Jew in Castilian was the

Proverbios Morales by Santob de Carrión (d. after 1345), also known as Shem Tov Ibn Ardutiel. Santob identified himself as a Jew in a self-deprecating tone,

> Many a sword of good and fine steel comes from a torn sheath, and it is from the worm that fine silk is made.... For being born on the thornbush, the rose is certainly not worth less, nor is good wine if taken from the lesser branches of the vine. Nor is a hawk worth less, if born in a poor nest; nor are good proverbs [of less value] if spoken by a Jew.[82]

Many of the book's teachings derive from other European proverb collections, though numerous examples clearly emanate from Jewish sources. For example, Santob's proverb "In truth, the world subsists through three things: justice, truth, and peace, which comes from these" (lines 1369–72) was an almost verbatim quotation of Rabban Shimon Ben Gamliel's statement in the Mishnah, "By three things is the world maintained: by justice, by truth and by peace" (Abot 1:18).[83] Other elements of the book may be traced to Arabic sources.[84] For these reasons, Américo Castro characterized the *Proverbios Morales* as an essential Jewish contribution to Spanish literature and hence Spanish civilization.[85]

The fifteenth century saw the first glimmerings of Judeo-Spanish, which became a normative language of Sephardic writing after the Expulsion. Although a complete Ladino[86] Bible did not appear until the sixteenth century, fragments survive of earlier translation attempts. Some of the earliest Judeo-Spanish compositions were translations of classic Jewish texts such as *The Sayings of the Fathers,* Judah Halevi's *Kuzari,* and a simplified prayer book for women. Other samples included original belletristic compositions such as the *Poem of Joseph* and a bilingual Hebrew-Spanish love poem.[87] Judeo-Spanish ballads among Jews in medieval Spain remained a part of the Sephardic oral tradition after the Expulsion down to the modern period.[88]

Conclusion

The literature of medieval Sephardic Jews in Hebrew, Arabic, Hispano-Romance, and Spanish elucidate the complex cultural environment of medieval Iberia. Through these texts, the modern reader could explore the degree of permeability between Jewish and non-Jewish culture. In al-Andalus and in Christian Spain, Hebrew retained premier status as the language of literature, demonstrating the impulse to maintain community and fortify identity. At the same time, Jewish writings in other languages and the influence of non-Jewish literature on Hebrew writing indicate the high degree of Jewish acculturation and the Jewish role in the formation of Spanish culture.

Following the Expulsion, Sephardic Jews carried many of the traditions developed in the medieval period with them. Liturgical compositions by Judah Halevi, Solomon Ibn Gabirol, and others adorned Sephardic liturgy throughout the Diaspora. A canon of Sephardic intellectual culture developed around Judeo-Spanish translations of classic works from the medieval period. In the peninsula and beyond, *conversos* composed works in Spanish that point to Jewish origins, testifying to the ongoing Jewish component in the development of Spanish culture.

NOTES

1. Solomon Ibn Gabirol, *Shirei ha-Hol shel Shelomo Ibn Gabirol*, ed. H. Brody and J. Schirmann (Jerusalem: Schocken, 1974), 169, l. 8.

2. Consuelo López-Morillas, "Language," in *The Literature of al-Andalus*, ed. María Rosa Menocal, Raymond P. Scheindlin, and Michael Sells (Cambridge: Cambridge University Press, 2000), 46–50; David J. Wasserstein, "The Language Situation in al-Andalus," in *Studies on the Muwashshah and the Kharja (Proceedings of the Exeter International Colloquium)*, ed. Alan Jones and Richard Hitchcock (Reading, England: Ithaca, 1991), 1–15. See for information on language in al-Andalus.

3. Américo Castro, *The Structure of Spanish History*, trans. Edmund L. King (Princeton, NJ: Princeton University Press, 1954). On the history and limitations of the term "*convivencia*," see Thomas F. Glick, "Convivencia: An Introductory Note," in *Convivencia: Jews, Muslims, and Christians in Medieval Spain*, ed. Vivian B. Mann, Thomas F. Glick, and Jerilynn D. Dodds (New York: Jewish Museum, 1992), 1–9; Thomas F. Glick and Oriol Pi-Sunyer, "Acculturation as an Explanatory Concept in Spanish History," *Comparative Studies in Society and History* 11 (1969): 136–54.

4. Joshua Blau, *The Emergence and Linguistic Background of Judaeo-Arabic: A Study of the Origins of Neo-Arabic and Middle Arabic*, 3d rev. ed. (Jerusalem: Ben Zvi Institute, 1999). Judeo-Arabic texts vary regarding their adherence to the rules of classical Arabic, often incorporate elements of colloquial usage, include Hebrew

and Aramaic terms specific to Jewish subjects, and exhibit grammatical peculiarities such as "hypercorrection" (i.e., making grammatical errors as a result of "trying too hard" to follow grammatical rules). See Blau's work.

5. The most extensive textbooks on the history of Hebrew poetry in Muslim and Christian Spain are the two volumes by Jefim Schirmann, *Toledot ha-Shirah ha-ᶜIvrit bi-Sefarad ha-Muslemit,* ed., supplemented, and annotated by Ezra Fleischer (Jerusalem: Magnes, 1995); and idem, *Toledot ha-Shirah ha-ᶜIvrit bi-Sefarad ha-Notzrit u-ve-Derom Tzarfat,* ed., supplemented, and annotated by Ezra Fleischer (Jerusalem: Magnes, 1997). Extensive information and bibliography on the periods and authors discussed in this essay can be found in these volumes.

6. Ezra Fleischer, *Shirat ha-Qodesh ha-ᶜIvrit bi-Yemei ha-Beinayim* (Jerusalem: Keter, 1975).

7. Aaron Mirsky, *Ha-Piyyut: Hitpathuto be-Eretz Yisraʾel u-va-Golah* (Jerusalem: Magnes, 1990). For examples in English translation, see T. Carmi, *The Penguin Book of Hebrew Verse* (New York: Penguin, 1981), 190–94.

8. On Saᶜadia Gaon in general, see Robert Brody, *The Geonim of Babylonia and the Shaping of Medieval Jewish Culture* (New Haven: Yale University Press, 1998), 235–332.

9. Yosef Tobi, "Saᶜadia Gaon, Poet-*Paytan*: The Connecting Link between the Ancient *Piyyut* and Hebrew Arabicised Poetry in Spain," in *Israel and Ishmael: Studies in Muslim-Jewish Relations,* ed. Tudor Parfitt (New York: St. Martin's, 2000), 59–77.

10. *Jews and Arabs: Their Contacts through the Ages* (New York: Schocken, 1964), 155–66. For an evaluation of Goitein's concept of "symbiosis," see Steven M. Wasserstrom, *Between Muslim and Jew: The Problem of Symbiosis under Early Islam* (Princeton, NJ: Princeton University Press, 1995).

11. A. S. Halkin, ed., *Kitab al-Muhadara wa'l-Mudhakara* (Jerusalem: Mekitzei Nirdamim, 1975); See also Raymond P. Scheindlin, "Rabbi Moses Ibn Ezra on the Legitimacy of Poetry," *Medievalia et Humanistica* n.s. 7 (1976): 101–15.

12. Ross Brann, *The Compunctious Poet: Cultural Ambiguity and Hebrew Poetry in Muslim Spain* (Baltimore: Johns Hopkins University Press, 1991), 95ff. Also, it should be kept in mind that Dunash's innovation was not utilized in every poem of the Sephardic School. Liturgical poems exist in three metrical forms: those that are composed in the style of the ancient *piyyut,* those that follow the Arabic system, and those that strike a compromise between the two systems. Particularly when adorning sections of the liturgy whose form was standardized in the ancient *piyyut,* the medieval poet would defer to the age-old protocols of traditional form.

13. Ángel Sáenz Badillos, "Hebrew Philology in Sefarad: the State of the Question," in *Hebrew Scholarship and the Medieval World,* ed. Nicholas de Lange (New York: Cambridge University Press, 2001), 38–59. See for a synopsis.

14. The phrase derives from Qurʾan 90:18.

15. Brann, *The Compunctious Poet*, 25.

16. Raymond P. Scheindlin, *Wine, Women, and Death: Medieval Hebrew Poems on the Good Life* (Philadelphia: Jewish Publication Society, 1986). See for information on wine and love poetry.

17. Jaroslav Stetkevych, *The Zephyrs of Najd: The Poetics of Nostalgia in the Classical Arabic Nasib* (Chicago: University of Chicago Press, 1993). See for information on the development of this and other themes.

18. Raymond P. Scheindlin, *The Gazelle: Medieval Hebrew Poems on God, Israel, and the Soul* (Philadelphia: Jewish Publication Society, 1991), 65. Selections reprinted from *The Gazelle*, © 1990, by Raymond Scheindlin, published by The Jewish Publication Society with the permission of the publisher, The Jewish Publication Society. Throughout this essay, I point the reader to some of the fine English translations of medieval Hebrew verse. Unless indicated otherwise, all translations are my own. Other English translations of poems by Moses Ibn Ezra may be found in *Selected Poems of Moses Ibn Ezra*, trans. Solomon Solis-Cohen (Philadelphia: Jewish Publication Society, 1945).

19. Colette Sirat, *A History of Jewish Philosophy in the Middle Ages* (Cambridge: Cambridge University Press, 1985), 57–112; Lenn E. Goodman, ed., *Neoplatonism and Jewish Thought* (Albany: State University of New York Press, 1992). See for information on Jewish Neoplatonism.

20. Scheindlin, *The Gazelle*, 203. See also Solomon Ibn Gabirol, *Selected Poems of Solomon Ibn Gabirol*, trans. Peter Cole (Princeton, NJ: Princeton University Press, 2001).

21. Tova Rosen and Eli Yassif, "The Study of Hebrew Literature in the Middle Ages: Major Trends and Goals," in *The Oxford Handbook of Jewish Studies*, ed. Martin Goodman, Jeremy Cohen, and David Sorkin (Oxford: Oxford University Press, 2002), 241–94. The enterprise of segregating "sacred" from "secular" verse is a modern construction of limited use since numerous poems do not fit neatly into one category or the other. "Secular" poems often assume a religious worldview while "sacred" poems do not always assume a liturgical context. On the history of the field, see the recent essay by Rosen and Yassif.

22. Samuel Ha-Nagid, *Diwan (Ben Tehillim)*, ed. Dov Jarden (Jerusalem: Hebrew Union College, 1966), 283, poem 132.

23. Scheindlin, *Wine, Women, and Death*, 19–33.

24. On roundness in poetry, see Gaston Bachelard, *The Poetics of Space*, trans. Maria Jolas (New York: Orion, 1964), chap. 10. See also the comments by Jaroslav Stetkevych, *The Zephyrs of Najd*, 180–81.

25. Jefim Schirmann, "The Ephebe in Medieval Hebrew Poetry," *Sefarad* 15 (1955): 55–68; Nehemiah Allony, "Ha-Tzvi ve-ha-Gamal be-Shirat Sefarad," *Otzar Yehudei Sefarad* 4 (1961): 16–42; Norman Roth, "'Deal Gently with the Young Man': Love of Boys in Medieval Hebrew Poetry from Spain," *Speculum* 57 (1982): 20–51. The homoerotic aspect of medieval Hebrew poetry has been the subject of

considerable discussion in scholarly and popular publications. The works by Schirmann, Allony, and Roth serve as examples.

26. Ha-Nagid, *Diwan*, 305. See translations in Scheindlin, *Wine, Women, and Death*, 69; Samuel Ha-Nagid, *Selected Poems by Shmuel HaNagid*, trans. Peter Cole (Princeton, NJ: Princeton University Press, 1996), 15.

27. On Judah Halevi, see Ross Brann, "Judah Halevi," in *The Literature of al-Andalus*, ed. Menocal, Scheindlin, and Sells, 265–81. For samples of Halevi's poetry in English, see *Selected Poems of Jehudah Halevi*, trans. Nina Salaman (Philadelphia: Jewish Publication Society, 1924; repr. 1974).

28. Leon Weinberger, *Twilight of a Golden Age: Selected Poems of Abraham Ibn Ezra* (Tuscaloosa: University of Alabama Press, 1997). Translations of some poems by Abraham Ibn Ezra can be found there.

29. Israel Levin, *Yalqut Avraham Ibn Ezra* (in Hebrew) (Haifa, Israel: Keren Yisrael Matz, 1985), 101–3.

30. Aviva Doron, "Arim ba-Shirah ha-Ivrit bi-Sefarad," in *Sefer Yisraʾel Levin*, ed. Tova Rosen and Reuven Tzur (Tel Aviv: 1994), vol. 1, 69–78.

31. Ahmad Ibn Muhammad Al-Maqqari al-Tilimsani, *Nafh al-Tib Min Ghusn al-Andalus al-Ratib*, ed. Ihsan ᶜAbbas (Beirut: Dar Al-Kitab Al-ᶜArabi, 1968), vol. 3, 522–30; see also Ross Brann, "The Arabized Jews," in *The Literature of al-Andalus*, ed. Menocal, Scheindlin, and Sells, 436.

32. The words "knife" (*sikkin*) and "inhabiting" (*sukna*) are both derived from the same root (*skn*).

33. S. M. Stern, trans., "Arabic Poems by Spanish Hebrew Poets," in *Romanica et Occidentalia à La Mémoire de Hiram Peri*, ed. M. Lazar (Jerusalem: Magnes, 1963), 258.

34. Halkin, *Kitab al-Muhadara wa'l-Mudhakara*, 78.

35. On Qasmuna, see María Ángeles Gallego García, "Approaches to the Study of Muslim and Jewish Women in the Medieval Iberian Peninsula: The Poetess Qasmuna bat Ismaᶜil," *Misceláne de Estudios Árabes y Hebraicos* 48 (1999): 63–75, Sección de Hebreo.

36. On the *muwashshah*, see Tova Rosen, "The Muwashshah," in *The Literature of al-Andalus*, ed. Menocal, Scheindlin, and Sells, 165–89; on the Hebrew *muwashshah*, idem, *Le-Ezor Shir: ʿAl Shirat ha-Ezor ha-ᶜIvrit bi-Yemei ha-Beinayim* (Haifa, Israel: Hotsa' At Sefarim Sel Universitat Haifa, 1985). See also María Rosa Menocal, *The Arabic Role in Medieval Literary History: A Forgotten Heritage* (Philadelphia: University of Pennsylvania Press, 1987).

37. Jefim Schirmann, *Ha-Shirah ha-ᶜIvrit bi-Sefarad u-ve-Provans* (Jerusalem: Mosad Bialik, DVIR, 1954–56), vol. 1, 442. Hereafter referred to as HHSP.

38. S. M. Stern, "Les vers finaux en espagnol dans les muwashshahs hispano-hebraïques: Une contribution à l'histoire du muwashshah et à l'étude du vieux dialecte espagnol 'mozarabe,'" *Al-Andalus* 13 (1978): 299–346.

39. See, for example, the discussion in Otto Zwartjes, *Love Songs from al-*

Andalus: History, Structure, and Meaning of the Kharja (Leiden, the Netherlands: Brill, 1997); James T. Monroe, "*Zajal* and *Muwashshah*: Hispano-Arabic Poetry and the Romance Tradition," in *The Legacy of Muslim Spain*, ed. Salma Khadra Jayyusi (Leiden, the Netherlands: Brill, 1992), 398–419.

40. HHSP, vol. 1, 210–12.

41. Literally, "only one." Cf. Psalm 22:21.

42. On this period in general, see Bernard Septimus, *Hispano-Jewish Culture in Transition: The Career and Controversies of Ramah* (Cambridge: Harvard University Press, 1982).

43. Gerson D. Cohen, *Sefer ha-Qabbalah: The Book of Tradition by Abraham Ibn Daud: A Critical Edition with Translation and Notes* (Philadelphia: Jewish Publication Society, 1967), 70–71, Hebrew section.

44. On Todros Halevi Abulafia, see Brann, *The Compunctious Poet*, 143–57; Ángel Sáenz Badillos, "Hebrew Invective Poetry: The Debate between Todros Abulafia and Phinehas Halevi," *Prooftexts* 16 (1996): 49–73; Aviva Doron, *Meshorer be-Hatzar ha-Melekh: Todros Halevi Abulafia—Shirah ʿIvrit bi-Sefarad ha-Notzrit* (Tel Aviv: Dvir, 1989).

45. Todros Halevi Abulafia, *Gan ha-Meshalim ve-ha-Hidot*, ed. David Yellin (Jerusalem: Weiss, 1934), vol. 2, 1 [714], 124–25; HHSP, vol. 2, 435–47, ll. 15–21.

46. HHSP, vol. 2, 434–35; translation in Brann, *The Compunctious Poet*, 145.

47. This area of poetry has not been studied sufficiently. See Raymond P. Scheindlin, "Secular Poetry in Fifteenth-Century Spain," in *Crisis and Creativity in the Sephardic World: 1391–1648*, ed. Benjamin R. Gampel (New York: Columbia University Press, 1997), 25–37.

48. Schirmann, *Toledot . . . ha-Muslemit*, 588–93.

49. Further on the *maqama* in Spain, see Rina Drory, "The Maqama," in *The Literature of al-Andalus*, ed. Menocal, Scheindlin, and Sells, 83–92; H. Nemah, "Andalusian *Maqamat*," *Journal of Arabic Literature* 5 (1974): 83–92. The most classical of Arabic *maqama* collections from al-Andalus is that by Abu al-Tahir Muhammad Ibn Yusuf al-Saraqusti, *Al-Maqamat al-Luzumiyah*, trans. James T. Monroe (Leiden, the Netherlands: Brill, 2002).

50. The Hebrew text *Neʾum Asher Ben Yehudah* may be found in HHSP, vol. 2, 554–65; for an English translation, see Raymond P. Scheindlin, trans., "Asher in the Harem," in *Rabbinic Fantasies: Imaginative Narratives from Classical Hebrew Literature*, ed. David Stern and Mark J. Mirsky (New Haven: Yale University Press, 1990), 253–67.

51. Raymond P. Scheindlin, "Fawns of the Palace, Fawns of the Field," *Prooftexts* 6 (1986): 189–203.

52. Scheindlin, "Asher in the Harem," 263.

53. It is possible that this story was originally one in a series of *maqamat* wherein Asher and the Adulamite are constant characters. This would be consistent with the classical *maqama* form. One fragment has been discovered with the

same opening phrase, "Asher Son of Judah spoke," but is too sketchy to allow for solid conclusions. See, however, Ezra Fleischer, "ʿInyanei Piyyut ve-Shirah," in *Meh qarei Sifrut Mugashim le-Shimʿon Halkin*, ed. Ezra Fleischer (Jerusalem: Magnes, 1973), 193–204, which argues for single authorship based on stylistic elements.

54. Hebrew text, *Sefer Shaʿashuʿim le-Rav Yosef Ben Meir Ibn Zabara*, ed. Israel Davidson (Berlin: Eshkol, 1925); English translation, *The Book of Delight by Joseph Ben Meir Ibn Zabara*, trans. Moses Hadas with an introduction by Merriam Sherwood (New York: Columbia University Press, 1932).

55. Merriam Sherwood compares stories in *The Book of Delight* with European folktales. See Hadas, *The Book of Delight*, 3–43.

56. Selections are published in HHSP, vol. 2, 67–86; the complete Hebrew text can be found in the dissertation of Matti Huss, "'Minhat Yehudah,' 'Ezrat ha-Nashim,' ve-'Ein Mishpat'—Mahadurot Madaʿiyot bi-Leviyat Mavo', Hilufei Girsa'ot, Meqorot u-Ferushim" (Jerusalem: Hebrew University of Jerusalem, 1991), vol. 2. A partial English translation is "The Misogynist," trans. Raymond P. Scheindlin, in Scheindlin, *Rabbinic Fantasies*, 269–94. On misogyny (and other themes) in medieval Hebrew literature, see the recent book by Tova Rosen, *Unveiling Eve: Reading Gender in Medieval Hebrew Literature* (Philadelphia: University of Pennsylvania Press, 2003).

57. HHSP, vol. 2, 71–72; Huss, "Minhat Yehudah," vol. 2, 5–6.

58. Huss, "Minhat Yehudah," 54ff.

59. On fictional devices, see Matti Huss, "Loʾ Haya ve-Loʾ Nivraʾ: ʿIyyun Mashveh me-Maʿamad ha-Bidayon ba-Maqama ha-ʿIvrit ve-ha-ʿAravit," in *Meh qarei Yerushalayim be-Sifrut ʿIvrit* 18 (2001): 58–104.

60. On variety, see Dan Pagis, "Variety in Medieval Rhymed Narratives," *Scripta Hierosolymitana* 27 (Jerusalem: Hebrew University Press, 1978), 79–98.

61. The book's title derives from the name of the father of one of King David's warriors in II Samuel 23:8; the root of the name (*hkm*) implies "wisdom."

62. Hebrew text, see Judah al-Harizi, *Tahkemoni*, ed. Y. Toporovsky (Tel Aviv: 1952). For a fine literary translation in English rhymed prose, see Judah Alharizi, *The Book of Tahkemoni: Jewish Tales from Medieval Spain*, trans. and explicated by David Simha Segal (London: Littman Library of Jewish Civilization, 2001). There is also a literal translation by V. E. Reichert, *The Tahkemoni of Judah Alharizi: An English Translation*, 2 vols. (Jerusalem: R. H. Cohen's Press, 1965–73).

63. A complete list of al-Harizi's translations can be found in Rina Drory, "Literary Contacts and Where to Find Them: On Arabic Literary Models in Medieval Jewish Culture," *Poetics Today* 14, no. 2 (1993): 277–302.

64. Moshe Ben Maimon, *Moreh ha-Nevukhim be-Tirgumo Shel Rabbi Yehuda al-Harizi* (Jerusalem: Mosad Ha-Rav Kook, 1953). The earlier translation of the *Guide* by Samuel Ibn Tibbon (produced in collaboration with Maimonides himself) may have been too cumbersome for some readers in Provence.

65. Al-Harizi explains this as the motive of the undertaking in the *Tahkemoni*, chap. 1.

66. Al-Hariri, *Mahbarot ʾIttiʾel*, trans. Judah al-Harizi, ed. Yitzhaq Peretz (Tel Aviv: Mosad ha-Rav Kook, 1955). The narrator 'Itti'el is named for a wise man in Proverbs 30:1.

67. Jefim Schirmann, *Die hebräische Übersetzung der Maqamen des Hariri* (Frankfurt: J. Kauffmann, 1930); Abraham Lavi, "A Comparative Study of al-Hariri's Maqamat and Their Hebrew Translation by al-Harizi" (Ann Arbor: University of Michigan Press, 1979).

68. Al-Harizi, *Tahkemoni*, ed. Toporovsky, 8.

69. Ibid., 12

70. Ibid., 14

71. The literature on the sources of the *Tahkemoni* is quite vast. For a convenient summary, see the dissertation by ʿAbd al-Rahman Marʿi, "Hashpaʿat Maqamot al-Hariri ʿal Mahbarot Tahkemoni" (Tel Aviv: Bar Ilan University, 1995).

72. Al-Harizi, *The Book of Takhemoni*, 8.

73. Ibid., 11. This is re-created in Segal's translation with a trilingual poem by Dr. Leofranc Holford-Stevens in English, French, and Latin.

74. Ibid., 11. Segal recreates this effect by including and omitting the letter "o."

75. Al-Harizi, *The Book of Tahkemoni*, trans. Segal, 216–17.

76. The Arabic poems are included in Joseph Sadan, "Rabi Yehudah al-Harizi ke-Tzomet Tarbuti," *Peʿamim* 68 (1996): 52–61.

77. Joseph Yahalom and Joshua Blau, *Masʿei Yehudah* (Jerusalem: Ben-Zvi Institute, 2002), 91–167.

78. At the same time, it is believed that aspects of medieval Spanish prose writing are indebted to *maqama* literature, though Arabic is generally considered a more immediate influence than Hebrew.

79. Pagis, "Variety in Medieval Rhymed Narratives."

80. However, Petrus Alfonsi (formerly Moses Sefardi), a famous Jewish convert to Catholicism, incorporated many maxims, proverbs, and folktales of Hebrew (and Arabic) origin in his celebrated *Disciplina clericalis*. See Lourdes María Alvárez, "Petrus Alfonsi" in *The Literature of al-Andalus*, ed. Menocal, Scheindlin, and Sells, 282–91 and bibliography therein.

81. The text survives in the Hebrew translation of Joseph Ben Shem Tov; the work has been translated into English by Daniel J. Lasker, *The Refutation of the Christian Principles* (Albany: State University of New York Press, 1992).

82. T. A. Perry, *The Moral Proverbs of Santob de Carrión: Jewish Wisdom in Christian Spain* (Princeton, NJ: Princeton University Press, 1987), 19–20, ll. 169–89. Perry argues that the "rose among thorns" motif is intended to alert Jewish readers of a Jewish-Christian polemic.

83. Ibid., 96.

84. Ibid., 79–80, where a passage is traced to a poem by al-Muʾtamid Ibn ʿAbbad of Seville, perhaps through the Hebrew translation of Rabbi Meir Abulafia.

85. Castro, *The Structure of Spanish History*, 551–57, 572–76. Castro especially credits Santob for introducing "intimate reality" into Spanish literature.

86. A register of Judeo-Spanish used in the translation of Hebrew texts that mimics the syntax of Hebrew. "Ladino" is often used more casually to refer to other registers of Judeo-Spanish.

87. On Judeo-Spanish texts in the fifteenth century, see Moshe Lazar, *Sefarad in My Heart: A Ladino Reader* (Lancaster, CA: Labyrinthos, 1999): vii–viii.

88. On the Sephardi ballad (and other Judeo-Spanish forms), see Samuel G. Armistead, Joseph H. Silverman, and Israel J. Katz, *Folk Literature of the Sephardic Jews*, 5 vols. (Berkeley and Los Angeles: University of California Press, 1971–1994).

Chapter 6

Medieval Sephardic-Oriental Jewish Bible Exegesis
The Contributions of Saadia Gaon and Abraham ibn Ezra

Isaac Kalimi

Introduction

In medieval times the Jewish Bible exegesis flourished in a variety of locations of the Jewish Diaspora, namely in Northern France, Provence, Spain, and the Middle East. During this period, Judaism interacted closely with Christianity and Islam. This interaction saved Judaism from becoming fossilized and nonproductive, and forced it to search for new horizons in Holy Scripture interpretations. Indeed, the disputes between Jews and non-Jews (especially Christians and Moslems) concerning a variety of theological issues in general and exegetical methods of the Hebrew Bible in particular, motivated many Jewish scholars to study the Bible for its own merit. They attempted to search and interpret the Scriptures by new methods that were profoundly different from that of the classical rabbis in Talmudic and Midrashic literature. Moreover, disputes among several internal Jewish groups, such as those between rabbinic Judaism and the Karaites, pushed—particularly the Sephardic Jewish scholars—to search for new directions in biblical studies and interpretation.

Jewish scholars under the Islamic realm were surrounded by the rich and well-developed Arabic language and philology. Thus, they were influenced and encouraged to develop their own literary languages, above all Hebrew. Here the Quran's interpretative methods and techniques were utilized for explanation of the Jewish Bible. Likewise, as the Arab interpreters attempted to harmonize between Greek philosophy and the

Quran, the Jewish exegetes tried to create some harmonies between the theologies of the Hebrew Bible and Greek as well as Arabic philosophies.

The Sephardic-Oriental Jewish Bible exegesis built up and established itself, especially in the Jewish communities under the Islamic realm, such as Egypt, Babylonia, Persia, and Spain. Yet it also developed in some Christian lands such as Italy and Christian Iberia (see below). Two essential clusters were distinguishable in the Sephardic-Oriental biblical interpretation: the Karaite biblical exegesis, and the rabbinic biblical exegesis.

The Karaite Bible Exegesis

Circa 750 CE, Anan ben David founded the Karaite movement in Persia. This swiftly spreading movement based Judaism on the Written Torah (i.e., *Mikra,* Jewish/Hebrew Bible, Tanak) rather than Written and Oral Torah simultaneously. Anan's well-known saying was "chapsu beOraita shaper" ("search the Torah well") in order to find out the proper *Halachot* ("Jewish laws").[1] The Karaite sect rebelled against rabbinic authority which interpreted Holy Scripture according to the methods passed through the generations. The Karaites preferred to ignore the entire rabbinic Bible expounding the so-called "Oral Torah" that developed over hundreds of years (particularly after the destruction of the Second Temple in 70 CE)[2] as reflected in Mishnah, Tosefta, Talmudim, and *Halachic* and *Aggadic* Midrashim.

The Karaite commentators lived in the Islamic lands, and therefore, composed mostly in Arabic. The Arabic words, however, were transliterated in Hebrew letters. Since there was no fear of the Moslems who could not read the writings, the compositions sharply criticized even the Islamic prophet, Mohammed.[3] Some important exegetes among the Karaites were: Benjamin ben Moshe Nahawendi (Nahawend, Persia, ninth century), Daniel ben Moshe al-Kumisi (North Persia, the second half of the ninth to beginning of the first half of the tenth centuries, Jerusalem), Abu Joseph al-Kirkassani (Kirkassn, Iraq, tenth century), and Jephet ben/ibn Ali (Basra, the second half of the tenth to beginning of the eleventh century, Jerusalem).

In the history of Judaism, the phenomenon of the Karaites' concentration on only the biblical writings[4] is most likely parallel to a phenomenon that appeared in the history of Christianity in the sixteenth century. During that time, the reformers of Martin Luther demanded *sola scriptura* ("Scriptures only") as opposed to the concept of the Church in Rome, of *scriptura et traditio* ("Scriptures and tradition").[5]

The Rabbinic Bible Exegesis

The rabbinic commentators desired the continuity of Judaism as it was based on the Written as well as the Oral Torah. They completely recognized the rabbinic authority and interpretation, especially those related to *Mitzvot* (commandments) and any *Halachic* issues. At the same time, however, these commentators strove to search and understand the Bible according to new and well-developed methods—specifically philological and/or philosophical ones. They strove to achieve the *peshat*, the simple meaning of the text. Here, one must count Saadia Gaon (see below) and the commentators from Provence—the Kimchi family from Narbonne: the father Rabbi Joseph Kimchi (ca. 1105–70) and his sons Rabbi Moshe Kimchi (died ca. 1190) and Rabbi David Kimchi (known by the acronym Radak; 1160–1235). It is worthwhile to also mention Rabbi Levi ben Gershon (Gershonides/Ralbag; Bagnolle, 1288–1344). Among the Spanish and Italian exegetes, there were Rabbi Abraham ben Meir ibn Ezra (see below), Rabbi Moshe ben Nachman (acronym: Ramban or Nachmanides; Gerona, 1194–1274, Acre), Rabbi Jeshaia from Tiranni (South Italy; died before 1260), and Don Isaac Abarbanel who lived during the time of the transition from the Medieval to the Renaissance era (Portugal, 1437–1508, Naples).[6]

These various groups of Sephardic-Oriental Jewish Bible exegetes harshly disputed with one another. Nevertheless, they both also sharply disputed with Islamic beliefs and religious views as well as with Christian doctrines and biblical allegorical interpretations.[7]

In the following sections, I will concentrate particularly on two very distinguished Bible commentators, philologists, and philosophers, namely Rav Saadia Gaon and Rabbi Abraham ibn Ezra. These prolific Sephardic exegetes share several common methodological approaches to biblical interpretation.[8] On the other hand, they disputed repeatedly with a variety of Karaite commentators.

Rav Saadia Gaon

Rabbi Saadia ben Joseph Gaon (acronym: Rasag) was born in 882 CE in Abu-Suweir, a small town in the district of Upper Egypt named Fayyum. Therefore, he was also called "Saadia ben Joseph al-Fayyumi," or in Arabic: Saʾid ibn Yusuf al-Fayyumi. No specific information is available about him, his family or what caused him to leave Egypt. Nevertheless, it is known that he studied several years in yeshiva (rabbinic seminar) in Eretz-Israel (Palestine). Afterward, he moved to Haleb (Aleppo, Syria) and later settled in Babylonia. He died in September 942 in Sura, Babylonia.

Saadia Gaon as Biblical Theologian and Philosopher

In 922, Rav Saadia was appointed by the Resh Galuta (the "Exilarch" or the "Chief of Exile"), David ben Zakkai, to serve as the head of the renowned Babylonian Talmudic Academy at Sura. Thus, he was entitled to use the epithet "Gaon" (rabbinic leader). Two years later, however, controversy erupted between Saadia and David ben Zakkai over an inheritance that Saadia refused to certify as legitimate. Saadia justified his refusal by saying that a large payment was made to ben Zakkai. According to Saadia, involving oneself in matters of inheritance contradicts *Halachic* teaching and therefore is illegal. As a result, Saadia Gaon was removed from his high position in Sura. Another scholar was appointed, and Saadia was forced to hide for approximately four years.

Saadia used this incident for productive writing and composed his magnum opus, *The Book of Beliefs and Opinions*.[9] This book, the first of its kind in Jewish literature, was written originally in flowing Arabic, the daily language of the Jews under the Islamic rule, and was called *Kitab al-Amanat wal-l'tiqadat*.[10] Undoubtedly, it is one of the most important and influential theological or Jewish religious-philosophical compositions of medieval Jewry. It is definitely comparable to the great composition by Rabbi Moshe ben Maimon's (acronym: Rambam or Maimonides; 1135–1204), *The Guide for the Perplexed* (Hebrew title: *Moreh Nevuchim*), written in the twelfth century.[11]

In *The Book of Beliefs and Opinions*, Saadia Gaon presents a comprehensible example of Jewish Bible theology. The book concentrates on ten core theological issues, such as the creation of the world; God's unity; the divine commandments; man's freedom either to obey or to disobey God; virtue and vice; man's soul and its immortality; the doctrine of resurrection; and the time of the Messiah and redemption. These subjects derived mainly from the interpretative biblical Scriptures.[12] Rasag's phenomenal and intimate knowledge of the rabbinic sources—*Halachic* and *Aggadic*—are also strikingly evident in the composition.

Nonetheless, the purpose of Saadia's work was—as he states in his introduction—to guide his contemporary, perplexed Jewish intellectuals in the Arab lands (North Africa, Babylonia, and Persia) and defend the consistent and logical foundations of Judaism. The book reflects a great deal of harmonization between the discovered Greek (Aristotle and Plato, in Arabic)[13] philosophical doctrines, and a variety of biblical theological topics. Thus, Saadia broke the Jewish custom of concentrating on only the limited Talmudic and *Halachic* studies.

Saadia Gaon as Hebrew Philologist

In the following years, Saadia appeased his opponents and became, once again, the head of the yeshiva in Sura, a position that he held until his final days. During this time, Rav Saadia Gaon established himself as one of the most prolific and thoughtful Jewish scholars in the Middle Ages. Saadia was aware of the intense correlation between Hebrew (and Aramaic), the language of the Holy Scripture, and an appropriate Bible interpretation, that is, rational understanding of the biblical text. This led him to compose several pioneer studies on Hebrew vocabulary and grammar. In the introduction to his *Sefer ha-Galui* (Arabic title: *Kitab al-ᶜarid*, i.e., *The Uncovered Book*) he states: "Since I saw that the Arabic and Nabatic languages were inherited by Jews ... they simply abandon their own language (Hebrew) and [have] forgotten its beautiful idioms."

His book *Ha'egron*, the first Hebrew dictionary, was classified in alphabetical order.[14] In another work, *Ktab Sachut Leshon ha-Qodesh* (Arabic title: *Kitab al-Lughah*, i.e., *The Book of Expressive Holy Language*), Rasag established, for the first time in the history of the Hebrew language, a scientific Hebrew grammar as an independent discipline that should be studied for its own merit. In his monograph *The Meaning of Seventy Words* (Arabic title: *Tafsir al-Sabᵒina Lafᵒah*) Saadia suggests explanations for a collection of rare words that appear only once in the biblical vocabulary. His method in this composition was, in essence, a comparative one. He compared the biblical words with those in rabbinical Hebrew as reflected in Mishnah and Midrashim on the one hand, and with the close-sounded Arabic words on the other. This work is the earliest research on *hapax legomena* in Hebrew Bible scholarship.[15]

Saadia Gaon as Bible Translator and Exegete

Saadia wrote two translations/commentaries on the Torah. One, "the long" commentary or as named by the Yemenite Jews *Tafsir al-Tafsir* (*The*

Commentary of Commentaries), offers linguistic and philosophical arguments in detail. Here, Saadia disputes with the Karaites on every occasion possible.¹⁶ Unfortunately, only some fragments remain from this commentary.¹⁷ The other, "the short" commentary, or *Tafsir al-Torah*, was abridged from the former. It offers a brief summary of Rasag's research and opinion without detailed philological and philosophical arguments. Indeed, in the introduction to his short commentary, Saadia Gaon wrote:

> I did not compose this book but for the request of a student who asked me to dedicate a unique composition on the simple meaning of the Torah, without correlating into all the philological matters such as the usage of the language, synonyms and antonyms.... And I will not bring the questions of the heretics [i.e., Karaites] as well as not my reply on them.... Rather I will translate/interpret the Torah verses only. I found indeed that this request has been beneficial for Torah students who will study the Torah matters, stories, commandments and rewards ordinarily and briefly. . . . If anyone would like to understand deeper any Torah commandments . . . and how to turn down the arguments of the heretics on the Torah portions, he may find all these in my other book.¹⁸

This translation/commentary reached us completely intact. It served well the ordinary Jews whose Hebrew and Aramaic had been shoved aside by Arabic since the rise of Islam. Indeed, Saadia's Arabic Bible translations in general and his Torah translation in particular are comparable to Septuagint, the Greek translation of the Pentateuch (and later on, other biblical books) in mid-third century BCE Alexandria. They are also comparable to Targum Onkelos, the Aramaic translation on the Torah (second century CE) in Eretz-Israel. As of today, Saadia's translation is still an authoritative source for many Jews. The Yemenite Jews, for instance, print Rasag's Arabic translation alongside the Hebrew text, and read it as תרגום שנים מקרא ואחד, that is, reading of Torah twice in its original language and once in Rasag's translation.

Controversy exists among scholars as to whether Rasag was the first to translate the Hebrew Bible into Arabic.¹⁹ It is also unclear if Rasag translated the entire Jewish Bible or only some parts into Arabic. Nonetheless, only Saadia's commentary on the Torah, Psalms, Five-Megilloth, Isaiah, Job, Proverbs, and Daniel, has become available to us. Seemingly, Saadia was mostly interested in Torah, liturgical books used in Synagogue (such as Psalms, Ruth, Esther, Lamentations, Qoheleth, and the Song of

Songs), and some prophetic and wisdom literature. He was, most likely, less interested in the biblical historical books of the Former Prophets, Ezra-Nehemiah and Chronicles, and consequently did not translate/interpret them.

In his translations/commentaries, Rasag strove to achieve the simple meaning (*peshat*) of the biblical text. His approaches were basically philological and philosophical. Rasag, however, did not apply both approaches on every biblical text. Rather, he used each method appropriately—sometimes independently—in interpretation of various texts. All this was done, as he says, "exactly according to the logic and the tradition" (והמקובל מדויק על-פי המושכל).[20] In his introduction to "the long" commentary on the Torah, Saadia Gaon stresses:

> Anyone who wishes to interpret [the Torah or any biblical text] must do it according to the simple meaning of all the words, according to the logics and the tradition.... It is worthwhile for everyone always to understand the Torah according to the simple meaning of the words as they were grasped by the linguistics and normally utilized, at least if the language (simple meaning) contradicts the common sense or any other biblical verse or prophetical tradition.[21]

The Confrontations of Saadia Gaon with the Karaites

In contrast to the weak reaction of the rabbis in the Jewish world, especially in the Land of Israel and Babylonia, Saadia opposed the Karaites' movement decisively and consistently. He was aware of the great threat of this sect to rabbinic authority, the continuity of Jewish life, and the unity and existence of the Jewish people in widespread Diaspora.[22] Saadia attempted, with all his authority and literary skills, to completely demolish the Karaites' fundamental arguments, methods, and biblical interpretation. Since he was deeply convinced that "our nation, the Children of Israel, is a nation only by virtue of its Torahs" (in plural, that is, both Torahs—Written and Oral),[23] he was always prepared to struggle with the Karaites' doctrines and interpretations, opinions, and beliefs. His endeavors found their expressions in three comparable ways. First, Saadia Gaon wrote a special manifest in which he uncovered the dishonest purposes of Anan ben David and his real reasons and motivations to found such a movement.[24] Second, he composed specific works—monographs, articles, and responsa—challenging the essential arguments and methods of the Karaites' biblical interpretation and *Halachah*. This was the goal of his famous polemical works such as *Book of Distinction* (Arabic title: *Kitab al-Tamyiz*, written in 926) and *Asa Meshali* (*I Will Take Up My Discourse*, composed in 927). Finally, he sharply disputed the Karaites' opinions on a variety of Scriptures in his biblical commentaries and translations. Saadia Gaon tried to dismantle the Karaites' biblical interpretation and approaches one by one. Apparently, Saadia was the most unpleasant controversialist ever to struggle with the Karaites.

Saadia Gaon: Estimation of the Man and His Work

Undoubtedly, Saadia was one of the greatest gaons of all time. His pioneer contributions to the study of Hebrew language, biblical exegesis, and theology are indispensable. He found new and valuable directions and opened fresh horizons in these fields of studies. Rasag's Arabic translations and his polemics against the Karaites strengthened rabbinic Judaism. Here it is noteworthy to mention also some of his *Halachic* works,[25] responsa, and his liturgical poetry, *Azharot*, which was preserved in his Siddur, *Siddor Rav Saadia Gaon*.

In the coming generations after his death, Saadia was considered the founder of the philological and philosophical approaches in Jewish biblical interpretation. The features of Saadia were later acknowledged by another biblical commentator and grammarian, Rabbi Abraham ibn Ezra. Ibn Ezra recognized Saadia as the first Hebrew philologist and "the elder of Holy Language."[26] Indeed, Saadia's philological works inspired further scholars to investigate Hebrew grammar and vocabulary. In general, ibn Ezra characterized Saadia's accomplishments as follows:

> He is the first and the chief of the commentators, one who interpreted the Hebrew Bible appropriately and correctly. From his wisdom studied all other commentators, and he knew the holy language properly.[27]

Maimonides, another towering Sephardic-Oriental Medieval Jewish scholar, said of Rasag:

וכמעט שתאבד תורת ה' לולא הוא (= רב סעדיה גאון). עליו השלום, לפי שהוא גילה מן התורה מה שהיה נעלם, וחיזק ממנה מה שנידלדל, והודיעו בלשונו ובכתבו וקולמוסו

If not for our master Saadia Gaon, Torah would have been forgotten from among the Jewish people. Since he discovered the hidden [matters of the Torah], strengthened all what was weakened and clarified it by his teaching and writing.[28]

Ibn Ezra: A Life of Wandering and Misery

Rabbi Abraham ibn Ezra (acronym: Raaba) was born in Tudela (on the bank of the Ebro, Navarre) in 1092 and died at the age of 75 (1167), probably in London. At the end of *Sephat Yeter* it has been remarked:

> On Monday, in the first day of the First-Adar, in the year 4827, was deceased ibn Ezra, God bless his soul, and he was 75 years old. He wrote a sign for himself before that time: "And Abraham was seventy-five years old as he got-out from blazing anger [of the Lord]."[29]

Indeed, the last part of the remark is understandable against Raaba's experience as a poor and painful wanderer.[30] He conceptualized his lifetime theologically as "blazing anger of the Lord" and expressed the easiness of separation from such a sorrowful life. Since he was forced to move out of Spain in 1140, ibn Ezra never established roots in any specific land.[31] He wandered with his wife (who died shortly after) and his only son, Isaac, first to the Jewish communities in Italy (at this time apparently, his son moved to Baghdad), and later to Provence, to northern France, and finally to England. Throughout these years, ibn Ezra struggled to obtain a suitable arrangement with decent income, however, without any success. Raaba expressed his unfortunate situation in his poetic writing, which in spite of everything contains a great deal of humor:

גלגל ומזלות במעמדם / נטו במהלכם למולדתי
לו יהיו נרות סחורתי / לא יחשך שמש עד מותי.
איגע להצליח ולא אוכל / כי עוותוני כוכבי שמי
לו אהיה סוחר בתכריכין / לא יגועון אישים בכל ימי

Planets in their orbits / turned aside at my birth.
If my merchant will be candles / the sun will not set until my death
I strive to succeed but decline / since the stars have made my path crooked
If I will merchant shroud / none would die during my entire lifetime.

In another poem, Rabbi Abraham ibn Ezra confesses, once again, his unsuccessful efforts to improve his difficult situation:

אשכים לבית השר / אומרים כבר רכב.
אבוא לעת ערב / אומרים כבר שכב.
או יעלה מרכב / או יעלה משכב
אויה לאיש עוי / נולד בלי כוכב

Early morning I go to the minister's residence / they say: "he rode out already."
I come at the evening / they say: "he is in bed already."
Either he rode / or went to bed
Woe to poor-man / who was burn luckless.

As already mentioned above, during his wandering years, ibn Ezra's son, Isaac, moved to Baghdad where he converted to Islam. However, he changed his mind after a short time. Until his death a few years later, Isaac lived in great grief and pain for his irresponsible conversion. Three years later, ibn Ezra learned about Isaac's death. The sorrowful father dedicated a thoughtful lamentation to the memory of his beloved young son.[32]

Ibn Ezra's Works and Methods

The tragic personal situation of Raaba stands absolutely in contrast to his unusual, talented, and fascinating intellectual ability and creativity. He proved himself as a skillful and prolific scholar in several branches of study. Thus, in addition to being one of the best Jewish biblical exegetes of the Middle Ages, he was also a philologist, poet, philosopher, mathematician, and astrologer. In other words, ibn Ezra was not only well versed in the wealth of Jewish literary sources, but also fluent in general secular experts of his time. Through his travels to a variety of cities and countries he met different cultures, societies, and sages, which undeniably enriched and broadened his vision and horizons. To be sure, these unusual intellectual resources served him perfectly in his exegetical works in general and in his commentary on the Pentateuch in particular. Moreover, Raaba utilized works of many other commentators and writers: rabbinic (such as, Talmudic and Midrashic scholars Rav Saadia Gaon, Rabbi Yehuda Halevi,[33] Rabbi Shelomo ibn Gabirol, Rabbi Shelomo Yitzhaki [acronym:

Rashi]) as well as Karaites (among others, Anan ben David, Benjamin ben Moshe Nahawendi, and Ben-Zuta).[34] Raaba debated with these scholars or strengthened his own interpretation against the background of their writing frequently. From time to time, ibn Ezra also dropped harsh words toward other commentators, especially Karaites, and made fun of their nonsensical methods and explanations.[35]

Ibn Ezra's commentaries are distinctive by a conglomerate of rich knowledge and opinions that were admirably elected and systemized in a lucid, attractive, poetic, short, sharp, and critical style. In his introduction on the Torah commentary, ibn Ezra characterizes himself as an independent commentator free from any bias or fear: "the Lord only I fear / and I will not prefer anyone while interpreting the Pentateuch." He details five "ways" (i.e., methods) in biblical exegesis. Four of them he negates, one after another, while the fifth is his own way:

1. Ibn Ezra mentions the gaonic method in the Arab lands. According to him, they commented too "long and wide." Thus, Rav Isaac[36] composed already two volumes on Gen 1:1–2:1 and still did not complete it! Raaba also counts here Rav Saadia Gaon and Rav Shamuel ben Chofni. These sages use secular disciplines as well, but in very worthless detail.
2. The second way is that of Karaites (who are named here Zadokites [Sadducees] because of the holding of similar beliefs),[37] such as Anan [ben David],[38] Benjamin [ben Moshe Nahawendi],[39] [Chasan] ben Mashiach and Yoshua, who did not accept the Oral Torah. They explained the Torah's commandments as they wished (i.e., not according to the rabbinic Sages)—even without knowledge of Hebrew language and grammar.
3. The third way is the Christian way that Raaba defines as "the way of black and darkness, which is out of the circle." Ibn Ezra negates their metaphorical and allegorical methods entirely. He stresses that "everything that is not against the rational judgment or common sense we must explain in the simplest way as possible ... and will not use the Biblical verses for our (theological) needs. And why should we cover the uncovered things?"
4. The fourth way is the Midrashic method of the classical rabbis of Talmudic and Midrashic literature and the commentators in northern France and Ashkenaz who re-wrote them. Ibn Ezra defines the Midrash "as clothes to body (that is, *peshat*)." He states that the "*derash* is, actually, endless."

5. The fifth is ibn Ezra's own way: "I will research the grammar of every word and then will explain it." In other words, his method is basically philological (see below). He praises the verbal translation of Onkelos and accepts completely the Sages' interpretation of the commandments.[40]

Indeed, in his exegetical works Raaba stresses, above all, the philological approach.[41] He strives to achieve the simple meaning of the Hebrew text —the *peshat*—or in his words, *haderch hayyshara* ("the straight way"), as it does not contradict the common sense, or the *mitzvot*. Thus, in his book *Sapha B'rura* he writes:

> Our elders, the copyists of the commandments, God bless their souls, interpreted the Biblical passages and verses separately, by words and letters, according to *derash* [rabbinic—generally *aggadic*—interpretation]. So it is in Mishnah, Talmud and *Beraitot*. Doubtless, they knew "the straight way," since they stated אין המקרא יוצא מידי פשוטו "a verse cannot depart from its plain meaning."[42] They considered *derash* as an additional explanation. The coming generations, however, considered *derash* as main and most essential [explanation]. Thus, Rabbi Shelomo [Rashi], God bless his soul, who interpreted the Bible on the way of *derash* and thought it is *peshat*. But actually one can find just very few *peshat* among thousand *derash* in his commentaries."[43]

Furthermore, Raaba introduces his exegetical methods at the very beginning of his foreword to the Torah commentary, even before the counting of the "five ways":

זה ספר הישר לאברהם השר / ובעבותות הדקדוק נקשר
ובעיני הדעת יכשר / וכל תומכו מאושר
נאום אברהם הספרדי הנזכר

This is the book of *hayyashar* [ibn Ezra's commentary on the Torah] by Abraham the poet / it is bound by cords of grammar / and approved by eyes of reason / happy are those who adhere to it.

In addition, it is noteworthy to mention Raaba's literary approach as well. He notices the existence of literary devices in biblical writing, such as chiasmus[44] and paronomasia (pun).[45] He also notes the importance and function of the number seven in biblical literature (Lev 12:2, 26:18; Num 23:1). Ibn Ezra does not defer also from making some historical notes (i.e.,

Gen 27:40; Lev 18:26; Deut 25:5; Ps 37:7) or even relating his personal experience (Exod 1:7, 10:22) on biblical texts. Moreover, as Simon remarks, "he frequently offers alternative interpretations when he cannot make an unequivocal decision as to which is better; nor is he afraid to acknowledge his inability to understand some verses[46]—an inability that stems, in part, from our limited knowledge of Biblical history (Gen 49:19; Zech 12:11), and our remoteness from the Biblical world (Gen 2:11, long commentary on Exod 30:23)."[47]

In contrast to Saadia Gaon who wrote generally in Arabic, ibn Ezra wrote his commentaries in Hebrew. Thus, his audience, which consisted of a variety of European Jewish communities, such as those in Italy, Northern France, and England, not versed in Arabic, would be able to read his compositions.

Ibn Ezra wrote commentaries on most of the Hebrew Scriptures. Some of them, for example, his commentaries on the biblical historical books (Joshua, Judges, Samuel, Kings, and Chronicles) as well as on some prophetic books (such as Jeremiah and Ezekiel), unfortunately did not reach modern times. The existence of ibn Ezra's commentaries on these books was learned about from his references to them in his commentaries on the Torah and Psalms, and from the references of other commentators.[48] The commentaries on Proverbs and Ezra-Nehemiah that were ascribed to him in *Mikraot Gedolot* (*Rabbinic Bible*) were written in fact by Rabbi Moshe Kimchi.[49] On the other hand, there are two commentaries from Raaba—complete or fragmentary—on Genesis, Exodus, the Twelve Prophets, Daniel, Psalms, Esther, and the Song of Songs.[50]

Without a doubt, the commentary on the Torah should be considered the crown of ibn Ezra's exegetical writing. He began composing this commentary in a late stage of his life, at the age of sixty-four, and worked on it for ten years. Raaba completed this work shortly before his death. In a poem that was dedicated on this occasion ibn Ezra writes:

לאברהם בנו מאיר יצו עז / יבינהו ומפיו כל תבונה

עזרהו עדי הלום / ומספר שני חייו שמונה על שמונה . . .

ונדרתי לאל נדר בחליי / לבאר דת בהר סיני נתונה

For His [God's] son, Abraham, He gave courage
and understanding since from Him all the wisdom
He helped him all these days
and his age is eight on eight [i.e., sixty-four] . . .

and I made vow to God at (the time of) my illness
to interpret the Law that had been given on Mount Sinai.⁵¹

Ibn Ezra clarifies the purpose of his writing a commentary on the Pentateuch at the end of his work:⁵²

זכר שמי תגיד חתימתי / אחר אשר אשוב לאדמתי
אכתוב ואזכותה / הכי ידי תכלה / ותשאר רק כתיבתי

My writing [literary signature] will relate [on] my name
after I will return to earth.
I write while keeping in mind
that my hand will perish
my writing, however, will survive.

The poor, lonely, and wandering ibn Ezra considered his work to be an eternal statute for his immortal name.

Abraham ibn Ezra: Evaluation of the Man and His Writing

The commentaries of Rabbi Abraham ibn Ezra were included in *Mikraot Gedolot*. Many scholars attempted to understand and clarify ibn Ezra's writings. There are several commentaries on his commentaries on the Torah. Biblical commentators throughout generations recurrently cite ibn Ezra. One such commentator was Nachmanides who argued with him, but at the same time also admired him. In the introduction to his Torah commentary, he wrote: רבי אברהם בן עזרא תהיה לנו תוכחת מגולה ואהבה מוסתרה ועם ("With Rabbi Abraham ibn Ezra we will have uncovered disputes with him, but covered appreciation for him"). The great Talmudic commentator, Rabbi Jacob Tam, Rashi's grandson, simply admired ibn Ezra, as is reflected in a poem that he wrote in ibn Ezra's honor⁵³ and from *tosefists* commentary on the Babylonian Talmud.⁵⁴ Generation after generation related countless legends about the man and his unusual wisdom.⁵⁵

Ibn Ezra is thought to be one of the earliest biblical-critical thinkers. His commentaries, which are often cited by Jewish and non-Jewish scholars, are considered among the best written in medieval times. However, one must admit as well that there were, and still are, some controversies about the man and especially his Torah commentaries since some of them contradict the classical rabbinic interpretation.[56]

Conclusion: Between Saadia Gaon and Abraham ibn Ezra

The established eminent Sephardic-Oriental Jewish scholars, Rav Saadia ben Joseph Gaon and Rabbi Abraham ibn Ezra, were profoundly versed in Jewish as well as non-Jewish sources and disciplines. Their vast educational training served them well in their biblical exegetical compositions. Both researched and expounded the Hebrew language as a main tool in their interpretation of biblical texts. Their mastery of the Arabic language and philology were very helpful in their linguistic and interpretive works. They strove to achieve the simple meaning—*peshat*—of the Hebrew text chiefly by stressing the philological approaches, using logic and philosophical methods, while at the same time, respecting the rabbinic interpretation, especially those concerning the commandments and *Halachic* issues.

From neither scholar do we obtain commentaries on early and late biblical historical books. Rasag and Raaba devoted years to commenting, first and foremost, on the Pentateuch and other biblical writings that were utilized in the Jewish liturgy—Five Scrolls (Megilloth) and the book of Psalms. Since the main audience of Saadia Gaon was in the Muslim Middle East, he composed in his contemporary *lingua franca*, Arabic. On the other hand, Rabbi Abraham ibn Ezra wrote his commentaries and other writings in Hebrew, since he primarily addressed them to the western European Jewish communities who, for the most part, did not know Arabic. By visiting in a variety of Jewish communities in Italy, France, and England, ibn Ezra spread the well-developed Sephardic-Oriental Jewish exegetical methods, Hebrew grammar, and lexical heritage as well as different secular disciplines.

Saadia Gaon and ibn Ezra raged a bitter battle against the Karaite movement. They disputed the Karaites' methods of biblical interpretation as well as their negative attitude toward Oral Torah and rabbinic authority concerning the commandments and Jewish life.

Saadia Gaon and Abraham ibn Ezra, each in his generation, considered their exegetical activities as a significant challenge to uncover new methods and other understandings of the biblical text for their contemporaries. They attempted—each within his specific religious-cultural and political context, as well as national and personal situation—to reinforce the ongoing eternal dialectical contact between the Jewish people and the "Book of Books."

NOTES

1. The term "Torah" here means not only the Pentateuch but also Prophets and Writing, that is, the Hebrew Bible in general. For the saying cited by Japhet ibn Ali from *Sefer ha-Mitzvot leAnan* (*The Book of Commandments by Anan*) in his commentary on the book of Zechariah, see A. Harkavy, *Aus den ältesten Karäischen Gesetzbüchern* (Studien und Mitteilungen 8; St. Petersburg, 1903), 132.

2. See I. Kalimi, "Die Auseinandersetzung mit den internen und äußeren Opponenten in mittelalterlich-jüdischer Schriftauslegung," *Zeitschrift für die alttestamentliche Wissenschaft* 115 (2003), 73–87.

3. See in detail Kalimi, "Die Auseinandersetzung mit den internen und äußeren Opponenten," 84–85.

4. The term "Karaite" derives from the Hebrew מקרא / קרא, and means "Biblist."

5. See I. Kalimi, "Die Bibel und die klassisch-jüdische Bibelauslegung—Eine Interpretations—und Religionsgeschichtliche Studie," *Zeitschrift für die alttestamentliche Wissenschaft* 114 (2002): 594–610, esp. 598.

6. Abarbanel's experience as a statesman in Iberia and his familiarity with philosophical theories greatly influenced his reading and interpreting of the Jewish Scripture. The life of this distinguished, prolific Jewish scholar did not follow a normal road. He wrote commentary on the Five Books of Moses, Former and Later Prophets. and the book of Daniel. Generally, he opens his commentary on the biblical books with an introduction that discusses a variety of comprehensive exegetical, theological, and other problems. See E. Schmueli, *Don Abravanel and the Expulsion of the Jews from Spain* (in Hebrew) (Jerusalem: Bialik Institute, 1963); E. Lawee, *Isaac Abarbanel's Stance toward Tradition: Defense, Dissent, and Dialogue* (Albany: State University of New York Press, 2000); A. F. Borodowski, *Isaac Abravanel on Miracles, Creation, Prophecy, and Evil: Between Medieval Jewish Philosophy and Biblical Commentary* (New York: Peter Lang, 2003).

7. See the variety of examples from Karaites and rabbinic commentators that were discussed by Kalimi, "Die Auseinandersetzung mit den internen und äußeren Opponenten," 73–87.

8. See the Conclusion in this chapter.

9. See S. Rosenblatt, *Saadia Gaon, The Book of Beliefs and Opinions: Translated from the Arabic and the Hebrew* (New Haven: Yale University Press, 1948; reprint, 1976).

10. It was translated for the first time by Rabbi Yehuda ibn Tibbon into Hebrew, *Sefer Emunut we-De'ot,* in the twelfth century. See also n. 23, below.

11. For the book, see S. Pines, *Moses Maimonides, The Guide for the Perplexed—Translated with an Introduction and Notes* (Chicago: Chicago University Press, 1963).

12. For more details, see I. Kalimi, "History of Israelite Religion or Hebrew Bible/Old Testament Theology? Jewish Interest in Biblical Theology," *Early Jewish Exegesis and Theological Controversy: Studies in Scriptures in the Shadow of Internal and External Controversies*, Jewish and Christian Heritage, no. 2 (Assen, the Netherlands: Royal Van Gorcum, 2002), 107–34, esp. 120–21.

13. Saadia was influenced by the *Mutazilites*—the rationalistic school in Islam.

14. For the critical edition of the book, see N. Alloni, ed., *Haʾegron: Kitab ʿusual al-shir al-eibrani* by Rav Saadiah Gaon (Sources and Studies 8; Jerusalem: Academy of the English Language, 1969; in Hebrew).

15. For a modern work on this topic, see, for example, F. E. Greenspahn, *Hapax Legomena in Biblical Hebrew: A Study of the Phenomenon and Its Treatment since Antiquity with Special Reference to Verbal Forms*, Society of Biblical Literature Dissertation Series, no. 74 (Atlanta: Scholars, 1984).

16. See the next section, below in this study.

17. Some fragments have been found in the Cairo Geniza; the commentary on Exodus has been found in Saint Petersburg's library. Many citations from Rasag's commentary remained in Rabbi Abraham ibn Ezra's commentaries on the biblical books and some other medieval scholars, such as Rabbi Abraham son of Maimonides.

18. See Saadia Gaon's introduction to his short commentary on the Torah, *The Commentaries of Our Rabbi Saadia Gaon on Pentateuch* (in Hebrew), trans. J. Kappach (Jerusalem: Mosad Harav Kook, 1963), 160–61.

19. See A. M. Halkin, "Saadia Gaon," *Encyclopedia Judaica* (Jerusalem: Macmillan, n.d.), vol. 14, 553–34, esp. 553.

20. See Saadia Gaon's introduction, Saadia Gaon, *The Commentaries of Our Rabbi Saadia Gaon on Pentateuch*, trans. Kappach, 161.

21. See ibid., 162.

22. On this issue, see in detail Kalimi, "Die Bibel und die klassisch-jüdische Bibelauslegung," 604–8.

23. See Saadia Gaon, *The Book of Beliefs and Opinions* (in Hebrew), ed. J. Kappach (New York: Yeshiva University, 1970), 132; S. Rosenblatt, *Saadia Gaon, The Book of Beliefs and Opinions*, 158.

24. See Saadia Gaon's *al-Kasaph* (*The Discover*), in which he recounts that Anan rebelled against the rabbis because they refused to appoint him to the position of Resh Galuta.

25. Thus, for example, Saadia Gaon's commentary on the thirteen rules of Rabbi Ishmael (in Hebrew translation only), and *Kelale ha-Talmud* (*The Methodology of Talmud*).

26. See, Abraham ibn Ezra's introduction to his book *Moznayyim*.

27. See Solomon Pharchon, *Machbarot ha-Orech* (in Hebrew) (reprint, Jerusalem: Makor, 1970), entry "פרח."

28. See I. Shilat, ed., *Iggerot ha-Rambam* (in Hebrew) (Jerusalem: Maʾalot, 1987), vol. 1, 144. The cited paragraph is from *Iggert Teman* (*The Letter [to the] Yemenites*).

29. Obviously, this is a paraphrase of Gen 12:4: "Abram was seventy-five years old when he left Haran." Raaba here used the word play between *Haran* (a town in northwest Mesopotamia) and *Haron-af* ("blazing anger").

30. For details, see below in this essay.

31. Most probably, ibn Ezra left Spain because of the Islamic zealous *al-Muchadein* persecutors who destroyed many flourishing Jewish communities. See the opening section of ibn Ezra's commentary on Lamentations: "and I, Abraham, son of Meir, from a distance land. The fierce anger of the persecutors forced me out of Spain." See also ibn Ezra's introduction to the book of Qoheleth (Ecclesiastes).

32. For the lamentation, see A. Weiser, *Ibn Ezra: The Torah Commentaries of Rabbi Abraham Ibn Ezra* (Hebrew) (Jerusalem: Mosad Harav Kook, 1977), vol. 1, 9.

33. See, for example, Raaba's commentary (in various editions of *Mikraot Gedolot*) on Exod 4:10, 13:14, 20:1, 24:11; Num 27:3; Deut 14:22, 33:5; Ps 18:5, 30:8, 82:8; Dan 9:2. See Weiser, "Rabbi Yehuda Halevi as Biblical Exegete in Raaba's Writing," in *The Torah Commentaries of Rabbi Abraham Ibn Ezra*, vol. 1, 52–58.

34. On this topic, see in detail Weiser, *The Torah Commentaries of Rabbi Abraham Ibn Ezra*, vol. 1, 59–71.

35. See the examples in Kalimi, "Die Auseinandersetzung mit den internen und äußeren Opponenten," 73–75; and ibn Ezra's commentary on Gen 36:31–32; Exod 20:23, 21:35, 31:18; 34:21; Lev 11:19; Deut 29:28; and below, in this essay.

36. Ibn Ezra mentions this Gaon also in his commentary on Gen 49:18 and Lev 5:7.

37. See also Ibn Ezra commentary on Lev 7:20, 11:19, 23:11.

38. Ibn Ezra mentions Anan also in his commentary on Exod 34:21.

39. For Benjamin ben Moshe Nahawendi see also Saadia Gaon, *The Book of Beliefs and Opinions*, 5, 6; Rabbi Yehuda Halevi, *The Book of Argument and Proof in Defence of the Despised Faith* (Arabic title: *Kitab al-Hazari*; Hebrew: *Sefer ha-Kuzari*), 3, 38. See H. Hirschfeld, *Book of Kuzari*, by Judah Hallevi, translated from the Arabic with Introduction, Notes and Appendix (New York: Pardes, 1946); idem, *An Argument for the Faith of Israel: The Kuzari* (New York: Schocken, 1971).

40. For the different versions of these "five ways," see Kalimi, "Die Auseinandersetzung mit den internen und äußeren Opponenten," 73–74 n. 3.

41. U. Simon notes, correctly, "a significant portion of ibn Ezra's commentary is devoted to precise and multifaceted linguistic clarifications, based on a critical adoption of major achievements of the Spanish school of Hebrew philology." See, U. Simon, "Abraham Ibn Ezra," in M. Sæbø, ed., *Hebrew Bible/Old Testament: The*

History of Its Interpretation, vol. 1, pt. 2, *The Middle Ages* (Göttingen, Germany: Vandenhoeck & Ruprecht, 2000), 377–87, esp. 378.

42. See the Babylonian Talmud, Shabbath 63a.

43. Compare to Raaba's introduction to his commentary on the book of Lamentations.

44. See, for instance, ibn Ezra's commentary on Exod 17:7, Josh 24:4, Joel 3:3 and the examples collected by E. Z. Melammed, *Bible Commentators* (in Hebrew), 2d ed. (Jerusalem: Magnes, 1978), vol. 2, 575–76. For this phenomenon in the biblical and ancient world literature, see I. Kalimi, *The Reshaping of Ancient Israelite History in Chronicles* (Winona Lake, IN: Eisenbrauns, 2004), 219–34, esp. 220 n. 6.

45. See, for example, Raaba's commentary on Gen 3:1 and Exod 22:5. For this literary device in the biblical and ancient Near Eastern literature, see I. Kalimi, "Utilization of Pun/Paronomasia in the Chronistic Writing," in *An Ancient Israelite Historian: Studies in the Chronicler, His Time, Place, and Writing* (Assen, the Netherlands: Royal Van Gorcum, in press), esp. n. 1, which refers to ibn Ezra's commentaries.

46. This feature of ibn Ezra's commentary is comparable with that of Rashi, for example in his commentary on Gen 43:11 and Exod 22:28.

47. See, Simon, "Abraham Ibn Ezra," 380.

48. See, for example, ibn Ezra's commentaries on Deut 34:4 (Joshua), Deut 29:19, 33:2 (Judges), Ibn Ezra's short commentary on Exod 27:21, Ps 51:2; as well as Rabbi David Kimche's commentary on 1 Sam 27:10 (Samuel), Deut 21:17 (Kings), Num 25:12 and Lev 26:34 (Chronicles), Lev 20:20 (Jeremiah); and ibn Ezra's short commentary on Exod 28:41 (Ezekiel). For more details, see Weiser, *The Torah Commentaries of Rabbi Abraham Ibn Ezra,* vol. 1, 14–15.

49. For a different opinion, see Weiser, *The Torah Commentaries of Rabbi Abraham Ibn Ezra,* vol. 1, 15.

50. Cf. Simon, "Abraham Ibn Ezra," 378.

51. For the poem, see D. Kahana, *Rabbinu Abraham Ibn Ezra: Raaba's Collection of Wisdom* (Warsaw: Ahiasaf, 1894), 46 (Hebrew; the English translation is mine).

52. A. Shatal, *Figures in Medieval Jewish Culture* (Tel Aviv: Hakibbutz Homeuchad, 1974).

53. For the poem, see Weiser, *The Torah Commentaries of Rabbi Abraham Ibn Ezra,* vol. 1, 10.

54. See, for example, the *tosefists* on the Babylonian Talmud, Taanit 20b; Kiddushin 37b; Rosh ha-Shanah 13a.

55. Some of the legends collected by A. Shatal, *Figures in Medieval Jewish Culture* (in Hebrew) (Tel Aviv: ha-Kibbutz ha-Meuchad, 1974), 57–60.

56. For this issue see detailed discussion of A. Mondschein, "Abraham ibn Ezra—Man against the Tide" (Hebrew), *Beit Mikra* 49 (2004): 137–55.

Chapter 7

Jewish Philosophy and Kabbalah in Spain

Moshe Idel

Jewish Philosophy and Kabbalah and Their Arrival in Spain

The history of elite culture of the Jews in medieval Spain[1] consists of different stages. During the first stage, the Andalusian Renaissance of the tenth and twelfth centuries, Jews adopted modes of thinking and writing found in the Islamic culture. In this stage, Jewish philosophy became the most prominent new form of thinking. The second stage related to the predominantly Christian parts of Northern Spain, and was characterized by structures of thought represented in Kabbalistic literature. This period paralleled the Christian world's twelfth-century Renaissance[2] and the Renaissance of Alfonso Sabio. Both stages involved accelerated creativity characteristic of Renaissance periods.[3]

The influence of these stages remained an integral part of Jewish Spanish culture long after their end, but the creative moments were limited to these periods of time. During the fourteenth century, the high Jewish culture in the provinces consisted of mediocre imitations of the two earlier phases of creativity. Though there were exceptions, like Hasdai Crescas in the field of philosophy and the Kabbalistic literature known as *Sefer ha-Meshiv*,[4] for a century and a half, the cultural processes in Spain declined. With their expulsion from Spain, Spanish Jews opened a new page in creativity, and during the next two generations, produced extensive literature that included major contributors like Isaac and Yehudah Abravanel, as well as a series of historical and Kabbalistic writings.[5]

The first full developments elaborated by Spanish authors were Jewish philosophy and the Kabbalah. Jewish philosophy made its first steps in other Jewish cultural centers—Babylonia, Egypt, and Southern Italy—

before it reached Spain.⁶ However, it became completed literature only through the writings of Spanish thinkers such as Shlomo ibn Gabirol, R. Abraham ibn Ezra, R. Yehudah ha-Levi, R. Abraham ibn Dawd, Maimonides, and Hasdai Crescas. The "Kabbalah" literature first consisted of short written documents that emerged in what the Jews called "Provence." R. Abraham ben David, R. Jacob the Nazirite of Lunel, R. Isaac the Blind, and R. Asher ben David, who authored the fragments during the twelfth century and early thirteenth century, were of Provençal extraction. The most elaborate expositions of the theosophical-theurgical brands of Kabbalah⁷ were found in Catalonia and Castile from the 1230s on. Just as Maimonides's *Guide of the Perplexed* represented the accomplished form of the medieval Jewish Aristotelianism, the book of the *Zohar* represented the peak of medieval Kabbalah.

Modern scholars regarded Jewish philosophy and Kabbalah as distinct speculative trends. Their adherents portrayed them as essentially diverse types of spirituality. Nevertheless, the ideas characteristic of literature known as philosophy and Kabbalah were intertwined in numerous writings. However, scholar Julius Guttmann's *Philosophies of Judaism*⁸ and scholar Gershom Scholem's *Major Trends in Jewish Mysticism* put this dichotomy in medieval Jewish speculation in sharper relief. Jewish mysticism was marginalized in Guttmann's *Philosophies of Judaism*, while Scholem rarely treated details of Jewish philosophy in his *Major Trends*. The extensive scholarly corpus of Harry A. Wolfson revealed a dramatic marginalization of Kabbalah. Gershom Scholem stated categorically that "Kabbalah certainly did not *arise* as reaction against philosophical 'enlightenment.'"⁹ Though he did not ignore the potential impact of the controversy concerning Maimonides' writings on the early Kabbalists, he regarded it as a secondary factor. He observed the affinity between the opponents to the Jewish philosopher and those who were mystically biased.¹⁰ Scholem emphasized the importance of the encounter between an alleged mythical Gnosticism transmitted in Jewish esoteric circles for centuries and the philosophical Neoplatonism represented by the various medieval versions as his main phenomenological description of the emergence of Kabbalah.¹¹ "Kabbalah," he said, in its historical significance, can be defined as the product of the interpenetration of Jewish Gnosticism and Neoplatonism."¹² To a certain extent, Scholem's attempt to disentangle the emergence of Kabbalah from an explanation that regarded it as a reaction to Neo-Aristotelianism was plausibly a response to the address of Heinrich Graetz.

Motivated by a deep aversion for Kabbalah, the most important nineteenth-century Jewish historian considered this lore a pernicious medieval innovation, or invention, aimed to counteract the influence of the "enlightening" Aristotelianism of Maimonides.[13] David Neumark and Franz Rosenzweig, however, expounded upon the "pendulum theory" in their writings.[14] The basic assumption of this theory was the existence of oscillations between the dominance of the speculative and the mystical in Jewish thought over centuries.

The initial strong demarcation between the two literatures remained less influential in subsequent scholarship of Jewish thought. The next generation of scholars: Georges Vajda[15] and Alexander Altmann[16] and—in their later writings—also Shlomo Pines,[17] Joseph B. Sermoneta,[18] Isadore Twersky,[19] Colette Sirat,[20] and Sarah O. Heller Wilensky,[21] were less predisposed toward strong dichotomies. The concept of "rational mysticism" highlighted the more mystical implications of those forms of thought.[22] Recent scholars of Kabbalah have adopted a similar stand.[23]

The stand of the great eagle himself in relation to mysticism was treated in the mid thirties: Gershom Scholem discussed the false attribution of mystical and quasi-mystical traditions and writings to Maimonides by Kabbalists.[24] Alexander Altmann, another important contributor to the topic, carefully analyzed the different approaches in crucial matters of religion as exposed by Maimonides and some Kabbalists. He resorted to Abraham Abulafia's commentaries on secrets of the *Guide*. More mystical readings of Maimonides' *Guide of the Perplexed* have been proposed by scholars,[25] while the wide range of the philosophical sources and speculative interpretations of the Kabbalistic types of thought received more attention.[26] The extreme polarization between the two lores was attenuated, and a variety of responses to the various parts of the Kabbalistic camp started with sharp criticism and ended with assumptions that Maimonides was, or became later in his life, a Kabbalist.[27]

Two West European Renascences and Spanish Kabbalah

The existence of philosophical trends and the emergence of some forms of Kabbalistic writings was part of a greater readiness by Jewish elites to engage in different forms of dialogues based on Greek and Hellenistic thinking found in Arabic literature.[28] Ashkenazi material available to the early Kabbalists in Provence, Catalonia, and Castile had an impact on the culture.²⁹ The theosophical-theurgical Kabbalah emerged as a literary phenomenon at the border of the southern Andalusian Jewish center and the northern French-Ashkenazi center in Provence and Catalonia.

Jewish thought emerged and flourished concurrently with Christian thought during the twelfth century. Jean Leclercq pointed out that Christian theology was less a full-fledged rebirth than a case of renewal.³⁰ However, in the case of Judaism, the twelfth century represented its birth, though others, such as Harry A. Wolfson, have argued that it was just a rebirth.³¹ The philosophical theologies of R. Abraham ibn Ezra, R. Yehudah ha-Levi, and Maimonides written in the 1100s, reverberated through centuries in vast theological literature.³² These treatises were composed under the spell of the Islamic thought of ibn Badjja, ibn Tufail, and Averroes from the region of Al-Andalus.³³ Petrus Alphonsi, a convert to Christianity from Judaism, was instrumental in mediating both Muslim and Jewish themes to Western civilization or, the Latin West, during this time.

Christian provinces in France and Spain experienced the effects of the Jewish philosophical treatises. However, in the Islamic regions, the influence of those books was less substantial. The dramatic change in Jewish philosophy, according to Maimonides, was a restoration of an ancient secret meaning—the rediscovery of an ancient corpus suppressed or forgotten for centuries. Maimonides' *Guide of the Perplexed* assumed that ancient esoteric knowledge of the canonical Jewish writings was lost for a vast period of time and rediscovered. This influential book mentions several instances of the occultation of the secrets of the Torah.³⁴ The *Guide* brought about a new phase in Jewish thought. It generated an entire philosophical Neoaristotelian literature, which flourished in Provence among Jewish Andalusian refugees like the ibn Tibbon and the Qimhi families. Those families imported the interest in Muslim and Jewish philosophy from Andalus in the Christian provinces and contributed their expertise and translations to the Jewish cultural renascence. Maimonides, along with those Andalusian families who left for Christian territories like Provence, restored the Andalusian proclivity to Neo-Aristotelian philosophy.³⁵

The Kabbalist R. Isaac of Acre expressed the feeling that Maimonides represented a change in the history of Jewish theology:

> I have contemplated the words of the prophets and sages about the hardship of the exile of Israel, as the prophet ... said³⁶ "There will be many days for Israel without Torah, without a priest and without the God of Truth." And the sages ... said³⁷ "The Torah is destined to be forgotten in Israel."

And I have seen that all this indeed happened, until the time of the believing rabbi[38] . . . in Egypt.[39]

The precise temporary boundaries of the period of the exile were not specified, but Maimonides represented the beginning of a broader movement that reflected the end of the oblivion of the Torah. The Kabbalist did not intend to marginalize the study of the Pentateuch or the entire Hebrew Bible. In a religious debate that took place in Barcelona in the early 1260s between Pablo Christiani and Nahmanides, Christiani described Maimonides as an eminent sage: "You [the Jews] did not have someone of his grandeur in the last four hundred years."[40]

The first Kabbalistic documents were created in the late twelfth century. The Maimonidean controversy and the impact of Maimonidean Aristotelianism in western Europe triggered some of these Kabbalistic texts. Maimonides represented the most universalistic approach in Judaism. Maimonides' thought served as the metaphysical and psychological underpinning of ecstatic Kabbalah in Barcelona after 1270.

R. Isaac of Acre's quote expressed the temporal proximity between the emergence of the theosophical-theurgical Kabbalah and the expansion of the Maimonidean philosophy:

> And R. Jacob the Nazirite and R. Abraham ben David [were] in Provence; and the faithful Rabbi [Nahmanides] . . . in Catalonia and R. Jacob ha-Kohen and R. Joseph Gikatilla in Segovia, and the book of the *Zohar*[41] [written] by R. Shimeon bar Yohai in *Sefarad*[42] since by these [persons] the number of the teachers of law easily increased, and the intellect increased by the intellect of philosophy to those whom God bestowed with philosophical spirit, but not with the Kabbalistic spirit. And the holiness of Kabbalah [increased] to those whom [God] bestowed with Kabbalistic spirit but not with philosophical spirit. However, happy is the person whom God bestowed [with] . . . the spirit of teaching, namely the religious spirit, and the philosophical spirit, and the Kabbalistic spirit, since he is for sure perfect and worthy that the Divine Presence will descend upon him, unless the generation would not be worthy of it.[43]

The two first figures related to Provence were the first known historical Kabbalists.[44] R. Isaac situated the emergence of the Kabbalistic Renaissance in Provence, though it was actually in Languedoc. The Catalan rabbi was the famous Nahmanides (1194–1270). All the others were Kabbalistic figures active in Castile. Thus, the Kabbalists put together the renewal of three different religious phenomena in the span of one hundred years: the religious, *Toriyy*, the philosophical, and the Kabbalistic. The explanation for the increase was revelation: the spirits were bestowed by God. This claim was reminiscent of a tradition connected to the earliest Provençal Kabbalists and to the importance of revelation in ecstatic Kabbalah in the generation before R. Isaac, but not found earlier among the Provençal or the Catalan Kabbalists.[45]

The biblical proof text adduced by R. Isaac was pertinent to the entire list of Kabbalists. The assumption of a historical gap was based upon the verse of prophecy about the absence of the Torah, priest, and God of truth.[46] This verse recurred twice in one of the early Kabbalistic writings, R. Ezra ben Solomon of Gerona's *Commentary on the Song of Songs*. In both cases, it related to the ignorance of Kabbalah, especially the theosophy related to the ten *sefirot* and the relationship between it and the meaning of the Jewish canonical texts, especially the theurgical significance of the commandments.[47] The ignorance of the secret doctrine related to the inner structure of the deity, constituting the absence of the awareness of the true God in the time of the exile.[48] The early Kabbalists offered new theologies that were related to ancient secret doctrines, which contributed to making the scriptures more arcane in the decades that followed.[49]

The re-emergence of an old oral tradition inspired the Kabbalistic lore, which skipped an important event in its history: the surfacing of the book of *Bahir*. The short, dense treatise contained mythical-theosophical traditions, which had an impact on Catalan Kabbalists from both the school of R. Isaac the Blind and that of Nahmanides.[50] According to Scholem and E. R. Wolfson, there were traces of earlier mythical themes in the book.[51] However other studies speculated that the book of *Bahir* was conceived of as the beginning of the theosophical-theurgical Kabbalah.[52]

In the subsequent history of Kabbalah, the pseudepigraphy became a tool of validation.[53] In addition to the temporary nexus between Maimonideanism and the emergence of Kabbalah, scholars drew attention to the direct impact of philosophical stands found in Latin thought on early Kabbalah.[54] The impact of the Christian cult of Mary on early Kabbalists, including the book of *Bahir*, had been postulated.[55] Unlike Jewish philosophy, the emergence of Kabbalah was based on an osmotic principle: The minority culture accelerated the elaboration of existing *mythologoumena*. Acceleration was evident when comparing the traditions of R. Abraham ben David, to those of his son, R. Isaac the Blind, and then to those of his grandson R. Asher ben David. Each generation multiplied the amount of material found from the earlier generation. While the grandfather hid the secret doctrines, his son wrote a commentary on *Sefer Yetzirah*, and his grandson wrote more than one hundred dense pages.[56] In Gerona, among the followers of R. Isaac the Blind, the most systematic expositions of the Provençal Kabbalah—which disappeared in southern France—were recorded.

The end of the acceleration of Kabbalistic creativity in Catalonia occurred around 1250 when the Kabbalistic traditions from the school of R. Isaac the Blind were no longer transmitted or elaborated on by students.[57] Another Catalan Kabbalistic school emerged under the leadership of Nahmanides that lasted in Barcelona for at least three generations.[58] A conservative figure, he and his cousin, R. Yonah Gerondi, obliterated the development of the other school. Nahmanides's school was part of a counter-Renaissance refusing to develop the esoteric traditions inherited from Kabbalistic sources other than those of R. Abraham ben David and R. Isaac the Blind.[59] The literary output of this later Kabbalistic school was conspicuously smaller than that of the Geronese school, despite its greater size and longer period of operation.

Together with the Safedian phase of Kabbalah (approximately 1540–1580), and the emergence of the Polish Hasidic movement (1740–1800), late-thirteenth-century Kabbalistic writings laid the foundation of the major paradigms in Jewish mysticism. The ha-Kohen brothers, R. Jacob and R. Isaac, sons of R. Jacob, were active in Castile (the new center of Kabbalistic activity). Their disciple, R. Moses of Burgos and his follower R. Todros ha-Levi Abulafia, were active in Toledo.[60] Castile led the Kabbalah in diverse literary genres and volume. Castilians, such as R. Joseph ben Abraham Gikatilla and R. Moshe ben Shem Tov de Leon participated in this. Few were recognized experts in matters of *Halakhah* (Jewish law) and were part of the secondary elite.[61] Free from inhibitions inherent in ancient Rabbinic thought regarding the dissemination of Jewish esotericism, these innovative Kabbalists underwent similar spiritual changes. Three Kabbalists, Abraham Abulafia and Moshe De Leon, born in 1240, and Gikatilla, born in 1248, initially interested in Maimonides' *Guide of the Perplexed*, shifted to Kabbalah, where they changed the lore in dramatic ways.[62]

Wide intellectual horizons opened at the court of Alfonso el Sabio, called The Wise (1226?–1284), king of León and Castile (1252–1282) and

Jewish translators contributed to the intellectual project of the king of Castile.[63] They translated mainly from Arabic into Latin and Castilian, but also from Hebrew.[64] This febrile activity took place in the immediate vicinity of the new Kabbalistic centers in Castile, especially Toledo, Burgos, and Avila, and influenced the Kabbalists.[65] The arrival of books from cultures other than Christian ones, contributed greatly to the development of the Renaissance atmosphere and conceptual structure of the Alfonsine culture. It opened to a variety of cultures, Muslim and Jewish, and themes, like astrology, mysticism, and magic.

The concern with magic during the late thirteenth century Kabbalah was more evident than in earlier forms of Kabbalah. This interest related to occultism, including magic, at the court of Alfonso Sabio. There was evidence, from the 1280s on, for magical interpretations of the most anti-magical thinker in Judaism, Maimonides.[66] Maimonides' work included the return of elements related to magic and a mystical-magical literature written in the Hellenistic period and attributed to Hermes Trismegistus, designated as Hermeticism. The broader context of this "occultist" Renaissance coincided with the "window of opportunities" of Kabbalah[67] during the Alfonsine Renaissance in Castile. This period introduced major Hermetic topics in European culture, especially by means of a translated Arabic text known in Latin under the title *Picatrix*.[68]

Reliable evidence in the 1250s and 1260s indicated the importance of occult material for a more energetic understanding of Judaism. Active in Morocco, R. Yehudah ben Nissim ibn Malka presaged a return to Judaism more consonant with thinkers like R. Abraham ibn Ezra, while completely ignoring Maimonides.[69] He did not continue the Hermetic views in the twelfth century, nor did he address Maimonides' critique of magic and astrology. In fact, he never mentioned their names. His main sources were Arabic texts.[70]

R. Dan Ashkenazi, an occultist from Cologne,[71] represented the Ashkenazi culture in Castile.[72] The Ashkenazi *Halakhah* and their customs influenced the book of the *Zohar*.[73] Influenced by Ashkenazi traditions, R. Abraham Abulafia's Kabbalah was represented in Castile. The arrival of new Kabbalistic material and the encounters between representatives of previously unknown forms of Jewish thought[74] were the main causes of religious effervescence in Castile.

Eschatological emphasis characterized the Jewish Castilian Kabbalah in the late thirteenth century.[75] The feeling of coming close to the end of time permitted the disclosure of secrets, which triggered intense oral and literary activities and hurried Kabbalistic creativity. This was evidenced in the writings of R. Abraham Abulafia, who pretended to reveal the secrets of the *Guide*.[76] Abulafia commented upon the *Guide* and disseminated it more than any other Spanish Jewish philosopher did.[77]

The philosophical Andalusian Renaissance provided the early Kabbalists with many themes and concepts as well as intellectual and religious challenges. The Kabbalists reorganized some of the earlier Jewish mythical themes, thus, sparking the emergence of the theosophical-theurgical Kabbalah and provided material for the second Kabbalistic Renaissance.

Literary Genres and Intellectual Disparity

The theosophical-theurgical Kabbalistic literature contributed two literary genres. One consisted of around 170 short and longer treatises on the ten *sefirot*.[78] The other, amounting to some tens of writings, consisted of commentaries on the rationales of the commandments.[79] No Spanish Christian prototype appeared that could have inspired any of the various forms of medieval Jewish mysticism. Kabbalah reached Spain from the north and remained influential in the northern parts of Spain: Catalonia, Valencia, and Castile.

The arrival of the esoteric traditions in northern Spain was not a simple case of *translatio scientiae* from one place to another. By that time the Kabbalistic lore was already divided into three types of traditions:

a) That represented by one of the earliest Kabbalistic documents: the book of *Bahir*.[80]
b) The Kabbalistic thought of R. Abraham ben David and R. Isaac Sagi Nahor and his disciples and R. Jacob the Nazirite from Lunel.[81]
c) The Kabbalistic traditions inherited by R. Moshe ben Nahman and continued by his followers.[82]

Though the *mythologoumena* of the book of *Bahir* influenced the mystical views of the schools of Sagi Nahor and Nahmanides, they were not the crucial trigger for the formulations of the "Kabbalah" written at these schools.[83] A division between views of Kabbalists regarding the specific details of mystical intention during the prayer was evident in Provence before the transition of Kabbalah in Spain. [84]

In Catalonia, Kabbalistic traditions combined with some elements of Christian thought. This happened in the Kabbalistic writings of both R. Azriel of Gerona[85] and Nahmanides.[86] Although Christian elements were influential, they remained secondary in relation to the general economy of the theosophical writings of these two Kabbalists. However, the Geronese Kabbalists knew Neoplatonic Arabic sources.[87] Both the Muslim and Christian influences contributed to the description of complex metaphysical systems, rather than in shaping the Kabbalists theurgical standards of ritual or their path of mystical contemplation. Similar influences were detected in the literature related to the *Book of Contemplation*.[88]

In the school of R. Isaac Sagi Nahor, where the Provençal Kabbalistic traditions were the necessary background for the further developments in Spain, the two phases of Provençal and Catalan were easily comparable. However, Nahmanides' traditions inferred the existence of antecedents. The assumption that Nahmanides' Kabbalah developed independently, despite the fact that he would vehemently oppose such an accusation of inventiveness, was debatable. Because this Kabbalist considered the genuine Kabbalah to be only those traditions transmitted orally by an authoritative master to the ear of a wise and competent student, written documents for Nahmanides' sources were difficult to locate.[89]

Despite the apparent advantage offered by the material from the school of R. Isaac Sagi Nahor, where two different geographical phases were discernable, subtle differences existed between the theories of the master and those of the disciples. Gerona Kabbalists expressed greater concern with philosophical stands than in the Provençal phase of either in the writings of R. Isaac the Blind or in that of his nephew, R. Asher ben David. The students of Isaac the Blind moved away from his theosophy toward a more "instrumental" concept of the role of the *sefirot*, in a way reminiscent of the views of *Sefer ha-Bahir*.[90]

The Centerness of Kabbalah and the Dis-Centeredness of Jewish Philosophy

While the centers of Jewish mysticism were intertwined with centers of Jewish traditional learning in general, this was not the case in many areas of Jewish philosophy. Philo (Jewish-Hellenistic philosopher, 20 BCE–50 CE) flourished in Alexandria, an important pagan cultural and religious center, and not in the land of Israel. Shlomo ibn Gabirol (Avicebrol),

Maimonides, Yehudah Abravanel (Leone Ebreo), Spinoza, Moses Mendelsohn, Solomon Maimon, Herman Cohen, Franz Rosenzweig, Joseph Dov Soloveitchik, and Emmanuel Levinas were active in centers of general culture but not places where Jewish lore, *Halakhah*, or exegesis, were the dominant forms of thought.

The speculative literature, more than any other Jewish literature, depended on external circumstances, namely, the developments of the Gentile environments that aided the formulation of the Jewish forms of philosophy. Because Jewish philosophy refracted, much more than the different forms of Jewish mysticism, questions, and problems posed by a great variety of foreign thought, it was more discontinuous than Jewish mysticism. For example: Neoplatonism, which was overcome by Aristotelianism, in Muslim philosophy, just as in the Jewish one, followed Kalam.[91] Similar to European thought, Jewish idealism was succeeded by dialogical and existential philosophy. It was an exception that R. Joseph ibn Caspi undertook a special journey at the beginning of the fourteenth century to find out the secrets of the *Guide of the Perplexed*.[92]

Jewish philosophers rarely addressed the idea of the existence of a continuous line of transmission of religious secrets, an idea critical to the Kabbalistic mindset. The only case was the claim of the Kabbalist Abraham Abulafia that implied he was the inheritor of a system of thirty-six secrets inherent in the *Guide of the Perplexed*.[93] Though it was possible to point out a relatively organic development that produced most of the forms of Jewish mysticism, the new commencements of Jewish philosophies were the results of encounters with alien types of speculation. Jewish philosophy was, like Jewish magic and poetry, one of the most cosmopolitan genres of Jewish writing.

The propagandistic approach of the Kabbalist is evident even so far as the *Guide of the Perplexed* was concerned. This is why the Kabbalist Abraham Abulafia spread a Kabbalistic understanding of the *Guide* long before any philosophical commentary on this book is known among the philosophers. Maimonides' refusal to share with R. Samuel ibn Tibbon, a highly educated person and one of his most extreme admirers, the secrets of the *Guide* was perhaps indicative of the more individualistic mood of the philosophers.

An exception was the circle of Don Hasdai Crescas in Barcelona at the beginning of the fifteenth century.[94] He was the first major Jewish philosopher to consider Kabbalistic themes, after a period when his Halakhic predecessors in Catalonia were quite reticent toward this lore.[95] Though

Abraham Abulafia seemed to be the first Kabbalist to create a heterogeneous school of individuals from different parts of the Jewish world in Messina,[96] his was the ecstatic Kabbalah alone, which was influenced by Maimonidean philosophy and did not emphasize the importance of group activity.

The Eastward Move of Spanish Kabbalah

The movement of the Kabbalah from the west to the east started in the second part of the thirteenth century with the visits of the ecstatic Kabbalist Abraham Abulafia, to Italy and Byzantium.[97] The Byzantine Empire eventually became one of the most important, though neglected, centers of medieval Kabbalah. Important books showing the impact of Spanish Kabbalah were composed in this region, including *Sefer ha-Temunah* and *Sefer ha-Qanah* and *ha-Peliy'ah*. Spanish Kabbalist R. Shem Tov of Folia's presence in Byzantium testified to the process of transmission of this mystical lore not only by passing manuscripts, but also by exchanges of masters.[98]

Ironically, the destruction of the material center of Kabbalah during the Jewish expulsion from Spain ensured its greater influence in larger parts of the Jewish world. The Sephardi Kabbalists established important centers in North Africa (especially Morocco and Algier),[99] the Ottoman Empire (basically modern Turkey), Italy, Jerusalem, Safed, and Hebron. The centers fostered dramatic contributions of Sephardi Kabbalistic material and authors.

In North Africa, in addition to the preservation of earlier traditions, Kabbalah, especially the book of the *Zohar*, became part of a *modus vivendi*, and shaped rituals of the Jewish communities in the Magreb. In both the Land of Israel and in North Africa, philosophy, including Jewish philosophy, played only a secondary role in the general development of Kabbalah. In the Ottoman Empire, the role of philosophy remained more conspicuous in the culture of Sephardi Jewish communities, though syntheses between those two forms of thinking were not manifested.[100]

In northern Italy, in Mantua, Florence, and Venice, encounters between the Spanish refugees and the emerging Renaissance culture took place. While in the other centers Spanish Kabbalah did not encounter strong forms of different culture, in northern Italy, the situation was different. Before the expulsion, the arrival of a Spanish Kabbalist in Italy provoked a reaction that became symptomatic of the relationship between the Spanish and the Italian Kabbalah. From the fifteenth century on, the particularistic, theosophical-theurgical Kabbalah in Spain rejected the more philosophical interpretation of this lore.[101] Still, the more open intellectual ambiance in Italy invited the Kabbalah to be interpreted in accordance with the philosophical concepts prevalent in that period.

The reaction of the Italians rarely included explicit criticism of the Sephardi Kabbalah. The feeling of Italian Jews that the great center of Kabbalah was indeed in Spain contributed to the absorption of the Kabbalah emanating from there. An adoption accompanied by adaptation of Kabbalah to the cultural background dominant in Italy, especially regarding its Neoplatonic and magical propensities, occurred.[102] While the first generation of Kabbalists among the refugees was more concerned with preserving the Spanish traditions of this lore, a more creative phase emerged with the second generation of Kabbalists active in Safed, a small town in the Galilee in the Land of Israel.[103]

The arrival in Italy of significant numbers of manuscripts from Spain dealing with an amalgam of philosophy, magic, and astrology, influenced the early Florentine Renaissance.[104] This corpus constituted an addition to the Greek-Hellenistic translation by Ficino and the translations made by Flavius Mithridates of mostly Kabbalistic writings stemming from Italy. The Italian printers preferred to print both Spanish philosophical and Kabbalistic writings over the literature in those fields generated by Italian thinkers.[105] Together with Yehudah Abravanel's contribution to Renaissance culture, those manuscripts enriched the forms of knowledge available to the nascent forms of thought in premodern Europe.

It was hard to find, in the structure of the Kabbalistic discourse, dominant messianic elements that transcended what was found in pre-expulsion Kabbalah. It was unlikely that Kabbalistic creativity was triggered by the trauma of the expulsion. Rather than being shocked by the event, Kabbalists were freed from the pressures of the Spanish authorities and inquisitions. The unusual creativity exhibited by the sixteenth-century Sephardi Kabbalists may be related to rebuilding the Sephardi communities in new places, rather than lamenting the lost Sepharad and the tribulations created by the expulsion.[106] Moreover, the need to react to new spiritual environments, as represented by non-Spanish Jews, or by non-Jewish cultures, triggered a more intense literary activity, which included both broad compendia of the earlier Kabbalistic literatures, as is the case in R. Meir ibn

Gabbai's and Joseph Alashqar's books, or original syntheses, as is the case of R. Moshe Cordovero's *Pardes Rimmonim*.

NOTES

1. To be sure, Spain as a unified geopolitical entity is a recent phenomenon, and I shall use it below in pure geographical terms, without assuming a homogeneous culture. This is the reason why I shall prefer in most cases to refer to Catalonia, Valensia, Castile, or Andalus. See n. 42 below.

2. Charles H. Haskins, *The Renaissance of the Twelfth Century* (Cleveland: Meridian, 1970) and entire literature written under his influence, discussed in detail in my study mentioned in the next footnote.

3. See my "On European Cultural Renaissances and Jewish Mysticism," *Kabbalah* 13 (2005). I draw in part on the following discussions, especially in the second section here, in some aspects of my treatment of this issue in this study.

4. For a description of this corpus and updated bibliography, see Moshe Idel, *Messianic Mystics* (New Haven: Yale University Press, 1998), 126–32.

5. "Jewish philosophy" and "Kabbalah" are generic terms. Thus, Neo-Aristotelianism and Neoplatonism not only are different in their sources, but also have different histories, and this is true also of the ways in which they were adopted in Judaism. "Kabbalah" is for me an umbrella term for different schools each having a separate though not necessarily independent history. Therefore, it is necessary to distinguish between them much more than is usually done in modern and recent scholarship. So, for example, we should not only distinguish between the theosophical-theurgical Kabbalah and the ecstatic one, but also between the various sorts of theosophical-theurgical tendencies from the very beginning of Kabbalah, as we shall see below.

6. This is the case also insofar as new genres of poetry and the study of Hebrew grammar and science are concerned. But despite the importance of this salient parallel, those branches of knowledge do not concern us here.

7. By this syntagma I refer to those Kabbalistic schools that assumed that the divinity includes a realm of emanated powers named *sefirot* (theosophy) and the interactions between the performance of commandments and those powers, namely theurgy.

8. See Julius Guttmann, *Philosophies of Judaism*, trans. D. W. Silverman (London: Routledge & K. Paul, 1964).

9. Gershom Scholem, *Major Trends in Jewish Mysticism* (New York: Schocken, 1967), 24, emphasis in the original. See also his "Mi-hoqer li-Mequbbal" (in Hebrew), *Tarbiz* 6 (1935): 91–92; "Maimonides dans l'ouevre des Kabbalistes," *Cahiers Juifs* 3 (1935): 104–5.

10. Gershom Scholem, *Origins of the Kabbalah*, trans. A. Arkush, ed., R. J. Zwi Werblowsky (Princeton, NJ: Princeton University Press; Philadelphia: Jewish Publication Society, 1987), 404–14.

11. Moshe Idel, "On Binary 'Beginnings' in Kabbalah-Scholarship," *Aporematha, Kritische Studien zur Philologiegeschichte* 5 (2001): 313–37.

12. Gershom Scholem, *Kabbalah* (Jerusalem: Keter, 1974), 45.

13. *Geschichte der Juden* (Leipzig, 1908), vol. 7, 385–402.

14. See, respectively, *Geschichte der juedischen Philosophie des Mittelalters* (Berlin, 1907), vol. 1, 179–236; and *Kleinere Schriften* (Berlin, 1937), 531. See also my remarks on this stand of Rosenzweig's in "Franz Rosenzweig and the Kabbalah," in *The Philosophy of Franz Rosenzweig*, ed. P. Mendes-Flohr (Hanover, NH: University Press of New England, 1987), 168–71.

15. Georges Vajda, "Un chapitre de l'histoire du conflit entre la Kabbale et la philosophie: La Polemique anti-intellectualiste de Joseph b. Shalom Ashkenazi," *Archives d'Histoire Doctrinale et Littéraire du Moyen Âge* 31 (1956): 45–127; idem, *Recherches sur la philosophie et la Kabbale dans la pensée juive du Moyen Âge* (Paris: Mouton, 1962); idem, "Comment le philosophe juif Moïse de Narbonne comprenait-il les paroles ecstatiques des soufis?" *Melanges a Georges Vajda*, ed. G. E. Weil (Hildesheim: Gerstenberg Verlag, 1982), 275–81; idem, "Recherches sur la synthese philosophico-Kabbalistique de Samuel ibn Motot," *AHDLMA* 27 (1960): 29–63.

16. Alexander Altmann, "The Ladder of Ascension," in *Studies in Mysticism and Religion Presented to Gershom G. Scholem*, ed. E. E. Urbach, R. J. Zwi-Werblosky, and Ch. Wirszubski (Jerusalem: Magnes, 1967), 1–32; "Moses Narboni's Epistle on *Shiʿur Qomah*," in *Jewish Medieval and Renaissance Studies*, ed. Alexander Altmann (Cambridge: Harvard University Press, 1967), 242–44; idem, "Lurianic Kabbalah in a Platonic Key: Abraham Cohen Herrera's Puerta del Cielo," *HUCA* 53 (19820: 321–24.

17. Shlomo Pines, "On the Term *Ruhaniyyut* and its Sources and On Judah Halevi's Doctrine" (in Hebrew), *Tarbiz* 57 (1988): 511–40; "Shi'ite Terms and Conceptions in Judah Halevi's Kuzari," *Jerusalem Studies in Arabic and Islam*, vol. 2 (1980), 165–251.

18. See, e.g., Giussepe Sermoneta, "Rabbi Yehudah and Immanuel of Rome: Rationalism whose End Is Mystical Belief," in *Revelation, Faith, Reason* (in Hebrew) (Ramat Gan: Bar Ilan University Press, 1976), 54–70.

19. Isadore Twersky, *Studies in Jewish Law and Philosophy* (New York: Ktav, 1982).

20. See especially the inclusion of Kabbalistic figures in her history of medieval Jewish philosophy. See also her "Juda b. Salomon Ha-Kohen: Philosophe, astronome et peut-être Kabbaliste de la premiere moitié du treizième siècle," *Italia* 1, no. 2 (1979): 39–61.

21. See Sara Heller Wilensky, "Isaac ibn Latif: Philosopher or Kabbalist?" in Jewish *Medieval and Renaissance Studies*, ed. A. Altmann (Cambridge: Harvard

University Press, 1967), 185–223; "The Guide and the Gate: The Dialectical Influence of Maimonides on Isaac ibn Latif and Early Spanish Kabbalah," in *A Straight Path: Studies in Medieval Philosophy and Culture, Essays in Honor of Arthur Hyman* ed. Ruth Link-Salinger, J. Hackett, M. S. Hyman, R. J. Long, and C. H. Manekin (Washington, DC: Catholic University of America Press, 1988), 266–78; and "Messianism, Eschatology and Utopia in the Philosophical-Mystical Trend of Kabbalah of the Thirteenth Century" (in Hebrew), in *Messianism and Eschatology*, ed. Z. Baras (Jerusalem: Merkaz Shazar, 1984), 221–38.

22. Pierre Hadot, *Exercices Spirituels et Philosphie Antique* (Paris: Albin Michel, 2002); Phillip Merlan, *Monopsychism, Mysticism, Metaconsciousness* (The Hague: Nijhof, 1963); Richard T. Wallis, "Nous as Experience," *The Significance of Neoplatonism*, ed. R. Baine Harris (Albany: State University of New York Press, 1976), 122 and 143 n. 1 for the pertinent bibliography; Michael Morgan, *Platonic Piety, Philosophy, and Ritual in Fourth-Century Athens* (New Haven: Yale University Press, 1990).

23. See my *Kabbalah: New Perspectives* (New Haven: Yale University Press, 1988), 251–53; idem, "Maimonides and Kabbalah," in *Studies in Maimonides*, ed. Isadore Twersky (Cambridge: Harvard University Press, 1990), 31–33; Moshe Idel, "Divine Attributes and *Sefirot* in Jewish Theology" (in Hebrew), in *Studies in Jewish Thought*, ed. S. O. Heller Willensky and M. Idel (Jerusalem: Magnes, 1989), 87–112; Mark Verman, *The Book of Contemplation: Medieval Jewish Mystical Sources* (Albany: State University of New York Press, 1992), 20–24; Dov Schwartz, "Contacts between Jewish Philosophy and Mysticism in the Rise of the Fifteenth Century" (in Hebrew), *Daat* 29 (1992): 41–68; Havah Tirosh-Rothschild, "*Sefiroth* as the Essence of God in the Writings of David Messer Leon," *Association of Jewish Studies Review* 7–8 (1982–83): 409–25; Nissim Yosha, *Myth and Metaphor* (in Hebrew) (Jerusalem: Ben-Zvi Institute and Magnes, 1994); Boaz Huss, "Mysticism versus Philosophy in Kabbalistic Literature," *Micrologus* 9 (2001): 125–35.

24. Scholem, "Mi-hoqer."

25. David Blumenthal, "Maimonides' Intellectualist Mysticism and the Superiority of the Prophecy of Moses," *Studies in Medieval Culture* 10 (1981): 51–67; Jose Faur, *Homo Mysticus: A Guide to Maimonides' Guide of the Perplexed* (Albany: State University of New York Press, 1999).

26. Moshe Hayyim Weiler, "Inquiries in the Kabbalistic Terminology of R. Joseph Gikatilla and its Relation to Maimonides" (in Hebrew), *HUCA* 37 (1966): 13–44; Elliot R. Wolfson, "Merkavah Traditions in Philosophical Garb: Judah Halevi Reconsidered," *Proceedings of the American Academy for Jewish Research* 57 (1991): 179–242; idem, *Abraham Abulafia: Hermeneutics, Theosophy, and Theurgy* (Los Angeles: Cherub, 2000); Charles Mopsik, "Philosophie et souci philosophique: Les deux grands courants de la pensée juive," *Archivio di filosofia* 61 (1993): 247–54; Dov Schwartz, "Divine Immanence in Medieval Jewish Philosophy," *Journal for Jewish Thought and Philosophy* 3, no. 2 (1994): 249–78; idem, "The

Study Program of Yohanan Alemanno" (in Hebrew), *Tarbiz* 48 (1979): 303–30; "The Magical and Neoplatonic Interpretations of Kabbalah in the Renaissance," in *Jewish Thought in the Sixteenth Century*, ed. B. D. Cooperman (Cambridge: Harvard University Press, 1983), 186–242; Moshe Idel, "Differing Conceptions of Kabbalah in Early Seventeenth Century," in *Jewish Thought in the Seventeenth Century*, ed. Isadore Twersky and Bernard D. Septimus (Cambridge: Harvard University Press, 1987), 137–200; Moshe Idel, "Kabbalah, Platonism, and *Prisca Theologia*: The Case of Menasseh ben Israel," in *Menasseh ben Israel and his World*, ed. Y. Kaplan, H. Meshoulan, and R. Popkin (Leiden, the Netherlands: Brill, 1989), 207–19.

27. See Moshe Idel, "Astral Dreams in Judaism: Twelfth to Fourteenth Centuries," in *Dream Cultures: Explorations in the Comparative History of Dreaming*, ed. David Shulman and Guy G. Stroumsa (New York: Oxford University Press, 1999), 235–38 and the bibliography adduced there.

28. See Moshe Idel, "Some Forms of Order in Kabbalah," *Daat* 50/52 (2003): xxxi–lviii.

29. See Scholem, *Origins of the Kabbalah*, 39–40; Joseph Dan, *The Esoteric Theology of Ashkenazi Hasidism* (in Hebrew) (Jerusalem: Mossad Bialik, 1968), 116–29; Moshe Idel, "The Mystical Intention in Prayer at the Beginning of Kabbalah: Between Ashkenaz and Provence" (in Hebrew), in *Porat Yosef: Studies Presented to Rabbi Dr. Joseph Safran*, ed. B. Safran and E. Safran (Hoboken, NJ: Ktav, 1992), 8–14.

30. See "The Renewal of Theology," in *Renaissance and Renewal in the Twelfth Century*, ed. Robert L. Benson, G. Constable, and C. D. Lanham (Cambridge: Harvard University Press, 1982), 68 ff.

31. See Harry A. Wolfson, *Philo: Foundation of Religious Philosophy* (Cambridge: Harvard University Press, 1982).

32. See, e.g., Uriel Simon, "Interpreting the Interpreter: Supercommentaries on Ibn Ezra's Commentaries," in *Rabbi Abraham ibn Ezra: Studies in the Writings of a Twelfth-Century Jewish Polymath*, ed. I. Twersky and J. M. Harris (Cambridge: Harvard University Press, 1993), 86–128.

33. See Shlomo Pines's analysis of Maimonides' philosophical sources in his introduction to Maimonides, *Guide of the Perplexed*, trans. Shlomo Pines (Chicago: Chicago University Press, 1963), ciii–cxxiii.

34. See Maimonides, *Guide of the Perplexed*, introduction, 6–10, 16, I:34, 77–79, I:71, 176.

35. See Steven M. Wasserstrom, "Jewish-Muslim Relations in the Context of Andalusian Emigration," in *Christians, Muslims, and Jews in Medieval and Early Modern Spain: Interaction and Cultural Change*, ed. Mark D. Meyerson and Edward D. English (Notre Dame, IN: University of Notre Dame, 2000), 69–87; and Moshe Idel, "Maimonides' *Guide of the Perplexed* and the Kabbalah," *Jewish History* 18, no. 2 (2004): 1–30.

36. Chronicles 15:3.

37. Babylonian Talmud, Sabbath, fol. 138b.

38. On the identification of this rabbi as Maimonides, see Moshe Idel, "Maimonides and Kabbalah," in *Studies in Maimonides*, ed. Isadore Twersky (Cambridge: Harvard University Press, 1990), 71–73, where the original Hebrew of the text as well as footnotes that concern some of the details of the passage can be found.

39. *Sefer ʿOtzar Hayyim*, Ms. Moscow-Ginzburg 775, fol. 183a, quoted in Idel, "Maimonides and Kabbalah," 71–72.

40. See *Kitvei ha-Ramban*, vol. 1, ed. Ch. Chavel (Jerusalem: Mossad ha-Rav Kook, 1963), 315.

41. The inclusion of the book of the *Zohar* in this context points to the view that despite its explicit attribution to the late antiquity figure R. Shimeon, R. Isaac envisioned its surfacing on the historical scene in Castile, no doubt as part of his acquaintance with the nexus between this book and the Castilian Kabbalist R. Moshe de Leon. On this issue see Isaiah Tishby, *The Wisdom of the Zohar*, trans. David Goldstein (Oxford, England: Littman Library, 1989), vol. 1, 13–18, and more in the next section.

42. Presumably the province of Castile, and not Spain in general as understood today.

43. Ms. Moscow-Ginzberg 775, fol. 183a, quoted in Idel, "Maimonides and Kabbalah," 72.

44. See Scholem, *Origins of the Kabbalah*, 205–38; Moshe Idel, "Kabbalistic Prayer in Provence" (in Hebrew), *Tarbiz* 62 (1993): 265–86.

45. See M. Idel, "On R. Isaac Sagi Nahor's Mystical Intention of the Eighteen Benedictions," *Studies in Kabbalistic Literature and Jewish Philosophy in Memory of Prof. Ephraim Gottlieb Massuʾot* (in Hebrew), ed. Michal Oron and Amos Goldreich (Jerusalem: Mossad Bialik, 1994), 25–52.

46. On the different interpretations of this verse in Midrashic, Kabbalistic, and Sabbatean literatures see more recently Abraham Elqayam, *The Mystery of Faith in the Writings of Nathan of Gaza* (in Hebrew) (Ph.D. dissertation, Hebrew University, Jerusalem, 1993), 49–62.

47. *Kitvei ha-Ramban*, vol. 2, 479, 514.

48. Ibid., 479.

49. See Moshe Idel, *Absorbing Perfections: Kabbalah and Interpretation* (New Haven: Yale University Press, 2002), passim.

50. See Scholem, *Origins of the Kabbalah*, 49–148.

51. Ibid., 68 ff; Moshe Idel, "To the Question of the Study of the Sources of the Book of Bahir," in *The Beginning of Jewish Mysticism in Europe* (in Hebrew), ed. Joseph Dan (Jerusalem, 1987), 55–72; Elliot R. Wolfson, "Hebraic and Hellenic Conceptions of Wisdom in *Sefer ha-Bahir*," *Poetics Today* 19 (1998): 46–76.

52. Arthur Green, *Keter: The Crown of God in Early Jewish Mysticism* (Princeton, NJ: Princeton University Press, 1997); and Peter Schaefer, *Mirror of His Beauty*

(Princeton, NJ: Princeton University Press, 2002). And also see, Moshe Idel, "On Binary 'Beginnings' in Kabbalah-Scholarship," *Aporematha, Kritische Studien zur Philologiegeschichte* 5 (2001): 313–37.

53. It should be mentioned nevertheless that an ancient book written by a Jewish author in late antiquity, has indeed surfaced in a Kabbalistic milieu, and was known and imitated by an early fourteenth-century Kabbalist: it is the Syrian version of the book *The Wisdom of Solomon*, a book never quoted in the Middle Ages by a Jew before Nahmanides. See Alexander Marx, "An Aramaic Fragment of the Wisdom of Solomon," *Journal of Biblical Literature* 40 (1921): 57–69; Gershom Scholem, "On *The Major Wisdom of Solomon* and R. Abraham ha-Levi the Older" (in Hebrew), *Qiryat Sefer* 1 (1924–1925): 163–64.

54. Scholem, *Origins of the Kabbalah*, 422–23, 425, 428–30, 439; Gabrielle Sed-Rajna, "L'influence de Jean Scot sur la doctrine du Kabbalist Azriel de Gerone," in *Jean Scot Erigene et l'histoire de la philosophie* (Paris, 1977), 453–62; Shlomo Pines, "Nahmanides on Adam in the Garden of Eden in the Context of Other Interpretations of Genesis, Chapters 2 and 3" (in Hebrew), *Exile and Diaspora: Studies in the History of Jewish People Presented to Prof. H. Beinart*, ed. A. Mirsky, A. Grossman, and Y. Kaplan (Jerusalem: Makhon Ben Zvi, 1988), 159–64; Amos Funkenstein, "Nahmanides' Symbolical Reading of History," in *Studies in Jewish Mysticism*, ed. J. Dan and F. Talmage (Cambridge, MA: Association of Jewish Studies, 1982), 129–50; and Mark Sendor, *The Emergence of Provençal Kabbalah: R. Isaac the Blind's Commentary on Sefer Yezirah* (Ph.D. dissertation, Harvard University, 1994), vol. 1, 115–16, 377.

55. Schaefer, *Mirror of His Beauty*, 147–216; Green, *Keter*, 160–61 n. 35; idem, "*Shekhinah*, The Virgin Mary, and the Song of Songs: Reflections on a Kabbalistic Symbol in Its Christian Context," *AJS Review* 26, no. 1 (2002): 1–52.

56. See Daniel Abrams, *R. Asher ben David: His Complete Works and Studies in his Kabbalistic Thought* (in Hebrew) (Los Angeles: Cherub, 1996).

57. Moshe Idel, "Nahmanides: Kabbalah, Halakhah, and Spiritual Leadership," in *Jewish Mystical Leaders and Leadership*, ed. M. Idel and M. Ostow (Northvale, NJ: Jason Aronson, 1998), 81.

58. Ibid., 82–84.

59. For other aspects of Nahmanides' conservatism see Moshe Halbertal, "Custom and the History of the Halakhah in Nahmanides' Thought" (in Hebrew), *Zion* 67, no. 1 (2002): 25–56.

60. On this Kabbalistic school see Scholem, *Kabbalah*, 55–57; and his studies in *Madaʿei ha-Yahadut* (in Hebrew), vol. 2 (Jerusalem: Hebrew University Press, 1927), 165–88; and the collection of his studies *The Study of Qabbalah of Rabbi Isaac ben Jacob ha-Kohen* (in Hebrew) (Jerusalem: ha-madpis, 1934); and R. Todros ben Joseph Abulafia, *Shaʿar ha-Razim*, ed. Michal Kushnir Oron (Jerusalem: Bialik Institute, 1989).

61. Moshe Idel, "Kabbalah and Elites in Thirteenth-Century Spain," *Mediterranean Historical Review* 9 (1994): 5–19.

62. An older Kabbalist with speculative propensities, R. Isaac ben Abraham ibn Latif, and a younger one, R. Nathan ben Sa°adya Harar, the author of *Sefer Sha°arei Tzedeq*, both underwent similar shifts from philosophy to Kabbalah. On this issue see Twersky, *Studies in Jewish Law and Philosophy*, 208.

63. See Jose S. Gil, *La escuela e traductores de Toledo y sus colaboratores judios* (Toledo: Instituto Provincial de Investigaciones y Estudios Toledanos, 1985), 57–87; Norman Roth, "Jewish Collaborators in Alfonso's Scientific Work," in *Emperor of Culture: Alfonso X the Learned of Castile and His Thirteenth-Century Renaissance*, ed. Robert I. Burns (Philadelphia: University of Pennsylvania Press, 1991), 59–71.

64. See now the important contribution of Alejandro Garcia Aviles, "Alfonso X y el Liber Raziel: Imagenes de la magia astral judia en el scriptorium alfonsi," *Bulletin of Hispanic Studies* 74 (1997): 21–39. This is an example of an early integration of astral magic with Hebrew material, which had an important career in the Renaissance, an issue that cannot be dealt with here. Another important contribution to the acquaintance of Jewish authors with Hermetic themes is the Hebrew translation of an Arabic text entitled *Sefer ha-Tamar*: Gershom Scholem, ed. and trans., *Sefer ha-Tamar: Das Buch von der Palme des Abu Aflah aus Syracus*, vol. 1 (Jerusalem: Workmen's Printing Press, 1926–27), vol. 2 (Jerusalem: Workmen's Printing Press, 1927).

65. See Idel, *Kabbalah: New Perspectives*, 251.

66. Moshe Idel, "Abulafia's Secrets of the Guide: A Linguistic Turn," in *Perspectives on Jewish Thought and Mysticism*, ed. A. Ivri, E. R. Wolfson, A. Arkush (Amsterdam: Harwood, 1998), 313–19.

67. Moshe Idel, "The Kabbalah's 'Window of Opportunities,' 1270–1290," *Me°ah She°arim: Studies in Medieval Jewish Spiritual Life in Memory of Isadore Twersky*, ed. E. Fleisher, G. Blidstein, C. Horowitz, and B. Septimus (Jerusalem: Magnes, 2001), 171–208.

68. On this book see H. Ritter and M. Plessner, *"Picatrix" Das Ziel des Weisen von Pseudo-Magriti* (London: Warburg Institute, 1962); Henri and Renee Kahane and Angelina Pietrangeli, "Picatrix and the Talismans," *Romance Philology* 19 (1965–66): 574–93; David Pingree, "Some of the Sources of the *Ghayat al-Hakim*," *Journal of the Warburg and Courtauld Institutes* 43 (1980): 1–15.

69. See Georges Vajda, *Juda ben Nissim ibn Malka: Philosophe juif Marocain* (Paris: Hesperis, 1954); idem, "La Doctrine Astrologique de Juda ben Nisim ibn Malka," *Homenaje a Millas Vallicrosa* (Barcelona, 1956), vol. 2, 483–500; idem, ed., R. Yehudah ibn Malka: Kitab Uns we-Tafsir (Ramat-Gan: Bar Ilan University, 1974); idem, "Les observations critiques d'Isaac d'Acco sur les ouvrages de Juda ben Nissim ibn Malka," *REJ* 115, n.s. 15 (1956): 25–71; and more recently *Judah ben Nissim ibn Malka: Judaeo-Arabic Commentary on the Pirkey Rabbi Eli°ezer with a*

Hebrew Translation and Supercommentary by Isaac b. Samuel of Acco, ed. Paul B. Fenton (Jerusalem: Daf Hen, 1991).

70. Moshe Idel, "The Beginning of Kabbalah in North Africa? A Forgotten Document by R. Yehudah ben Nissim ibn Malka" (in Hebrew), *Pe˓amim* 43 (1990): 4–15.

71. See R. Schlomo ben Abraham ibn Adret [Rashba], "Responsum," in *Teshuvot ha-Rashba*, ed. Hayyim Dimitrovsky (Jerusalem: Mossad ha-Rav Kook, 1990), vol. 1, no. 548, 105–6.

72. See Israel Ta-Shma, "Rabbeinu Dan Ashkenazi" (in Hebrew), in *Studies in Jewish Mysticism, Philosophy, and Ethical Literature Presented to Isaiah Tishby*, ed. J. Dan and J. Hacker (Jerusalem: Magnes, 1986), 385–94.

73. See, e.g., Israel M. Ta-Shma, "Be'erah shel Miriam" (in Hebrew), *Jerusalem Studies in Jewish Thought* 4 (1985): 267–70; idem, "Pores Sukkat Shalom: Berakhah ve-Gilguleiah" (in Hebrew), *Assufot* 2 (1988): 186–89; idem, *Ha-Nigle She-Banistar: The Halakhic Residue in the Zohar* (in Hebrew), 2d ed. (Tel Aviv: Hakibutz Hameuhad, 2001).

74. As to the importance of encounters between diverse forms of Jewish mysticism for the effervescence of the Safedian Kabbalah, see Moshe Idel, *Studies in Ecstatic Kabbalah* (Albany: State University of New York Press, 1988), 126–40.

75. See Joseph Dan, "The Emergence of Messianic Mythology in Thirteenth Century Kabbalah in Spain," in *Occident and Orient: A Tribute to the Memory of A. Schreiber* (Leiden, the Netherlands: Brill, 1988), 57–68; Yehuda Liebes, *Studies in the Zohar* (Albany: State University of New York Press, 1993), 1–83; Idel, *Messianic Mystics*, 58–125.

76. See Idel, *Messianic Mystics*, 58–100.

77. See Idel, "Abulafia's Secrets of the Guide."

78. See the list compiled by Gershom Scholem, "The Key of the Commentaries on Ten Sefirot" (in Hebrew), *Qiryat Sefer* 10 (1933–34): 498–515.

79. A detailed list of the Kabbalistic commentaries on this topic is still a desideratum.

80. Scholem, *Origins of the Kabbalah*, 49–198; see also Daniel Abrams's introduction to his work *The Book Bahir: An Edition Based on the Earlier Manuscripts* (Los Angeles: Cherub, 1994), 1–31; Wolfson, "Hebraic and Hellenistic Conceptions of Wisdom in *Sefer ha-Bahir*."

81. Scholem, *Origins of the Kabbalah*, 199–309, 365–460.

82. See Idel, "Nahmanides."

83. See Joseph Dan, *Hugei ha-Mequbbalim ha-Rishonim* (in Hebrew), ed. I. Agassi (Jerusalem: Academon, 1976), 178–79; M. Idel, "Sefirot above Sefirot" (in Hebrew), *Tarbiz* 51 (1982): 239.

84. Scholem, *Origins of the Kabbalah*, 208–16; Moshe Idel, "Prayer in Provencal Kabbalah" (in Hebrew), *Tarbiz* 62 (1993): 265–86.

85. See note 61, above.

86. See note 61, above.

87. Scholem, *Origins of the Kabbalah*, 422, 428–30.

88. Amos Goldreich, "The Theology of the *Iyyun* Circle and a Possible Source of the Term of *Ahdut Shavah*" (in Hebrew), in *The Beginnings of Jewish Mysticism in Medieval Europe*, ed. J. Dan (Jerusalem: National and University Library, 1987), 141–56.

89. See Nahmanides' introduction to his *Commentary on the Pentateuch*, ed. Ch. Chavel (Jerusalem: Mossad ha Rav Kook, 1959), vol. 1, 7–8; Idel, "Nahmanides," 42–53; Daniel Abrams, "Orality in the Kabbalistic School of Nahmanides: Preserving and Interpreting Esoteric Traditions and Texts," *Jewish Studies Quarterly* 3 (1996): 85–102.

90. See Idel, *Kabbalah*, 141–44.

91. See the comprehensive survey of Guttmann, *Philosophies of Judaism*.

92. I. Last, ed., *Tirat Kesef* (in Hebrew) (Pressburg: Alkalay, 1905), 18–19.

93. Idel, *Studies in Ecstatic Kabbalah*, 29 n. 110; idem, "Abulafia's Secrets of the Guide," 289–329.

94. See Aviezer Ravitzki, *Crescas' Sermon on the Passover and Studies in His Philosophy* (in Hebrew) (Jerusalem: Israeli Academy, 1988); Shalom Rosenberg, "The *Arbaʿah Turim* of Rabbi Abraham bar Judah, Disciple of Don Hasdai Crescas" (in Hebrew), *Jerusalem Studies in Jewish Thought* 3 (1983–84): 525–621.

95. Ze'ev Harvey, "Kabbalistic Elements in R. Hasdai Crescas' book *ʾOr ha-Shem*" (in Hebrew), *Jerusalem Studies in Jewish Thought* 2 (1983): 75–109. See also idem, *Physics and Metaphysics in Hasdai Crescas* (Amsterdam: J. C. Gieben, Amsterdam Studies in Jewish Thought, 1999). It should be mentioned that after a generation in which Kabbalah has been regarded with suspicion by two Catalan important mid- and late fourteenth-century rabbis, R. Isaac bar Sheshet and R. Nissim Gerondi, two major fifteenth-century thinkers, Crescas and Joseph Albo were much more open to this lore.

96. See my introduction to R. Nathan ben Saʿadyah Harʾar, *Le porte della giustizia*, trans. Maurizio Mottoleze (Milan: Adelphi, 2001), 22–34.

97. See Idel, "Maimonides and Kabbalah," 60–61.

98. Efraim Gottlieb, *Studies in the Kabbalah Literature* (in Hebrew), ed. Joseph Hacker (Tel Aviv: Tel Aviv University, 1976), 117–21; Joseph Hacker, "The Connection of Spanish Jewry with Eretz-Israel between 1391 and 1492" (in Hebrew), *Shalem* 1 (1974): 114–16, 133–36; idem, "Links between Spanish Jewry and Palestine, 1391–1492)," in *Vision and Conflict in the Holy Land*, ed. Richard Cohen (New York: St. Martin's Press, 1985), 111–39.

99. On the arrival of Spanish Kabbalah to North Africa after the expulsion, see Moshe Hallamish, *The Kabbalah in North Africa: A Historical and Cultural Survey* (in Hebrew) (Tel Aviv: Hakibbutz Hameuchad, 2001); Moshe Idel, *Introduction* to *R. Joseph ben Moshe Alashqar, Sefer Tsafnat Paʿaneah* (in Hebrew) (Jerusalem: Misgav Yerushalayim, 1991).

100. Joseph Hacker, "The Intellectual Activity among the Jews in the Ottoman Empire in the Sixteenth and Seventeenth Century" (in Hebrew), *Tarbiz* 53 (1994): 569–603. See also his "On the Intellectual Character and Self-Perception of Spanish Jewry in Late-Fifteenth Century" (in Hebrew), *Sefunot*, vol. 2 (17) (1983): 52–56. See also Rachel Elior, "The Struggle on the Status of Kabbalah in the Sixteenth Century" (in Hebrew), *Jerusalem Studies in Jewish Thought* 1 (1982): 177–90; and my "Neglected Treatises by the Author of Sefer *Kaf ha-Qetoret*" (in Hebrew), *Pe'amim* 53 (1993): 75–89.

101. See Moshe Idel, "Inquiries in the Doctrine of *Sefer Ha-Meshiv*" (in Hebrew), *Sefunot*, vol. 2 (17) (1983): 232–40.

102. Moshe Idel, "The Magical and Neoplatonic Interpretations of Kabbalah in the Renaissance," in *Jewish Thought in the Sixteenth Century*, ed. B. D. Cooperman (Cambridge: Harvard University Press, 1983), 186–242, reprinted in *Essential Papers on Jewish Culture in Renaissance and Baroque Italy*, ed. David B. Ruderman (New York: New York University Press, 1992), 107–69.

103. See Moshe Idel, "On Mobility, Individuals, and Groups: Prolegomenon for a Sociological Approach to Sixteenth-Century Kabbalah," *Kabbalah* 3 (1998): 145–76.

104. Stephane Toussaint, "Ficino's Orphic Magic or Jewish Astrology and Oriental Philosophy? A Note on *Spiritus*, the Three Books on Life Ibn Tufayl and Ibn Zarza," *Accademia* 2 (2000): 19–33; Franco Bacchelli, *Giovanni Pico e Pier Leone da Spoleto: Tre filosofia dell'amore e tradizione cabalistica* (Florence: Leo Olschki, 2001), 15, 21–30, 100–102; Moshe Idel, "Jewish Mystical Thought in the Florence of Lorenzo il Magnifico," in *La cultura ebraica all'epoca di Lorenzo il Magnifico*, a cura di Dora Liscia Bemporad e Ida Zatelli (Florence: Leo Olschki, 1998), 17–42.

105. On this issue I shall elaborate in a separate study. The printing of R. Menahem Recanati's writings is, however, an exception.

106. See Moshe Idel, "Religion, Thought and Attitudes: The Impact of the Expulsion on the Jews" in *Spain and the Jews: The Sephardi Experience, 1492 and After*, ed. Elie Kedourie (London: Thames and Hudson, 1992), 123–39.

Part II

From Expulsion to the Modern Era
Exile, Decline, and Revival

Chapter 8

Hispanic Culture in Exile
Sephardic Life in the Ottoman Balkans

Annette B. Fromm

Introduction

The Edict of Expulsion of 1492 by no means meant the end of Spanish or Sephardic Jewry. However, the actions leading to the actual expulsion brought an important era in Jewish history to a close. In medieval Spain, a richness of secular and sacred creativity influenced by the unique interactions of Jews, Christians, and Muslims flourished. The Jewish Hispanic traditions that developed there continued to grow and prosper in a number of different forms in the Ottoman Balkans long after the forced departure of the Jews from the Iberian Peninsula.

The Sephardic exile from Spain was led into two geographical directions: to northwestern Europe and to the eastern Mediterranean and North Africa. Descendants of the Spanish Jews lived in a large number of social settings. Their histories, modes of religious expression, languages, and large body of traditional culture reflect great diversity, reflected upon their Spanish heritage and the cultures of the lands in which they established residence.

Sephardic Jews eventually assimilated into the prevalent cultures of northwestern Europe (Holland, France, and England) and ultimately, by extension, the Americas. In the Ottoman Empire and North Africa, Sephardim established major communities in which their special Iberian Jewish culture fostered and grew. Despite the economic and intellectual stagnation of the eighteenth and nineteenth centuries, Ottoman Sephardic culture survived until the eve of the Holocaust. Largely due to twentieth century settlement of Sephardim in North America and Israel, Sephardic identity and culture enjoyed a revival.

Medieval Spain: A Multicultural Context

Muslims from North Africa ruled all of the Iberian Peninsula for 700 years, from the early eighth century to the late fifteenth century. Under Muslim law, Jews and Christians were viewed as "peoples of the Book" and were generally tolerated. Under the repressive rule of the Almohades in the mid-twelfth century, however, many Jews fled northward to Christian-ruled areas of Spain and south to Morocco and then Egypt. Most notable among these early exiles fleeing to Morocco was the scholar Maimonides.

The Jewish population of Spain evolved from small communities to sizable populations in the major cities. Toledo was known as the "Jerusalem of the Spanish Jews." In the eleventh and twelfth centuries, it was home to the "School of Translators," where Jewish, Christian, and Muslim scholars studied and worked together. The period was characterized by a flowering of Jewish scholarship and Hebrew literature as creative minds shaped the intellectual world there.

Other cities with significant Jewish communities included Seville and Barcelona. When King Ferdinand III captured Seville, the leaders of the Jewish community presented him with the "keys to the city" inscribed in Hebrew. The Jews of Barcelona were prominent in the royal court as diplomats, physicians, bankers, artists, and traders as well as landowners and farmers. Significantly, Spain was the last European country in the Middle Ages with a large and economically flourishing Jewish community. Changes occurred as Catholic rulers gained ascendancy in the Spanish states. Anti-Jewish riots broke out in several cities in 1391, most notably in Seville. There, a series of forced baptisms created thousands of conversos.

Exile

The Inquisition, the search for heresy by the Catholic Church, first emerged in northern Italy and southern France, then in Spain. The Spain of three religions—Christianity, Islam, and Judaism—followed the example of other European nations. The Catholic monarchs, Ferdinand and Isabella, signed the edict that led to the expulsion of Jews (from Castile and Aragon) who refused to convert to Catholicism.[1] The edict blamed the Jews for influencing many of their former coreligionists who forcibly chose Christianity in the fourteenth century but reverted to Judaism.

Many Spanish Jews converted and remained in Spain with the distinctive title of New Christians. About one-half of the Jewish population chose to leave, paying a hefty exit tax for this right. Many sought refuge in the relatively close territories of Portugal, the Kingdom of Navarre, the French region of Provence, and several Italian states. In these places, the Jews had a short reprieve and could still practice Judaism openly. But in 1497, Portugal expelled its Jews, and the tiny kingdom of Navarre followed suit in 1498. The proximity of North Africa drew others, although they were not universally welcomed by indigenous North African Jews. The gradual process of exile spanned many decades, but the most significant waves left between 1492 and 1512.

The nearly 200,000 Spanish Jews who were sent into exile were called Sephardim. The origin of the root term Sepharad was found in the biblical reference in Obadiah 1:20. "The exiles of Jerusalem who are in Sepharad will inherit the cities of the Negev."[2] Through interpretation of this sentence, Sepharad came to refer to the Iberian Peninsula. The Jews who lived there and their descendants have thus been referred to as Sephardim.

Following the Edicts of Expulsion against the Jews of Spain and Portugal, overwhelming numbers of Jews from the Iberian Peninsula settled in Ottoman territories, where they were welcomed. From the 1490s, and in increasing numbers throughout the first quarter of the sixteenth century, boatloads of Sephardic Jews arrived there. Constantinople, Izmir, Safed, and Thessaloniki became the centers for Sephardic Jewry. Other communities were established in cities in Anatolia, the Balkans, in what became Bosnia, Macedonia, Bulgaria, Rumania, Greece, and in Arab lands that were later absorbed into the empire. The Jews enjoyed a period of prosperity and cultural efflorescence during the sixteenth century.

This transition from the Iberian Peninsula to the Ottoman Balkans was not always accomplished smoothly. Several factors played a role in the transition. On one hand, the Sephardim found Jews already living in the region when they arrived. The historical background of these Jews was quite different. Many longtime residents of the Byzantine Empire, known as Romaniote Jews, were deeply entrenched in Byzantine culture. Their heritage in the Balkans and Anatolia actually predated the early Christian Empire and dated to antiquity.[3]

Furthermore, among the Sephardim were many conversos, Jews who converted to Christianity in the fourteenth century or later. Their return to Judaism was sometimes difficult, and their pride and sense of cultural superiority caused friction in their dealings with Romaniote Jews. Despite these difficulties, the former Byzantine Romaniote communities of Constantinople, Edirne, Thessaloniki, and Rhodes were forced, by the weight of numbers and cultural superiority, to adopt, not only the minhag, or custom, but also the language of the newcomers. According to Bowman, "In a matter of a few generations the demographic composition and the very character of this Jewish population in [the] Ottoman [Empire] had changed beyond recognition" (ix).

Multicultural Milieu prior to the Ottomans

The history of the Jews in the Balkan Peninsula and Anatolia started many centuries before the migration of the Sephardic Jews. Remnants of Jewish settlement from the fourth century BC were uncovered in the Aegean region. Ancient synagogue ruins were found in Sardis, near Izmir, dating from 220 BCE, and traces of other Jewish settlements were discovered near Bursa, in the southeast, and along the Aegean, Mediterranean, and Black Sea coasts.

The capital of the Roman Empire was moved to the east by Constantine the Great, in the fourth century. At that time, the Empire, now known as the Byzantine Empire, adopted Christianity as the state religion. The first anti-Jewish laws were written there. Jews were seen as heretics, and the church, as ruling authority, was the guardian of orthodoxy.[4]

Compared to the situation in western Europe, life for the Jews in Byzantium was never as restrictive. Jews could own land, engage in most occupations, continue to practice their religion, and build their synagogues. Their niche was primarily in trade, especially in the silk industry. They were also physicians and interpreters in both imperial and private sectors.[5]

The presence of Jews in the Byzantine Empire was documented by the twelfth-century Spanish rabbi Benjamin of Tudela. Benjamin found that Constantinople was home to 2,000 Jewish families and 500 Karaite families who lived in quarters separated by a wall from the others. Among the 500 or so Jews at Thessaloniki, many were scholars "[who busied] themselves in the craft of silk." Benjamin found 2,000 other families in Thebes who were "the most eminent manufacturers of silk and purple cloth in all of Greece.... The town of Saluniki ... contains about five hundred Jewish inhabitants ... who live by the exercise of handicrafts."[6]

Other evidence of the position of Jews in the Byzantine period included the two Golden Bulls (Chrysobulla) of Andronicus II, dated 1319 and 1321.

At this period, Andronicus II united Ioannina and Epirus, in northwestern Greece, with the Byzantine Empire. According to Charanis, his "attitude toward the Jews was that of absolute toleration."[7] The first Golden Bull "was issued in favor of the city of Janina, with a principal aim to define the status and privileges of that important fortress."[8] Considered to be the most important document regarding Christian-Jewish relations in the Balkans, the first Golden Bull asserted that the Jews of Ioannina were to be free and unmolested like the rest of their fellow citizens. The rights of the Jews were thus reaffirmed. The Second Golden Bull (1321) specifically mentioned the sons of three Jews in service to the Metropolitan of Ioannina—Namer, David, and Samaria.[9]

The Byzantine Jews were joined by other exiles over time. For example, many Jews entering the Balkans from the north and northwest were the descendants of refugees expelled from England, France, and the German states during the 1200s and 1300s. A long tradition of Jewish autonomous communal rule in the Byzantine Empire attracted Jews from other parts of Europe despite the fact that they had the status of second-class citizens.[10]

Enter the Ottomans

Early in the fourteenth century, the Turkish tribal chieftain Othman (Osman) founded an empire in western Anatolia (Asia Minor) that endured almost six centuries. This empire grew through the conquering of lands of the Byzantine Empire and beyond. At the height of its power, it came to include all of Asia Minor; the countries of the Balkan Peninsula; the islands of the eastern Mediterranean; parts of Hungary and Russia; Iraq, Syria, the Caucasus, Palestine, and Egypt; part of Arabia; and all of North Africa through Algeria.[11]

From the beginning of the conquest of Constantinople in 1453, Sultan Mehmet II, or Mehmet the Conqueror, had clear plans for his new capital. It was not to be an exclusively Turkish or Muslim city; but a world city worthy of his land. It would reflect the enormous racial and cultural diversity of his expanding empire. Mehmet II was of mixed race and imagined himself in the image of Alexander the Great. One of the favorite Ottoman epithets, both of the sultans and their city, soon became alem penah, "refuge of the world."

Multiculturalism became the essence of Constantinople. At one point, it was calculated that 72.5 nationalities from 40 major cities and towns in

Western Anatolia made their homes in Constantinople.[12] In the fifteenth century, national differences, based on history and geography more than race, were acutely felt. Gennadios, the first ecumenical patriarch under the Ottomans, called the Greeks a race than which there had been none finer on earth. Mustafa Ali, a prominent sixteenth-century historian, extolled the number of nationalities in the Empire—Turks, Greeks, Franks, Kurds, Serbs, Arabs, and others—as a source of strength. A nineteenth-century minister of the Sultan, Cevdet Pasha, called the Ottoman Empire a great society because of the population diversity that brought languages, traditions, and economic skill.

The principal reason for Constantinople's variety of nationalities was a strategically calculated policy known as *surgun,* or forced transfer of populations. This policy of massive forced movements of people was carried out throughout the entire empire. Because of the fighting between the Ottomans and the Byzantines, the populations of most of the major cities were depleted. Mehmet II moved entire ethnic communities to the capital and other cities to fill voids brought about by years of fighting.[13]

One custom in Constantinople following the transfers of communities was for each quarter, or *mahalle,* to retain the name of its inhabitants' city of origin. Each *mahalle* had its own places of worship, shops, fountains, and night watchmen. Inhabitants maintained distinctive customs, language, and styles of architecture. Muslim Turks were the first and largest group that the sultan brought to Constantinople. In the years following its capture in 1453, the city remained a ruin devastated by plague. The sultan used *surgun* to move Turks to his new capital. Mehmet II personally went to Bursa to force artisans and merchants of this rich trading city to move to the capital.

The conqueror also imported Greeks to Constantinople. Some areas of the city never lost their Greek population. Psamatya, present-day Koca Mustafa Pasha, in the southwest part of the city, surrendered separately. It was, therefore, spared pillage—which explains the large number of churches there today. As Mehmet II increasingly conquered more neighboring territory and as his empire expanded, more Greeks were forcibly brought to Constantinople. Greek slave peasants, who were freed in the next century, settled in villages outside the city in order to ensure its food supplies.

Christian Greeks were regarded as "people of the Book" by the Muslim Turks: their religion was superseded by, but was not wholly alien to, Islam. According to Islamic law, Christians were given the status of *dhimmi,* or protected persons. In return for paying a poll and other taxes, they were granted the right to worship in freedom and to live by their own laws. Armenians were another Christian group brought to Constantinople by the sultan. They were a distinct nationality that had lived in eastern Anatolia and the Caucasus since at least the sixth century BCE. Their use of the Armenian language and alphabet maintained their distinct identity, despite the disappearance of the last Armenian kingdom in southern Anatolia in the fourteenth century. They were prominent in the eastern Mediterranean as jewelers, craftsmen, and traders and were naturally appealing to the Conqueror.

When he captured Constantinople in 1453, Mehmet II encountered a preexisting Byzantine, Romaniote Jewish community that welcomed him with enthusiasm. By the fourteenth century, according to Bowman, "some twenty-seven former Byzantine cities in the Balkans, Greece, and the islands [were] known to have harbored Jews" (95). The first 50 years of Jewish life under the Ottomans was dominated by these Byzantine, Romaniote Jews.

The Ottomans established their first capital at Edirne, or Adrianople, in the early fourteenth century. Byzantine Jews had long been established there. When the Ottomans entered Bursa in 1324, they found a Byzantine Jewish community in residence. The Jews welcomed the Ottomans as saviors. Sultan Othman gave them permission to build the *Etz ha-Hayyim*, "Tree of Life," synagogue that remained in service until the mid-twentieth century. Other Jews from Europe, including Karaites, migrated to Edirne.[14] Similarly, Jews expelled from Hungary, France, and Sicily found refuge in the Ottoman Empire.

In the 1420s, Jews from Thessaloniki, which was then under Venetian control, also fled to reestablish themselves in Edirne.[15] In 1470, Jews expelled from Bavaria found refuge in the Ottoman Empire.[16] A letter sent by Rabbi Yitzhak Sarfati in Edirne to Jewish communities in Europe invited his coreligionists to leave the torments they endured in Christendom and to seek safety and prosperity in Turkey.[17]

By the third quarter of the fifteenth century, the Ottoman Empire supplanted the Byzantine Empire. A flowering of Romaniote intellectual activity took place at the same time. Independent schools and academies were established in Constantinople as well as Adrianople. The Hebrew lament, by Shabbetai Kohen Balbo (a Jewish scholar and poet from Crete), documented the fall of Constantinople, the enslavement and deportation of the Jews, and the cruelty of the Ottomans.[18]

Jews from Edirne, Thessaloniki, and other locales in the Ottoman Empire were brought to Constantinople by *surgun*. They were distinct from other Jewish populations, which were voluntary migrants, or *kendi gele*. The former were forbidden to leave without official permission. They regarded themselves as "ensnared in the net of captivity." Until the nineteenth century, the *surgunlu* remained distinct in ritual and tax payments from the *kendi gele*.

Mehmet's son and successor, Bayazid II (1481–1512), saw the expulsion of Jews from Spain as an incomparable opportunity. He proclaimed that Jews from Spain would be welcome in his empire. Sultan Bayazid II's offer of refuge gave new hope to the persecuted Sephardim. In 1492, the Sultan ordered the governors of the provinces of the Ottoman Empire not to refuse the Jews' entry. Bayazid II was made famous by the remark that the Catholic monarch Ferdinand was wrongly considered wise, since he impoverished Spain and enriched Turkey by the expulsion of the Jews. Thus, the Sephardic Jews were encouraged, assisted, and sometimes compelled to settle in the Ottoman lands. Constantinople was the largest and most thriving economic center of the empire, followed by Thessaloniki. The former emerged as the largest and most prosperous Jewish community of the empire.

Twenty-four years after the conquest, a census taken for the personal information of the Sultan revealed that there were 80,000 inhabitants. In the capital and neighboring Galata, there were 9,486 houses inhabited by Muslims; 3,743 houses inhabited by Greeks; 1,647 houses inhabited by Jews (11 percent of the total); 434 houses inhabited by Armenians; 332 houses in Galata inhabited by Franks; and 31 houses inhabited by gypsies. Half a century later, 8,070 Jewish houses were listed in the city.[19] Soon afterwards 36,000 Jews left Sicily, many of whom settled in the Balkans.[20]

An increasing number of European Jews continued to settle within the boundaries of the Ottoman Empire. In 1537, the Jews expelled from Apulia (Italy) migrated eastward. In 1542, those expelled from Bohemia by King Ferdinand found a safe haven in the Ottoman Empire. In March of 1556, Sultan Suleiman "the Magnificent" wrote a letter to Pope Paul IV asking for the immediate release of the Ancona Marranos, whom he declared to be Ottoman citizens. The Pope had no choice but to release them. The Ottoman Empire became the "superpower" of those days.

The immigration of the Sephardic Jews was welcomed by the Ottomans because of the economic stimulation it brought. In "the refuge of the world," there were no restrictions on freedom of trade and few limits on the construction of synagogues. The sultans consistently protected Jews from Christian attacks and never gave the slightest credence to blood libels. Constantinople and many other urban settings in the Ottoman Empire, were distinct from those in Europe because the words "pogrom," "ghetto," and "inquisition" had no meaning. The multilingual Spanish Jews soon flourished as perfumers, blacksmiths, carpenters, technicians, gold workers, gunsmiths, mapmakers, creators of navigational instruments, and, in exceptional cases, tax farmers, bankers, and doctors. Jews came to occupy administrative posts and play important roles in intellectual and commercial life throughout the empire.

From the late fifteenth century onward, the centers of Jewish life in Constantinople were the districts of Balat and Haskoy, on either side of the Golden Horn. Jewish settlements in these neighborhoods dated to before the conquest. All Jewish immigrants in Constantinople and other Ottoman cities established communities in proximity to their synagogue, which they named after their city of origin. Among the Sephardic congregations established were the Gerush (expulsion) and Cordova. The *surgun kehillot* came from locations in the Balkans and Anatolia, and took the names of these places, such as Istanbul, Bursa, and Sinope.

The synagogue dominated Jewish life. There, the customs and rituals of the locality from which the congregants came were maintained, local schools and benevolent societies were run, and the payment of taxes to the government was arranged. Rabbis acted as judges in the Jewish courts, which enjoyed remarkable independence and had the power to legislate for Jews.

In 1493, the first Hebrew printing press was established in Constantinople by two Jewish brothers exiled from Spain—Samuel and David ibn Nahmias. Their first book was published in 1497.[21] Other Jewish presses soon followed in various cities, notably Thessaloniki. This was one of the most significant innovations that Jews brought to the Ottoman Empire. The Muslim ban on printing in Arabic and Turkish remained in effect until the eighteenth century and kept this new technology from spreading to the Muslim population earlier.

Ottoman diplomacy was often carried out by Jews. Joseph Nasi, the Duke of Naxos, was the former Portuguese Marrano Joao Miques.[22] Another Portuguese Marrano, Aluaro Mandes, was named Duke of Mytylene in return of his diplomatic services to the sultan. Salamon ben Nathan Eskenazi arranged the first diplomatic ties with the British Empire. Most of the court physicians were Jews, including Yakup Pasha, Joseph and

Moshe Hamon, Daniel Fonseca, and Gabriel Buenauentura. The story of Yakup Pasha was one of the most successful and outstanding Jews in Constantinople. Originally named Giacomo di Gaeta, he fled the Renaissance of Italy for the haven of the Ottoman Empire. Di Gaeta served as physician to Sultan Mehmet II, converted to Islam, and took the name Yakup Pasha. He was awarded tax exemption for himself and his descendants, whether Jewish or Muslim, because of his service and accomplishments. Yakup Pasha moved with ease between different worlds. He frequented the sultan's palace, as well as the house of the Venetian Bailo in Galata. He negotiated with the Venetian policymakers on behalf of the Sultan.[23]

Jewish women, such as Dona Gracia Mendes Nasi, known as La Seniora, and Esther Kyra, exercised considerable influence in the court. Esther Kyra was one of a phenomenon of highly placed ladies in the Ottoman court who were employed by the ladies in the palace.[24] They were known by the Greek title "kyra," "mistress" or "lady." These Jewish women crossed several boundaries in their service as they moved between the world outside the court and inside its hidden reaches, the harem. In addition, their work allowed them to move between men and women.

In the relatively free air of the Ottoman Empire, Jewish literature flourished. Joseph Caro, a native of Toledo who settled in Safed, compiled the Shulhan Arouh, the standard code of Jewish law. Shlomo haLevi Alkabetz composed the Lekhah Dodi, the hymn that welcomed the Sabbath according to both Sephardic and Ashkenazi ritual. Yaakov Culi began to write the famous Meʾam Loʾez. This commentary on the Torah included *halakhah*, midrash, and ethical guidance along with stories and parables. Rabbi Abraham ben Isaac Assa became known as the father of Judeo-Spanish literature. By the mid-nineteenth century, over 300 Judeo-Spanish newspapers were published in the Sephardic world. Judeo-Spanish drama flourished; works were translated from French for performance in the vernacular.[25]

The second largest center of Sephardic Jewry in the eastern Mediterranean was Thessaloniki. When the Spanish Jews arrived there, the city was occupied by the Ottomans, and the titular offices were held by Muslims. Manufacturing, finance, distribution, and transportation were in the hands of the Jews and Christians. The port, filled by Jewish stevedores, was closed on the Sabbath and Jewish holidays. Despite the Turkish occupation and raids from pirates, the Jews of Thessaloniki excelled in the production of silk, wool, and cotton fabrics. They built international trade and maintained close commercial ties with the families they left in other parts of Europe and North Africa. As in Constantinople, Jewish printing houses were established and associated with businesses in the capital and Amsterdam. According to the fifteenth-century poet Samuel Usque, Thessaloniki was "a metropolis of Israel, city of righteousness, loyal town, mother of the Jewish nation like Jerusalem in its time," Madre d'Israel. Stavroulakis described it as "a Jewish city in its heart" and "a Sephardic island."[26] The Ottoman census of 1470 recorded no Jews resided there; many had been forcibly removed to the capital. By 1519, there were 3,143 households and 930 tax-paying bachelors resident in Thessaloniki.[27] By 1553, there were 20,000 Jews there. By the beginning of the seventeenth century it was estimated that about 30,000 Jews lived there. In fact, Thessaloniki remained a major center of Jewish population until the early decades of the twentieth century.

The influx of Iberian Jews caused Thessaloniki to have a proportionately large Jewish presence, predominated by a Spanish-Jewish nature and the Judeo-Spanish language. Although some indigenous, Greek-speaking Byzantine Jews also lived there. At the end of the fifteenth century, Thessaloniki became a melting pot for European Jewish communities. Each new Jewish group brought to the city its own traditions and attained different levels of assimilation. As in Constantinople, the exiles established communities centered adjacent to their synagogues. Among its 30 separate Jewish communities *kehillot* were many named for the regions and cities of origin of the Sephardic Jews such as Castile, Aragon, Saragoza, and Toledo. A large number of Portuguese conversos, Jews forced to convert to Christianity during the Spanish Inquisition, also settled there. Each group spoke the language of its country of origin, but eventually, they all embraced Judeo-Spanish. Jews from eastern Europe were drawn to the city's superior yeshivot. Through the seventeenth century, Thessaloniki continued to be a center of rabbinic and Kabbalistic studies. There, the Jews developed a strong and active scholarly, intellectual, and religious life. The responsas of its rabbis were accepted as the interpretation of the law throughout the Sephardic world.

Ottoman Multiculturalism: The Millet *System*

Ottoman policy toward minorities was based on Islamic law, which recognized both Jews and Christians as a separate nation, or *millet,* with religious and legal autonomy within their own communities. One of the most noteworthy attributes of Ottoman Muslim rule was toleration of different religious beliefs. The Turks of the Ottoman Empire were Muslims, but they did not force their religion on others. Christians and Jews in the empire prayed in their own churches or synagogues, taught their religion in their own schools and seminaries, and went about their business, sometimes amassing great fortunes. Each religious or national community was responsible for its own courts, schools, and welfare system. Separate *millets* even built roads, water fountains, and communal buildings for their neighborhoods. Certain rules evolved to create order in the relations between Muslim and non-Muslim. Muslims were not allowed to convert to other religions, nor could non-Muslims attempt to convert Muslims. In various places, non-Muslims were restricted in certain ways.

Constantinople's multicultural character was evident in the names and the dress of its inhabitants. Whatever their religion, people living in the capital generally wore simple robes or tunics. Until the nineteenth century, in order both to demonstrate Muslim superiority and to foster national rivalries, the Ottoman government enforced distinctions of dress between the different communities. In addition, non-Muslims were repeatedly forbidden to live near mosques, to build tall houses, or to buy slaves.

The toleration of other religions or national groups was in the interest of the Ottoman Muslims. The Ottomans took over a vast area where the population was primarily Christian, especially in the Balkans. Religion was the most important element of personal identification to these people. By allowing Christians and Jews to practice their religions, the Ottoman Muslims defended themselves against revolt.

Ottoman religious toleration was not perfect, however. The Ottoman Empire was definitely a Muslim state and gave preference to Muslims in many parts of government. Only in the last decades of the empire were non-Muslims allowed to gain and hold high office. Muslims always had greater rights and responsibilities than non-Muslims did. Official toleration did not mean that prejudices disappeared among Ottoman Muslims, Jews, or Christians.

Multicultural Character of Ottoman Jewry

Diversity was equally evident among the Jews in the Ottoman Empire. Byzantine or Romaniote Jews who traced their origins to classical times prospered as craftspeople and merchants in many of the urban areas incorporated by the Ottomans. Like other minority groups, they were permitted to retain their autonomy while paying taxes to the Sultan. In the late fifteenth century, these Greek-speaking Jews were literally submerged by enormous numbers of Jewish exiles seeking refuge from the Inquisition. The latter brought with them a distinct Spanish-Jewish culture. Due to their overwhelming numbers, reverse assimilation took place in most parts of the empire, and this culture dominated the Greek-influenced Byzantine culture. Periodically, immigrants from Ashkenazi traditions also established small communities in the Ottoman urban centers. Among the other components of Ottoman Jewish diversity were two other communities, the Karaites and the Donme, or Ma'min.[28]

Early in the Ottoman period, the Karaites were recognized as an independent group. During the ninth century, a number of sects within Judaism arose that denied the existence of oral Torah. They came to be known as Karaites (literally, "People of the Scripture"), and were distinguished from the Rabbanites or Rabbinical Judaism. The Karaites believed in strict interpretation of the literal text of the Scripture, without rabbinical interpretation. They believed that rabbinical law was not part of an oral tradition that had been handed down from G-d, nor was it inspired by G-d, but was an original work of the sages. They found rabbinical teachings to be subject to the flaws of any document written by mere mortals. The most common difference between Rabbanites and Karaites was the approach to the Sabbath. The Karaites also followed a slightly different calendar than the Rabbanites. According to the Karaites, their movement at one time attracted as much as 40 percent of the Jewish people.

A significant event in the life of seventeenth-century Ottoman Jews was the schism led by Shabbetai Zvi, the pseudo-Messiah. Shabbetai Zvi was born in Izmir, on the coast of Anatolia in 1626. It was a typical Ottoman city with mixed populations including Greek Christians, Spanish Jews, and Muslim Turks, as well as others. Zvi showed early promise as a Talmudic scholar, and even more as a student and devotee of Kabbalah. He was also known for strange mystical speculations and religious ecstasies. He traveled widely. His strong personality and his alternately ascetic and self-indulgent behavior attracted and repelled both the rabbis and the populace.

First reports about Shabbetai Zvi reached Europe from the Ottoman communities early in October 1665. In such cosmopolitan European cities as Venice, Livorno, and Amsterdam the leading rabbis and sophisticated men of affairs were caught up in the messianic frenzy. From many places, delegations left bearing written statements signed by the leaders of the community that acknowledged Zvi as the Messiah and king of Israel.

Zvi was expelled from Thessaloniki by its rabbis for staging a wedding service with himself as bridegroom and the Torah as bride. His erratic behavior continued. For long periods, he was a respected student and teacher of Kabbalah; at other times, he was given to messianic fantasies and unusual acts. The basic cohesion of the Ottoman Jewish community was challenged by Shabbetai Zvi. Thus, he was condemned by rabbinical authorities. Levy considers the affairs of Zvi and his followers as a "watershed in the history of Ottoman Jewry" (87) because of the major destructive impact made on the Jewish community there.

On September 15, 1666, Shabbetai Zvi was brought before the sultan. Because of the turmoil his messianic claims stimulated, he was faced with the choice of conversion to Islam or death. Prudently, he chose the former, setting a turban on his head to signify his conversion to Islam. With that choice, he was rewarded with the honorary title "Keeper of the Palace Gates" and took the name Mehmet Aziz Effendi. He was granted a pension of 150 piasters a day. This turn-about shocked the Jewish world. Leaders and followers alike refused to believe it. Many continued to anticipate a second coming, and faith in false Messiahs continued through the eighteenth century. The vast majority of believers were disillusioned and disgusted by Zvi and set about to erase all evidence, even mention, of the pseudo-Messiah. Pages were removed from communal registers, and documents were destroyed.

However, many of his adherents followed in his footsteps and also converted to Islam. Shabbetai Zvi attracted some 200 Jewish families to Islam. At his death, nearly 300 more families converted. They came to be known as Donme, or "converted" or "turncoats." Among themselves, the converted former followers of the pseudo-Messiah were referred to as Maʾmin, "faithful." In both Thessaloniki and Constantinople these people maintained their historical identity. They considered themselves neither Turkish nor Jewish. Endogamy was one of their customs. Donme did not intermarry with Muslims who were not from a Donme heritage. They were characterized by the Jewish-based mysticism they have perpetuated.

The Donme community flourished, especially in Thessaloniki, with a population of some 25,000. A very strong association between Shabbetai Zvi and Thessaloniki had a major effect on the community identity. He announced his mission there even though he eventually renounced it by converting to Islam. Another tie to Thessaloniki was the presence of the synagogue where he announced himself as the Messiah. Other Donme communities continued in his home, Izmir, and to a lesser degree in Constantinople.

Decline of the Ottoman Empire

During Suleiman the Magnificent's long reign, the Ottoman Empire was at the height of its political power and close to its maximum geographical extent. Although the Sephardim left all their valuables behind when they were compelled to flee from Spain, they brought with them their rich cultural heritage, which dated from the Andalusian Golden Age. The Golden Era of Ottoman Jewry spanned the sixteenth and seventeenth centuries. Jews took part in the economic and political life of the empire, especially in the sixteenth century. The seeds of decline, however, were already planted. The eighteenth and nineteenth centuries were marked by commercial, spiritual, and scholarly decline throughout the crumbling empire.

Few sultans after Suleiman had the ability to exercise real power when the need arose. This weakness at home was countered by a growing power in the west. The age of nationalism in Europe was emerging from the shroud of the Middle Ages as nascent nation states started taking shape under strong monarchies. Armies and navies powerful enough to attack the decaying Ottoman military, were being built by European rivals. The Ottomans began losing territory from their vast empire. In 1683, a final futile attempt to overrun Vienna failed. Russia and Austria fought the empire by direct military attack and by fomenting revolts by non-Muslim subjects of the sultan.

Reform efforts undertaken by seventeenth-century sultans did little to deter the onset of decay. Economic crises coupled with military failures and administrative misrule affected the empire as well as the cultural and economic expansion of the Jewish community. The expansion of direct trade with China and the collapse of the Venetian market directly affected the Jews of Thessaloniki. The growth of textile imports from European competitors drained the self-sufficiency of the community. The ensuing stagnation over the next two centuries included new taxes that were imposed on the Jews and other minority nations in the empire.

As the central government became weaker, large parts of the empire began to act independently, retaining only nominal loyalty to the sultan. Local rulers, called notables, carved for themselves permanent regions in which they ruled directly, regardless of the wishes of the sultan in Constantinople. They formed their own armies and collected their own taxes, sending only nominal contributions to the imperial treasury.

The Greek War of Independence brought disaster to the Jewish communities in the Peloponnesus, where the revolution erupted in 1821. The Jews, because of their close association with the Ottoman administration, were disfavored by the Christian Orthodox Greeks. Thousands of Jews in Greece were massacred alongside the Ottoman Turks. The ancient Jewish communities of Mistras, Tripolis, and Kalamata were decimated.[29] The few survivors moved north to settle in Chalkis and Volos, which were still under Ottoman rule. The ancient Jewish community of Patras, on the Gulf of Corinth, was destroyed.

Jewish nationalism was an emerging concern of the Jews in the Ottoman Balkans. Two Balkan Zionist rabbis—Judah Bibas and Judah Alkalai—were influential. Bibas was the rabbi of Corfu. Through Corfu, Western ideas reached Greece and the Jews in the Balkans. In 1839, Bibas met Rabbi Alkalai of Zemun. In his writings, Alkalai reinterpreted the religious concept of *teshuvah*, "repentance," from its root *shivah*, "return," and argued for a physical return to Eretz Israel by individual Jews. He valued a Jewish presence in Palestine primarily as spiritual. By 1840, the notion of a Jewish return to the Eretz Israel became a part of Balkan Jewish consciousness.

The early nineteenth-century sultan Mahmud II was committed to reform and valued the multicultural nature of his empire. In 1830, he declared that there was no distinction between the Muslims, Christians, and Jews aside from their faith. His sentiments were perpetuated by his son, Sultan Abdulmecid. Abdulmecid carried out further reforms, especially in education and law. Under Ottoman tradition, each non-Muslim community was responsible for its own institutions, including schools. Abraham de Camondo established a modern Jewish school in Constantinople, "La Escola." This innovation caused a serious conflict between conservative and secular rabbis, which was only settled by the intervention of Sultan Abdulaziz in 1864. The same year, the Takkanot haKehillah, the by-laws of the Jewish community, were published, defining the structure of the Jewish community of Constantinople. Despite these and other attempts at reform, by mid-century it was evident that the Ottoman efforts were hopeless.

Jewish trade, particularly in Thessaloniki experienced a brief renaissance. The establishment of rail connections allowed for the development of close contact with western Europe.[30] More than half of the city's population was Jewish, about 80,000 people. One-third of the population was Greek, and the balance was made up of Turks, Bulgars, and other nationalities. The Jewish population was varied and included both Karaites and Donme, followers of the seventeenth-century pseudo-Messiah Shabbetai Zvi. The language of government and law was Osmanli, or Ottoman Turkish, but general commercial life of the city was conducted in Judeo-Spanish. Thirty-eight of 56 of the largest trading houses, including banks, were dominated by Jews.[31] They were not only traders and bankers, but also filled all parts of the economic structure, from laborers to officials and industrialists.

By 1900, the Jewish community of Thessaloniki supported more than 50 synagogues, 20 Jewish schools, and numerous Jewish institutions and associations.[32] It continued to be a center of Torah learning for all of Europe. With modernization, most of the upper strata of the Jewish community was drawn into a movement of secularization. Among the many aspects of western culture they adopted, was the French language and modern education. The French schools transformed the Jews of the Ottoman Empire into citizens of the modern world, starting them on the road of assimilating into Western culture, almost at the expense of losing their centuries-old Spanish Jewish culture.

A series of events in the early decades of the twentieth century laid the ground for irreparable change to the Jewish community. The Balkan Wars of 1912–13 brought about territorial shifts. Thessaloniki became part of Greece in 1913, leading to the emergence of fears that the economic territory the Jewish merchants had exploited would shrink as national borders transected the former empire. Even prior to the Balkan Wars, Greece attempted to regain the southern Balkan territories historically associated with Greek history and language. Jews and other ethnic groups were subjected to planned "Hellenization," a movement to force them into accepting Greek customs and language. The Greek-speaking Romaniote Jews of southern and northwestern Greece had long been Hellenized to a large extent. Hellenization was mostly problematic for the Judeo-Spanish–speaking Sephardim who only came under Greek rule after the Balkan Wars of 1912–13, for example in the northeastern provinces of Thrace and Macedonia. The Hellenization movement sought to absorb Thessaloniki, the former medieval and Ottoman city, into contemporary Greek life. Fears of this policy, however, were quelled when a pro-Jewish policy was adapted by the new state.

A massive fire on September 18, 1917, destroyed most of the center of

Thessaloniki and with it the core of Jewish life, allowing for extensive modern building in the center of the city, where the ancient cemetery was also located.[33] In 1922, the young Greek nation attempted to carry out an ill-conceived plan to reconquer all of Anatolia that, in ancient times, had fallen under the rule of Alexander the Great. They did not expect to be so thoroughly defeated and routed by the Turkish army. Both Christians and Jews were victims to the wrath of the Turks at that debacle.

Greek refugees from Asia Minor were taken from the towns and villages they had lived in for centuries, and they flooded Thessaloniki and areas of Athens. Muslim inhabitants of Ottoman Greece were removed from their homes and resettled in the new Turkish nation. The subsequent Jewish emigration to Athens, Paris, South Africa, the United States, and Palestine put a considerable dent in the Jewish population of Thessaloniki.

At the time of the population transfer, the Donme were among the Muslims who made new homes in the new Turkish nation. The Donme claimed Spanish and Jewish origins as a means to remain in Thessaloniki. On halakhic grounds, the rabbis denied the applicability of this claim because of their connection to Islam. Thus, they were removed to Constantinople with the other Turkish Muslims. The movement to Hellenize the new populations and others strengthened. Several factors within this movement disrupted the Spanish Jewish culture in northern Greece. By 1939, there were approximately 56,000 Jews left in Thessaloniki.

The Nazis destroyed the population of Thessaloniki—almost totally wiping it out.[34] Synagogues were destroyed and properties lost. Suffice it to say that after the massive deportations and despite the assistance of some Greek Christians and the underground in hiding Jews, only about 1,950 Jews from Thessaloniki survived to return to their homes.

Hispanic Culture

Up to the thirteenth century, the Jews of Spain spoke Arabic. With the ascendancy of the Christian Spaniards, Judeo-Spanish (also known as Ladino and Judezmo) developed as their vernacular. Judeo-Spanish served to distinguish Jews from other residents of the eastern Mediterranean. As the language evolved in communities outside of Spain, the archaic fifteenth-century Castilian was soon considered specifically Jewish. The Spanish of the time of Cervantes was characterized by heavy additions of Turkish, Arabic, and Greek. In general, the Spanish Jews integrated into existing Jewish communities and adopted their language after a certain time.[35] However, in the north of Morocco and in the Ottoman Empire, they retained their Spanish language and imposed it on the resident Jews. Even non-Jewish communities used the language in trade relations.

The variety of forms of traditional literature expressed in Judeo-Spanish ranged from romantic poetry to evocative proverbs to folktales concluded with moralistic endings. The ballads, "*romansas,*" served as one genre in which the form and content of the medieval European ballads were preserved. Sephardic "*romanceros,*" ballad singers, borrowed from the popular poetry of the peoples among whom the Sephardim lived after their exile from Spain. Proverbs, "*refranes,*" formed a rich body of Judeo-Spanish folk literature that was used daily. It reflected the unique philosophy of life of Balkan Sephardic Jews.[36] The proverbs were often a phrase describing a situation or elaborating, poking fun at, or changing an idea. The function of the proverbs essentially was to teach, for example:

> Seas bienvenido mal si vienes solo.
> Bad things never come alone.

Early Sephardic synagogues in the Balkan Ottomans were influenced by *mudijar,* "Moorish," style of synagogues in Spain.[37] This holdover can be seen in the curves and archways in the synagogue interiors. When they went into exile, few Sephardim were able to carry with them the wealth of ritual Judaica they had used in Spain and Portugal. No more than a dozen pieces survived to the twentieth century.

Cuisine also preserved the Hispanic origins of the Ottoman Sephardim. Even the Donme traced some of their food traditions to customs preserved from Spain.

Conclusion

Two particular elements of worldview remained with the Sephardic exiles who reestablished themselves in the Ottoman Balkans. First, after their very reluctant departure from Spain, they retained an intense pride in and connection to their Iberian origins. Countless synagogues were established in their new homes, providing religious and communal centers for the Sephardim. In recognition of their origins, the *kehillot* were given names like Aragon, Castile, Toledo, and Magrebi, reminiscent of a time long before in a land abandoned in desperation and sadness. Second, the Ottoman Sephardim placed a strong emphasis on the purity of their descent. Family names and genealogies preserved the Spanish and Portuguese connections as well as the hierarchy in the social order in exile.

The pattern of Sephardic Jewish life arose in the multicultural setting of the Iberian Peninsula. It continued to take a unique shape as they followed a new path in the pluralistic setting of the eastern Mediterranean. The Sephardic Jews carried the experience and knowledge of successful multicultural experiences with them in exile. Music and poetry expressed this unique historical experience through the use of Iberian modes in Judeo-Spanish. This rich Iberian tradition was the essential bond between the Jewish communities in the Mediterranean basin. The system of spiritual and cultural values and institutions, which grew in Spain, was steadfastly maintained by the exiles from Spain and Portugal.

Traditional Ottoman Balkan Jewish life was defined by religion, family ties, and local communities. It was not very different from the Orthodox Christian communities in the area, but Jews experienced very different treatment from their neighbors in different parts of the region. The Jews were distinct because they were exiles who brought their language and many other aspects of Judeo-Spanish culture to the Balkans. In many places, the Sephardim, with their energy, resources, training, and vitality, quickly took a leading role in local Jewish cultural and religious life. For the Sephardim, their Spanish culture was a means of preserving their Jewish identity.

NOTES

1. Yitzhak Baer, *A History of the Jews in Christian Spain* (Philadelphia: Jewish Publication Society, 1961–66), vol. 2, 433.

2. Mair Jose Benardete, *Hispanic Culture and Character of the Sephardic Jews* (New York: Sepher-Hermon, 1982). Many discussions of the origin of the term "Sephardic" appear.

3. Steven B. Bowman, *The Jews of Byzantium, 1204–1453* (Birmingham: University of Alabama Press, 1985). See for a discussion of Byzantine Jews.

4. Ibid.

5. A. Asher, *The Itinerary of Rabbi Benjamin of Tudela*, vols. 1–2 (London-Berlin, 1840–41), 47. The writings of the itinerant Spanish Rabbi Benjamin of Tudela documents demographic information about Jews in the Eastern Mediterranean at this time.

6. Ibid.

7. Peter Charanis, "The Jews in the Byzantine Empire under the First Palaeologi," *Speculum* 22 (1945): 76.
8. Ibid.
9. See Sp. Lambros, "Chrysobull of Andronicus I Palaiologos in Behalf of the Church of Ioannina," *Neos Hellenomnemon* 12 (1915): 36–40.
10. For more on this subject, see Bowman, *The Jews of Byzantium*.
11. Avigdor Levy, *The Sephardim in the Ottoman Empire* (Princeton, NJ: Darwin, 1992). See for more information on the development of the Ottoman Empire.
12. Ibid.
13. Michael Kritovoulos, *History of Mehmed the Conqueror* (Princeton, NJ: Princeton University Press, 1954).
14. Mark Allen Epstein, *The Ottoman Communities and Their Role in the Fifteenth and Sixteenth Centuries* (Freiburg, Germany: Klaus Schwarz, 1980).
15. Joseph Nehama, *Histoire des israélites de Salonique*, vols. 1–2 (Salonika, Greece: Librairie Molho, 1935).
16. Abraham Galante, *Histoire des juifs de Turquie* (Istanbul: Isis, 1985).
17. Bernard Lewis, *The Jews of Islam* (Princeton, NJ: Princeton University Press, 1984).
18. Bowman, *The Jews of Byzantium*, 178.
19. Levy, *The Sephardim in the Ottoman Empire*.
20. Ibid.
21. Nehama, *Histoire des israélites*, chap. 12.
22. Levy, *The Sephardim in the Ottoman Empire*, 32.
23. Ibid., 30.
24. For more about the Jewish kyras see Levy, *The Sephardim in the Ottoman Empire*, 29–30.
25. See Nehama, *Histoire des israélites*, for more on the various forms of literature.
26. Nicholas Stavroulakis, *The Jews of Greece: An Essay* (Athens: Talos, 1990), 50, 51.
27. Levy, *The Sephardim in the Ottoman Empire*, 6.
28. See Stavroulakis, *The Jews of Greece*, for a brief discussion of the Donme.
29. Steven Bowman, "The Jewish Settlement in Sparta and Mistra," in *Sonder-Abdruck aus dem XXII* (Athens: Verlag der Byzantinisch-Neugriechischen Jarhbucher, 1979). See for more on this period.
30. Nehama, *Histoire des israélites*; Benardete, *Hispanic Culture and Character of the Sephardic Jews*.
31. Elias V. Messinas, *The Synagogues of Salonika and Veroia* (Athens: Gavrielides, 1997).
32. Elis Petropoulos, *Agada Shel Pesach* (Thessaloniki: Ekdosis Israelitikis Koinotitos Thessalonikis, 1970). See for more information on the synagogues in Thessaloniki.

33. Elis Petropoulos, *Salonique: L'incendie de 1917* (Salonika: Barbounakes, 1980).

34. Raul Hilberg, *The Destruction of the European Jews* (Chicago: Quadrangle, 1961).

35. Benardete, *Hispanic Culture and Character of the Sephardic Jews.*

36. Cynthia Crews, *Recherches sur le judéo-espagnol dans les pays balkaniques* (Paris: Librairie E. Droz, 1935); Max A Luria, "Judeo-Spanish Proverbs of the Monastir Dialect," *Revue Hispanique* 81 (1933): 256–71. These are two of the foremost collections of early twentieth-century Sephardic proverbs.

37. For more on the Sephardic synagogues of the Balkans see Messinas, *The Synagogues of Salonika and Veroia.*

Chapter 9

Sephardic Jurisprudence in the Recent Half-Millennium

Zvi Zohar

In 1492, an estimated 150,000 Jews chose exile over conversion to Christianity and departed from Spanish soil. Since the riots of 1391, their situation had become increasingly difficult, and, during the century leading up to the expulsion, a change in mood and orientation was in process within Spanish-Jewish culture. Part of the community gradually became less involved in Judaism; others tended toward forms of pietism and mysticism, which attached only limited significance to the study and elaboration of halakha per se. The very enterprise of Torah qua study and the application of Jewish law became less than central to the community's own self-definition.[1]

Against the backdrop of the decline of Torah in the last century of Jewish existence in Spain, a figure of great brilliance stood out—Rabbi Yitzhak Canpanton (1360–1463). Canpanton's hermeneutic was based on the insight that a close inner affinity existed between medieval semantics and Talmudic reasoning and argumentation. Thus, it was possible to achieve a synthesis of the two and formulate a rigorous methodology of Talmudic study both in perfect "fit" with the Talmudic suggiyot themselves—and completely justifiable on the basis of general semantic theory. His revolutionary approach restored to the study of Talmud a sense of intellectual novelty, profoundness, and challenge, unmatched perhaps since the heyday of Tosafist innovation in twelfth-century France. His four major disciples formed a vanguard that "conquered" the world of Sephardic Talmudic study; their own disciples were the great scholars of the sixteenth-century Sephardic dispersion—described below.[2]

Canpanton's achievements notwithstanding, major rabbis from Spain established a "Sephardic Diaspora" in the wake of the events of 1391. Algiers was in political ascendance, and it was there that such masters as Yitzhak bar Sheshet (RIBaSH, 1328–1408) and Shim'on ben Zemach Duran (1361–1444) relocated themselves and assumed positions of community leadership. Both composed lucid, analytic responsa that became mainstays of halakhic decision making. For several generations during the sixteenth century, Shim'on's descendants were the outstanding scholars of Algeria.[3] Thus, it was not in Spain, but among Sephardic émigrés and exiles in North Africa and in the countries of the eastern Mediterranean, that the heritage of Sephardic culture enjoyed a renewed efflorescence.

Sephardic Torah—Renewal in Exile

North Africa

Toward the end of the fifteenth century, émigrés from Spain settled in all Mediterranean lands that would accept them; in many of the communities they settled in, Torah was at an ebb, and the impact of the Sefaradim was enormous. An outstanding instance is that of the city of Fez in Morocco.

FEZ

In medieval times, Fez was an important center of Jewish life and creativity, boasting first-rate scholars, such as Rabbi Isaac alFasi ("of Fez," 1013–1103). But during the fifteenth century, the community experienced severe decline. Not many years after the exiles from Spain and Portugal (*megorashim*) arrived, only one synagogue retained allegiance to the customs and liturgy of the earlier local community (the *toshavim*), with close to 20 others following Spanish (i.e., Sephardic) rite. The *megorashim* brought with them from Spain the tradition of enacting halakhic ordinances (*taqqanot*) to create legally binding local norms, ordinances that in several cases effectively abrogated classic biblical and Talmudic law. The collected enactments of Fez reflected a continuous legal activism up to the middle of the eighteenth century.[4]

Torah Returns from the West to the East

Up to the year 1000, the "center of gravity" of Torah gradually shifted from the Middle East—Babylonia, Eretz Israel, and the Byzantine Empire

—to the West, with the emergence of major centers in North Africa, Spain, and Northern Europe. Five hundred years later, it shifted again, to the east. Great centers of learning were created by Sephardic masters in the major cities of the Ottoman Empire. In northeastern Europe—Poland and Lithuania—a remarkable efflorescence of "Ashkenazic" Torah took place.

SALONIKA

From the second half of the fifteenth century to the first half of the sixteenth, thousands of refugees—from Spain, Portugal, Italy, Sicily, North Africa, Germany, and France—flocked to Salonika. Increasingly relegating the indigenous ("Romaniot") community to the sidelines, they established over thirty separate congregations, each serving those of a specific country or town of origin: Kahal Lisbon, Kahal Sicilia, and so on. Each congregation followed the customs and practices of its original locale; each had its own rabbi ("marbiz Torah") and its own yeshiva. Salonika maintained a "beit midrash" for religiously inspired vocal art, and a "beit midrash" for secular subjects, where students could acquire astronomy, medicine, and the natural sciences.[5]

Most of the scholars of Salonika were disciples of the multifaceted Joseph Taitatzak (c. 1480–c. 1540). The greatest halakhist of them all was clearly Samuel (ben Moshe) di Medina (MahaRaShDaM) (1506–1589). He established and headed a great Yeshiva, supported by the munificent Donna Gracia Mendes, "Nasi," in which he educated numerous disciples in the Talmudic hermeneutic of Rabbi Yitzhak Canpanton. His independence of mind and ability to integrate legal reasoning, ethical-religious principles, and general policy considerations were evident in his numerous responsa. Another important scholar was Moses Almosnino (c. 1515–c.1580), an expert authority in halakha, polished rhetoretician, biblical commentator, ethicist, and social historian and a mystic.[6]

ISTANBUL

The communal composition of Istanbul was similar to that of Salonika; here, too, tens of discrete congregations maintained their own institutions and customs. Yet Istanbul's mosaic structure preceded that of Salonika. The most fascinating and original of Istanbul's masters was of indigenous Romaniot origin—Rabbi Eliyahu Mizrahi (c. 1450–1526). His responsa are outstanding for their logical structure, lucid argumentation, and deep analysis; his supercommentary on Rashi to the Torah was a classic of its genre. Mizrahi pursued "secular" knowledge.[7] Sephardic scholars who settled here included such luminaries as Tam Ibn Yahya (d. 1542), Elijah ben Hayyim (1530–1610), and Joseph ibn Lev.[8]

Sephardic Influence in Sixteenth-Century Poland

Perhaps the most well known Jewish scholar in Poland was Moshe Isserles (ReMAh, c. 1525–1572). Upon completing his studies in Lublin, he moved to Cracow, and established a yeshiva whose students were supported by stipends he funded. Like Eliyahu Mizrahi, and in a manner similar to the vein of Sephardic masters, ReMAh integrated a wide range of topics in his studies. He wrote on Halakha, philosophy, kabbala, biblical commentary, and astronomy. As he was not versed in Latin, his knowledge of "general" topics was derived from Hebrew sources—written by Sephardim: philosophy via Maimonides and Albo, astronomy via the fourteenth-century "Yesod Olam" composed by Yitzhak ben Yoseph Israeli of Toledo. He was in close contact with the Torah world of the contemporary Ottoman Empire; an illustration of this is his rapid response to Joseph Caro's *Shulhan ʿArukh*. Caro's work was first published in Venice in 1564–65, the ReMAh's glosses to the entire *Shulhan ʿArukh*, entitled *Mappah*, were published in the Cracow edition of the work which was printed in 1569–1572.[9]

In a sense, the Cracow edition of the *Shulhan ʿArukh* with the *Mappah* reflected an unprecedented interconnectedness of the cultural world of Torah. The great masters of the far-flung Ottoman Empire and of Italy were in intensive contact with each other—and corresponded with Ashkenazic masters of Poland and central Europe. A major reason for this was that Eretz Israel regained the function of the pivot and center of Torah for the entire Jewish world. The focal point of that center was the town of Safed, high in the mountains of Upper Galilee.

Safed

Many of the exiles from Spain, and their immediate descendants, perceived their fate as an event of cosmic import. They were convinced that the expulsion of Spanish and Portuguese Jewry was not just another act of Christian cruelty, but rather, a harbinger of the Messianic age.[10]

THE REESTABLISHMENT OF SEMIKHA

In Tannaitic times, the designation of a scholar as a fully competent master of Torah was performed by the symbolic act of "Semikha" ("ordination"). Only one who possessed Semikha could so invest another. As Semikha could be performed only in Eretz Israel, the emergence of Babylonia as a center of Torah in the first centuries of the Common Era created a situation in which leading masters lacked Semikha. Formally, Amoraim (Talmudic masters) of Eretz Israel—who continued to posses Semikha—enjoyed certain prerogatives that their Babylonian counterparts lacked; the former also continued to be entitled "Rabbi," while the latter had the title "Rav."

Throughout the Gaonic period (seventh to eleventh centuries CE), scholars of Eretz Israel continued to extend the chain of Semikha from generation to generation, yet the chain was eventually broken, and the last ordained master ("musmakh") died without ordaining another. For the sixteenth-century rabbis expecting the immanent advent of the Messiah, Semikha seemed an overwhelming necessity, for two reasons:

a) Only masters invested with Semikha served as members of the Sanhedrin (high court). Since restoration of the Sanhedrin was believed to be an event that had to occur before the coming of the Messiah, lack of Semikha might constrain the flow of history toward its ultimate culmination.
b) It was expected that the Messianic age would include the Day of Judgment; many became greatly concerned over their soul's expected standing in divine estimation. While repentance could ameliorate God's negative judgment, this might not include cardinal sins mandating the extreme sanction of Karet ("extinction of the soul"). Yet the Mishnah had already cited a recipe for escaping Karet: if a sinner worthy of Karet were to receive "Malkot" (lashes) from a duly constituted court, heaven would no longer regard him as liable for Karet. However, only masters invested with Semikha ("Musmakhim") could constitute courts authorized to administer bona fide ritual punishments of "Malkot." Therefore, a court of Musmakhim was urgently needed by those who wished to enjoy the wonders of Messianic times unthreatened by the terrible fate of Karet.

The crucial necessity of Semikha was thus apparent. In his *Mishne Torah*, Rabbi Moshe ben Maimon (1135–1204), Maimonides, offered a solution as to how Semikha could be attained. He wrote, that if all the significant scholars of Eretz Israel agreed to designate one master as worthy of Semikha, that person would acquire the status of musmakh. Once ordained, he could then invest others with Semikha—and the chain of Torah transmission would be renewed.[11]

In the great yeshiva he established and headed in Safed, Yaʾakov Beirav (1474–1546) advocated the implementation of Maimonides' procedure.[12] Gradually, the masters of Safed designated him musmakh. However, controversy erupted when the scholars of Jerusalem felt slighted by the Galileans' unilateral move, which seemed to intimate that the Torah community of Eretz Israel (whose consensus was required for renewal of Semikha by Maimonides' method) was coextensive with the Yeshiva of Safed. They debated, and ultimately rejected the validity of Beirav's project and his nomination as musmakh. When Rabbi Beirav was forced by the Turkish authorities to move to Damascus, the entire project foundered.[13]

Shulhan ᶜArukh: *The Reestablishment of "One Torah"*

The scholarly justification of Rabbi Joseph Caro's *Shulhan ᶜArukh* (literally, "A Set Table") rested on Caro's magnum opus *Beit Yoseph*.[14] In that work, Caro (known to later Sephardic scholars as "Maran" ["our master"]) traced every halakhic topic from its talmudic roots down to his time. The *Shulhan* was much briefer. Here, he "only" sets forth the functional "bottom line" on each topic: what, exactly, is the correct praxis for a contemporary Jew? Rabbi Caro's stated goal was to eliminate the confusing multiplicity of halakhic rulings that had evolved, and to establish a standard, uniform set of norms: "Having cited all opinions and sources, it seemed appropriate to me to determine the correct halakha and to decide between the various options; for that is the goal—that we should all have one Torah and one Rule."[15]

The condition of all Israel having "One Torah" existed, traditionally, only in the heyday of the Sanhedrin;[16] Caro hinted that he sought to recreate a halakhic situation similar (in unity of Torah praxis) to that which existed in Sanhedric times. His agenda bore a significant similarity to that of Beirav. Caro's language also pointed to his far-reaching aspirations: "I am assured by Divine Grace that through the vehicle of this book the Earth will be filled with knowledge of God."[17]

This was a clear reference to Isaiah 11:9, where the eschatological reality was described as one in which "the Earth will be filled with knowledge of God, as the sea is full with water." In the twelfth century, Maimonides sought to establish his legal magnum opus, *Mishne Torah*, as the one standard halakhic code. He was criticized for omitting source references and for failing to justify his rulings.[18] Joseph Caro learned well the lesson of *Mishne Torah*'s failure: his source references were the entire *Beit Yoseph*. Above citing all his sources, Caro avoided the need for analytic justification of specific rulings:

> I realized, that if I were to attempt to decide between the positions of previous authorities by employing logical arguments based on Talmudic texts—why, the Tosafot, and the Ramban in his novellae, and the Rashba, and the RaN[19]—are all full of arguments and proof-texts for each of the competing positions. Who would be so bold as to adduce more arguments and texts, and who would deign to stick his head between such great mountains and to decide by analysis and argument who is right and who is wrong?! . . . In addition, even if such a course could be followed, it would be folly to embark upon it, for it would require a tremendous length of time.[20]

Rabbi Caro then explained how halakha was determined:

> As all the House of Israel rests (halakhically) on three pillars—the RIF, the Rambam and the Rosh[21]—I concluded that whenever two of them agree on a point of halakha, halakha should be ruled in accordance.[22]

In other words, the consensus of halakhic scholars in regarding those three great codifiers as paramount authorities enables, ipso facto, an identification of the valid practical norm without requiring cognitive justification of its content. This method of determining halakha was to serve Caro as Alexander's sword, cutting through the Gordian knot of halakhic argumentation that, by its very subtlety and complexity, threatened to thwart halakha's primary goal of providing clear normative guidelines for living Jews. It must be stressed, that this method was completely novel, introduced ex nihilo by Caro. Nevertheless, its spiritual roots grew from conceptual premises closely akin to those which led Rabbi Beirav to reconstitute Semikha (with Caro's participation). The premises were the following:

1) The belief that univocal halakhic leadership was a pressing necessity for their time, which contributed to the creation of Messianic reality.
2) The strategic employment of "rabbinic consensus" to outflank the major procedural obstacle to such univocality.

Rabbi Joseph Caro's project of the *Shulhan ᶜArukh* may be seen as an attempt to realize a central strategic goal of the 1538 abortive renewal of Semikha, taking into account the lesson of its collapse: Caro's move was to substitute an irrefutable claim of accumulated historical consensus (for RIF, Rambam, Rosh)[23] for Beirav's claim of current, live consensus (for himself as musmakh). While overtly less daring than renewal of the Sanhedrin, the goals of the *Shulhan ᶜArukh* were, nevertheless, to create a halakhic condition functionally similar to that which would prevail in Messianic times: "One Torah" for all Israel and an "Earth filled with knowledge of God."

Reception of the Shulhan

While the Messiah did not arrive in sixteenth-century Safed, Rabbi Joseph Caro's hopes for the *Shulhan ᶜArukh* were not completely in vain. It attained an almost sacrosanct status in halakhic discourse. In the lands of the Ottoman Empire, the *Shulhan*'s dominance was achieved quite rapidly. By the end of the sixteenth century, Rabbi Eliahu bar Haim (Turkey, c. 1530–c. 1610) declared unequivocally: "He [Joseph Caro] has been accepted by us here as our Master, and we have committed ourselves to follow his rulings."[24] An oral tradition related that two hundred contemporary rabbis convened and voted to accept Caro's innovative procedure of determining halakha by following the majority of Rif, Rambam, and Rosh. While that convention may well be a myth, the myth itself reflected a widespread attitude regarding the *Shulhan*'s validity.[25] In the Torah centers of eastern and central Europe, a high status was not easily obtained by the *Shulhan*.[26] Nevertheless, by the seventeenth century, the *Shulhan* became the authoritative work of halakha.[27]

The Shulhan ᶜArukh *as Supreme Authority—Myth and Fact*

The widespread reception of the *Shulhan* resulted in increased uniformity. This implied a dual assault: on the independence of local rabbinic authorities and on the particularity of local communities. In what may be seen as a reaction to these threats, communities asserted their uniqueness and independence by stressing local customs and mores, an area considered independent of the *Shulhan*'s rule. As put by Rabbi Joseph Molkho (Salonika, eighteenth century): "We are obligated to his [i.e., Caro's] decisions only in matters in which no specific practice or custom previously obtained. But as for matters in which long accepted norms were practiced . . . custom continues to prevail, despite the spread of his rulings."²⁸

When adopted as basic policy by rabbis, such an attitude can lead to what may be termed halakhic insularity: almost any praxis claimed to be locally normative is ipso facto rendered impervious to material deliberation or critique (especially by nonlocal masters). Concomitantly, halakhic works by masters of other communities can be regarded as of purely academic interest, since only "local" authorities are ultimately binding. Such virtual "islands" of halakha must, of course, be understood as an "ideal type" never fully realized. Yet, the centrifugal force of this position may well account for much of the halakhic differentiation that continued to characterize Sephardic jurisprudence after the sixteenth century, despite the canonization of the *Shulhan ᶜArukh*, improved communication, and the diffusion of printing. It was only in the second half of the twentieth century that a centripetal counterforce emerged, in the form of Rabbi Ovadia Joseph's major campaign to instate the hegemony of Rabbi Caro throughout all Jewish ethnic groups.

An analogous vector on the level of individual halakhic insularity became increasingly popular in Sephardic communities during the sixteenth and seventeenth centuries: the legal tactic of *kim li*, literally: "I hold according to . . ." The arena of such a claim was a court, in which, for example, Mr. X is suing Mr. Y for money that Y purportedly owes him. It becomes clear that the case is going in favor of Mr. X, as the weight of halakhic opinion supports him: almost all rabbinic authorities who wrote on this topic agree that Mr. Y is in the wrong. At this point, Mr. Y (perhaps on the advice of his learned attorney) announces that it just so happens that he holds with the one or two minority views, according to whom he need not pay a cent to Mr. X. Sephardic jurisprudents in the late sixteenth and the seventeenth centuries hotly debated the validity of such a claim. While some strongly rejected it, many others agreed that since it was impossible to know for certain which position was correct in the eyes of God, any court taking money from Y and handing it over to X might, in fact, be robbing Y of money that was really his. Therefore, the halakhic maxim to be followed in such cases was: when in doubt, desist. Even rabbis who in all other matters regarded the *Shulhan* as decisive might refrain from ruling according to the *Shulhan* against Y, if Y adduced some obscure rabbi whose position buttressed Y's case and Y said "*kim li* according to that rabbi."²⁹

Sephardic Halakha in the Seventeenth Century

The major culture-area of Sephardic Torah during the seventeenth century flourished in the lands of the eastern Mediterranean; focal communities were Istanbul and Izmir in Asia Minor, Salonika in Greece, Jerusalem in Eretz Israel, and Cairo in Egypt. Joseph Trani was born and educated in Safed but lived in Istanbul, where the yeshiva he headed became the major center of study for Turkish Jewry. He wrote responsa and derashot entitled *Tzafenat Paʾaneah*, commentaries to the Talmud, and a work on the design of the Temple.³⁰ Trani's disciple, Hayyim Benveniste, composed a massive critical anthology of halakhic literature relating to all sections of both the Turim and the *Shulhan ʿArukh*. This eight-volume work, entitled *Kneset HaGedolah* ("The Great Assembly") was regarded by halakhists as an authoritative and invaluable reference work. He also authored an important collection of responsa, entitled *Ba'ei Hayyei*.³¹ In Salonika, Hayyim Shabbetai was a leading halakhic authority, head of a yeshiva, and chief rabbi. He composed responsa *Torat Hayyim* in three volumes, Talmudic commentaries, and monographs on specific legal topics.³²

In Eretz Israel, Israel Yaʾakov Hagiz headed a yeshiva in Jerusalem. He continued the Sephardic traditions of combining Torah study with secular learning and delved into medicine, philosophy, astronomy and grammar. His writings included the responsa *Halakhot Ketanot*, *Tehillat Hokhma*, and *Etz HaHayyim*, and others. His disciple Moshe Habib (1654–1696) devoted special attention to issues relating to the legal termination of marriages in his works *Get Pashut* and *Ezrat Nashim*. He also wrote Talmudic commentaries *Shamot baAretz* and *Pnei Moshe*. During this century, Cairo was home to Mordekhai HaLevi (d. 1685), author of the responsa *Darkei Noam*, and his son Avraham HaLevi (1650–17??), author of *Ginat Veradim*.³³

Italy continued to maintain its own distinctive style in halakha. Its masters combined Torah and worldly studies and concerns with originality and flair. While not a native, Moshe Zacuto (1620–1697) was a representative example of Italian masters. He composed a collection of responsa, as well as commentaries on the Mishna and on the Talmud of Eretz Israel.

Yet his main fame and influence were in the field of Kabbala. Italian Jewry's openness to "general" culture was reflected in the fact that his poem "Tofteh Arukh," depicting a soul's experiences in hell, was inspired by Dante's *Divine Comedy*. He also pioneered as a dramatist, composing Yesod Olam, the first biblical drama in Hebrew.[34]

While all of the above-mentioned scholars related in their halakhic works to the *Shulhan ʿArukh*, another strand united them. While nonhalakhic, its implications for the realm of halakha were subsequently great—the meteoric appearance—and drastic eclipse—of Shabbetai Zvi, the false Messiah who ignited tremendous enthusiasm in all the far-flung lands of the Diaspora—and whose subsequent conversion to Islam resulted in bitter disillusionment for most Jews, and to the formation of secret sects by others. While personally opposed to Shabbetai, Haim Benveniste equivocated when his peer Aaron Lapapa was deposed in Smyrna for opposing the "Messiah," and Benveniste later failed to support Lapapa's reinstatement. Benveniste's policy reflected the fragility of a halakhist's status vis-à-vis popular sentiment. Zacuto first supported Shabbetai Zvi, but after the latter's conversion, firmly opposed the Sabbatean sect. The spirit of the times was reflected, however, in the fact that two of Zacuto's leading disciples failed to follow him back to "mainstream" Judaism, remaining believers of the apostate Messiah.[35]

Most Jews remained loyal to halakhic praxis. Yet, in the opinion of several scholars, one significant cause—and result—of the rise and fall of Shabbetai Zvi, was the growing importance of nonhalakhic modes of thought and expression in the Jewish world.

Sephardic Halakha in the Eighteenth Century

Halakhic creativity during this century was widespread. Italy continued to be an independent halakhic community. Rabbi Isaac Lampronti pioneered the massive halakhic encyclopedia *Pahad Yitzhak*, in two series consisting of 155 volumes, most still in manuscript. He also edited what may be considered the first periodical for rabbinic and halakhic writing. Another outstanding Italian scholar was Rabbi David Pardo, whose commentaries on the Tosefta (*Hasdei David*) and on the Sifrei (*Sifrei deVei Rav*) were considered by many to be the best on these classic texts. He also composed responsa, a commentary on the Mishna, liturgical poems, and other scholarly works. Rabbi Ishmael haCohen of Modena was perhaps the last great

Italian halakhist, author of the three-volume responsa *Zera Emet* and advocate of integrating advanced Torah achievements with the learning of secular studies.[36]

In the Balkans and Turkey, leading masters of the eighteenth century included the Salonikan scholars Solomon Amarillo and his sons Aharon and Hayyim; Ephraim Navon in Istanbul; Moshe Israel and his son Eliyahu in Rhodes; Eliakim Gatigno of Izmir; and many more.[37]

North Africa experienced a flowering of Torah during this period. In Morocco, perhaps the most outstanding was Rabbi Raphael Berdugo, whose halakhic works included responsa, a commentary to the *Shulhan ᶜArukh*, and Talmudic novellae. Of special interest were his methodological and theoretical positions regarding the study and interpretation of classic rabbinic texts, positions that have been analyzed as prefiguring, in certain senses, those of modern scholars.[38] Another prominent halakhist in Morocco was Yaᵓakov ibn Tsur, whose responsa *Mishpat Utsedaka bᵓYaᵓakov* were analytical and original.[39] A leading Algerian rabbi was Yehuda ᶜAyyash of Algiers (d. 1760) who authored *Lehem Yehuda* on Maimonides' codex *Mishne Torah*, responsa *Beit Yehuda*, *Matteh Yehuda*, and *Shevet Yehuda* on Caro's *Shulhan ᶜArukh*, and other works.

Eretz Israel's small Jewish community was home to several important rabbis, including two members of the AlGhazi family, who in turn held the post of Rishon Lezion. Israel Yaᵓakov AlGhazi (incumbent from 1745 to 1756) authored ten volumes of responsa, commentaries, halakha, and sermons. His son, Yom Tov AlGhazi, held the post from 1782 to 1802 and also published several learned works.

Two outstanding masters who represented, respectively, the Torahworlds of the Sephardic Middle East and of eastern Europe were Hayyim Joseph David Azulai (known by the acronym of HIDA, 1724–1806) and Eliyyahu of Vilna (the GRA; 1720–1797), known as "the Vilna Gaon." The HIDA was a prolific writer who composed works on a wide range of topics, including glosses to the *Shulhan ᶜArukh*, responsa, bibliography, kabbala, folk-tales, liturgy—and a personal travel diary.[40] The GRA was regarded as a virtual realization of the ideal type of a halakhic master. He attained a near-mythic status in the European yeshiva world. He wrote no responsa, all of his literary efforts were devoted to determining the correct wording and meaning of classic texts in the Bible, rabbinic literature, halakha, and kabbala. He also studied and composed treatises on general topics that he believed would facilitate these endeavors.[41]

Although these two great masters were both widely versed in the full range of halakhic literature, their attitudes to that corpus were strikingly different: The GRA held only Tannaitic and Amoraic literature to be actually binding and considered with all subsequent scholarship only an attempt at correct explication of those classic texts. Consequently, he devoted much effort to determining the precisely correct textual variants of ancient works and felt free to disagree with any authority when convinced that their ruling was Talmudically wrong. The HIDA, on the other hand, saw current praxis as depending on the incremental, organic growth and development of halakha throughout its entire history. Thus, study of post–*Shulhan ᶜArukh* halakhic masters was, to him, of greater significance than the creation of error-free Talmudic manuscripts. He devoted a significant part of his work to summing up the literary production of post-Talmudic scholars of Torah.

Both men believed that a halakhic scholar should know more than Judaic texts. Yet the GRA never left his study in the Jewish quarter of Vilna, devoting almost 22 hours a day to the perusal of works on Torah. The HIDA not only wrote, but also traveled extensively, preaching to a wide range of congregations and meeting many Jews and Gentiles throughout the Middle East and Europe. Both men were public leaders, intensively involved in the polemics of their day. Rabbi Eliyyahu was the great and implacable leader of the Mitnagdim, who fought against the spread of the new Hasidic movement founded by Israel Baʾal Shem Tov. Deeply convinced that elements of Hassidism were tantamount to heresy and to worship of idols, he refused any compromise with its adherents. His disciples were moved to revivify Torah learning in eastern Europe, one result of which was the innovation of the institutional framework of Torah-study known as the "Great Yeshiva"—the first example of which was the Yeshiva of Volozhin, founded in 1802.

The HIDA, during his residence in Livorno (Leghorn) and travels in Europe, witnessed the beginnings of the breakdown of traditional Jewish society in both central and western Europe. He condemned moves to reject traditional customs for the sake of current convenience and was involved in some early controversies against the forerunners of Reform. Yet, he realized that certain changes produced by modern developments called for bold halakhic solutions. His support of the rabbis of Trieste in instituting conditional betrothal (*Kiddushin al Tnai*) in response to changes in the general legal structure prevailing in that city were illuminating.[42]

The Nineteenth Century

The nineteenth century was a time of change in Europe as well as in the centers of Sephardic culture. While virtually all lands in the Mediterranean region and in the Middle East began this century with a vital cadre of rabbinic scholars, several communities experienced a significant waning of Torah: Italy, the Balkans, Turkey, Tunisia, and Algeria. Great scholars in these lands included Raphael Asher Covo and Abraham Gatigno, the great Hayyim Palache, and his sons, Isaac, Abraham, and Joseph, in Izmir.

While Westernization led to a decline of traditional scholarship in the modernizing city of Tunis, the island of Jerba in southern Tunisia began to develop an intensive culture of Torah study and authorship, reaching its peak in the first half of the twentieth century. The Jewish community of Baghdad, which had been in eclipse for more than half a millennium, began to develop renewed scholarship in the late eighteenth century, and in the nineteenth century was a flourishing center of halakha. Two major figures were ʿAbdallah Somekh and Joseph Hayyim.

Rabbi Somekh (1813–1889) established a center of Torah learning whose graduates were the rabbis of Iraqi Jewry until the mass ʿaliyya to Israel a hundred years later. His halakhic works included *Zivhei Zedeq,* an erudite and detailed commentary on *Shulhan ʿArukh, Yoreh Deʾah,* and responsa that reflected his position as halakhic authority not only of Iraq and Iran, but also of the far-flung Iraqi-Jewish Diaspora in India, Burma, Hong Kong, and Shanghai.[43]

Joseph Hayyim (1835–1909) was a blend of halakhist, kabbalist, and *maskil*. He authored *Ben Ish Hai,* a systematic presentation for laypersons of the norms of Jewish life that became a standard practical guide for many Sephardic-Oriental Jewish communities. He also authored several works of responsa, glossa on the *Shulhan ʿArukh,* sermons, and mysticism. An avaricious reader of contemporary Hebrew newspapers from Europe, he supported reform of the traditional education system to include religious and secular studies and modern-style learning facilities. In the introduction to his four-volume work of responsa, *Rav Peʾalim,* he presents his views on halakhic methodology. He explains that while precedent is not absolutely binding, halakhic decisions must be justified by argumentation, and the more sources a master is acquainted with, the more grounds he has for justification of his decisions. Sephardic rabbis should not limit themselves to local or to specifically Sephardic sources, but rather take into consideration all rabbinic scholarship they can become cognizant of.

Creativity and originality are the hallmark of halakhic greatness, but the more one knows, the more creative one can be within the universe of halakhic discourse.[44]

In Egypt, halakhist Israel Moshe Hazan (1808–1863) dealt in his responsa with the topic of *huqqot hagoyyim,* that is, what aspects of non-Jewish culture and religion must be rejected by Jews. He concluded that only norms that were essentially arbitrary were forbidden. Thus, any norm based on universal human traits and culture was permissible to Jews, even if it was already included by other faith communities in their religious praxis.[45] This reflected Rabbi Hazan's deep identification with the rational universal values characteristic of classic Sephardic culture in the High Middle Ages. Rabbi Hazan was opposed to contemporary reform, but also to the ultra-Orthodox reaction to modernity that he characterized as "fanaticism." He published an annotated scholarly edition of Gaonic responsa (*Iyyei haYam*) and was one of the first scholars to discover the Cairo Geniza (c. 1858).[46]

Eretz Israel continued to be an important center of Sephardic halakha in the nineteenth century. It attracted scholars, some of whom, for example, Raphael Joseph Hazzan, reached the high position of Rishon LeZion, chief rabbi of the holy city of Jerusalem. However, more salient were locally educated masters, who had come to Jerusalem with their parents at a tender age. These included Yaʾakov Moshe ʿAyyash, Hayyim Avraham Gaguin, Avraham Ashkenazi, and Raphael Meir Panigel.

Perhaps the most prominent Rishon LeZion of this period was Yaʾakov Shaʾul Elyashar, a "dayyan" ("judge") in Jerusalem from 1853 and Rishon LeZion from 1893 to his decease in 1906. Elyashar authored ten volumes of responsa, Talmudic commentaries, religious poetry, and sermons.[47] During the nineteenth century, ʿ*aliyya* to Eretz Israel increased from all Sephardic communities. Especially noteworthy was the ʿ*aliyya* from Algeria and from Morocco in which scholar Rabbi David Ben-Shimʾon of Rabat emerged. In 1854, he established an autonomous Moroccan communal framework there. He authored several works (e.g., *Shaʾar heHatser* and *Shaʾar haMatara*), focusing on the norms and customs of Eretz Israel and the religious significance of life in the Holy Land.[48] Interestingly, one of the most erudite masters of this period, Hayyim Hezqiyya Medini, was born in Jerusalem (1835), completed his magnum opus over the course of 45 years in Istanbul and in far-off Crimea, and returned only in 1899 to Eretz Israel, where he served as chief rabbi of Hebron until the end of his life (1905). He authored the great halakhic encyclopedia *Sdei Hemed.*

During the second half of the nineteenth century, issues relating to European modernization became increasingly directly relevant for Sephardic communities and rabbis. They were aware of the ultra-Orthodox reactionary policy toward modernity, but consciously adopted a position more analogous to that of the moderate *Haskalah* in Europe. For example, the great majority of Sephardic rabbis supported the creation of an integrated curriculum for local schools, integrating Torah study and general knowledge in one educational framework.[49]

The Twentieth Century

This century saw great transformations in Jewish life throughout the world, including in Sephardic and Oriental communities. Most Sephardic communities became increasingly influenced by western European culture and lifestyle and experienced a rise in their economies. This attracted talented young men, who in previous generations would naturally have aspired to Torah scholarship, to choose other, more profitable occupations. In many Sephardic communities such as Turkey, Iraq, Syria, Egypt, the Balkans, and Italy, there was a paucity of local halakhic scholarship.

Nevertheless, Egypt enjoyed first-rate rabbinic leadership by rabbis educated in Jerusalem: Rabbi Eliyyahu Hazan and Raphael Aharon Ben-Shimʾon. Together, the rabbis of Egypt initiated a bold halakhic response to a modern challenge, by formulating and executing an enactment invalidating all acts of "private betrothals."[50]

Morocco continued to be an important center of halakhic scholarship. In the series of original and bold enactments, halakhic lacunae and archaic norms considered inappropriate to contemporary realities were superceded by Jewish legal norms decided upon by the assembled scholars. This included areas of marriage, divorce, inheritance, kashrut, and so on. These enactments were not undertaken in the spirit of European reform, which sought to deny the authority of Talmudic and rabbinic halakha, but rather in the grand tradition of halakha that had always empowered rabbis to innovate rules that they deemed appropriate to the current socioreligious context.[51]

In North Africa, the Island of Jerba stood out as a beacon of halakhic creativity in the first half of the twentieth century, and tens of works were authored there by leading scholars. Rabbi Moshe Khalfon HaCohen (1874–

1949) authored the nine-part responsa work *Shoel veNishal, Brit Kehuna,* and *Beiᵓer Moshe* on the norms and customs of Jerba according to the order of the *Shulḥan ᶜArukh,* works on specific halakhic topics such as the laws of divorce, of ritual kashrut of meat, of philanthropy, and so on. He also authored works on religious ethics and thought, and was a leader and spiritual patron of the Zionist movement of Jerba.[52]

By the mid-twentieth century, the world center of Sephardic halakhic scholarship and creativity returned to where it had been four centuries before: Eretz Israel. The centrality of Eretz Israel had been growing since the latter part of the nineteenth century, as increased security under late Ottoman rule and improved international transportation made ᶜ*aliyya* an increasingly real option for (*inter alia*) Sephardic scholars and their families, of whom we can note but a few.

From Iraq came Yaᵓakov Sofer (1870–1939), author of *Kaf haHayyim* on *Shulḥan ᶜArukh Orah Hayyim*; Yitzhak Nissim (1896–1981), who was to serve as Rishon LeZion and Sephardic chief rabbi of Israel from 1955–73; and Ovadia Joseph (b. 1924), who emerged as the leading Sephardic halakhic master in the second half of the century. From Syria, a significant cohort of rabbis from Aleppo moved to Jerusalem in the 1890s and up to World War I. They and their descendents engaged both in halakha and in Kabbala and had a significant impact as faculty of the Porat Joseph Sephardic yeshiva (e.g., Ezra ᶜAtiyya, 1887–1970), as kabbalists and as halakhic authorities (e.g., Ovadiah Hadaya, 1890–1969). From Morocco came ᶜAmram Aburabi'a (1892–1966), author of *Netivei ᶜAm* on the halakhic norms of Eretz Israel; Eliyahu Iluz (1860–1929), author of *Hilkhot Ishut* and of *Maᵓaseh Eliyahu* on laws of marriage and divorce, the responsa *Yesh Me-Ayyin,* sermons, and biblical commentaries; from Algeria, Nissim Binyamin Ohanna (1882–1962), author of the responsa *Naeh Meshiv,* and translator of several Talmudic tractates from Aramaic to Hebrew.

These rabbis joined scholars born in Eretz Israel, such as Yaᵓakov Moshe Toledano (1880–1960), halakhist and researcher of rabbinic texts and chief rabbi of Tel Aviv beginning in 1942; Ben-Zion Koinca (1867–1938), gifted teacher, initiator and editor of the international rabbinic journal *HaMeᵓasef* (1896–1915), dayyan, and communal leader; and Eliyahu Pardes (1893–1972), chief rabbi of Ramat Gan and then of Jerusalem. Together, they formed a scholarly community in a paradox-bound situation: while the Jewish people renewed itself in its homeland and regained independence after more than 2,000 years, processes of secularization led to a decline in both the observance and study of Torah and in the social status of rabbinic scholars. Nevertheless, Sephardic rabbis such as those noted above made significant contributions to halakha.

A son of illustrious Sephardic rabbinic lineage, Rabbi Ben-Zion Meir Hai Uzziel (1880–1953)[53] was born and educated in the Jewish quarter of the Old City of Jerusalem. He combined serious traditional scholarship with a spirit of creativity and was appreciative of central strands of contemporary Western life. A fine example was his position with regard to the notion that basic legal and political rights follow from man's creation "in God's Image."

When Palestine was conquered by Great Britain in 1917–18, the Jewish community (Yishuv) included two major constituent elements: the "Old Yishuv," that is, Jews whose ancestors chose to live in Eretz Israel because it was the Holy Land, and the "New Yishuv" who came to Eretz Israel in order to participate in the creation of a national home for the Jewish people. Each of these subdivided again. The Ashkenazic Old Yishuv, of European lineage, mostly arrived in Palestine during the nineteenth century. The group rejected Zionism. The Sephardic Old Yishuv, of Sephardic-Oriental lineage, were traditionally religious. The New Yishuv subdivided into the "Bourgeois" New Yishuv, conservative farmers and town-dwellers. The Socialist New Yishuv included several thousand Jews who had immigrated to Palestine over the past 15 years and whose vision included the establishment of a Socialist Jewish national society in Palestine. Both sections of the New Yishuv were staunch Zionists.

Toward the end of the war, representatives of these groups began internal negotiations, with the goal of electing an assembly that would evolve into an institution that represented them vis-à-vis the local British authorities. Not surprisingly, the Old Yishuv rejected the notion of women's suffrage; surprisingly, they were supported in this matter by Rabbi Isaac haCohen Kook, whose Zionist credentials were impeccable. Those who rejected women's suffrage in the name of Jewish tradition argued that precedent supported their position—in premodern Jewish communities women never had political rights. Thus, Rabbi Dr. Ritter of Rotterdam asserted that women had been accorded no recognized status in the biblical definition of the Israelite polity: they were not regarded as Kahal nor as ʾEdah and were not counted in the biblical census nor included in Israel's genealogical lists.

So be it, responded Rabbi Ben-Zion Meir Hai Uzziel:

Let us grant that they are neither Kahal, nor Edah . . . nor anything. But are they not creatures, created in the Divine Image and endowed with intelligence? And are they not connected to matters within the competence of the proposed assembly or of the committee it shall designate, whose directives they shall be required to obey . . . ? ("Mishpetei Uzziel, Hoshen Mishpat," responsum 6; reprinted in *Piskei Uzziel bi-Shelot ha-Zeman* [Jerusalem, 1978], responsum 44).

Thus, the fact that women were "created in the Divine Image and endowed with intelligence," and that they would be expected to obey the decisions of the Yishuv's elected leadership entailed that Torah acknowledged women's inalienable right to vote. Uzziel affirmed the halakhic validity not only of the biblical notion of man's Divine Image—but also of the modern political implications derived from that notion.[54]

In the second half of the twentieth century, Sephardic halakhic creativity was concentrated almost exclusively in Israel. Scholars who were still active in Morocco in the 1950s and 1960s, such as Moshe Malka and Shalom Mesas, eventually arrived in Israel in the 1960s and 1970s, where they were elected to major posts. Joseph Mesas (1892–1974), after a long and distinguished career in Morocco and Algeria, went to Israel in 1964 and served for a decade as chief rabbi of Haifa. One of his many bold rulings was his decision that modern European changes in public mores with regard to women's apparel make it unnecessary, and in fact inappropriate, for halakha to require that married women cover their hair for reasons of modesty (cf. Joseph Metsas, *Otsar Hamikhtavim*, vol. 3, 212). In a European-Ashkenazic context, such a ruling would immediately tag a rabbi as nonorthodox. The very ability of rabbi Mesas to advocate such a position openly, and the willingness of other Sephardic rabbis to continue to accept him as part of their community of discourse, was symptomatic of a significant difference between Ashkenazic and Sephardic halakha in modern times.

The two major figures of Sephardic jurisprudence in the second half of the twentieth century were Jerusalemites: Hayyim David HaLevi (1924–1998) and Ovadia Joseph (b. 1924). Hayyim David HaLevi was born in Jerusalem and became a disciple of Rabbi Uzziel; from 1973 until his death, he served as chief rabbi of Tel Aviv. He intentionally wrote in a simple and lucid style, so that his writings would be accessible to laypersons. He wrote, among other works, many responsa (nine volumes of ʿ*Aseh Lekha*

Rav and three volumes *Mayyim Hayyim*) and an innovative five-volume handbook of applied halakha, *Meqor Hayyim HaShalem,* in which he integrated the legal and the ideational/religious/ethical aspects of the halakhic norms. He was a firm halakhic advocate of democracy as the best form of political life (at least in non-Messianic reality), of civil rights for non-Jews in a Jewish state, of recognition of Christians as monotheists, and of the importance of universal ethics and the resolution of international conflict by peaceful means. His marriage of traditionalism and rationalism together with originality, innovation, and the notion of halakha as an open-ended process was the epitome of major trends within Sephardic halakha.[55]

Ovadia Joseph was born in Baghdad but educated from an early age in Jerusalem. His virtually absolute command of all halakhic sources from the earliest to the most contemporary, combined with his total lack of qualms in enunciating unequivocal rulings, contributed to his meteoric rise to the post of Rishon LeZion. After completing his term of office in 1983, he became spiritual and political leader of a Sephardic/right-wing-Orthodox religious-political movement, Shas. His blunt political/social pronouncements tended to becloud his image as halakhic master in the eyes of some; however, his impact on the world of Sephardic halakha was overwhelming.[56]

Rabbi Ovadia's major works of halakha include nine volumes of extremely erudite responsa *Yabi'a Omer*; six volumes of the more "popular" responsa, *Yehavveh Da'at, Halikhot ʿOlam,* in which he presented and contested the halakhic rulings of the great Iraqi rabbi Joseph Hayyim; *Taharat HaBayyit* on the norms of "family purity," and *Hazon ʿOvadiah* on the norms of Passover and on the Haggada of the Seder night. In addition, his sons and disciples compiled tens of volumes of halakhic compendiums and handbooks, all presented as summaries and expositions of his decisions.

A central tenet and axis of Rabbi Ovadia Joseph's halakhic activity was the motto LeHahazir ʿAtarah le-Yoshna ("Returning the Crown to Its Ancient Glory"). Meaning, all Jews of all ethnic origins should follow one common halakhic path—that set forth by Rabbi Joseph Caro, in his *Shulhan ʿArukh.* Unity would be reached by setting aside all other halakhic traditions in favor of wholesale adaptation of the one true way, that of the local Eretz Israel Sephardic religious culture as exemplified by Joseph Caro.[57]

The tradition of halakha was a forward-looking, innovative religious phenomenon, transforming itself organically through the "built in" dynamic response of halakhic masters to changes in sociohistorical and cultural life. Thus writes Rabbi Uzziel:

> In every generation, conditions of life, changes in values, and technical and scientific discoveries create new questions and problems that require solution. We may not avert our eyes from these issues and say "Torah prohibits the New," i.e., anything not expressly mentioned by earlier sages is ipso facto forbidden. A-fortiori, we may not simply declare such matters permissible. Nor, may we let them remain vague and unclear, each person acting with regard to them as he wishes. Rather, it is our duty to search halakhic sources, and to derive, from what they explicate, responses to currently problematic issues.[58]

"Torah Prohibits the New" means no new halakhic ruling can be introduced. This dictum was, and still is, the leading motto of European Orthodoxy. Declaring matters "simply permissible" in disregard of halakha was a characterization of classical Reform Judaism. Rabbi Uzziel rejected each of these options, advocating a halakha that responded dynamically in response to "conditions of life, changes in values, and technical and scientific discoveries," continuing the path begun by earlier sources, but saying what they never were called upon to say, since the realities of their times were different from those of the present.

Rabbi Eliyyahu Hazan, writing in 1874, phrased the matter thus:

> Since the Holy Torah was given to physical human beings, who are always subject to changes stemming from differences in history and time, in rulers and decrees, in nature and climate, in states and realms—therefore, all Torah's words were given in marvelous, wise ambiguity; thus, they can receive any true interpretation at any time. . . . Indeed, the Torah of Truth, inscribed by God's finger, engraved upon the Tablets—will not change nor be renewed, forever and ever.[59]

Torah was eternal, engraved in stone upon the Tablets.[60] Its ambiguity was not a fault, but a supreme virtue, enabling it to be responsive to change in human realities, without sacrificing its authenticity. Rabbi Hayyim David HaLevi, 150 years later, responded to a criticism leveled at him by an Orthodox rabbi who said true adherence to halakha meant absolute lack of change with regard to the *Shulhan ᶜArukh*; conversely, any change was ipso facto departure from true halakha. HaLevi replied that dynamic but organic change was in fact the very lifeblood of halakha. Indeed, the eternal relevance of Torah over millennia had been

> possible only because permission was given to Israel's sages in each generation to renew halakha as appropriate to the changes of times and events. Only by virtue of this was the continuous existence of Torah in Israel possible, enabling Jews to follow the way of Torah.... There is nothing so flexible as the flexibility of Torah.... It is only by virtue of that flexibility that the People of Israel, through the many novel and useful rulings innovated by Israel's sages over the generations, could follow the path of Torah and its commandments for thousands of years.[61]

We thus see that the two greatest Sephardic rabbis of recent times, Joseph and Halevi, express two very different religious-cultural visions: reattainment of a glorious ancient mythic unity versus continuation of a multivocal organic and open-ended process.

Halakha in Our Times: An Overview

Despite the denial of communal autonomy, Emancipation, assimilation, and other changes that radically transformed the conditions of Jewish existence, halakhic activity continued during the nineteenth and twentieth centuries in a seemingly unabated manner, through an abundance of major works and by reaching an extensive geographical area.

Nevertheless, during the past two centuries, the character of halakhic creativity, and the relationship between that activity and the Jewish people and community, changed significantly. Recent trends, such as sweeping political and social changes, have catalyzed a growing decline in the status of halakha and of halakhic authority. These changes include:

1) Denial of legal recognition to corporate subsocieties in European countries—a policy subsequently followed also by governments in the Middle East and North Africa. In consequence, many areas of halakha pertaining to communal and civil matters have fallen into desuetude.
2) The growing perception of religion as a private matter that should not be subject to public determination; In consequence, conformity

with halakhic norms has become even more differentiated from conformity with social norms.
3) The "Enlightenment," one of whose effects was a growing focus on nontraditional topics and modes of study, at the expense of the beit midrash and yeshiva, even for Jews who have continued to be concerned with the religious aspects of Judaism. In consequence, persons of superior intellectual capabilities, now study a broad range of non-Judaic subjects—or study Judaic subjects in an academic mode, rather than studying the halakha.
4) The appearance of new religious ideologies of Judaism, some of which deny the importance of halakha. Many Jews have become convinced of the nonrelevance of halakha for contemporary Jewish religiosity. On the other hand, many European and North American halakhic masters have reacted with a policy of "haHadash Asur min haTorah" ("halakhic innovation is prohibited by Torah"). This policy, first explicitly formulated by Moshe Sofer, has made modern halakhists much less free than medieval masters in applying halakha to novel situations—in an era in which such novel situations have increased tremendously in variety and depth. Such Orthodox attitudes have increasingly influenced students and scholars of Sephardic ethnic extraction.[62]

All of the changes noted above relate to the devaluation or constraining of halakha within the context of basically religious orientations to Judaism. For many, a sense of Jewish peoplehood or nationality informs their consciousness; most, however, see their Jewish birth as a relatively unimportant fact. Thus, the entire enterprise of seeking "knowledge of God," whether in halakha or elsewhere, seems absent from the agenda of most contemporary Jews.

On the positive side, the numeric growth of the Jews (from 4.75 million around 1850 to 16.6 million around 1939, and over 13 million today) and their global dispersion led to a situation in which Halakhic creativity became unprecedentedly far flung. The rapid spread of the printing press enabled thousands of scholars to impart their halakhic opinions to contemporaries and to posterity. Thus, an information explosion occurred, in contrast to the medieval condition in which far fewer scholars wrote.

On the negative side, during the past 200 years, social and technological change became increasingly rapid. Thus, scholars were faced with an ever-increasing range of novel questions, whose solutions cannot be conveniently derived from any premodern code. Contemporary projects designed to enable halakhists to cope with this situation (such as the Talmudic encyclopedia) were of some help. One response to this problem took the form of intentional (or de facto) limitation of the sphere of issues acknowledged as relevant to halakhic discourse to the range of topics covered by premodern scholars. Conversely, new technological and social realities were "shut out" from the halakhic consideration of many scholars and their communities. The gamut of issues presented by the (halakhically unprecedented) reestablishment of Jewish sovereignty in Israel were examples of issues affected by this strategy, as was the whole range of questions raised by changes in the education and social position of women.

Another typical response to this reality was the crystallization of what may be called pseudosectarian halakhic islands, that is, communities or groups who saw themselves as committed only to the positions outlined in the teachings of a quite limited subset of recent halakhic authors. Thus, certain Hassidic groups regarded only their rebbe's ancestors as relevant figures in halakhic matters. This strategy simplified the problem of ruling in halakhic matters, but severely limited real discourse and cross-fertilization within the broad spectrum of contemporary halakha.

Postscript

Rabbi Caro's aspiration that through his *Shulhan ᶜArukh* the world would be filled with the knowledge of God implied, that in some significant sense, "knowledge of halakha" was (at least, to an important degree) synonymous with "knowledge of God." Yet, developments since Caro's time have rendered this premise increasingly problematic, as more and more Jews have come to regard other (or no) spheres of Jewishness as of primary religious significance, and as halakhic development and creativity have become increasingly fragmentary and sectarian. Thus, the hope for "the Earth" (at least, the Jewish world) to be filled with halakha and (ipso facto) with the knowledge of God—seems today to be further from realization than perhaps ever before.

Many, however, would not conclude with a prognosis for the future of halakha, and especially that of Sephardic halakha, based on its current problematic status in the real life of many Jews. Our society may well be headed for a renaissance of the religious dimension in both personal and social spheres. Within that renaissance, a growing recognition of the importance of religious community, as opposed to purely personal modes of religiosity, may be discerned. Throughout the course of the past two millennia, halakha—through the creativity of its masters—contributed decisivly to formulating the structure and content of Jewish communal religiosity. Thus, at the outset of the twenty-first century, it would seem wiser to base a prognosis for halakhic study and praxis on the religious and intellectual potential inherent within Sephardic halakha's rich spiritual heritage—a potential that, as every student of halakha came to realize, was truly great.

NOTES

1. On Spanish Jewry during this period see Yitzak Baer, *The Jews in Christian Spain*, trans. L. Schiffman, vol. 2 (Philadelphia: Jewish Publication Society, 1993), 167–219.

2. An excellent presentation and analysis of Canpanton's Talmudic methodology and its theoretical understructure, as originated by himself and developed by his disciples, is to be found in D. Boyarin's *Darkam baKodesh* (Jerusalem: Publication Society of America, 1989), especially chap. 2, 47–68.

3. On Yizhak bar Sheshet, see A. Hershman, *Rabbi Isaac ben Sheshet Perfet and His Times* (1945). On the Durans see several articles in *Encyclopedia Judaica*, vol. 6, 298–99, 301–7.

4. On the enactments of Fez, see Menahem Elon, *Jewish Law: History, Sources, Principles*, trans. from the Hebrew by Bernard Auerbach and Melvin J. Sykes (Philadelphia: Jewish Publication Society, 1994), chap. 20.

5. On Salonika during this period see J. Nehama, *Histoire des israélites de Salonique* (1935); Minna Rozen, "Individual and Community in the Jewish Society of the Ottoman Empire" and "Salonica in the Sixteenth Century," in *The Jews of the Ottoman Empire*, ed. Avigdor Levy (Princeton, NJ: Darwin, 1994), 215–73.

6. On MahaRaSHDaM see M. S. Boodblatt, *Jewish Life in Turkey in the Sixteenth Century as Reflected in the Legal Writings of Samuel de Medina* (1952); J. Hacker's article in *EJ*, vol. 11, 1212–14. On modes of Torah study in sixteenth-century Salonika and Turkey, see H. Bentov, "Methods of Torah Study in the Yeshivot of Salonica and Turkey" (in Hebrew), *Sefunot* 13 (1977–78): 5–107. On Almosnino, see *EJ*, vol. 2, 669–71.

7. On rabbi Mizrahi, see Y. Friedman, "Eliahu Mizrahi—The Man and His Works" (Ph.D. dissertation, Yeshiva University, 1974).

8. The jurisprudence of Joseph ibn Lev has been analyzed in depth by S. Morell, *Precedent and Judicial Discretion: The Case of Joseph ibn Lev* (Atlanta, 1991).

9. On Moshe Isserles see Y. Ben-Sasson, *Mishnato haʾIyyunit shel haRemah* (Jerusalem, 1984). A. Ziv, *HaRemah* (Jerusalem, 1957); Elon, *Jewish Law*, chap. 36.

10. For an overview and context of Safed in this period, see Raphael Jehuda Zwi Werblowsky, "The Safed Revival and Its Aftermath," in *Jewish Spirituality*, vol. 2, *From the Sixteenth-Century Revival to the Present*, ed. Arthur Green (New York: Crossroad, 1987), 7–33.

11. Cf. *Mishne Torah*, Laws of Sanhedrin, 4:11.

12. On Rabbi Beirav and his yeshiva in Safed see H. Dimitrovsky, "The Beit Midrash of Rabbi Yaʾakov Beirav in Safed," *Sefunot* 7.

13. See: Yaʾakov Katz, "The Dispute between Jacob Berab and Levi ben Habib over Renewing Ordination," in *Binah: Studies in Jewish History, Thought, and Culture* 1 (1989): 119–41.

14. On the *Beit Yosef*, the *Shulhan ʿArukh* and the relation and interconnection between them, see Elon, *Jewish Law*, chap. 36.

15. From Caro's introduction to the *Beit Yosef*, printed at the beginning of all standard editions of Rabbi Ya'akov Bar Asher's opus *Arbaʾa Turim*. My translation.

16. This characterization of the "golden age" of the Sanhedrin (which supposedly persisted until the death of Hillel and Shammai) is set forth by the Tanna Rabbi Yossi (second century CE) in a baraita quoted in *BT Sanhedrin* 88b. It was endorsed by Maimonides who cites it in *Mishne Torah*, Hilkhot Mamrim, 1:4.

17. From Caro's introduction to *Shulhan ʿArukh*, printed at the beginning of *Shulhan ʿArukh Hoshen Mishpat* in all standard editions. My translation.

18. Cf. Elon, *Jewish Law*, chap. 34.

19. Caro refers here to the great talmudic commentators of medieval times: Tosafot are the talmudic scholars of twelfth- to thirteenth-century France and Germany; Ramban is Rabbi Moshe ben Nahman, 1194–1270, Spain; Rashba is Rabbi Shmuel ben Adret, 1235–1310, Spain; RaN is Rabbi Nissim Gerondi, 1310–1375, Spain.

20. From the introduction to *Beit Yosef*.

21. RIF is Rabbi Isaac AlFasi, 1013–1103, North Africa and Spain, author of a condensed edition of the Talmud, in which he also indicated which halakhic position should be followed. Rambam is Rabbi Moshe ben Maimon (Maimonides), author of the great codex *Mishne Torah*, in which he summed up the "bottom line" of all issues dealt with in the entire Talmudic literature. Rosh is Rabbi Asher ben Yehiel, 1250–1327, Germany and Spain, codifier of the Ashkenazic halakhic position in his systematic condensation of the Talmud.

22. Introduction to *Beit Yosef*.

23. Ibid. It should be noted that when citing the Rosh (Asher ben Yehiel) as one of the "three pillars" of halakha, Rabbi Caro is including, and perhaps primarily relating to, the positions of Rosh as recorded in his son's *Arbaʾah Turim*.

24. Rabbi Eliyyahu bar Haim, *responsum*, no. 92.

25. The tradition was supposedly transmitted orally and was first recorded by Haim Joseph David Azulai ("the HIDA," eighteenth century, Eretz Israel) in his work *Birkei Yossef* on *Shulhan ᶜArukh Hoshen Mishpat,* chap. 25, para. 29.

26. One of these was Haim bar Bezalel (1520–1588), who wrote that halakhic codes invariably lead to superficial decision making, as rabbis read from the codex onto reality without checking the sources and (consequently) without true comprehension even of the meaning of the brief entry in the codex itself. What's more, the "sanctification" of a codex severely curtails halakhic discretion and originality, and compels the adoption of a false consistency, which runs against the true natural openness of halakha. Rabbi Haim bar Bezalel added, that even regarding exactly similar cases, halakhic consistency in praxis is not necessarily a virtue:

> For a person's understanding varies over time, and perhaps today it seems correct to him to rule otherwise than he ruled yesterday. And this need not reflect any fickleness or deficiency, nor should it be said that through him "the Torah is split into two Torot," Heaven forbid. To the contrary: such is the way of Torah, and "both this and that are the words of the living God."

Codification of halakha is, thus, opposed to its very nature. Other masters who held similar attitudes (although phrased in a less striking manner) were Shemuel Eidles (the MaHaRSHA, 1555–1631) and Meir of Lublin (MaHaRaM miLublin, 1558–1616). These also included Shlomo Luria (the MaHaRSHaL, 1510–1574), author of *Yam Shel Shlomo* in which halakha was directly related to the Talmud, and Yom-Tov Lippman Heller (1579–1654), who attempted to relate halakha directly to the Mishna in his work *'Tosafot Yom-TOV.* Mordekhai Yaffe (1530–1612) accepted the notion of an independent codex, yet thought that much more extensive grounding in earlier sources was required than that supplied in the *Shulhan*; his code *Levush Malkhut* sought to provide the necessary alternative to Caro's opus.

27. Responsa *Zemah Zedek,* Amsterdam 1675, responsum 9.

28. Joseph Molkho, *Shulkhan Gavoah* (Salonika, 1755), 2–3.

29. *Kim Li* has been the topic of several articles by Hanina ben Menachem, most recently in *Dinei Israel* 20–21 (2001): 13–41, in which he compares the doctrine of *Kim Li* with the Catholic theological doctrine of probabilism.

30. Cf. *EJ,* vol. 15, 1314–15, and also H. Bentov, *Shalem* 1 (1974): 195–228.

31. On Benveniste see *EJ,* vol. 4, 559–61 (includes bibliography); and Elon, *Jewish Law,* chap. 38.

32. Cf. *EJ,* vol. 7, 1512.

33. On these and other Egyptian scholars, see S. Havlin, "Rabbi Abraham Halevi (Author of Responsa "Ginath Vradim") and the Scholars of His Time and Place" (Ph.D. dissertation, Hebrew University, 1983).

34. On Zacuto see *EJ,* vol. 16, 906–9, and bibliography there; more recently Andrea Yaakov Lattes, "L'opera letteraria di Rabbì Moshè Zacuto," *Rassegna Mensile di Israel* 63,2 (1997): 1–25.

35. The classic and exhaustive account of the rise and fall of the celebrated false Messiah is Gershon Scholem's *Sabbatai Sevi The Mystical Messiah* (Princeton, NJ, 1973).

36. On Italian halakhic writing from the eighteenth century onward, see David Malkiel, "Texts and Themes in the Halakhic Literature of Italy in Modern Times" (in Hebrew), *Pe'amim* 86–87 (2002): 258–96.

37. See Leah Bornstein-Makovetsky, "Halakhic and Rabbinic Literature in Turkey, Greece and the Balkans, 1750–1900" (in Hebrew), *Pe'amim* 86–87 (2002): 67–123.

38. On Berdugo, see H. Bentov, "The Contribution and Methodology of Rabbi Raphael Berdugo in the Study of Talmud and Halakha" (in Hebrew), in *Judaisme d'Afrique du Nord aux dix-neuvième au vingtième siècles*, ed. M. Abitbol (Jerusalem, 1980), 141–49.

39. On Moroccan halakhic creativity in this and subsequent centuries, see H. Bentov, "Rabbinic Literature North Africa in the Last 250 Years" (in Hebrew), *Pe'amim* 86–87 (2002): 214–32; and Shalom Bar Asher's article in that same volume, 233–57.

40. M. Benayahu has written and edited the definitive works on HIDA, including *Rabbi Hayyim Joseph David Azulai* (Jerusalem, 1959), *HaHIDA* (1960); *Sefer HaHIDA* (1959).

41. Several books have been written on the GRA. The most recent and comprehensive is I. Etkes, *The Gaon of Vilna: The Man and His Image*," trans. Jeffrey M. Green (Berkeley: University of California Press, 2002).

42. Cf. A. H. Freiman, *Seder Kiddushin veNissuin* (Jerusalem, 1964), 314–20.

43. On Rabbi Somekh, see A. Ben Ya'akov, *Rabbi 'Abdallah Somekh* (in Hebrew) (Jerusalem, 1949); Zvi Zohar, *The Luminous Face of the East* (in Hebrew) (Tel Aviv: Hakibbutz HaMeuhad, 2001), chap. 1.

44. On Joseph Hayyim see A. Ben Ya'akov, *Rabbi Joseph Hayyim: One of the Greatest Rabbis of Iraq* (Jerusalem, 1972); Zohar, *The Luminous Face of the East*, chaps. 2 and 3.

45. Cf. *Responsa Kerakh Shel Romi*, #1.

46. On Rabbi Israel Moshe Hazan, see Avi Sagi, "Rabbi Israel Moshe Hazan— Between Particularism and Universalism" (in Hebrew), *Judaism between Religion and Ethics* (Tel Aviv, 1998).

47. Cf. N. Efrati, *The Role of the Eliachar Family in Jerusalem* (in Hebrew) (Jerusalem, 1975); Zohar, *The Luminous Face of the East*, chap. 11.

48. Cf. J. Barnai, *The Moroccan Community in Jerusalem, 1830–1918* (Jerusalem: Hebrew University, 1971).

49. Cf. Yaron Harel's article in *AJS Review* 26, no. 2 (2002): Hebrew section, 1–58.

50. Zvi Zohar, "Halakhic Responses of Syrian and Egyptian Rabbinical Au-

thorities to Social and Technological Change," *Studies in Contemporary Jewry* 2 (1986): 18–51.

51. On the enactments of the Moroccan rabbinate in the mid-twentieth century see M. Bar-Yudah, ed., *Halakha and Openness (Halakha u-Petihut)* (Tel Aviv, 1985).

52. On Rabbi HaCohen, see M. ElHarar, *A Giant in Torah and Lover of Zion, Rabbi Moshe Khalfon HaCohen* (in Hebrew) (Jerusalem, 1997); Zvi Zohar, "Religious Justification of Secular Nationalist Zionism," in *Israel* N.S. 2 (Tel Aviv: Tel Aviv University, 5762–63), 107–26.

53. On Rabbi Uzziel, see M. D. Angel, *Loving Truth and Peace: The Grand Religious Worldview of Rabbi Benzion Uziel* (Northvale, NJ, 1999.)

54. Uzziel's position on the issue of women's suffrage is analyzed and contrasted with that of Rabbi Kook in Zvi Zohar, "Traditional Flexibility and Modern Strictness: A Comparative Analysis of the Halakhic Positions of Rabbi Kook and Rabbi Uzziel on Women's Suffrage," in *Sephardi and Middle Eastern Jewries: History and Culture*, ed. Harvey Goldberg (Bloomington: Indiana University Press, 1996), 119–33.

55. On Rabbi HaLevi, see Zvi Zohar, "Sephardic Religious Thought in Israel: Aspects of the Theology of Rabbi Haim David HaLevi," in *Critical Studies on Israeli Society, Religion and Government*, vol. 4, ed. Walter Zenner and Kevin Avruch (Albany: State University of New York Press, 1997), 115–36. An anthology of scholarly articles on the halakhic and theological works of Rabbi HaLevi, edited by A. Sagi and Z. Zohar, is scheduled to appear in 2004.

56. At least two doctoral dissertations written at Bar Ilan University have been devoted to Rabbi Ovadia Joseph's *oeuvre*: B. Lau (2002) and A. Picard (2004).

57. On Rabbi Ovadia's doctrine of "Returning the Crown to Its Ancient Glory," see Z. Zohar, "Sephardic Religious Thought in Israel."

58. Rabbi Ben Zion Meir Hai Uzziel, responsa *Mishpetei Uzziel*, vol. 1 (Tel Aviv, 1935), author's introduction.

59. Rabbi Eliyyahu Hazan, *Zikhron Yerushalayyim* (Livorno, 1874), 57.

60. Rabbi Hazzan alludes here to a classic Talmudic midrash upon the verse "And the tablets were the work of God, and the writing was the writing of God, engraved upon the tablets" (Exodus 32:16). The midrash says: "Do not read *Harut* ['engraved'] but *Heirut* ['freedom']" (cf. Mishna, tractate Avot 6:2 and parallels). On Rabbi Hazan's reading, these are two sides of a coin: the engraved words are totally ambiguous, thereby enabling total freedom of interpretation.

61. Responsa ʿ*Aseh Lekha Rav*, vol. 7 (1986), Responsum 54.

62. Cf. J. Lupu, "La metamorphose ultra-orthodoxe des jeunes juifs du Maroc: L'influence lituanienne du début du vingtième siècle jusqu'à l'apparition du phenomène Chass en Israel" (Ph.D. dissertation, University of Paris, 2002); idem, "The Rescue of Moroccan Jewry for Torah: The Transfer of Moroccan Students to "Lithuanian" Yeshivot after the Shoah" (in Hebrew), *Peʾamim* 80 (1999): 112–28.

Chapter 10

Safed Kabbalah and the Sephardic Heritage

Morris M. Faierstein

After the Jews were exiled from Spain in 1492, the Spanish kabbalists fled to three Diasporas including North Africa, Italy, and the Ottoman Empire, to continue their teachings.[1] Of these diasporas, it was the kabbalists who migrated to the Ottoman Empire who were responsible for shifting the kabbalistic tradition into new directions. They created a major revolution in Jewish life and spirituality[2] by first moving to the major Jewish centers in Greece and Turkey and ultimately converging in the small Galilean town of Safed.

The kabbalistic response to the trauma of the exile varied widely, ranging from a quietistic approach adopted by the Italian[3] and North African[4] kabbalists, to a more activist apocalyptic approach which sought signs of the imminent redemption.[5] The expulsion was seen by many as the tribulation that would herald the beginning of the messianic age as foretold in rabbinic literature.[6] The spiritualization of religious life culminated in the creative outburst of religious innovation in Safed in the second half of the sixteenth century as a response to the expulsion. This spiritual revolution spread from Safed and transformed the practice of Judaism throughout the Jewish world. It is this spiritual revival that I will concentrate on in this study. Beginning in the 1530s, Safed became the most important spiritual center of the sixteenth century. There were two major factors that attracted a number of important kabbalists to the center. On the mundane level, it provided a solid economic base for the Jewish community as the center of the wool trade.[7] Spiritually, it was near the graves of Rabbi Simeon bar Yohai and his colleagues who were the heroes of the *Zohar,* the central kabbalistic text. The development of Safed Kabbalah, which has become an important means of understanding the Jewish mystical tradition, was enhanced through practices that included direct communion with the spirits of the deceased mystical figures at their graves.

Joseph Karo and Solomon Alkabetz

Joseph Karo (1488–1575) and Solomon Alkabetz (c. 1505–1584) were among the leading figures that aided in bringing Safed to its peak. Karo, the author of the *Bet Joseph* and *Shulkhan Arukh*, was well known for being the most significant halakhic authority of the sixteenth century. Though his works betrayed little evidence of his mystical interests, Karo was deeply immersed in mystical practices. Even before his arrival in Safed in 1535, Karo received a heavenly messenger—a *maggid*, the personification of the *Mishnah*, that both encouraged his mystical practice and admonished him when his spiritual intensity flagged.[8]

This *maggid* was experienced by others as well. Solomon Alkabetz described in a letter how the *maggid* entered Karo on the first night of Shavuot and began to speak through his mouth so that others present, including Alkabetz, were able to hear it.[9] They spent the whole night awake, studying selections from biblical, rabbinic, and mystical texts in preparation for receiving the Torah on Shavuot. This is the first record of the ritual known as "Tikkun Layl Shavuot" which later became widespread.[10]

Alkabetz, author of the hymn "Lekha Dodi," formed a mystical brotherhood of disciples who agreed to lead their lives according to certain spiritual principles and practices (*hanhagot*). As an example, the *hanhagot* of Moses Cordovero, one of Alkabetz's disciples and his brother-in-law, contains thirty-six practices expected of members of his brotherhood. The majority are traditional practices associated with a pious lifestyle, such as not getting angry, being punctilious in prayers and study, and living a generally ascetic life, refraining from overindulgence in material pleasures. Among the more unusual expectations were weeping during the prayers[11] and confessing one's sins to colleagues, particularly on Friday afternoon as part of the preparations for the Sabbath. The mystical practice of *gerushin* (divorces) was also initiated by Alkabetz and Cordovero.

Moses Cordovero

Moses Cordovero (1522–1570) was the most important kabbalist in Safed before Isaac Luria. He was taught by Karo in halakhah and Alkabetz in

Kabbalah. Cordovero was influential as both an author and a teacher, numbering most of the key Safed kabbalists among his disciples. Even Isaac Luria was his disciple for the few months that he was in Safed before Cordovero's death.

In his kabbalistic writings, Cordovero endeavored to systematize the diverse kabbalistic theologies that had arisen in the wake of the *Zohar*. His major work, which he completed by the age of twenty-seven, was the *Pardes Rimmonim* (The Garden of Pomegranates). Another systematic treatise was *Elimah Rabbati*. He also wrote a variety of other works, including an introduction to Kabbalah[12] and a commentary on the prayer book (*Tefillah le-Moshe*). His largest work, *Or Yakar* (Precious Light), a massive commentary on the *Zohar* that runs over thirty volumes, was only recently published. It was previously known from the extensive quotations in Abraham Azulai's *Zohar* commentary, *Hesed Le-Abraham*.

Cordovero was also the author of a small ethical treatise, *The Palm Tree of Deborah*,[13] which formed the basis for a whole new genre of kabbalistic ethical literature. The book, focusing on *imitatio dei* (the imitation of God), contains ten chapters that correspond to the ten *sefirot*. Its core concept is that ethical behavior is dependent on the inner structure of the *sefirot* and should be reflected in one's deeds. Joseph Dan commented: "It is not the system of ethics that is meaningful; it is the mystical idea that by following simple, everyday ethical commandments a person can participate in the inner developments within the Godhead, and become a part of the united divine and earthly divine providence."[14]

Some of Cordovero's disciples included Elijah De Vidas, Abraham ben Eliezer ha-Levi Berukhim, Abraham Galante, Eleazar Azikri, and Hayyim Vital. There was a legend that before his death, his disciples asked him who would replace him as their teacher. He responded that whoever would see a pillar of fire over his grave would be worthy to be his successor. The story concluded that Isaac Luria was the one who saw the pillar of fire.[15] Indeed, Luria became the dominant figure in Safed after Cordovero's death in the summer of 1570.

Isaac Luria

Isaac Luria Ashkenazi (AR"I)[16] was born in Egypt in 1534 and came to Safed in 1570.[17] Orphaned at an early age, Luria was raised by his uncle. He received an excellent rabbinic education, studying with Rabbi Bezalel Ashkenazi, a leading rabbinic authority of the period.[18] One day in the synagogue, Luria saw a visiting merchant hold a manuscript. When Luria inquired about its contents, the merchant answered that he was of converso background and could not read it. Luria looked at it and realized that it contained mystical secrets.

The merchant gave the manuscript to Luria after he promised to intercede with his uncle concerning duties owed by the merchant. Luria withdrew to a small hut near the Nile where he studied the manuscript, which was a part of the *Zohar*, for six years. He came home only for Sabbaths and holidays. Eventually he was worthy of having Elijah come and teach him the mysteries of the text. When he reached the age of thirty-six, Elijah told him that the time had come for him to travel to Safed and teach disciples. He traveled to Safed but did not "reveal himself" until after the death of Moses Cordovero. After his public revelation, he gathered a group of disciples.

Isaac Luria came to be identified as the central figure of the kabbalistic revolution in Safed during the second half of the sixteenth century. He was the initiator of a new school of kabbalistic thought known as Lurianic Kabbalah that initiated many new religious practices and traditions that became widespread throughout the Jewish world. Luria's authority was not based on his halakhic or Talmudic knowledge, but on his mystical attainments and personal charisma.

Stories began to circulate about Luria that spoke of his mystical and magical abilities. He could look at a person's forehead and tell what sins he or she had committed.[19] He knew the sources of a person's soul,[20] could understand the language of birds and animals, and was able to expel evil spirits that possessed people. Luria was also seen as a messianic figure. There was an expectation that the Messiah would come in 1575 and that Luria would be the Messiah.[21]

After only two years of teaching in Safed, Luria died. At that time, his status was reinterpreted as a Messiah of Joseph figure whose death would be an early part of the messianic drama. His disciple Hayyim Vital, who assumed leadership of the disciples after Luria's death, took over some of these messianic aspirations.[22]

Lurianic Kabbalah found its expression in two distinct areas. One area was esoteric, the theoretical teachings of Luria and his disciples, and the other was exoteric, the rituals and traditions that first began as the practices of the mystical brotherhoods in Safed. I will first examine the theoretical aspects of Lurianic Kabbalah and then consider the new rituals and their impact on the Jewish religious tradition.

Isaac Luria left behind very few writings, including fragmentary *Zohar* commentaries and three well-known Sabbath hymns.[23] Luranic writings were, in fact, the teachings of Luria as they were copied and interpreted by his disciples. The body of literature traditionally called "kitvei ha-AR"I" (the writings of the AR"I) were Luria's ideas mediated by his primary disciple and successor, Hayyim Vital. After Luria's death, Vital made the other disciples sign a document in accepting him as the only authorized interpreter of Luria's teachings. He also asked all of them to turn over any notebooks or other written materials they had containing records of Luria's teachings.[24]

Despite these draconian measures, several other interpretations of Luria's teachings have survived from Joseph ibn Tabul, Moses Jonah, and Israel Sarug.[25] The differences between Vital's interpretation of Luria's teachings and those of the others are in details that are primarily of interest to scholars of Kabbalah.

Luria's theoretical writings were intended for only a very small elite group of disciples, and not for public dissemination. Vital also felt very strongly about this and kept his writings in a locked cabinet. He even asked that his writings be buried with him after his death. Once when Vital was seriously ill and in a coma, the richest Jew in Safed bribed Vital's brother to allow access to his writings so that they might be copied. Working feverishly, a group of scribes copied as much as they could during the few days that Vital was in the coma.

An example of the secrecy that surrounded Luria's teachings concerned Vital's teacher in halakhah, Rabbi Moses Alsheikh. Alsheikh was a great exegete and homilist and gave Vital his rabbinic ordination. His commentary on the Torah, *Torat Moshe,* was "the most quoted authority in East European and Mediterranean Jewish homiletics."[26] Yet despite all this, Vital did not want to initiate Alsheikh into the mysteries of Lurianic Kabbalah. He had been informed by Luria that Alsheikh's soul was not worthy to receive these teachings.[27] In the end, Vital relented. Seven days before his death, Luria told Vital that he had contributed to his early death through his revelation of the teachings to Alsheikh and some others who had implored him.[28]

Secrecy pertaining to Luria's teachings continued long after Vital's death in 1620. Vital's corpus was transmitted orally and through manuscripts. It wasn't until the end of the eighteenth century that Vital's writings began to be published by disciples of the Maggid of Mezhirech. The first work, the *Etz Hayyim* was published in Koretz in 1782. The whole corpus of Vital's writings finally appeared in print in the beginning of the twentieth century.

The core of Lurianic Kabbalah was the extremely complicated doctrine of creation. The details of the process varied according to the different versions of Luria's teachings found in the writings of his disciples.[29] We can discuss only the central ideas of this process in a somewhat simplified form in this context. According to Luria, creation occurred in three stages, *zimzum* (contraction), *shevirat ha-kelim* (breaking of the vessels) and *tikkun* (repair).

The first act in the process of creation was *zimzum*, God's self-contraction leaving an empty space for creation to take place. In the beginning, the divine presence (*Ein Sof*) filled the universe leaving no room for a separate creation. Before this, all the divine forces within the godhead were balanced and equally distributed. God's withdrawal was equal in all directions and produced a circular space in which creation could take place. A residue of *Ein Sof* (*reshimu*) remained in this space.

The divine light shone into this empty space and created the first configuration of the *sefirot* called Adam Kadmon (primordial Adam). The light of the *sefirot* flowed from Adam Kadmon's eyes, mouth, ears, and nose in an undifferentiated form. However, the light emanating from the eyes emanated in a differentiated form and formed each of the *sefirot*. The individual *sefirot* were not yet in a stable arrangement, and they were given "vessels" made of a thicker light in which they could arrange themselves and function. The vessels of the first three *sefirot* were able to contain the divine light that flowed into them, while the seven lower vessels were not able to and therefore shattered. The vessel of the last *sefirah*, Malkhut, also shattered but not to the same extent as the six *sefirot* above it. This was the second stage, the breaking of the vessels (*shevirat ha-kelim*).

Different reasons were offered for the existence of the imperfections in the vessels that caused them to shatter. Some attributed it to the presence of residues of *Din* in the vessels. Others pointed to the imbalanced nature of the emanation that created the differentiated *sefirot*. However, regardless of the explanation, the results were the same. Some of the light was trapped by the broken shards (*kelipot*) and gave substance to the dark forces of the *sitra achra* (the evil side).

After the breaking of the vessels, the light reassembled in a new configuration, the countenances (*parzufim*). These *parzufim* took the place of the original *sefirot* as the manifestations of Adam Kadmon. They were composed of materials damaged in the breaking of the vessels along with newly emanated materials. The first countenance (*parzuf*) was Arikh Anpin (the long face) that was the reconfigured *sefirah* of Keter. The second and third sefirot of Hokhmah and Binah became Abba (Father) and Imma (Mother). From the coupling of these two *parzufim* a new *parzuf* was born, Zeir Anpin (the short face or the impatient face), which consists of the next six *sefirot* from Hesed to Yesod. The last *sefirah* Malkhut was converted into the *parzuf* of Nukvah de-Zeir (the female of Zeir). The evolution of these *parzufim* is the first stage in the process of *tikkun*. This configuration of *parzufim* is also identical with the first of the four worlds found in earlier Kabbalah, Azilut (emanation).

From the world of Azilut, a divine light descends downward to the lower three worlds of Beriah (creation), Yezirah (formation), and Assiyah (action). At the bottom of each world there was a "curtain" that filtered out the sefirotic substance of that particular world and allowed the other light to pass through. Each of the lower worlds reflected the structure of Azilut and had its own structure of *parzufim*. As a result of the breaking of the vessels, each of the worlds stood one level lower than originally intended. For example, Azilut now stood in the place originally intended for Beriah and so forth. Assiyah, the lowest world, descended so low that it was in contact with the realm of the *kelippot* and the physical world.

As Gershom Scholem has commented on Lurianic Kabbalah:

> The main concern of Lurianic Kabbalah, as has been mentioned, is with the details of the process of *tikkun* and the developments that take place in the *parzufim* of the different worlds, in the "*Adam* of *azilut*," the "*Adam* of *beriah*," etc. . . . The crucial point in the various Lurianic discussions of these developments is that although the *tikkun* of the broken vessels has been almost completed by the supernal lights and the processes stemming from their activity, certain concluding actions have been reserved for man. These are the ultimate aim of creation, and the completion of *tikkun*, which is synonymous with the redemption, depends on man's performing them. Herein lies the close connection between the doctrine of tikkun and the religious and contemplative activity of man, which must struggle with and overcome not only the historic exile of the Jewish people but also the mystic exile of the Shekhinah, which was caused by the breaking of the vessels.[30]

Luria's doctrine of the soul was closely related to the processes of *shevirat ha-kelim* and *tikkun*. Adam's soul contained within it all the souls of humanity. It had 613 limbs, corresponding to the 613 commandments of the Torah. It was Adam's purpose to lift them up spiritually. Each of these 613 limbs was considered a great root which contained within itself a further 613 small roots. Some sources have said that each great root contained 600,000 small roots.

As a result of the world of Assiyah's falling from its original place and interacting with the *kelippot*, Adam became materialized and assumed a physical body, in contrast to his original purely spiritual state. The unity of his soul was disrupted, and the bulk of the souls that were within him fell into the *kelippot* and were subjugated by them. These souls are required to go through the process of transmigration (*gilgul*) in order to achieve their *tikkun*. A few souls remained within Adam. These holy souls were not contaminated by the *kelippot* and were exempt from the process of *gilgul*.

Adam's sin was the human equivalent of the breaking of the vessels in the sefirotic realm, although the precise nature of this sin was never specifically defined in kabbalistic literature. There are differing theories, but none of them have achieved widespread acceptance. One interesting Lurianic explanation was that the first sin occurred because Adam was anxious to complete the *tikkun* before its appointed time, which should have been the first Sabbath of creation. Instead, Adam misunderstood and tried to finish the *tikkun* before the onset of the Sabbath.

Man's role in the process of *tikkun* is played out through the commandments of the Torah and prayer. The proper observance of the commandments, with the proper intentions (*kavvanot*), helped restore the outer aspects of the world. Each person had a role to play based on the spiritual level of his or her soul and the task assigned to him or her. Prayer played a role in the human-divine dialogue that began with the Revelation at Sinai. Prayer was the human response to the divine revelation that spoke at Sinai and continued to speak to humanity, allowing Israel to occupy a central place in the process of *tikkun* that will ultimately lead to the final redemption and the messianic age.

Scholem understood the innovation of Lurianic Kabbalah as a result of the expulsion of the Jews from Spain. He wrote:

> After the catastrophe of the Spanish Expulsion, which so radically altered the outer aspect of the kabbalah if not its innermost content, it also became possible to consider the return to the starting point of creation as the means

of precipitating the final world catastrophe, which would come to pass when that return had been achieved by many individuals united in a desire for "the End" of the world.[31]

Recent scholars questioned Scholem's assumptions, both about the centrality of messianism in Lurianic Kabbalah and about the innovative nature of its theology. Moshe Idel convincingly demonstrated that messianism was not the central motif in kabbalistic literature after the expulsion.[32] Idel also argued that Luria's teachings were not well known or easily understood by kabbalists. It was well into the eighteenth century that Lurianic teachings were widely disseminated.[33]

Another important aspect of Scholem's interpretation of Lurianic Kabbalah that has been revised by recent scholarship was his concept of the various schools of Kabbalah as distinct entities, with one school following another in historical progression. The more recent understanding of the development of Kabbalah sees it as a more organic process in which later schools built on certain themes of earlier schools and developed them in new directions. For example, the major motifs of Lurianic Kabbalah could be traced back to concepts found in certain parts of the Zoharic corpus, particularly the *Idrot*.[34] Specific concepts that were thought to be Lurianic innovations could be traced back to earlier periods in the history of Kabbalah. The concept of *zimzum* is one such instance.[35] However, these new perspectives did not detract from the importance of Lurianic Kabbalah. Rather, they only placed it in the broader development of the Jewish mystical tradition.

New Rituals and Practices

Like many of the theoretical aspects of Lurianic Kabbalah, the rituals and practices that were first popularized in the wake of the Safed kabbalistic tradition had their roots in earlier rabbinic and kabbalistic traditions, particularly the *Zohar*. The major innovation of Safed was to put into practice concepts and ideas that had previously been theoretical.

The primary rituals we will consider are the two types of *tikkunim*.[36] The first type includes the night vigils on the festivals of Shavuot, Passover, and Hoshanah Rabah.[37] The second is the daily night vigil that relates to the exile and redemption of the Shekhinah called *tikkun hazot* (the *tikkun* of midnight).[38] The *tikkun* for the first night of Shavuot during which Joseph Karo received his *maggid* was mentioned previously. It was Luria's disciple, Hayyim Vital, who created the order of study for the first night of Shavuot. The order was reprinted in special booklets for this purpose and has been followed to the present day.[39]

The *tikkun* for the seventh night of Passover is related to the concept that the following day commemorated the Israelites' crossing of the Red Sea. Isaac Luria also connected it to the mystical relationship between Zeir Anpin and the *Shekhinah*. The *tikkun* for Hoshanah Rabah differs from the other two in that it is heavily referred to in earlier medieval kabbalistic writings and works concerning customs. Because the decrees concerning life and death issued on Yom Kippur were finalized on Hoshanah Rabah, it was a time of prayer and repentance.

The other type of tikkun is *tikkun hazot*, the nightly ritual initiated by Rabbi Abraham ha-Levi of Jerusalem (c. 1460–after 1528). Like many other Safed rituals, its roots could be found in Talmudic and Zoharic statements. But it was in Safed that it became a ritual that was practiced and disseminated.[40] The purpose of *tikkun hazot* was to lament the exile of the Shekhinah and pray for the redemption of the Shekhinah and Israel.

The ritual had two parts, the *tikkun* of Rachel and the *tikkun* of Leah. The *tikkun* of Rachel was the lamentation over the exile of the Shekhinah. The *tikkun* of Leah looked forward to the hope for the redemption. There was a set liturgy that was composed of selected psalms and hymns written by various kabbalists.[41]

The ritual of Yom Kippur Katan (the small Yom Kippur), the last day of the month before the New Moon (Rosh Hodesh), was set aside as a day of fasting and repentance. The moon is a symbol for the Shekhinah, and its waning was seen as a symbol of the exile of the Shekhinah.[42]

Sabbaths and Festivals

The centrality of the Sabbath and rituals associated with it were discussed in the Zohar and other kabbalistic literature before Safed.[43] However, it was in Safed that these rituals were actively put into practice. Additional rituals added to those found in earlier sources. It is impossible to describe fully all of the rituals relating to the Sabbath, we can give only an overview.

The preparations for the Sabbath began on Thursday night. Staying awake the whole night and studying was considered especially meritorious. It was a good way of atoning for any sexual transgressions such as nocturnal emissions, which was considered a significant sin needing penance.[44] Preparations for welcoming the Sabbath began early in the afternoon with immersion in the *mikvah* (ritual bath). After the *mikvah*, the Song of Songs was read. Some kabbalistic brotherhoods in Safed gathered to review their sins of the previous week and confess them to their fellows in the brotherhood. They participated in setting the Sabbath table and obtaining myrtle branches that would be smelled after the *Kiddush*.

Welcoming the Sabbath Queen, the Shekhinah coming out of her exile temporarily for the Sabbath, began shortly before sundown. Some of the kabbalists dressed in white and would go out to the edge of town to welcome the Sabbath with psalms and hymns. This ritual has been transformed into the part of the synagogue liturgy called Kabbalat Shabbat (welcoming the Sabbath). Its centerpiece is the hymn "Lekha Dodi" (Come My Beloved), which was composed by Solomon Alkabetz.

After the synagogue service, the kabbalists came home for the Sabbath eve meal. "Eshet Hayil" (The Woman of Valor) from Proverbs 31 was sung before reciting the *Kiddush*. The "woman" to whom this was sung was not the kabbalist's wife, but the Shekhinah.[45] Then a special *kavvanah* (intention) ascribed to Isaac Luria would be recited dedicating the meal to the "Holy Apple Orchard," another term for the Shekhinah. The other two obligatory Sabbath meals were dedicated to the Attika Kadisha (Ancient Holy One) and the third to Zeir Anpin. Many of the hymns associated with the Sabbath meals were written by figures in Safed or later kabbalists influenced by them. Isaac Luria himself composed three hymns, one for each of the Sabbath meals.

The tradition of Friday night's being auspicious for marital relations has Talmudic roots, but was mystically reinterpreted by the Safed kabbalists. The sexual relations were an earthly reflection of the union of Zeir Anpin and the Shekhinah in the sefirotic realm.

The Sabbath ended with a fourth symbolic meal, the Melaveh Malkah (Accompanying the Queen). This meal was a means of extending the Sabbath as long as possible and bidding farewell to the Shekhinah. Isaac Luria believed that the souls in Gehenna who rested from their torments on the Sabbath did not return to their torments until after the Melaveh Malkah.

Synagogue and Festivals

Because the contributions of the Safed kabbalists to the prayers and practices of liturgy, synagogue, and the celebration of festivals have become so common, they are assumed by many to have their origins in the mists of antiquity. An excellent illustration is the ritual of taking the Torah out of the Ark when the Torah is read in the synagogue. "It was the custom of my teacher (Luria), of blessed memory, to kiss the scroll of the Torah and to accompany it, walking behind it when it is brought from the Ark to the Reader's table in order to read it."[46]

Luria's disciples would not have recorded this practice if it were common or customary previously. We can assume that the practices listed in the *hanhagot* were innovative or departed in some way from the norm. Otherwise, why would they feel the need to record them for posterity?

Many "universal" Jewish customs began in Safed. Some that are more well known include the reciting of the "*Shema* before Sleeping"[47] and "Mode Ani"[48] in the morning upon awakening, kissing the mezuzah when entering and leaving, and the *mayim achronim* before the grace after meals.[49] One often-misunderstood custom is the practice of putting the *talit* over one's head during the recitation of the *amidah*. It is often interpreted as a sign of special piety or concentration, shutting out distractions. The recitation of the *amidah* raised spiritual forces that facilitated the union of the *sefirot* of Tiferet and Malkhut and the kabbalist was modestly averting his gaze from the sefirotic union.

The festivals were also influenced by the Safed kabbalists. Three of the better-known festivals related to the *ushpizin*, the *lulav* and *etrog*, and *hakafot* on Simhat Torah. The seven *ushpizin* (divine guests) were seven biblical heroes—Abraham, Isaac, Jacob, Moses, Aaron, Joseph, and David—representing the seven lower *sefirot*. On each night that one sits in the *sukkah*, one of these divine guests was specially invited into the *sukkah* to join the assembled in celebrating the festival. It was also considered meritorious by the *Zohar* to invite paupers or beggars to share in the festivities of the *sukkah*.

Though the commandment of taking the four species was biblical,[50] the kabbalists added their own distinctive elements to this commandment. The practices not found before Safed included the idea of holding all four species in contact with each other while reciting the blessing over the *lulav*.[51] Immediately after reciting the blessing, one shook the four species in a specific pattern that included the four points of the compass and above and below. The seven *hakafot* (circumambulations) with the Torah on Simhat Torah and many other rituals of this festival were also an innovation of the Safed kabbalists.[52]

Tu B'Shevat (the fifteenth of Shevat), the New Year of trees is mentioned in the Talmud.⁵³ However, the idea of turning it into a day of special observances began in Safed. Later, a special liturgy was developed based on the model of the Passover seder. It was attributed to Nathan of Gaza (1643–1680), the prophet of Sabbatai Sevi. This liturgy was developed and expanded into a separate book, *Pri Etz Hadar* (1753). The observance of Tu B'Shevat and the seder associated with it was more widely practiced among Sephardi communities until recent years when many Ashkenazim also began to have Tu B'Shevat seders.

Scholarship on Safed Kabbalah has tended to concentrate on its more esoteric and theoretical aspects, but there have been specific studies that looked at aspects of the Safedian influence on Jewish life and religious practice.⁵⁴ However, the question of how a small group of elite mystics living in a remote corner of the Jewish world spread the influence of their ideas and affected virtually every aspect of Jewish religious life remains to be answered.

Sabbatai Sevi and the Sabbatean Movement

The Sabbatean movement of the seventeenth century is unique in the history of Jewish messianic movements in that Jews in all corners of the Diaspora could be found among its followers. Even after the apostasy of its Messiah, Sabbatai Sevi (1626–1676), the movement's followers still accepted him as a messianic figure for more than a century after his death.⁵⁵

Sabbatai Sevi was born on the ninth of Ab, 1626,⁵⁶ into a wealthy merchant family in Smyrna (Izmir). He received a traditional rabbinic education and earned rabbinic ordination at the age of eighteen from one of the leading rabbis in Smyrna. Sabbatai was attracted to an ascetic lifestyle but was tormented by sexual temptations. In his early twenties, he began to be afflicted by manic-depression. He experienced periods of exaltation and euphoria and periods of deep melancholy and depression.

During his manic periods, or periods of illumination, as they were called, he committed acts that violated Jewish religious law. Sabbatai pronounced the Ineffable Name of God, the Tetragrammaton and spoke about a "mystery of the Godhead" that had been revealed to him. In addition to this and other violations of halakhah, he began to speak of himself as the Messiah. He was considered mentally unbalanced by many in Smyrna and was not taken seriously. Eventually, around 1654, he was banished from Smyrna and spent the next decade wandering around the

Ottoman Empire, mainly Turkey, Israel, and Syria. During this period, he unsuccessfully attempted to rid himself of his personal demons through practical Kabbalah.

In 1664, word spread of the appearance of a holy man in Gaza who could reveal the source of a person's soul and prescribe a *tikkun* for his or her spiritual afflictions. This holy man was Nathan of Gaza. Sabbatai Sevi decided to visit Nathan to seek a cure for his soul. By the time Sabbatai visited Nathan in Gaza in the spring of 1665, Nathan had already heard about Sabbatai and his concerns. Two months earlier Nathan had had a vision that Sevi was the awaited Messiah. Nathan tried to convince Sabbatai that he was not suffering from a spiritual illness, but rather, that he was the awaited Messiah. Sabbatai did not believe him at first, but on the night of Shavuot Nathan had another vision, and he publicly announced Sabbatai's messiahship to a group of assembled rabbis. Two weeks later, during a period of illumination, Sabbatai publicly announced that he was the Messiah, and the whole Jewish community of Gaza was swept up in the event.

News of Sabbatai's announcement quickly spread to other Jewish communities in Israel. Many important rabbis strongly opposed him and spoke out against him. In the next months Nathan sent letters to various Jewish communities spreading the news that the Messiah had come. He also declared periods of repentance to prepare for the advent of the messianic age.

Nathan and Sabbatai traveled to various communities in Israel, Syria, and Turkey gaining support and little opposition. Sabbatai returned to Smyrna, and during the week of Hanukkah in 1665, he began to violate different aspects of Jewish law openly. One Passover, Sabbatai sacrificed and roasted a lamb, along with the forbidden fats, and convinced his followers to eat it. He did this while reciting the blessing "He who permits the forbidden (*matir issurim*)."[57] The ultimate moment came when about 150 people fell into a trance and began to "prophesy" that Sabbatai Sevi was the Messiah.

Shortly afterwards, Sabbatai, Nathan, and a group of followers sailed for Constantinople to confront the sultan. Sabbatai was arrested upon arrival in February 1666 and imprisoned. But the vizier took no immediate action. Sabbatai's imprisonment did not diminish the enthusiasm of his followers and the dissemination of the messianic propaganda. However, events reached a crisis in September 1666 when Sabbatai was called before the vizier and given the choice of death or conversion to Islam and renouncing his claims to be the Messiah. He accepted conversion over death. This created a profound disturbance and crisis among his followers. Some of them left the movement, but many still remained.

Upon hearing news of Sabbatai's acceptance of conversion, Nathan began to interpret the events as part of the messianic mystery. He explained that the task of the Jewish people had been to restore the sparks of their own souls helping the process of *tikkun*. However, there were still sparks that were captives of the *kelippot*, and only the Messiah could redeem these sparks. The only way that the Messiah could accomplish this mission was from within the *kelippot*. That is, the Messiah had to appear to join the forces of evil in order to redeem the sparks they held captive. The redemption of these final sparks would be the final act in the messianic drama.

Though living outwardly as a Muslim, Sabbatai Sevi was well known to continue to practice Judaism in private and even to celebrate Jewish holidays with followers who visited him. In his last letter, written six weeks before his unexpected death on Yom Kippur in 1676, he asked friends in a nearby Jewish community to send him a prayer book for the upcoming High Holy Days. Nathan responded to Sabbatai's death by propagating the idea that Sabbatai had not died, but had "occulted." That is, he had ascended to heaven and had been absorbed in the "supernal lights." Nathan himself died not long after, in January 1680, and others took up the mantle of leadership of the Sabbatean movement.

Sabbatai Sevi's death accelerated the defections from the movement, but a corps of believers remained. They may be divided into two main groups, the radicals and the moderates. The radicals followed Sabbatai Sevi into apostasy and followed his practice of being a Muslim externally while secretly remaining believers in Sabbatai Sevi and his Messiahship. This group became known as the Doenmeh. They practiced a version of Messianic Judaism based on Sabbatean teachings. The group numbered about 200 families originally, though there was another mass conversion in the 1680s that added several hundred families to the group. The traditions and internal history of this group were not well known until the twentieth century when some of their writings came to light. The center of this community was in Salonika until 1924, when there was a major population transfer in the wake of the Greco-Turkish war. There is sketchy evidence that the Doenmeh still exists as an organized group.[58]

The majority of Sabbatean believers were moderates. They remained practicing Jews. But they believed that Sabbatai Sevi was indeed the awaited Messiah, and his "occultation" was a temporary part of the messianic process. The extent to which they participated in Sabbatean activities was held under secrecy. Among the intellectual leaders of the movement, many confined expression of their Sabbatean sympathies to references and allusions in their writings that would attract the attention only of fellow believers or modern scholars. One author who successfully hid his Sabbatean affiliation was Rabbi Elijah ha-Cohen of Smyrna (d. 1729) until Gershom Scholem brought it to light.[59] He wrote one of the important religio-ethical treatises, *Shevet Musar,* which was frequently reprinted and translated into Ladino, Yiddish, and Arabic.[60]

In contrast, one scholar who made his Sabbatean sympathies public was Abraham Miguel Cardozo (1626–1706). When news of Sabbatai Sevi reached Cardozo, he became one of his most ardent supporters and spent the rest of his life traveling and spreading the teachings of Sabbateanism. He composed many books and treatises defending and justifying Sabbatean theology. Attempts were made to publish some of his books, but the local rabbis stopped them. An important aspect of his teachings was his anti-Christian polemics, based on a sound knowledge of Christian theology. He saw the basic Christian doctrines as distortions of the true kabbalistic teachings. His own converso background made him particularly sympathetic to Sabbatai Sevi's apostasy, seeing it as a reflection of his own experience. His writings also illuminated the attraction of Sabbateanism to many former conversos who found themselves uncomfortable with the transition from their former lives to the acceptance of rabbinic Judaism.[61]

A variety of explanations have been offered for the relative success of Sabbateanism. The dominant explanation has been that of Gershom Scholem, who saw Sabbateanism as a natural outgrowth of Lurianic Kabbalah.[62] Gershom Scholem suggests five factors that contributed to the success of Sabbatai's proclamation of his messiahship: 1) The messianic call came from the Holy Land; 2) the renewal of prophecy with the conspicuous figure of Nathan, the brilliant scholar and severe ascetic-turned-prophet; 3) the efficacy of traditional and popular apocalyptic beliefs, whose elements were not relinquished but reinterpreted; 4) the prophet's call to repentance played a decisive role; 5) there was, as yet, no differentiation between the various elements in the movement.[63]

More recently, Moshe Idel has questioned Scholem's theory. Idel's argument is based on the finding that Lurianic Kabbalah's esoteric doctrine was known to only a small elite group of kabbalists before the late eighteenth century and thus could not serve as the catalyst for a mass movement.[64] Instead, Idel argues, Sabbatean theology was based on earlier kabbalistic works that were better known and more influential than Lurianic Kabbalah.

The various controversies surrounding the Sabbatean movement and its aftermath did not adversely affect the continuing influence and continued observance of religious practices popularized in Safed. The popular eighteenth-century work *Hemdat Yamim* was an anonymous work that was first published in Smyrna in 1731.[65] Influenced by Lurianic Kabbalah and Sabbateanism, it stressed the mystical importance of the commandments and explained how the pious Jews could participate in the mystical process of *tikkun*. It was one of the most important anthologies of popular kabbalistic practice that became normative in many Jewish communities.

The influence of Safed on Sephardic Jewish life and religious practice has been profound. In this essay, I have attempted to trace the origins and development of kabbalistic ideas and practices that originated in Safed and spread to all sectors of the Jewish community. Since the eighteenth century there has been no aspect of Jewish life that has not been touched by the innovations of Safed. Without an understanding of this influence, one cannot understand Sephardic religious life and practice in the last centuries.

NOTES

1. My thanks to Professor Ron Kiener for reading an earlier draft of this paper and making helpful comments and suggestions.

2. M. Idel, "Spanish Kabbalah after the Expulsion," in *Moreshet Sefarad: The Sephardi Legacy*, ed. H. Beinart (Jerusalem: Magnes, 1992), vol. 2, 166–78. See for an overview of Spanish Kabbalah after the expulsion.

3. M. Idel, "Encounters between Spanish and Italian Kabbalists in the Generation of the Expulsion," in *Crisis and Creativity in the Sephardic World, 1391–1648*, ed. B. Gampel (New York: Columbia University Press, 1997), 189–222.

4. M. Halamish, *The Kabbalah in North Africa from the Sixteenth Century: A Historical and Cultural Overview* (in Hebrew) (Tel Aviv: Ha-Kibbutz Ha-Meuhad, 2001). See for information on the history of Kabbalah in North Africa.

5. Among the kabbalists who saw apocalyptic significance in the expulsion were Abraham ha-Levi of Jerusalem and Solomon Molcho. See, M. Idel, *Messianic Mystics* (New Haven: Yale University Press, 1998), 132–34, 144–52.

6. The classic rabbinic passage is M. Sotah 9:15. See also, R. Elior, "Messianic Expectations and Spiritualization of Religious Life in the Sixteenth Century," *Revue des Études Juives* 145 (1986): 36–37.

7. Concerning the economic life of Safed in the sixteenth century see S. Avit-

sur, "Safed: Center of the Manufacture of Woven Woolens in the Sixteenth Century," *Sefunot* 6 (1962): 41–69.

8. On Karo and his *maggid* see, R. J. Z. Werblowsky, *Joseph Karo: Lawyer and Mystic* (Philadelphia: Jewish Publication Society, 1977).

9. The letter can be found in, L. Jacobs, *Jewish Mystical Testimonies* (New York: Schocken, 1977), 99–104.

10. This and similar rituals will be discussed below.

11. On the kabbalistic significance of weeping see, E. Wolfson, "Weeping, Death, and Spiritual Ascent in Sixteenth Century Jewish Mysticism," in *Death, Ecstasy, and Other Worldly Journeys,* ed. J. Collins and M. Fishbane (Albany: State University of New York Press, 1995), 209–47.

12. I. Robinson, *Moses Cordovero's Introduction to Kabbalah: An Annotated Translation of His "Or Neʾerav"* (New York: Yeshiva University Press, 1994).

13. L. Jacobs, *The Palm Tree of Deborah* (London: Vallentine, Mitchell, 1960). The Hebrew edition is only about twenty pages long.

14. J. Dan, *Jewish Mysticism and Jewish Ethics* (Seattle: University of Washington Press, 1986), 86.

15. R. Shloimel Dresnitz, *Shivhei ha-Ari* (Jerusalem: Ahavat Shalom, 1998), 11.

16. Luria is known by the acronym "AR"I" which stands for "the divine Rabbi Isaac."

17. The biographical information on Luria is derived from the hagiographical biography *Shivhei ha-Ari* (Praises of the Ari), which is based on a series of letters by Shelomo Dreznitz. Dresnitz came to Safed at the beginning of the sixteenth century and sent a series of letters to a friend in which he collected the tales about Isaac Luria that he had heard in Safed.

18. Rabbi Bezalel Ashkenazi was the author of the important halakhic compendium *Shita Mekubezet.*

19. L. Fine, "The Art of Metoposcopy: A Study in Isaac Luria's Charismatic Knowledge." *AJS Review* 9 (1986): 79–101.

20. The fourth part of Vital's mystical autobiography, *The Book of Visions* (*Sefer Hezyonot*) consists of what Luria told Vital about the source of his soul. See, M. Faierstein, *Jewish Mystical Autobiographies: Book of Visions and Book of Secrets* (Mahwah, NJ: Paulist Press, 1999), 156–243.

21. D. Tamar, "The Messianic Expectations in Italy for the Year 1575" (in Hebrew), *Sefunot* 2 (1958): 61–88.

22. D. Tamar, "Luria and Vital as the Messiah ben Joseph" (in Hebrew), *Sefunot* 7 (1963): 169–77.

23. G. Scholem, "The Authentic Kabbalistic Writings of R. Isaac Luria" (in Hebrew), *Kiryat Sefer* 19 (1942): 184–99; J. Avivi, *Binyan Ariel* (Jerusalem: Misgav Yerushalayim, 1987).

24. G. Scholem, "A Charter of the Students of the AR"I" (in Hebrew). *Zion* 5 (1941): 131–60.

25. R. Meroz, "Faithful Transmission versus Innovation: Luria and His Disciples," in Gershom Scholem's *Major Trends in Jewish Mysticism Fifty Years After*, ed. P. Schaefer and J. Dan (Tuebingen, Germany: Mohr, 1993), 257–74.

26. Dan, *Jewish Mysticism and Jewish Ethics*, 79.

27. Faierstein, *Jewish Mystical Autobiographies*, 48.

28. Ibid., 205f.

29. See, G. Scholem, *Kabbalah* (New York: Quadrangle, 1974), 128–44.

30. Ibid., 142f.

31. G. Scholem, *Major Trends in Jewish Mysticism* (New York: Schocken, 1961), 245f.

32. M. Idel, *Messianic Mystics* (New Haven: Yale University Press, 1998), 126–82.

33. Ibid., 175–78; M. Idel, "'One from a Town, Two from a Clan'—The Diffusion of Lurianic Kabbalah and Sabbateanism: A Re-Examination," *Jewish History* 7 (1993): 79–104.

34. P. Giller, *Reading the Zohar* (New York: Oxford University Press, 2001), traces the relationship between the Zoharic corpus and Lurianic Kabbalah.

35. M. Idel, "On the Concept of *Zimzum* in Kabbalah and its Research" (in Hebrew), *Jerusalem Studies in Jewish Thought* 10 (1992): 59–112; B. Sack, "R. Moshe Cordovero's Doctrine of *Zimzum*" (in Hebrew), *Tarbiz* 58 (1989): 207–37.

36. The term literally means "repair." However, in this context it is used in the sense of "order of service or ritual."

37. Y. Wilhelm, "The Orders of the Tikkunim" (in Hebrew), in *Alei Ayin—Salman Schocken Jubilee Volume* (Jerusalem, 1948–52), 125–46.

38. On the popularization of this ritual see, E. Horowitz, "Coffee, Coffeehouses, and the Nocturnal Rituals of Early Modern Jewry," *AJS Review* 14 (1989): 17–46.

39. Wilhelm, "The Orders of the Tikkunim," 125–30.

40. G. Scholem, "Tradition and New Creation in the Ritual of the Kabbalists," in *On the Kabbalah and Its Symbolism* (New York: Schocken, 1965), 146–50; M. Halamish, "The Place of Kabbalah in Customs," in *The Customs of Israel: Sources and History* (in Hebrew), ed. D. Sperber (Jerusalem: Mosad Harav Kook, 1994), vol. 3, 219–20.

41. The text of *tikkun hazot* can be found in many prayer books.

42. Scholem, "Tradition and New Creation," 151–52; Halamish, "The Place of Kabbalah in Customs," 221f.

43. E. Ginsburg, *The Sabbath in the Classical Kabbalah* (Albany: State University of New York Press, 1989); idem, *Sod Ha-Shabbat: The Mystery of the Sabbath* (Albany: State University of New York Press, 1989).

44. Halamish, "The Place of Kabbalah in Customs," 218.

45. Ibid., 209.

46. L. Fine, *Safed Spirituality* (New York: Paulist Press, 1984), 73.

47. A group of prayers recited immediately before falling asleep, attributed to Rabbi Isaac Luria. See, Halamish, "The Place of Kabbalah in Customs," 218.

48. A prayer recited immediately upon waking. Found in *Sefer Seder Ha-Yom*, by R. Moses ibn Machir, a Safed kabbalist of the generation before Rabbi Isaac Luria.

49. This is a symbolic washing of the hands after the meal and before the grace is recited. See, Halamish, "The Place of Kabbalah in Customs," 180.

50. Lev. 23:40.

51. The *lulav* is the only one of the four species specifically mentioned in the blessing.

52. On the kabbalistic influence on Simhat Torah, see A. Yaari, *History of the Festival of Simhat Torah* (in Hebrew) (Jerusalem: Mosad Harav Kook, 1964), 259–318.

53. M. Rosh Hashanah 1:1.

54. Among the more important recent studies are Z. Greis, *Hanhagot Literature* (in Hebrew) (Jerusalem: Mosad Bialik, 1989); M. Halamish, *Kabbalah: In Prayer, Halakhah, and Custom* (in Hebrew) (Ramat Gan: Bar Ilan University Press, 2000).

55. The most comprehensive study of this movement is G. Scholem, *Sabbatai Sevi: The Mystical Messiah* (Princeton, NJ: Princeton University Press, 1973).

56. There is a rabbinic tradition that the Messiah will be born on the ninth of Ab. The possibility must be considered that this date was later manipulated to conform to the tradition.

57. The original blessing is "matir assurim" (who releases the captives) and is part of the morning liturgy. This is a play on the Hebrew words.

58. On the Doenmeh and their history, see Scholem, *Kabbalah*, 327–32.

59. G. Scholem, "R. Elijah ha-Cohen ha-Itamari and Sabbateanism" (in Hebrew), *Alexander Marx Jubilee Volume,* ed. Saul Lieberman (New York: Jewish Theological Seminary, 1950), 451–70.

60. On the various editions and translations, see C. Friedberg, *Bet Eked Sefarim* (Tel Aviv, 1954), vol. 3, 962. Friedberg lists more than forty editions.

61. On Cardozo and his writings, see D. Halperin. *Abraham Miguel Cardozo: Selected Writings* (Mahwah, NJ: Paulist Press, 2001).

62. A convenient summary of Scholem's explanation can be found in his *Major Trends in Jewish Mysticism*, 287–324.

63. Scholem, *Kabbalah*, 259, describes these factors in greater detail.

64. M. Idel, "'One from a Town, Two from a Clan.'"

65. The authorship of this work has been discussed by a number of scholars. The most important studies are A. Yaari, *The Propaganda of a Book: Who Wrote "Hemdat Yamin"* (in Hebrew) (Jerusalem: Mosad Harav Kook, 1954); I. Tishby, "The Sources of *Hemdat Yamim*": Paths of Faith and Heresy (in Hebrew) (Tel Aviv: Masada, 1964), 108–68.

Chapter 11

Jewish Women in the Ottoman Empire

Paméla Dorn Sezgin

Ottoman Women's Historiography

The life of a woman in the Ottoman Empire, whether she was Muslim, Jewish, Greek, or Armenian, was oriented toward domestic, private, family space until the sweeping reforms and social upheavals of the nineteenth century. Public space was predominantly male space: the areas of commercial, educational, court, and religious life. In contrast, women were centered in their families and communities. Notable exceptions occurred for some elite women in the Ottoman court or for widows who, upon necessity, took over the family business. For the most part, however, urban women's lives were lived behind the veil, latticework, and the high walls of the household garden or courtyard. Women could move about in public, but only in groups at specific times. This gender separation and regulation of women's social space makes tracking their lives, particularly the lives of working-class women difficult.

Whereas shipping registers, tax records, court proceedings, and guild rosters documented the participation of men from the various Ottoman ethnic groups and social classes in public life, women's lives, principally those of Jewish women, were hidden and almost undocumented in the usual Ottoman sources. Jewish women relied upon rabbinical law, rather than the Ottoman *kadi* courts, to settle disputes. Nonelite women were, for the most part, unschooled and illiterate prior to the late nineteenth century. Therefore, diaries, letters, and their own accounts had to wait until foreign-sponsored educational movements (1860–1923) gave them voice. Instead, sources of information from the sixteenth through the eighteenth centuries were from the occasional European traveler's accounts or Ottoman records that made mention of notable women at the *saray* (palace) and in major cities.

The nineteenth and early twentieth centuries, in contrast, provided a rich treasure of documents, paintings, textiles, photographs, diaries, school records, musical recordings, and newspaper accounts. European female travelers provided an abundance of descriptions about the lives of Jewish, Muslim, and Christian women in this period of rapid social change. Oral narratives of women who lived during the early twentieth century enhanced ethnographic reports that rounded out the understanding of women's activities, ideas, and actions.[1]

The study of Jewish women in the Ottoman Empire must proceed at two levels. First, I examine the general, sociocultural, and historic milieu in which women of different social classes lived, contrasting the lives of minority women with those of their Muslim counterparts (the majority and dominant cultural group). Their behaviors, ideas, and environments are compared. Second, elements that were specific to Jewish women are investigated. These include their status within Jewish law (*halakha*), which helps explain the uniqueness of Sephardic women's existence and adaptation to the historical events and cultural contexts in which they lived. The geographic and cultural area in which Iberian Jews settled upon leaving Spain and arriving in the Ottoman Empire in 1492 was transformed by an emergent Ottoman Jewish culture. Women's interactions within their own community and their intercommunal mixing are topics that round out the discussion. I will close with a look at the changes of the nineteenth century that not only foresaw the end of the empire, but also the demise of a rich, vibrant Sephardic world that existed for almost 450 years outside of Spain.

The Judeo-Spanish Culture Area

Sephardic Jewish life, characterized by Judeo-Spanish language and its related literary and cultural traditions, dominated other Jewish traditions in the Ottoman Empire with the arrival of somewhere between 50,000 to 150,000 Iberian Jewish refugees in the empire in 1492.[2] Sultan Beyazit II was looking for people to repopulate the newly conquered areas that had been depleted of Byzantine subjects in the intervening years since his father's (Fatih Sultan Mehmet's) conquest of Constantinople in 1453.

The newly arrived Iberian Jews held skills useful to the empire. They were doctors, merchants, bankers, artisans, boatmen, entertainers, and tradesmen with European contacts. Their Spanish experience with Muslim rule made them no strangers to the Islamic legal system (Shariʾah). They already knew how to be useful as tax farmers (collectors/landlords), provisioners, and administrators knowledgeable in different languages. Instead of adopting the local *minhag* (custom) of the resident Jewish community, which in this case was Byzantine, the Sephardim clung to their own traditions.[3] Their success with the Ottomans was also due to their connections to Europe, which enhanced their local dominance. Also, their sheer numbers overwhelmed the existing Jewish communities who became subsumed by them—except in rare instances like the Greek-speaking community of Ioannina in northern Greece, which preserved its distinctiveness.

For approximately 450 years (from 1492 until World War II), the Judeo-Spanish cultural area extended from the Ottoman Empire in southeastern Europe (the Balkan peninsula), to Asia Minor (Anatolia), into the Levant (the portion of the Middle East that borders the Mediterranean Sea), and into limited areas of North Africa. However, its strongest influences manifested themselves in the Balkans and Anatolia, where Judeo-Spanish speakers came to dominate Italian, Ashkenazic, and preexisting Byzantine Jews. Arabic-speaking Jewish communities in Morocco, Libya, Tunisia, Egypt, Ottoman Palestine, and Greater Syria (including what today would be Israel, Jordan, Syria, Lebanon, and portions of the Arabian peninsula) had their own distinct cultures, coexisting with much smaller, Ottoman Turkish Jewish communities in their midst.

Ottoman Social Organization

The unique social structure of the Ottoman Empire permitted the Iberian Jewish refugees and their descendants to create a distinctive Judeo-Spanish culture that thrived until the twentieth century and had surprising continuity from community to community despite regional variations. Jews, as non-Muslims, were recognized as *dhimmi* (in Turkish: *zimmi*), "people of the book"—a monotheistic minority with certain rights and restrictions. These restrictions included paying special taxes; wearing distinctive clothing to mark their identity; not riding certain animals; and observing architectural covenants.[4] Minority houses, according to the official legal code, were not permitted to be next to mosques, nor were they to be more than two stories in height. Though they remained on the books, these restrictions were not always enforced. In mid-eighteenth-century Aleppo, for example, Jewish homes were located next to a mosque, and Muslim homes were adjacent to a synagogue. The prime factors determining residence patterns were location and class, not ethnicity or religion.[5]

The Ottoman social system was segmental in nature. Subject peoples were classified according to their religious status as distinct communities retaining their own laws and customs. Within these communities, there were differences of wealth and class. For personal matters, the Ottoman officials recognized non-Muslim, religion-based, legal systems under the *millet* system, with the Ottoman code taking precedence in criminal cases. It was not a perfect system because non-Muslims as witnesses or plaintiffs were not equal to Muslims. Also, women, both Muslim and minority, were viewed as being one half as important as men—that is, two women witnesses were needed to be the equivalent of one male witness's testimony. However, women were recognized as property owners. Elite women even had recourse to divorce proceedings or to refusing potential spouses in arranged marriages.[6] Non-Muslims sometimes went to the Ottoman court system for inheritance or commercial issues, although they were not compelled to litigate in the Muslim system. The Ottoman imperial state recognized groups and corporate entities, dividing tax-paying subjects, *reaya*, from the ruling class. For the Jewish community, this meant that groups were organized around specific synagogues, *kehalim*. The synagogues initially were organized by the local residents' place of origin, and later, by neighborhoods. The Ottomans learned this organization from the Byzantines. The Sephardic Jews adopted it, retaining their place names of origin as congregational names.

Later, the communities of each Ottoman city were reorganized as a *kehillah* organization. These community associations were under the jurisdiction of a rabbi (*hakham*) and religious court (*bet din*). By the eighteenth century, large communities exerted administrative influence over smaller ones in their region. Influential Jewish men who had connections in the Ottoman bureaucracy, lay leaders, came to have important roles of leadership. This was also true of tax assessors and *parnasim* or *memunim*, operations managers who ran the day-to-day business of the community.[7]

There were no restrictions on Jewish travel, trade, or settlement, other than periods of the *sürgün* in the fifteenth and sixteenth centuries, when the Ottoman government moved populations—both Muslim and non-Muslim—to repopulate conquered areas and encourage commercial life. The Ottoman system continued with subtle variations, until 1839, when the Tanzimat Reforms instituted major changes using European-inspired legal and governmental models.

Jewish Women in the Ottoman Context

Sixteenth-century accounts mention a few exceptional Jewish women who served the royal women of the sultan's family by bringing silks, pearls, gold bracelets, and other luxury goods to the palace. These Jewish women also brought news from the outside world, to which the cloistered harem women had limited access. Esther Kyra was perhaps the most famous of these women. During the reign of Murad III (r. 1574–1595), she was the trusted confidant of Murad's mother, the *vâlide sultan*, Nur Banu. Esther was the wife of Rabbi Eli Handeli (also Handali) an Istanbul merchant. "*Kyra*" was a Greek honorific for a woman of importance; her name was similar to "Lady Esther." Esther became wealthy from her connections in the palace and her control of Istanbul customs, from which her son profited handsomely. She was useful for diplomacy, acting as a go-between for the palace women and foreign embassies. Esperanza Melchi (or Malkhi) was the agent for Safiye, mother of Mehmed III (r. 1595–1603). Esperanza Melchi was an Italian Jewish immigrant who wrote letters on the Ottoman queen's behalf to Elizabeth I of England. The *kyras* were highly political and took part in palace intrigues, promoting the appointments of regional governors and military administrators. This led to jealousy, sometimes resulting in murder by the Janissaries. Jewish *kyras* continued to be active in Ottoman diplomacy and court politics through the 1730s.[8]

Dona Gracia Mendes, the aunt of Don Joseph Nasi, was the most famous Ottoman Jewish woman of the sixteenth century. She was from a prominent *converso* family in Portugal and became a banker after the death of her husband, Francisco. Dona Gracia made loans to Hapsburg and French monarchs. During her exile in Belgium and Italy, she returned openly to Judaism. In 1553, she transferred her wealth from Vienna, and reestablished herself in the Ottoman Empire. She and her nephew were of great help to Sultan Selim II. They established a network of business enterprises and charitable works in Jewish communities in the Holy Land and Ottoman-dominated Mediterranean.[9]

Some Ottoman Jewish women also engaged in commerce, selling jewelry, silks, and other luxury goods to elite women in their homes. Other women had real estate interests, following the pattern of elite Ottoman women from all ethnic groups, who held their own property. Less affluent women worked in family businesses, mostly at home or in workshops, producing embroidery, sewing decorative textile goods (e.g., fancy linen towels, tablecloths, and handkerchiefs), making lace, and producing custom-made clothing, or cleaning and pressing it for wealthier families. Others worked in the silk industry around the town of Bursa, where Jewish and Greek women raised silk worms and spun and loomed textiles.[10] The poorest women worked as servants in the homes of wealthy Jewish families, who might provide their *dota* (dowry) and otherwise finance and arrange their marriage, following an Ottoman pattern shared by Muslims and Christians.

The lives of most Jewish women in the Ottoman Empire were not as glamorous as that of Dona Gracia or Esther Kyra. Jewish women dominated the domestic sphere of activities. Their husbands, for the most part, handled the public dimension, interacting with the multiethnic mix of Ottoman society in the market place. In the seventeenth century, population statistics for Istanbul showed that 15 percent of the Jewish community lived in poverty, and another 15 percent was extremely rich. The vast majority of families, the remaining 70 percent, were small-business owners, that is, shopkeepers.[11]

The women's lives revolved around their extended families and the *kortijo* (interior courtyard). Ottoman houses had either a protected garden or a central courtyard in which women often spent the day doing their chores or embroidering luxurious textiles for the home, and supervising their servants. Female neighbors visited, as did female relatives. Women took coffee breaks, reading their fortunes from the grounds of the Turkish coffee, exchanging gossip and news with one another, and planning advantageous marriages for their children. To calm babies and fill the time, women also sang the *romansas* (epics) their ancestors brought with them from Spain, and later, improvised *kantigas* (songs) in the style of Italian, Greek, and Turkish urban, popular songs of the times. They also told *konsejas* (moralistic stories) as a means of teaching their children ethics and good conduct.[12]

Women were the primary transmitters of the Judeo-Spanish language and culture. The majority of the women before the nineteenth century were not formally educated. Elite families and the families of religious officials, such as rabbis and cantors, may have engaged tutors for their daughters or taught them at home themselves. However, the majority of women were ignorant of the languages and formal religious training their husbands received in the *meldars* and *Talmudei Torah* schools in Hebrew and Ladino, the formalized Judeo-Spanish that was used for printing religious books.

The use of both Ladino and Judeo-Spanish is an example of what linguists call diglossia. The same language had two, distinct forms: a formal one for printing and educated discourse, and an informal one for everyday life. Ladino was composed of Spanish and Hebrew and was used for religious discourse. Judeo-Spanish was the vernacular, used informally in the family and in the Jewish community. Unlike Ladino, during its long sojourn in the Ottoman Empire it became mixed with Greek, Turkish, Italian, Arabic, and French, as well as with Hebrew words and word endings.[13]

Until the nineteenth century, when they received formal instruction in French and other European languages, Judeo-Spanish was often the only language that women used. It was not until the twentieth century that most Jewish women learned and became fluent in Turkish. Of course, elite women knew other languages. Such women included Dona Gracia, who came from Europe in one of the later migrations of *conversos* (some 100 years after the first Sephardic migration), and the women of *los Frangos* (the Europeans), who were Italian Jews who maintained ties to Italy and went back and forth throughout the Ottoman period. The vast majority of Jews were not in the elite. Working-class women and the wives of the shopkeepers were Judeo-Spanish speakers, particularly outside of Istanbul in Anatolian and Balkan towns and cities.[14] Crews in 1932 observed that while older Jewish men in Monastir (Bitola, Macedonia) were "able to read and write Hebrew" and "many of them knew [in addition to Judeo-Spanish] Greek, Turkish and Macedo-Serbian," the women of the same generation were generally illiterate and knew no other language than Judeo-Spanish. The women "lived exclusively in a small Jewish circle."[15]

Women's religious life and responsibilities were focused around maintaining a proper Jewish home and raising children. Their religious knowledge came from their mothers and, not surprisingly, mixed Judaic tradition with a rich system of folk belief. In contrast, their husbands received rudimentary, formal instruction in the *meldars* and stayed in contact with rabbis and other religious leaders through the synagogue. Women's beliefs were more flexible. Until the formal religious education of women in the late nineteenth century as part of the women's educational movement, most women learned only the domestic aspects of Judaism: keeping a kosher home, home-based activities for major holidays, life-cycle events (such as birth, *brit millah,* weddings, and death), religious observances concerning the *mikvah,* and women's purity requirements.

Unlike the majority of women, rabbis' daughters often learned formal religious knowledge simply because their fathers and brothers engaged in Talmudic debates at home and hosted other religiously observant men for study on Shabbat afternoons and holidays. Listening in the kitchen or sitting next to their fathers as very young children, these women acquired religious knowledge from the male domain. But they were the exception and not the rule.[16]

Women's belief systems, while based in Sephardic Judaism, revolved around general Middle Eastern and Mediterranean folk religion. Infant mortality was a constant problem, as was jealousy from neighbors, relatives, and friends. There was a belief in the evil eye (*ojo malo*) and its related practices such as amulet (*kameya*) wearing, or the heating of lead in water to break bad luck. Blessings to bring good fortune and curses to ward off disaster were common. Much of folk religious practice revolved around health concerns.

Because children were the focus of adult women's lives, infertility gave rise to many practices. Ottoman Jewish women in Cairo, for example, stayed overnight in the Maimonides Synagogue and said special prayers. Elsewhere, these prayers were said at the tombs of famous rabbis or holy men (*tzadikim*).[17] Such practices were similar to those of Muslim women, who implored dead Sufi saints (*pir*[s]) throughout Turkey and the Balkans for help in conceiving, as well as for assistance in curing relatives of terminal illnesses and finding suitable marriage partners for their children.[18] There were many rituals and special formulaic sayings, called *endulkos*, for curing illnesses.[19] Men also engaged in folk religious practices, but not to the extent that women did. Rabbis and *soferim* (scribes) wrote the prayers and magical names of angels that filled the parchments giving the *kameya*(s) their power.

Jewish women were not restricted, as their Muslim neighbors were, to staying within their own courtyards and houses. However, if one went to *kal* (synagogue), the women's gallery often had a latticework in place or lace curtain so that the women would not be visible to the men below who were praying. The Marquis de Villeneve (1728–1741), who was the French ambassador to the Ottoman Empire under Louis XV, wrote that, while Jewish women were permitted freely to leave their houses, they preferred to stay home and embroider, sending their slaves or servants out for errands and shopping.[20] Perhaps one reason that Jewish women felt more comfortable in their own homes was that it was an environment in which they could let down their guard. Jewish women, like Muslim women, in the Ottoman Empire, lived by a strict moral code. The Jewish code, which demanded the just and proper conduct of women, was one upon which the family's reputation depended. The quality of one's name was paramount. Jewish women were careful to avoid being a topic of gossip, for the appearance of a transgression, even if it was erroneous, was just as bad as the actual transgression. Sephardic *refranes* (proverbs) reflect these attitudes: "Ajo sin pajo, no ay" (There is no garlic without the chaff), meaning that there was no gossip without a grain of truth to it. One did not want to be "de la boka de la gente" (in the mouth of the people), meaning the topic of people's conversations.[21] However, there was safety in numbers, and women enjoyed going on family picnics, particularly on the shores of the Halič, the Golden Horn in Istanbul.

The status of an individual Jewish woman was determined by two factors: (a) the family into which she was born, and (b) the family into which she married. Marriages were monogamous and continued well into the twentieth century to be arranged by the parents of the prospective bride and groom. However, the young people had the right to refuse a potential match. Among middle-class and affluent families, the *dota* (dowry) given to her new husband was paid by the bride's father. He paid a sum of money and/or provided a house and furnishings for the couple and, if possible, took the new son-in-law into the bride's family's business.

Sometimes, the new couple lived with the bride's family, which was called *masa Franka* (European table). The *dota* custom ensured a level of good treatment for the bride from her new husband. If the husband was out of line, he would quickly hear from his father-in-law, the person upon whom he was dependent for earning a living! This system favored the brides, so much so that potential grooms worried about being controlled by their fathers-in-law. It gave rise to the *refrane* "Abasha eskalon toma mujer, suve eskalon, toma haver" (Step down the stairs for a wife, step up for a business partner). The meaning of the proverb was that one should take a wife from the same or lower social level as oneself, but take a business partner from a higher socioeconomic group.

Winds of Change: Europeanization and Modernization

The Ottoman Empire began an economic decline in the seventeenth and eighteenth centuries as trans-Atlantic trade became increasingly important to Europe, and the Ottoman—Italian connections had less impact in the global economy. The Netherlands, Spain, Portugal, France, and England built rival empires based upon colonialism, the transfer of slaves, and silver currency. Their empires spanned the world, as they included North and South America, Africa, the Indian subcontinent, and China. Improvements in European military technology and the eventual development of mechanized industrial production did not go unnoticed by the Ottoman rulers. The Ottoman elite began to familiarize itself with European languages and cultures, importing rococo architecture, Italian bandmasters, French painters, and tutors to the *saray*.

This awareness of Europe and interest in new forms of technology and social organization resulted in the Tanzimat Reforms, beginning in 1839. Changes in the Ottoman legal system did away with the *dhimmi* system and granted equality before the law for all subjects, regardless of religion. In the 1850s and 1860s, special taxes on non-Muslim minorities were abolished. French commercial and penal codes were adopted in 1850 and 1858. Civil, commercial, and criminal cases were heard by state courts, while Christian and Jewish religious and lay councils were formally recognized by the government. These community courts heard matters of personal status such as divorce and inheritance disputes. The Young Turk Revolution of 1908 resulted in further changes, including actual military service for minorities, which was implemented in 1909.[22]

The active role played by European powers in these reforms, as well as in the growing nationalism of Christian Ottoman subjects in the Balkans, resulted in increasing contacts with European travelers, merchants, governments, and missionaries by the mid-1800s.[23] Presbyterian and Congregational missionaries started schools throughout the Balkans and Levant, and Jews, Christians, and to a lesser extent, Muslims attended them. Greeks and Jews became agents for European embassies and commercial interests.

Greek, Bulgarian, and Armenian national movements were supported by European powers and resulted in instability in the empire, prolonged wars, famine, hardship, suffering, and population movements. This was particularly true in Thrace, Macedonia, and the Greek Islands, where Turks and Jews fled, seeking refuge in Istanbul and more secure Ottoman towns. Whereas the Turks mostly left the Jews to run their own communities, Greek and Bulgarian Orthodox Christians jealously plotted to remove the Jewish communities from or boycott Jewish commercial activities in the territories now coming under their jurisdiction. Accusations of blood libels against the Jews surfaced in Balkan and Syrian communities at this time, with one of the most infamous occurring in Damascus in 1840.[24]

European Jewish philanthropists, such as the Montefiore, Cremieux, Rothschild, and Hirsch families, took notice of the extreme hardships their Eastern brethren were experiencing. They made visits to the Ottoman

Empire or sent their representatives, advocating European Jewish intervention to upgrade living conditions and bring modern education to the Ottoman Jews. These efforts resulted in the formation of several Jewish schools, which were eventually taken over by the Alliance Israélite Universelle (henceforth referred to as Alliance), a French Jewish organization founded in 1860 in Paris with the purpose of emancipating and protecting Eastern Jewry.

The schools began utilizing Alsatian Jewish faculty and organizing local committees in Ottoman and Middle Eastern cities and towns. They were established using funds from Baron de Hirsch and his wife, Clara, as well as from the member fees (paid by subscribers) and tuition (from families who could afford to pay). Scholarships were arranged for poor children. Eventually, Ottoman and Middle Eastern Jews were trained at the Ecole Normale Israélite Orientale in France, and they worked as directors and teachers in the schools—but not in their own communities (for example, an Istanbul Jew ran the Casablanca school).

The educational program promoted by the Alliance was meant to transform its students. The goal was not simply to teach French and other foreign languages or give students a trade in which to work. Rather, it was to remake students into modern citizens of the countries in which they lived with a decidedly pro-European and "rational" outlook. Alliance directors subscribed to the late Victorian idea of "civilizing the peoples of the East." Even the directors who were born in the Ottoman Empire and the Middle East, developed a kind of ambivalence about their own Sephardic culture, embracing the "advancement" of European ideology.[25]

The rigorous curriculum of the schools promoted a general elementary-through-middle-school program, including a variety of subjects: basic mathematics; sciences; general history; geography; Jewish history and religion; Hebrew language (for religious purposes, not as a living language); French language (penmanship and literature); a second language (such as modern Spanish, German, English, or the language of the country in which the school was located); and vocational subjects. The vocational part of the curriculum included embroidery and sewing for girls, and business education or a skilled trade for boys. The Alliance promoted new, manual trades for Jewish boys, such as metalworking, mechanics, cabinetry, typography, mattress making, locksmithery, and coach building. This moved away from the traditional trades of the lower classes in petty commerce such as "hawking," or peddling, and money lending. Some schools in Ottoman Palestine also promoted agricultural work.

The Alliance, more than any other institution, changed Ottoman Jewish women's role as culture bearers almost overnight. Whereas Jewish women were the most important influence in the almost 450-year maintenance of Judeo-Spanish language and culture in the Ottoman Empire, the Alliance transformed them into agents of change. The Alliance leadership saw women's education as paramount to transforming the Ottoman Jewish family because women had an immediate impact on future generations. So women went from being transmitters of tradition to advocates of change.

It was the first opportunity women had for a formal education, and they liked it. The Alliance established girls schools by the 1870s. While most schools were gender segregated—boys and girls attended separate schools—in some communities, like Chorlu in Thrace, there were co-educational schools. This was a radical idea which went against Ottoman social conventions. The gender-mixed schools were rare and occurred mostly in small towns like Chorlu. Perhaps their existence can be attributed to cost-saving measures designed to make the modern, European education system accessible even in remote areas, where otherwise the communities might not be able to support a school.

Despite any discomfort regarding new social mores and ideas advanced by the Alliance, girls and their families saw the Alliance as a way of advancing their marriage prospects. The alliance taught them new domestic skills, with updated views about hygiene and modern science in the home, including practices that enhanced the survival of their infants.

The Alliance forced its students to wear European clothes to school, a practice that Ottoman Jewish women readily and happily adopted. Family photographs from the 1890s and early 1900s show younger women wearing European fashions while their mothers and grandmothers still maintained Ottoman Jewish dress. The European *fustan blanka* (white dress) became the norm for Istanbul weddings in the early 1900s, replacing the traditional Ottoman wedding dress, the *bindalli*, which became restricted in use for Purim festivities as an exotic costume.[26] The Turkish *bindalli* had been the standard wedding dress for Muslim, Armenian, Bulgarian, and Jewish women in Ottoman towns, its heavy dark-burgundy or navy-blue velvet embroidered with gold or silver threads. Valuable and special, it was lovingly cut into covers for the *teva* (the reader's desk in the synagogue) or refashioned into a *parokhet* (the curtain before the ark) by generations of Jewish women. This change to European fashions also came about when they began to be mass-produced in the Ottoman Empire and marketed by Jewish stores in the larger cities.[27]

Education opened up new worlds for Ottoman Jewish women. While a woman attending the Alliance schools generally married and became the *nikochera* (housewife) as her mother had done, albeit a more efficient and literate one than her mother was, a few women went on to have careers. Female teachers were needed in the Alliance schools, which, between 1880 and 1914, existed in all Jewish centers from Morocco to Iran. The most promising students, male and female, were sent to Paris by the Alliance to be trained as teachers and directors for the schools. The first were Fortunée and Rachel Béhar, sister of Nissim Béhar, also an Alliance teacher, from Jerusalem and Istanbul.

The story of one early female student from Adrianople (Edirne) illustrates the difficulties experienced by young Ottoman Jewish women at the Ecole Normale, the Alliance teacher training school in Paris. She described some of the hardships that the Eastern students endured, such as teasing by the Parisian girls. The writer from Adrianople went to Paris at age of fourteen and almost had to come home because of gossip. Her mother's friends insisted that the daughter was not really going to school and implied that perhaps she was involved in something unsavory, since Paris was the center of all kinds of vices. Luckily, the girl's uncle intervened, a Turkish Jewish merchant doing business in India, whose experiences in the world made him a better judge of the school and the people in charge.[28]

Women's schools also opened up new ideas and opportunities. A few literate Jewish women became newspaper owners and journalists in the Ottoman Empire early in the twentieth century. One was Esther Azhari Moyal (1873–1948), who was born in Beirut and contributed to several Arabic-language newspapers in Cairo and Jaffa. She attended the World Columbian Exposition in Chicago in 1893 and later returned to the Middle East and married her husband, Shimon, a medical doctor who translated the Talmud into Arabic. In 1899, she started her own newspaper, *al-ᶜAᵓlia*, writing about literary subjects and world affairs, particularly the Dreyfus affair in France. She later wrote a biography of Emile Zola in Arabic and translated popular and classic French novels. In 1908, she and her husband moved back to Jaffa where she started a women's organization and ran a bilingual Arabic/Hebrew newspaper, *Sawt al-ʿUthmaniyya* (The Ottoman Voice). After her husband's death, she migrated to France but returned to Jaffa in the 1940s, fleeing the Nazis in Europe.[29]

Marguerite Saltiel was another Ottoman Jewish female journalist. She worked briefly as a contributor to the local Judeo-Spanish press in Salonika prior to her 1923 emigration to the United States. Her articles documented the aftermath of the Balkan Wars, the transition to Greek government in Salonika, and the hardships experienced by the Jewish community.[30]

Literacy and education had interesting consequences for Ottoman Jewish women. Women's work was accepted as a temporary situation, before marriage, or as an emergency measure in the case of economic hardship for the family, but the idea of women's having careers as a norm was not widely accepted. Middle-class Jewish families discouraged manual work, even though the Alliance schools promoted a kind of socialist attitude toward the benefits and inherent goodness of manual labor.

Ottoman Jewish society, however, was status-conscious. The mark of a well-to-do family was that its women stayed home, that they did not have to work. Yet, a few women had romantic ideas about working and became entertainers and entered public life. For example, the great Greek singer Rosa Eskenazi, was from an Istanbul family that relocated to Salonika. Her career began when soldiers walking by in the street heard her singing at home while doing chores and asked her to perform at a *taverna* in the city. Her career meant, though, a complete break from her Jewish background. Performing in public was something that respectable Jewish women did not do. Armenian and Greek women worked as entertainers in the Ottoman Empire, but rarely did Jewish and Muslim women.[31]

Women's literacy also made them open to new ideas. French novellas were translated into Judeo-Spanish and serialized in the Judeo-Spanish press. The women attending the Alliance schools read classic French novels and poetry in which the characters married for love, not because their parents had made an economically and socially appropriate match for them. Some women took this idea to heart. Nobel Prize–winner Elias Canetti wrote in his memoir, *The Tongue Set Free*, about his early years in Ruschuk, Bulgaria, that his parents met at school in Vienna and married for love (circa 1904; Canetti was born in 1905) despite the objections of his mother's family. They shared a common passion for the theater and German literature. Her family, the Ardittis, was composed of wealthy merchants in Bulgaria. His father's people, the Canettis, were Jews from Adrianople of modest means: "Grandfather Canetti had pulled himself up by his bootstraps; an orphan, cheated, turned out of doors while young, he had worked his way up to prosperity."[32] Grandfather Arditti viewed the Canettis as socially inferior to his family, but he gave in to his daughter's wishes.

Marrying for love was a new and very European idea. It was expressed in many of the *kantigas,* popular Sephardic songs of the late nineteenth and early twentieth centuries.[33] Many women in the second generation to attend Alliance schools, around the time of World War I, had dreams of marrying for love. But due to respect for their parents and practical circumstances, they still made arranged marriages, keeping their first, real love a secret.[34]

No Turning Back: The End of an Empire

The discussion of Ottoman Jewish women's lives properly ends with the empire itself. World War I and its aftermath were devastating to the empire. The European powers, particularly Britain, could not wait to divide the spoils. Perhaps they were surprised at the strength of Gazi Mustafa Kemal (later, Atatürk) and his followers who fought for the independence of modern Turkey in 1923 and rebuilt it from the ashes of the empire. Population exchanges ensued, other national movements having changed the face of the Balkans and the Near East to make the maps that defined the twentieth century. Growing Arab Muslim and Balkan Christian nationalisms left little room for Jewish diversity. However, Jewish communities continued in the Balkans until World War II and the destruction of European Jewry, and into the 1950s in Iraq and Egypt, until the rise of pan-Arab nationalism. Some Ottoman Jews emigrated to western Europe because of their Alliance pro-European mind-set in the early twentieth century. Others went to the New World, going to New York and the southern United States prior to 1924, when federal laws limited immigration. Others went to Cuba, Mexico, and Uruguay where their Judeo-Spanish was quietly transformed into modern Spanish. Many Turkish Jews embraced Jewish nationalism in British-mandated Palestine and, during Israel's independence, literally arrived by the boatload.[35]

The distinctive Judeo-Spanish culture, preserved by almost 450 years of Ottoman rule, gave way to national cultures in which mandatory schooling for women, women's emancipation in terms of voting participation and working outside of the home, and fluency in the national languages took precedence. The Alliance schools prepared Ottoman Jewish women and their daughters to enter these changing social and cultural circumstances. It was not the adoption of French language and European social mores that dealt the deathblow to Judeo-Spanish culture. Instead, it was the changing political boundaries of Europe, the Middle East and North Africa in the twentieth century that allowed little room for a distinctive Eastern Jewish culture.

Judeo-Spanish culture continued in certain families, nostalgically associated with the memories of dear mothers and grandmothers; preserved in memoirs and the Judeo-Spanish press; collected for museum exhibits and archives in the modern land of Israel; and lovingly analyzed by folklorists, anthropologists, and linguists for the past 100 years. Just recently, in the postmodern, transnational world, has it begun to be understood and respected, taking its rightful place in history. The Ottoman Empire, as much, if not more so, than the Jewish Pale of Settlement in Eastern Europe, enjoyed a rich and lengthy Jewish presence, a cosmopolitan and socially diverse world of Judeo-Spanish culture that declined by the mid-twentieth century but remains in many unexplored documents waiting in Jewish and Ottoman archives, and in the fading recesses of family memories.

NOTES

1. My own ethnographic fieldwork with Sephardic communities in the United States, Turkey, and Israel in the 1970s and 1980s included narratives by women who as children lived through World War I, remembering stories of their mothers and grandmothers in that period, as well as stories of contact with foreign soldiers garrisoned in their Ottoman communities. See Paméla J. Dorn, "Change and Ideology: the Ethnomusicology of Turkish Jewry" (Ph.D. dissertation, Indiana University, Bloomington, 1991). Other ethnographic work documenting these women includes Cynthia Crews, "Judeo-Spanish Folktales in Macedonia" *Folklore* 43 (1932): 193–225; and Isaac Jack Levy and Rosemary Levy Zumwalt, *Ritual Medical Lore of Sephardic Women: Sweeting the Spirits, Healing the Sick* (Urbana: University of Illinois Press, 2002), an exploration of folk religious belief. Memoirs are good sources, too, such as Rebecca Amato Levy, *I Remember Rhodes/Mi Akodro de Rhodes* (in Judeo-Spanish and English) (New York: Sepher-Hermon, 1987).

2. These population statistics primarily come from Ottoman tax registers as quoted in Esther Benbassa and Aron Rodrigue, *Sephardi Jewry: A History of the Judeo-Spanish Community, Fourteenth to Twentieth Centuries* (Berkeley: University of California Press, 2000), xxiii. Given that there was a trend to underreport members of the Jewish community so as to minimize paying taxes, there is no definitive number but rather a range for the population of the Judeo-Spanish-speaking community. See also Stanford J. Shaw, *The Jews of the Ottoman Empire and the Turkish Republic* (New York: New York University Press, 1991); and Avigdor

Levy, *The Sephardim in the Ottoman Empire* (Princeton, NJ: Darwin, 1992) for further statistical information based upon Ottoman sources and distinctions between waves of Iberian and Italian Jewish immigration to the Balkans, Levant, and Anatolia.

3. The Byzantine Jewish community is often called Romaniyot or Romanist, something of a misnomer as these Jews were Greek-speaking.

4. Minorities started to wear Western clothing in the eighteenth century until an imperial decree in 1758 specifically addressed the issue, forcing a return to traditional dress. See Fatma Müge Göcek, *East Encounters West: France and the Ottoman Empire in the Eighteenth Century* (New York: Oxford University Press, 1987), 119, 124. For specific taxes that Jews were required to pay, see
Shaw, *The Jews of the Ottoman Empire and the Turkish Republic*, 75. For detailed descriptions of the dress of Ottoman Jews, see Esther Juhasz, ed., *Sephardi Jews in the Ottoman Empire: Aspects of Material Culture* (Jerusalem: Israel Museum, 1990); Alfred Rubens, *A History of Jewish Costume* (New York: Crown, 1973); and Yedida Kalfon Stillman and Norman A. Stillman, *Arab Dress: A Short History* (Leiden, the Netherlands: Brill, 2000).

5. According to Donald Quataert, *The Ottoman Empire, 1700–1922* (Cambridge: Cambridge University Press, 2000), "The inhabitants of this important Arab city often preferred to live with others of similar wealth rather than common religion. Elsewhere, as in Istanbul and Ankara, rich and poor and middling often resided together in the same neighborhoods. In sum, when Ottoman families choose their home sites, they used a host of criteria and not simply religion" (178).

6. Göcek, *East Encounters West*, presents a detailed analysis of *kadi* court records in the Galatasaray district of Istanbul, an area of Jewish settlement, but finds almost no mention of Jewish women using these courts. Instead, they preferred the Jewish religious courts in Balat, a district of dense Ottoman Jewish settlement on the Golden Horn, not far away. For comparisons of the legal status of Jewish, Greek and Muslim Ottoman women, see Suraiya Faroqhi, *Subjects of the Sultan: Culture and Daily Life in the Ottoman Empire* (London: I. B. Tauris, 2000); and Madeline C. Zilfi, "'We Don't Get Along': Women and the *Hul* Divorce in the Eighteenth Century," in *Women in the Ottoman Empire: Middle Eastern Women in the Early Modern Era*, ed. Madeline Zilfi (Leiden, the Netherlands: Brill, 1997), 264–96.

7. For more details about communal organizations, see Jacob Barnai, "On the History of the Jews in the Ottoman Empire," in *Sephardi Jews in the Ottoman Empire*, ed. Juhasz.

8. Godfrey Goodwin, *The Private World of Ottoman Women* (London: Saqi, 1997).

9. Cecil Roth, *The House of Nasi: Dona Gracia* (Philadelphia: Jewish Publication Society, 1947).

10. Women's commercial and work activities are discussed in Fernand Braudel, *The Mediterranean and the Mediterranean World in the Age of Philip II*, trans. Sian Reynolds, vol. 2 (New York: Harper & Row, 1973), 814; Levy, *The Sephardim in the Ottoman Empire*, 36–37; and Donald Quataert, ed., *Consumption Studies and the History of the Ottoman Empire, 1550–1922* (Albany: State University of New York Press, 2000), 137. Faroqhi, *Subjects of the Sultan*, presents interesting information on "women's markets" and reports Ottoman women, Muslim and minority, were able to patronize neighborhood markets freely from the sixteenth through the nineteenth centuries (119–20).

11. Benbassa and Rodrigue, *Sephardi Jewry*, 32.

12. For examples of *konsejas* in their original language, see Matilda Koen Sarano, *Konsejas i kosejikas del mundo djudeo-espanyol* (In Judeo-Spanish) (Jerusalem: Kaza Editora Kana, 1994).

13. For a discourse on the distinctions between these two forms of the language, see Haim Vidal Sephiha, *La ladino: Judéo-espagnol calque* (Paris: Editions Hispaniques, 1973); and idem, *L'agonie des judéo-espagnols* (Paris: Editions Entente, 1979).

14. Abraham Galanté's published works (1927 to 1956) map the extensive settlement of Jews throughout the Ottoman Empire in places large and small. Galanté's materials have been reprinted as Abraham Galanté, *Histoire des juifs de Turquie*, 9 vols. (Istanbul: Editions Isis, 1985).

15. Crews, "Judeo-Spanish Folktales in Macedonia," 196.

16. The formal religious practices of Sephardic Jews are explained in Nissim Behar, *El gid para el praktikante* (in Ladino), 2d ed. (Istanbul: Türkiye Hahambašiligi, 1967); and in Herbert C. Dobrinsky, *A Treasury of Sephardic Laws and Customs* (New York: Yeshiva University Press, 1986). My assertions about women's religious knowledge were based upon ethnographic field experiences in Turkey and Israel. Mme. Rashel Ben Habib Levy, daughter of an Ottoman rabbi, Moshe Ben Habib, and Mme. Janti Behar, daughter of a cantor, were among several narrators, all daughters of religious specialists, having formal, Judaic knowledge which they had received at home (my field notes, 1982).

17. Information about these practices comes from fieldwork with Egyptian Jews in Cincinnati (1980) and from Egyptian Jewish friends.

18. Telli Baba is one such shrine in modern Istanbul along the Bosphorus, where the *pir* is known for his posthumous ability to help potential brides find spouses and make happy marriages.

19. See Levy and Zumwalt, *Ritual Medical Lore of Sephardic Women*, for a description of folk religious practices and curing among Sephardic women in the Judeo-Spanish culture area. The film by Gregori Viens, *Island of Roses: The Jews of Rhodes in Los Angeles* (video) (Los Angeles: California Council for the Humanities, 1995) illustrates some of these folk medical practices.

20. From my translation of the French as quoted by Abraham Galanté, *Nouveau recueil de nouveaux documents inédits concernant l'histoire des juifs de Turquie* (Istanbul: Fakulteler Matbaasi, 1952), 39.

21. A study investigating the influence of gossip on women's behavior illustrated by Judeo-Spanish *refranes* (proverbs) is my article published as Paméla J. Dorn, "Gender and Personhood: Turkish Jewish Proverbs and the Politics of Reputation," *Women's Studies International Forum* 9, no. 3.

22. Benbassa and Rodrigue, in *Sephardi Jewry*, maintain that many of these reforms were actually instigated to appease the European powers upon whom the Ottoman Empire was becoming economically dependent (69).

23. An excellent account of Ottoman Jewish and other women in this period is by Lucy M. J. Garnett, *The Women of Turkey and Their Folklore*, vols. 1 and 2 (London: David Nutt, 1893).

24. Blood libels usually were brought by Orthodox Christians against Jews as charges of ritual murder when a Christian child disappeared. Ottoman Turkish authorities intervened and protected the accused Jew from an angry mob of Christian peasants. Eventually, the charges were proved false when it was discovered that the child fell into a well and drowned or experienced some other type of accident that rationally explained the disappearance.

25. The Alliance social philosophy and its promulgation by Ottoman Jewish teachers who expressed both their enthusiasm and cognitive dissonance for it is discussed by Aron Rodrigue, *Images of Sephardi and Eastern Jewries in Transition: The Teachers of the Alliance Israélite Universelle, 1860–1939* (Seattle: University of Washington Press, 1993). He analyzes French Jewish relations with Ottoman Jews in depth in his *French Jews, Turkish Jews: The Alliance Israélite Universelle and The Politics of Jewish Schooling in Turkey, 1860–1925* (Bloomington: Indiana University Press, 1990).

26. Pictures collected during my fieldwork from Sephardic families in the United States, Israel, and Turkey support this statement. Rebecca Amato Levy, in *I Remember Rhodes*, also provides illustrations of the change in use of the *bindalli*.

27. The change from Ottoman to European dress is explored in articles by Charlotte Jirousek, "The Transition to Mass Fashion System Dress in the Later Ottoman Empire" (201–42) and by Elizabeth B. Frierson, "Cheap and Easy: The Creation of Consumer Culture in Late Ottoman Society" (243–60), both in *Consumption Studies and the History of the Ottoman Empire*, ed. Quataert. Frierson discusses the distribution of Singer sewing machines in the Ottoman Empire and gives examples of print advertisements, such as one from Haim Mazza and Sons' dry good store in the Corapci Han of Istanbul, which featured a sketch of unveiled women shopping in their establishment.

28. See Rodrigue, *Images of Sephardi and Eastern Jewries in Transition*, 34–35.

29. See Beth Baron, *The Women's Awakening in Egypt: Culture, Society, and the Press* (New Haven: Yale University Press, 1994).

30. Marguerite Saltiel's biography was written by her daughter, Gloria Sananes Stein, *Marguerite: Journey of a Sephardic Woman* (Morgantown, PA: Masthof, 1997).

31. Rosa Eskenazi's account of how she became a professional singer was provided in an interview that was later published by the journalist Costas Hadjidoulis, *Rosa Eskenazi: Auto pou Thimami* (in Greek) (Athens: Cactus Editions, 1982). A parallel example is that of Mazeltov Matsa who became the Greek-American singer, Amalia. She was divorced by her Jewish husband, Jack Saretta, when she insisted on having a career as a *rebetisa* (Ottoman Greek urban singer) in New York after her arrival in 1912. Amalia later converted to Greek Orthodox Christianity, the faith of her second husband.

32. Elias Canetti, *The Tongue Set Free: Remembrance of a European Childhood*, trans. from the German by Joachim Neugroschel, 1979 (New York: Farrar, Straus & Giroux, 1983).

33. Examples of *kantigas* (Sephardic popular songs) like "*Tres de la Noche*" and "*Los Kaminos de Sirkeci*" which illustrate the active participation of young people in courtship rituals and the changing notions about arranged marriages can be found in my dissertation, Dorn, "Change and Ideology."

34. Elder women, who were in the 80-to-95-years-of-age range when I interviewed them in the 1980s, had stories about the great loves of their lives. Usually the men were teachers or directors of the Alliance schools. Due to family circumstances, World War I, emigration, and differences in social classes, these young women were not allowed to marry their beloved. Following their parents' wishes, they consented to arranged matches with others. The husbands chosen by their parents were good providers and family men. Their arranged marriages lasted 50 or 60 years, a lifetime. Yet, the elder women when I interviewed them still secretly treasured their memories of their first loves.

35. The entire Jewish population of Tyre in southern Turkey was resettled in Yehud, Israel, by the political party Betar in 1948 during the War of Independence (my ethnographic field notes, Yehud, Israel, 1982).

Part III

Sephardic Jewry in the Modern Era and Special Topics

Chapter 12

Early Modern Sephardim and Blacks
Contact and Conflict between Two Minorities

Jonathan Schorsch

While scholarship has traditionally focused on relations between Jews and their host societies, it has rarely noticed relations between Jews and other minority groups. An investigation of early modern Jewish-black relations shows how Jews shared the denigrating antiblack attitudes and behavior of their host societies, whether Catholic or Protestant; how Jews wielded antiblack discourse as a means of positioning themselves as insiders, as whites; and how black slaves constituted an opportunity for Jews to obtain the kind of servile labor forbidden to them from among the members of their Muslim or Christian societies.[1]

Originally as residents of Portugal and Spain, the two countries that initiated the Atlantic slave trade and modern industrial slavery, Sephardic Jews had immediate familiarity with blacks and the general discourse concerning them. The few black slaves who belonged to Sephardim or former Conversos in the eastern Mediterranean faced treatment no different than that of any other slaves. However in the Atlantic region, Sephardic attitudes toward blacks hardened considerably by the seventeenth and eighteenth centuries. Several Sephardic communities instituted their own versions of the increasingly transnational *sistema de castas,* or racialized caste system. Here, nonwhites, even those who converted to Judaism, confronted marginalization and exclusion from various forms of public and ritual participation in the life of the community. This chapter seeks to understand this transformation within the Sephardic world from Eastern slavery, mostly a system of domestic help lived under the guidance of *halakha*, to Western slavery, a heavily racialized, industrial system approached solely in accord with civil practice.

Medieval Images of Blacks to an Early Modern Transformation

The attitudes of early modern Sephardim toward blacks stemmed from a double heritage. The first was internal—rabbinic and medieval Jewish sources. The second was external—Muslim and Christian sources. From the Hellenistic period onward, Jewish sources partook of the increasingly negative general attitude toward blacks. It is apparent that denigrations of blacks and blackness were related to the growing number of black Africans kidnapped or purchased into slavery. However, it is not clear whether the socioeconomic reality generated antiblack discourse or whether antiblack attitudes helped justify the enslavement of black Africans. By the eleventh century, Muslim enslavement of black Africans had become a vital commerce.

Though the Bible lacks any sort of denigration of blacks, rabbinic texts manifest a growing aversion toward blacks and blackness. As wielded in midrashic literature, Noah's curse of Ham seems to target Ham and his descendants *as blacks.* Later exegetes associate their punitive servitude from the biblical text with a blackness that appears to derive from their accursedness. Medieval Jewish sources cite these rabbinic statements within a discourse influenced by Muslim thought's absorption of classical philosophy and natural science.[2] The most outrageous rabbinic depiction of Ham appears in one version of a relatively vague text of obscure origin, the early medieval *Midrash Tanhuma*:

> And because Ham saw with his eyes the nakedness of his father, his eyes were made red; and because with his mouth he told his brothers, his lips were distended; and because he turned back [to look at his father's nakedness], the hair on his head and beard was singed; and because he did not cover the nakedness [of his father] he went about naked and his foreskin was elongated.[3]

This passage did not mention blackness, yet its combination of elements is parallel to the many similar statements in contemporary Muslim discussion drawn from earlier classical sources. Ibn al-Faqih wrote (ca. 902–3) that with "the Zanj, the Ethiopians, and other blacks who resemble them," "the child comes out something between black and murky, malodorous, stinking, woolly-haired, with uneven limbs, deficient mind and depraved passions."[4] The *Tanhuma* passage closely resembled the similarly detailed attention to physiognomy in the Arab historian Masʾudi (d. ca. 956).

The view that blacks as a whole were cursed with either servitude or blackness, or both, may have been fairly widespread among medieval thinkers. Rashi reinforced the link between the curse of Ham and blacks when commenting on the talmudic passage conveying Ham's being stricken in his skin that "from him came Kush."[5] A century later Ibn Khaldun and Ibn Ezra explicitly refuted such a notion in a manner that implied its popularity: the biblical story "mentioned Kenaʾan [Gen. 9:18] and not Kush because he/it [Noah/the Bible] cursed Kenaʾan." "There [were] those," continued Ibn Ezra, "who [said] that the Kushites [were] slaves because Noah cursed Ham, but they forgot that the first king after the flood came from Kush [i.e., Nimrod]."[6]

Medieval Sephardic authors of various intellectual stripes imagined blacks through a lens refracting theology, rationalism, natural science, and ethnography. Medieval rationalists such as Rambam/Maimonides or Yehuda ha-Levi saw blacks as incompletely formed humans, lacking the faculties of speech, intelligence, or religious culture, which defined civilized people. Rambam wrote in a famous parable:

> Those who are outside the city [that is, most distant from God, but also most removed from the *polis,* the site of civility] are all human individuals who have no doctrinal belief, neither one based on speculation nor one that accepts the authority of tradition: such individuals as the furthermost Turks found in the remote North, the Negroes found in the remote South, and those who resemble them from among them that are with us in these climes.[7]

Blacks frequently served as examples of human ugliness, distinguished negatively from "normal" European appearances. One popular thirteenth-century Hebrew critique of marriage featured a plot in which the hero's beautiful beloved was secretly replaced at the wedding with "a quarrelsome hag, black as a crow, with lips like two inflated bladders—anyone who saw would gasp."[8] Blacks, who often represented the fearsome in medieval discussion from all three major monotheisms, appeared as tormentors in dreams. In one such description of a traumatic dream, Shem Tov b. Yosef Falaquera (ca. 1225–1295; northern Spain) utilized as tormentors two ugly Kushites who sought to stab the dreamer with their spears as he trudged through a desert wasteland.[9] The sources for this trope came to Falaquera from Islamic roots. According to the Islamic author Ishaq ibn Imran (ninth or tenth century), one patient suffering from melancholia "saw negroes who wanted to kill him, as well as trumpeters and cymbal players who played in the corners of his room."[10]

Isaac Abravanel commented on Genesis 10:1 with an extensive discussion of Noah's son Ham, wherein the physical and metaphysical become elided. Abravanel noted that he was called "Ham [i.e., Cham, meaning "hot"] either because his heart was hot within him [paraphrase of Deut. 19:6] to chase after his desires or because he was black and ugly and had attributes like a Kushite." In good Aristotelian fashion, Abravanel allegorized the three sons: "Ham was the sign for the animal life and therefore he saw his father's nakedness and did not show mercy for his honor, as a fool he did not know the degrees of respecting one's father and mother and uncovering nakedness." Hence the appropriateness of Noah's curse of servitude.

> And you will see how the characteristics of these three fathers are found in the nations which come from them, for from Ham comes "Kush and Egypt and Libya and Kenaʾan" [Gen. 10:6], for they are all until today ugly looking and their figures are black as a raven, steeped in licentiousness and drawn after the animal lusts, lacking intelligence and knowledges and lacking [political] states and the degrees of good qualities and bravery.[11]

By Abravanel's time, at the end of the fifteenth century, the Portuguese began importing sub-Saharan Africans on a regular basis to serve as slaves. The Spanish quickly followed suit. Like their Christian counterparts, elite Jews in Portugal and Spain owned and traded in slaves, frequently blacks. Jews were prohibited from owning Christian slaves, and sometimes even from employing Christian servants. However, elite medieval Jews owned Muslim slaves. Pagan blacks, whose Christianization was not enforced until the sixteenth century, became an opportune labor force for Jews seeking "help."[12] In response to allegations to the Portuguese Cortes "that generally [people saw] in these kingdoms the Jews being masters of many slaves, white as well as from Guinea, which they [bought] to serve them," a royal decree of 1490 stated that "no Jew may buy male or female Moors from Guinea under penalty of losing them."[13] Many Jews or Conversos fleeing to eastern lands, especially after 1492, brought their black slaves with them.[14]

The few Jews who owned slaves treated them no differently than did Muslim masters. As in the Iberian Peninsula, the number of slaves owned by Jews was not significant. A survey demanded by the Ottoman Sultan in 1559 produced a mere 32 slaves and 51 old freed maidservants that belonged to (or lived with) the tens of thousands of Jews and Christians in the Ottoman capital.[15] A 1612 Ottoman edict required all slaves of the Jewish and Christian communities who had been manumitted within the previous six years "to secure a new proof from the *sicill* (judicial record)" within three days. An "unprecedented number of manumissions" followed, approximately 60 in all.[16] On the whole, it appeared that Jewish masters and rabbinic authorities treated slaves within the framework of *halakha*: frequently male slaves were circumcised, male and female slaves ritually immersed, and slaves manumitted according to ritual procedure.[17] The lack of racialized treatment of black slaves reflected the multiethnic background and demographic fragmentation of the slave population.

Blackness in the Atlantic World

The rise of anti-Jewish sentiment and activity in Spain and Portugal culminated in the expulsion from Spain in 1492 and the forced conversion of the entire Portuguese Jewish community in 1497 and 1498. The tragic and miserable fate of Sephardic Jewry led many exiled Sephardim to seize conceptually upon the growing numbers of blacks in Iberian lands. Despite their enslavement, these blacks seemed to integrate smoothly into their new host community's Catholicism, especially in northwestern Europe. Blacks after the fifteenth century thus provided a more specific textual fulcrum for the working out of Sephardic self-identity. They served two opposite purposes in the triangulation of "national" or "ethnic" desires and repulsions. On the one hand, their blackness threatened to apply to Jews themselves. On the other hand, Jews were able to argue their own whiteness.

Some of the sensitivities of Sephardim and Conversos regarding blacks derived from a specific connection not infrequently voiced in the Iberian peninsular and colonial orbit. In the eyes of many inquisitors and proponents of "blood purity" statutes, Jews and Muslims, or, more accurately, their converted descendants, occupied similar positions as disloyal Christians and citizens and potential heretics. But Jews were also seen as bearing a certain kinship with decidedly "primitive" peoples. Several priests drew on a connection already made by Nicolas de Lyra based on Jeremiah 13:23 that "it [was] impossible for the Jews to repent of their errors, as it [was] impossible for the black to change his skin or the leopard to change his spots."[18] Writing against the New Christians around 1541, Francisco Machado wistfully imagined "Portugal . . . cleansed of heresies and of Jewish ceremonies, and of Moors and blacks." To Machado, it is clear that the constant shaming and humiliation of Jesus in Portugal stems directly from the fact that "where there are Moors, blacks, Indians, Jews, it is inevitable that each one follows his own path and sect."[19]

It is no surprise to find Conversos in Iberian territories wielding blacks as a contrastive example. They saw in them a lower group accorded (in some ways) higher status. Mutual animosity often based itself on prevailing religious and racial stereotypes, especially since Jewish Conversos shared in the general discourse's negative perceptions about the other group. Watching the 1540 Lisbon auto-da-fé, in which the judaizer and messianic pretender Diogo de Montenegro was burned alive at the stake, one Conversa allegedly reacted with visible rage. Some neighbors told the accused judaizer "how a black looked with evil intention at Montenegro, and [the accused judaizer] responded that in the same way would she watch the black dragged [through the streets]."[20] The "evil" look of a black in the crowd, whether it happened or was invented by the neighbors, proved to be an effective taunt to the suspected judaizer, perhaps even because of the racial makeup of the look's giver.

A year later, a black woman of Lisbon testified against a woman friend, Maria Rodrigues, already imprisoned for several months on charges of judaizing. According to her statement, the black woman had invited Maria to go see an auto-da-fé by the Teja riverside in Lisbon. Maria responded, "God's evil inferno for King Dom Manuel who made us Christians by force!" Maria further asked the witness if she would prefer to be turned white, to which the witness responded that she would like it. Maria Rodrigues retorted: "Well, so we will turn ourselves into good Christians like you will yourself turn white!"[21]

This black Christian expressed the desire to turn white as a means of convincing the Inquisitors that she sought "conversion" in a manner directly opposite the stubborn refusal of the accused judaizer. Such a desire manifests a distinct similarity to her interest in watching an auto-da-fé to begin with and her later denunciation of a friend formerly but mistakenly thought to share her Christian desires, both for spectacle and otherwise. She equates turning white with turning Christian, and equates the judaizer's emphasis on the inability of blacks to turn white into a denial of the potency of the universalizing Christian mission. Whether these are accurate depictions of blacks' reactions or not, these testimonies deftly, and perhaps even inadvertently, assized the contestatory group dynamics that could be so overheated in the crucible of a mass exorcism of "heresy."

A woman named María, accused of judaizing in Mexico, appeared fond of an insulting blasphemy that linked black inferiority to that of Christianity. Her denouncer related to the inquisitors how many times María was in the habit of speaking badly about the saints whom the Church had canonized and beatified. María did not believe that there could be saints in the evangelical law. She asked of Saint Benito of Palermo, the black, "how could a black be a saint?"[22]

Antiblack attitudes could serve downtrodden whites of the wrong religion well as a component of insults slung against the "Christian Empire." Hence the particular gall in one imprisoned crypto-Jew's comment from the 1640s that he regretted having come to Mexico, "to this awful land, . . . where there are . . . the type of people who treat honorable men worse than blacks."[23] In this view, persecuted Jewish new Christians possessed an inner "honor" or "nobility," though their outward circumstances appeared worse than those of the lowliest black slaves, who by implication lacked the "honor" that would make their fate undeserved.

An Atlantic Sephardic Sistema de Castas?

The seventeenth century marked the historical moment in which blacks became a significant presence in Europe and its colonies. Between 1500 and 1580, some 74,000 Africans had been forcibly boarded onto boats for transshipment to the Americas. Between 1580 and 1640, roughly 714,000 Africans found themselves in the same dire circumstances, a tenfold increase.[24] By the end of the seventeenth century, slavery constituted a nearly universal foundation of European colonial governance.

Despite the intense medieval theological politics surrounding the Jewish ownership of Christian slaves and the official nonrecognition of slavery in most European metropolises, Sephardic polities reconstituting themselves after their expulsion or flight from Spain and Portugal made efforts to ensure their rights to owning domestic or servile labor.[25] This can be gleaned from many of the charters granted to Sephardim in their new places of residence or for the purpose of colonial settlement. As "pagans," blacks offered Jews a unique opportunity to control the kind of "help" they could not obtain from Christians. Evidence seems to indicate that the first blacks and mulattos in Amsterdam belonged to the "Portuguese"

Jewish elites in the city. For reasons of state, Jewish ownership of slaves in the newly established colonies was (with few exceptions) not curtailed or prohibited. Hence, in Dutch Brazil, Barbados, Surinam, Curaçao, Jamaica, and elsewhere, Sephardim increasingly participated in the local subculture of slaveholding.

The perception in northern Europe that Jews were not exactly white exacerbated Sephardic anxieties along racial lines. In 1691, François-Maximilian Mission, one of the influences for Buffon's *Natural History*, wrote against such views of Jewish somatic blackness, "Tis also a vulgar error that the Jews are all black. . . . Those [Jews] I have seen at Prague, are not blacker than the rest of their countrymen."[26]

Numerous early modern travelers noted the blackness of Jews, especially Sephardim, in a manner wavering between the physical and metaphysical.[27] By the seventeenth century, whiteness carried quite real social effects such as determining one's profession, what organizations one could join, and whom one could marry (even in the European metropolises lacking enormous populations of black slaves). Various pieces of evidence conveyed the impression that Sephardim in these regions actively attempted to prove their whiteness. Mission agreed that Portuguese Jews were extremely dark. It became essential to refute the problematic blackness often assigned to Jews.

Contrasts of the situations of Jews and blacks can be found in early seminal works of Sephardic literature. Samuel Usque fled Portugal in the 1530s for Italy. He wondered about the justice of idolaters' and evildoers' living peacefully throughout the world while the Jews suffered the fates they did in the Iberian lands: "In Africa, the people commit turpitudes beyond all human comprehension. . . . And above all, they are not Mohammedans, or Jews, or Christians, nor do they have any religion or offer prayer to any thing; rather they live like the beasts of the field."[28] In a similar vein, ex-Converso Daniel Leví (Miguel) De Barrios (1635–1701) stated in one work that the first people to fail to honor wisdom and, by implication, lack the fear of God, were certain descendants of the biblical Kush. These De Barrios opposed the God-fearing supporters of Solomon, who conquered them. De Barrios links these Kushite scorners of wisdom and religion with unreason or insanity, calling them "*locos.*"[29]

De Barrios's work, a history of the Amsterdam Sephardic community, comprises an amazing hodge-podge of genealogical and other efforts to glorify the Jewish descendants of Shem. Noah acclaimed God the creator, who was "not [the God] of Iamphet, nor of Cham, but rather of Sem, because Sem conveyed his true knowledge to the Hibrim," the Jews. Elsewhere, De Barrios exerts himself in refuting genealogical linkage between the Jews and the Indians or Ethiopians.[30] De Barrios wrote against authors such as the Mantuan Jesuit Antonio Possevino (ca. 1533–1611), who cited Prester John as an authority for the fact that the Abyssinians, in general, originated from Solomon and their aristocracy from Abraham.[31] Bernardo José Aldrete (1565–1645), canon of the church at Cordoba, argued that ancient Hebrew had (d)evolved into Ethiopian after the exile of the Jews to that locale.[32] Ancient writers such as Sulpicius Severus (ca. 360–ca. 425) argued that the barbarian nations, such as the Parthians, Medes, Indians, and Ethiopians, descended from the Jews. But the early modern writers, including De Barrios, probably were influenced by the appearance of the first Spanish translations of the Ethiopian royal chronicles, the *Kebra Nagast*, which detailed the Solomonic ancestry of the Christian kings of Ethiopia.[33] De Barrios's distancing of Jews from Ethiopians was no mere genealogical exercise. Instead it was part of vividly living Iberian polemics about the cultural status of Jews, as is evident from its odd appearance in a history of the Sephardim of Amsterdam.

The communal and rabbinic leadership of seventeenth-century Sephardic Amsterdam sought to suppress seemingly problematic traditional *halakhic* behaviors concerning slaves. Slaves were almost exclusively black at this time. In Amsterdam, the number of black and mulatto slaves belonging to Sephardim was not particularly high. According to archival sources, over the course of the seventeenth century, some 30 nonwhites were buried in a section of the communal cemetery set apart for them.[34] In the colonies, blacks constituted an often hostile and threatening population, frequently numbering far more than their white overlords. Sephardic ownership of slaves was at times significant there. In Dutch Brazil, Sephardic merchants appeared to have been major purchasers of slaves at the auctions of the West India Company. Records from seventeenth-century Barbados show 105 Jewish households owning 565 slaves, while evidence from eighteenth-century Jamaica reveals 312 Jewish households owning 3,073 slaves. In 1744, Curacoan Jews owned 310 slaves and in 1765, 860. In Surinam, Jews must have owned well over 10,000 slaves over the course of the seventeenth and eighteenth centuries.[35] Due to this novel sociological setting, the Sephardic community of Amsterdam instituted a series of communal ordinances that reflected and constructed the desired "racial" transformation of the Jews by gradually excluding nonwhite Jews and nonwhite slaves from participation in the community. Related measures appeared in Sephardic Brazil and Surinam as well.

In 1627, an ordinance was passed by the Amsterdam Sephardic governing council restricting access to burial at the community's cemetery. The ordinance read, in part: "No black person nor mulatto will be able to be buried in the cemetery, except for those who had buried in it a Jewish mother. . . . None shall persuade any of the said blacks and mulattos, man or woman, or any other person who is not of the nation of Israel to be made Jews."[36] The specification of blacks and mulattos reflects the reality of their presence as slaves and servants in the Amsterdam Jewish community.

The Sephardic exclusionary burial practices participated in a wave of similar legislation inspired by the conflicted social consequences of black slavery. The 1627 ordinance of the Amsterdam Mahamad (governing council) discouraged community members from bringing nonwhites into Judaism. Though the ordinance aimed to exclude all non-Jews, blacks and mulattos obviously bore the brunt of the intention again. Similarly, from the outset of English colonization on Barbados (ca. 1625), slaves (Africans), but not servants (Europeans) faced "exclusion . . . from the Christian church," language that assumedly included baptism.[37]

Other exclusionary ordinances soon followed within the seventeenth-century Amsterdam Sephardic community. In 1641, the communal board ordered that Sephardic women not send their black and mulatto girls (slaves) to reserve seats for them in the synagogue's women's gallery. It should be remembered that women's seats were not assigned, unlike those in the men's section, according to the 1639 merger agreement of the three Sephardic congregations. At the same time, the Mahamad decreed that the doors to the women's section of the sanctuary were not to be opened before six in the morning. This was done in order to prevent the congregating of the slave women and other servants on the street, clearly perceived as a public nuisance or embarrassment. Further, the nonwhite serving women who remained were now allowed to sit in the women's section, only in the eighth row or farther back.[38]

Three years later, the men of the communal board decreed that "circumcised Negro Jews" were not to be called to the Torah or given any honorary commandment to perform in the synagogue, "for such is fitting for the reputation of the congregation and its good government."[39] Again, such measures to institute distinctions within the community, now faced with an influx of "different" outsiders, did not arise *ex nihilo*. Dutch Protestant planters in Brazil had been making it difficult for their slaves to attend church services, as early as a 1636 report to that effect by a Dutch Protestant pastor.⁴⁰

In 1647, a separate section of the Sephardic cemetery was established for "all the Jewish blacks and mulattos." Exceptions were limited to those "who were born in Judaism, [their parents] having [been married] with *quedosim* [with *kiddushin*, i.e., properly, according to Jewish law], or those who were married to whites with *quedosim*."⁴¹ In other words, very few if any blacks or mulattos now qualified for burial in the Jewish cemetery proper.

An ordinance of 1650 reiterated the *ascama* (ordinance) from the *ascamot* issued with the unification of the three congregations banning the circumcision or ritual immersion of non-Jews. This new pronouncement explicitly targeted blacks and mulattos and confirmed the earlier penalty of excommunication for their circumcision or ritual immersion.

> Renewal of the escama of 1639 which treats the circumcising of *goyim*. The Gentlemen of the *Mahamad* declare that the same penalty of *herem* [the most stringent form of excommunication] [will apply] to any [person] circumcising blacks or mulattos and also any immersing them or [any who] should be a witness for them [as required by *halakha*], seeing [their] immersing, or [that of] any other person or woman who is not of our Hebrew nation.⁴²

The practice of bringing slaves or former slaves into even a minimal level of Judaism continued. The latter part of the ordinance made an exception for leaders of the community, who could choose whether or not to circumcise or ritually immerse, perhaps in private, any child born to them from a non-Jewish mother (the text defines Jewish parentage with *judeu*, that is, only in the masculine). These wealthy members of the Mahamad of course comprised the men most likely to own slaves. The "occasion" of their siring a child with a female slave remained a prerogative the Mahamad did not want to threaten.

The spirit of this particular Sephardic ordinance mirrored, and may have derived from, certain results of the 1618 Synod of Dordt. The leaders of the Reformed Church there failed to reach a conclusion on the issue of "whether slaves born in Reformed households should be baptized and of whether baptism would free them," since the latter case would "discourage slaveowners from allowing [baptism]." Ultimately, in the face of disagreement over the consequences of baptism for the slave and master, the Reformed Church sages "favoured leaving the discretion on whether to baptize to the head of household."[43] Robert C.-H. Shell, Blackburn's source, framed this step in a manner that well illuminates the trajectory of the Jewish discourse under discussion, "Baptism, a public imperative for the Catholic church, became a household choice for the Reformed Christian."[44]

Even in Iberian colonial territories, the religious absorption of slaves was not as uncontested as imagined by contemporary scholarship. Writing about Andalusian slavery between 1450 and 1550, Alfonso Franco Silva noted that some masters freed their slaves on the condition that they be baptized. This indicates that, especially early on in the Iberian enslavement of blacks, the taking on of the sacrament of baptism could remain a voluntary decision.[45] On Santo Domingo, some clergymen argued that the baptism of newly arrived slaves should not be automatic, but given only when the slave assumed the mantle of Christian doctrine and understood the significance of God and baptism. This view, whose popularity is undetermined, would have provided far greater latitude for masters and slaves to avoid the latter's Christianization.[46] When the archbishop of Seville issued an instruction calling for the automatic baptism of all slaves departing from African ports on slave ships in 1614, it became clear that many slaves still had not been receiving baptism, much less any instruction in Christian doctrine.[47] Yet, in 1622, the Provincial Dominican Council on Santo Domingo felt the need to call for an inquisition to investigate the continued failure of many slave traders to have the slaves baptized.[48] Though the responses differed, the varied and often conflicting interests regarding the religious absorption of slaves comprised a transnational phenomenon.

In 1658, the *Mahamad* decided that mulatto boys would no longer be admitted for study in the Amsterdam yeshiva of the Sephardim.[49] Based on talmudic precedent, Maimonides had already prohibited teaching slaves Torah. The Jesuit College of St. Peter and St. Paul in Mexico City, founded in 1582, included in its constitution a clause expressly forbidding the admission of blacks and mulattos.[50] Indeed, from the mid-1500s on, full-blooded American Indians and blacks were not allowed to receive holy orders or hold sacerdotal office in the viceroyalties of Mexico or Peru.[51]

By the early seventeenth century, exceptions aside, the Jesuits and other religious orders working in the Congo and Angola "refused to admit either blacks or mulattos to their own ranks."⁵² The 1622 Provincial Dominican Council on Santo Domingo reiterated that "Blacks [were] not to be admitted to the Sacred Orders . . . nor Ethiopians and other Blacks, vulgarly called mulattos. Because from this, as experience and concrete cases show, originate scandals and scorn of the Church." Neither could blacks or mulattos "wear the clerical habit" unless they were three generations removed from "the Ethiopian trunk (*tronco*)," that is, if "their ancestors had been of white color and free from all servitude."⁵³ These ordinances from Iberian colonial territories did not exactly correspond with the 1658 exclusion from the Sephardic yeshiva. But they established a pattern of segregating nonwhites from attainment of religious knowledge beyond the necessary minimum, and of religious authority.

The wealthy, cosmopolitan Sephardic merchants in Amsterdam who signed into law these exclusionary ordinances (many of them born and bred as Christians in Spain or Portugal, some of them possibly temporary residents of colonies under Iberian control) could not have been unaware of the *sistema de castas*. At this time, it was increasingly regnant in the Iberian colonies. In many ways, this system marked a logical extension of Iberian practices of *limpieza de sangre* first established in the mid-fifteenth century and intimately known by these former Conversos. In R. Douglas Cope's summation of colonial Mexico,

> the evolution of the sistema de castas is far from clear. . . . Gonzalo Aguirre Beltrán states that the sistema came into effect during the seventeenth century; John K. Chance believes that it was functioning in Oaxaca by 1630. . . . The parishes of Santa Veracruz and Sagrario Metropolitano [in Mexico City] began to keep separate marriage registers for the castas in 1646.⁵⁴

In Surinam, as in Amsterdam, a group of colored Jews arose and became large enough to cause community leaders discomfort. Surinam constituted the most significant plantation economy created by Sephardim, who operated over 400 plantations around the mid-eighteenth century. The language of the Surinamese Sephardic *ascamot* followed closely that of Amsterdam, to whose practice they alluded. In 1665 the leadership decided to demote the status of Jahidim (full members) who married mulattas.⁵⁵ In the 1734 *ascamot*, it was stipulated that mulatto Jews in Jodensavanne "may not have any *Mitsvahs* on Holiday or Sabbath days, but only on *Rosh Chodesh* [the New Moon] and the minor fasts and are also required to sit behind the *Theba* [the central table whence prayers were led and the Torah read]."⁵⁶ These non-*halakhic* mechanisms relegated nonwhite Jews to receiving honors only on lesser, and poorly attended holidays and to sitting only in undesirable seats. The following ordinance appeared in the 1754 community *ascamot*, translated here by Robert Cohen: "Since experience has taught how prejudicial and improper it would be to admit Mulattos as *Yahidim* [full members], and noting that some of these have concerned themselves in matters of the government of the community, it is resolved that henceforth they will never be considered or admitted as *Yahidim* and will solely be *Congreganten,* as in other communities."⁵⁷ The formerly acceptable participation of nonwhite Jews in the self-organization of the community had clearly become intolerable to the Parnasim by this time.

Further racial restrictions obtained in the 1754 regulations. Members who married mulatto women, "either according to our Holy Law or solely in front of the Magistrates," would have their children considered mulattos by the community as punishment. Mulatto Jews had to sit at the bench of mourners located at the synagogue's margin. They could not receive certain public blessings (*Misheberah*). No woman who was black, mulatto, or Indian could enter the prayer hall, not even to tend to her master's children, "considering the Respect of the Holy Place."⁵⁸ Similarly, the Curaçao congregation Mikve Israel passed an ordinance, in 1751, "not to bring into the synagogue Black or mulatto women in order not to remove the devotion which there needs to be."⁵⁹ This happened to be in the wake of a 1750 slave uprising, but a specific connection need not exist. According to a 1753 document, the Jodensavanne synagogue in Surinam possessed a separate door for blacks (*porta dos negros*), of unclear origin or location, though its function can be guessed.⁶⁰

The *halakhic* framework for some of the specific terms, which were legislated, can easily be identified. Beginning in 1665, the offspring of relationships with mulattos were to be considered mulatto until the third generation. They could then reenter the congregation as Yahidim if they were "legitimately born from a marriage with a white."⁶¹ This stipulation clearly echoed the *halakhic* system of accepting into the community the third-generation offspring of Egyptian and Edomite converts based on Deuteronomy 23:8–9. Similarly, the statement in the *ascamot* that these mulattos could not become Yahidim "by learning the Jewish laws and customs" derived from rabbinic precedent.⁶²

The Demise of Halakhic *Slavery*

The Sephardic efforts at social engineering bore repercussions in the religious realm. The holding of slaves no longer fell under the rule of *halakha*. Many of the seventeenth- and eighteenth-century books of blessings made no reference to the traditional blessing said when purchasing or circumcising a slave. Other works, including many by prominent rabbis, also ignored, without explanation, the seemingly critical and clear biblical commandment to circumcise male slaves. The works include a 1683 Hebrew compendium of the commandments; a 1692 digest of the commandments in Spanish; the list of commandments at the back of a 1695 Spanish translation of the Five Books of Moses; a 1713 compendium of the commandments; a similar Hebrew compendium from 1753; a 1763 verse rendition of the commandments according to Rambam; and a 1768 circumcision booklet.[63] Nearly all the authors of these works lived in western Europe or in the Dutch or English colonial orbit.

Even Jews in traditional and observant communities in the Mediterranean region and westward often failed to observe *halakhot* pertaining to the circumcision and/or immersion of slaves. By the eighteenth century, Caribbean Sephardim treated their slaves almost with total disregard for *halakhic* tradition. Slaves were dealt with under the civic law of the colony. Only the smallest minority of slaves of Surinamese Jews converted to Judaism, and these were overwhelmingly from the lighter-skinned houseslave population. In Surinam, a 1762 survey found in the Jewish community 27 free mulattos and blacks whose religious affiliations are not clear but who most likely converted to Judaism. "Almost 100 free Jewish mulattoes" were found in 1788.[64] On Curaçao, nonwhites were simply and consistently denied participation in the community. Not a single black or mulatto was buried in the Jewish cemetery there. Perhaps the only *halakhic* stipulation to be followed by Sephardic slave owners in the Caribbean was to allow their slaves to rest on the Sabbath. Though even here slaves were frequently given wages in order to make it seem as though their labor was voluntary and not a transgression, as was done in Curaçao and Surinam.

Central to the Converso and Sephardic wielding of the hegemonic discourse about blacks was its redemptive logic. In both Iberian Catholic and northwest European Protestant colonial spheres, Conversos and Sephardim found antiblackness useful in helping forge an identity that enabled them to see themselves (and be seen) as part of the dominant culture and class, as whites, regardless of their religious Otherness. The aspects of *limpieza de sangre* or of the *sistema de castas* put into place by Sephardim were not internalized or appropriated as if they had come from without; they derived from aspects of the Jewish culture these Sephardim (re)appropriated at home again in exile, from aspects of the Iberian and then northern European culture to which these Spanish and Portuguese Jews felt they belonged as insiders from the perspective of classical culture, of monotheism, even, despite frequent ambivalence, of color.

NOTES

1. Jonathan Schorsch, *Jews and Blacks in the Early Modern World* (New York: Cambridge University Press, 2004). Much of this essay is drawn from the fuller depiction provided there.

2. Abraham Melamed, *The Image of the Black in Jewish Culture: A History of the Other* (London: Curzon, 2002); David H. Aaron, "Early Rabbinic Exegesis on Noah's Son Ham and the So-Called Hamitic Myth," *Journal of the American Academy of Religion* 63 (1995): 721–59; Benjamin Braude, "The Sons of Noah and the Construction of Ethnic and Geographical Identities in the Medieval and Early Modern Periods," *The William and Mary Quarterly*, 3d series 54, no. 1 (January 1997): 103–42; David M. Goldenberg, "The Curse of Ham: A Case of Rabbinic Racism?" in *Struggles in the Promised Land: Toward a History of Black-Jewish Relations in the United States*, ed. Jack Salzman and Cornel West (New York: Oxford University Press, 1997). For a thorough survey of rabbinic and medieval Jewish views of blacks and blackness see Melamed's work. See the works of Aaron, Braude, and Goldenberg for further information on the curse of Ham. Goldenberg's book, *The Curse of Ham* (Princeton, NJ: Princeton University Press, 2003), was not yet available at the time of this writing.

3. *Midrash Tanhuma*, assembled from various manuscripts, ed. Shlomo Buber (Jerusalem: Ortsel, 1963), parshat Noah, no. 13.

4. Bernard Lewis, *Race and Slavery in the Middle East: A Historical Inquiry* (New York: Oxford University Press, 1990), 33–34.

5. B.T. Sanhedrin 108b.

6. Abraham ibn Ezra, *Perush al ha-Torah*, on Gen. 9:25.

7. Moses Maimonides, *The Guide to the Perplexed*, trans. and ed. Shlomo Pines (Chicago: University of Chicago Press, 1963), vol. 2, 618–19 (bk. 3, chap. 51); S. Harvey, "A New Source of the Guide of the Perplexed," *Maimonidean Studies* 2 (1991), 31–60. Rambam's sentiments may well have derived directly from Muslim discourse.

8. Judah ibn Shabbetai, *Minhat Yehuda Sone ha-Nashim*, written in Toledo, 1208, translated in Tova Rosen, "Sexual Politics in a Medieval Marriage Debate," *Exemplaria* 12, no. 1 (spring 2000): 170–71.

9. *Sefer ha-Mevakesh* 1260s; cited in Melamed, *Image of the Black*, 9.

10. Manfred Ullman, *Islamic Medicine* (Edinburgh: Edinburgh University Press, 1978), 75.

11. Isaac Abravanel, *Perush al ha-Torah*, on Gen. 10:1.

12. A. C. de C. M. Saunders, *Black Slaves and Freedmen in Portugal, 1441–1555* (Cambridge: Cambridge University Press, 1982), 62; Schorsch, *Jews and Blacks*, chap. 2.

13. Livros das cortes 19–45, Aclamacóes e cortes, 14–15 sec., Archivo Nacional Torre do Tombo, Arch. A. 46, Central Archives for the History of the Jewish People, Jerusalem (hereafter cited as CAHJP), microfilm HM2 5302, unpaginated; cited also in Maria José Pimenta Ferro Tavares, *Os Judeus em portugal no século XV*, 2 vols. (vol. 1, Lisbon: Universidade Nova de Lisboa/Faculdade de Ciências Sociais e Humanas; vol. 2, Lisbon: INIC, 1982–84), vol. 1, 246, and see vol. 1, 297; Saunders, *Black Slaves and Freedmen*, 63.

14. Ruth Lamdan, *The Holding of Maidservants in the Jewish Community in Israel, Syria, and Egypt in the Sixteenth Century* (in Hebrew) (Tel Aviv: University of Tel Aviv Press, 1996), 360; Simcha Asaf, "Slaves and Slave Trading among Jews in the Middle Ages" (in Hebrew), *Zion* 4 (1939): 91–125; Asaf, "Slaves and Slave Trading among Jews in the Middle Ages: Addenda" (in Hebrew), *Zion* 5 (1940): 271–80. It must be emphasized that Conversos who owned slaves did so as Christians.

15. Haim Gerber, *The Jews of the Ottoman Empire in the Sixteenth and Seventeenth Century: Economy and Society* (in Hebrew) (Jerusalem: Zalman Shazar Center for the Study of Jewish History, 1982), 82–83 (docs. 2–3); Lamdan, *The Holding of Maidservants*, 356.

16. Yvonne Seng, "A Liminal State: Slavery in Sixteenth-Century Istanbul," in *Slavery in the Islamic Middle East*, ed. Shaun E. Marmon (Princeton, NJ: Markus Wiener, 1999), 31.

17. Schorsch, *Jews and Blacks*, chaps. 2–3; Asaf, "Slaves and Slave Trading"; Lamdan, *The Holding of Maidservants*.

18. Elias Lipiner, *Izaque de Castro: O mancebo que veio preso do brasil* (Recife, Brazil: Fundaeao Joaquim Nabuco/Editora Massangana, 1992), 103; Yosef Hayim Yerushalmi, *Assimilation and Racial Anti-Semitism: The Iberian and German Models*, Leo Baeck Memorial Lecture no. 26 (New York: Leo Baeck Institute, 1982), 16. The quote, which appears in Lipiner's work, is from an incident in the 1640s. Already in the first decade of the same century, Fray Prudencio de Sandoval voiced the same sentiment, as seen in Yerushalmi's book.

19. My translation; Francisco Machado, *The Mirror of the New Christians* (*Espelho de Christaos Novos*) *of Francisco Machado*, ed. and trans. Mildred Evelyn

Vieira and Frank Ephraim Talmage (Toronto: Pontifical Institute of Mediaeval Studies, 1977), 75, 323.

20. Antonio Baiao, *A Inquisição em Portugal e no Brasil. Subsidios para a sua historia. A inquisição no seculo XVI* (Lisbon: Edição do Arquivo Historico Portugues, 1921), 117.

21. The new Christian was Maria Rodrigues; testimony given in 1541. Baiao, *A Inquisição em Portugal e no Brasil*, 121–22.

22. Boleslao Lewin, ed., *Proceso de María de Zárate: Racismo inquisitorial* (Puebla, Mexico: J. M. Cajica Jr., 1971), 99. The accused was Doña María de Zárate, charged in 1656 for judaizing.

23. Juan de León, also known as Salomón Machorro (1646), quoted in Boleslao Lewin, ed., *Confidencias de dos criptojudíos en la cárcel de la Inquisición* (Buenos Aires: n.p., 1975], 78.

24. David Eltis, "Atlantic History in Global Perspective," *Itinerario* 23, no. 2 (1999): 151, table 1.

25. Schorsch, *Jews and Blacks*, chap. 2.

26. François-Maximilian Mission, *A New Voyage to Italy* (London: Printed for R. Bonwick, 1714), vol. 2, 139; cited by Sander Gilman, *The Visibility of the Jew in the Diaspora: Body Imagery and Its Cultural Context*, B. G. Rudolph Lecture in Judaic Studies, Syracuse University, 1991 (Syracuse: Syracuse University Press, 1992), 3.

27. Schorsch, *Jews and Blacks*, chap. 7. See examples.

28. Samuel Usque, *Consolation for the Tribulations of Israel*, trans. Martin A. Cohen (Philadelphia: Jewish Publication Society, 1965), 221; Samuel Usque, *Consolação a tribulações de Israel: Edição de Ferrara, 1553*, with an introduction by Yosef Hayim Yerushalmi (Lisbon: Fundação Calouste Gulbenkian, 1989), vol. 2, 227–28.

29. Daniel Levi (Miguel) De Barrios, *Triumpho del govierno popular, y de la antiguedad holandesa* (N.p., n.d. [1683]), 66.

30. De Barrios, *Triumpho del govierno popular*, 48, 54–58.

31. Antonio Possevino, *Bibliotheca selecta de ratione studiorum* (1607 [orig. 1603?]), bk. 15, ch. 19.

32. *Varias antygvedades de España Africa y otras provincias* (Amberes, Spanish Netherlands [Belgium]: A Costa de Iuan Hasrey, 1614), 165.

33. Enrique Cornelio Agrippa, *Historia de las cosas de Etiopía* (Toledo, 1528) and Manuel Almeida (1580–1646), *Historia de Etiopía*, for example, the latter not published in its entirety.

34. Schorsch, *Jews and Blacks*, chap. 3.

35. Ibid., chap. 2. The owners in all of these places were overwhelmingly Sephardic. The numbers given are conflations of different data and stem from a variety of sources.

36. Libro dos termos da ymposta da nação, principiado em 24 de Sebat 5382, 20 Tamuz 5387 (1627), GAA 334, no. 13, fol. 42, CAHJP microfilm HM2 1512, no pagination.

37. Gary Puckrein, *Little England: Plantation Society and Anglo-Barbadian Politics, 1627–1700* (New York: New York University Press, 1984), 23.
38. Livro dos acordos (undated [1640]), GAA 334, no. 19, CAHJP microfilm HM2 1518, fol. 165.
39. Livros dos acordos, fol. 173, CAHJP microfilm HM2 1518, fol. 258.
40. B. N. Teensma, "The Brazilian Letters of Vicent Joachim Soler," in *Dutch Brazil*, vol. 1: *Documents in the Leiden University Library*, ed. Cristina Ferrão and Jose Monteiro Soares (Rio de Janeiro: Editora Index, 1997), 61.
41. Livro dos acordos, 24 Nisan 5407 (1647), fol. 224, CAHJP microfilm HM2 1518, no pagination.
42. GAA 334, no. 19, fol. 281, CAHJP microfilm HM2 1518, no pagination.
43. Robin Blackburn, *The Making of New World Slavery: From the Baroque to the Modern, 1492–1800* (London: Verso, 1997), 64.
44. Robert C.-H. Shell, *Children of Bondage: A Social History of the Slave Society at the Cape of Good Hope, 1652–1838* (Hanover, NH: Wesleyan University Press / University Press of New England, 1994), 334.
45. Alfonso Franco Silva, *La esclavitud en Andalucia, 1450–1550* (Granada, Spain: Universidad de Granada, 1992), 128.
46. The date was 1576. José Luis Saez, *La Iglesia y el negro esclavo en Santo Domingo: Una historia tres siglas* (Santo Domingo, 1994), 136. The same view prevailed in peninsular Jaén, enacted in the 1624 constitution of the town's church. Manuel López Molina, *Una década de esclavitud en Jaén, 1675–1685* (Jaén, Spain: Ayuntamiento de Jaén, 1995), 125.
47. Alonso de Sandoval, *Un tratado sobre la esclavitud*, trans. and ed. Enriqueta Vila Vilar (Madrid: Alianza Editorial, 1987), 493–503.
48. Saez, *La Iglesia y el negro esclavo en Santo Domingo*, 152–57.
49. Livro dos acordos, 9 Shvat 5418 (1658), fol. 426, CAHJP microfilm HM2 1518, no pagination.
50. Colin A. Palmer, *Slaves of the White God: Blacks in Mexico* (Cambridge: Harvard University Press, 1976), 54.
51. C. R. Boxer, *The Church Militant and Iberian Expansion, 1440–1770* (Baltimore: Johns Hopkins University Press, 1978), 15–16. In 1555, the first Mexican Ecclesiastical Provincial Council declared Indians, mestizos, mulattos, descendants of Moors, Jews, and persons sentenced by the Inquisition "inherently unworthy of the sacerdotal office." The Third Provincial Council (1585) relaxed this somewhat, admitting "Mexicans who are descended in the first degree from Amerindians, or from Moors, or from parents of whom one is a Negro." By implication, full-blooded Indians and blacks remained unacceptable for admission.
52. Boxer, *Church Militant*, 9.
53. Reprinted in Saez, *La Iglesia y el negro esclavo en Santo Domingo*, 155–56.
54. R. Douglas Cope, *The Limits of Racial Domination: Plebeian Society in Colonial Mexico City, 1660–1720* (Madison: University of Wisconsin Press, 1994), 24;

G. Aguirre Beltrán, *La población negra de Mexico, 1519–1810*, 2d ed. (Mexico City: Fondo de Cultura Económica, 1972), 163; John K. Chance, *Race and Class in Colonial Oaxaca* (Stanford, CA: Stanford University Press, 1978), 126, 193. For the Santa Veracruz parish, see Edgar F. Love, "Marriage Patterns of Persons of African Descent in a Colonial Mexico City Parish," *Hispanic American Historical Review* 51 (1971): 79–91.

55. "Reducçao das Ascamot," tratado 1, Concernente a obrigaçao, Liberdade & Prerogativa dos Jehidim & Congreganten, art. 1, fol. 7ff., microfilm reel 177, American Jewish Archives (hereafter cited as AJA). The document is dated 17 August 1665 and was drawn up under the British government of Lord Willoughby.

56. My translation; cited in J. Meijer, *M. J. Lewenstein's Opperrabbinaat Te Paramaribo (1857/58–1864): Analyse Van Het Surinaamse Jodendom in Zijn Crisisperiode* (Amsterdam: Uitgeverij de Driehoek, n.d. [1959]), 45.

57. Robert Cohen, *Jews in Another Environment: Surinam in the Second Half of the Eighteenth Century* (Leiden, the Netherlands: E. J. Brill, 1991), 161.

58. Ibid.

59. Congregation Mikve Israel, Congregational records, 1672–1817, entry from 5511, SC-13505, AJA.

60. Mentioned in a list of debts owed by the synagogue to Ishak Arrias, 1753, records of the Portuguese Jewish Community, fol. 177, microfilm reel 180, AJA: "hum Par ditto [Engonsos] para a Porta dos Negros." The list seems to differentiate between this entry and "the doors and windows of the kitchen/as Portas y ginelas d cosinha."

61. "Reducçao das ascamot," tratado 1, art. 3, microfilm 177, fol. 7, AJA; see also Cohen, *Jews in Another Environment*, 161.

62. Cohen, *Jews in Another Environment*, 161.

63. Selomoh de Oliveyra, *Darkhei ha-Shem* (Amsterdam: David de Castro Tartas, 1683); Abraham Vaez, *Arbol de vidas en el qual se contienen los dinim mas necessarios que deve observar todo Ysrael* (n.p. [Amsterdam?], 1692); "Dinim tocantes á los Preceptos siguientes," printed at back of Jósef Franco Serrano, *Los cinco libros de la Sacra Ley* (Amsterdam: Mosseh Diaz, 1695); Moshe b. Ya'akov Hagiz (1672–1751?, Jerusalem, Amsterdam), *Sefer Eleh ha-Mitzvot* (Amsterdam, 1713); Binyamin Rafael Dias Brandon, *Orot ha-Mitzvot* (Amsterdam: Jan Janson, 1753); Avraham Gabay Yzidro, *Yad Avraham: Ve-Hu Khibur ha-Azharot* (Amsterdam: Leib b. Moshe Zusmans/Jan Janson, 1758); Selomoh Levy Maduro, *Brit Yitshak* (Amsterdam: Gerard Johann Janson/House of Mondui, 1768).

64. Cohen, *Jews in Another Environment*, 159; Jacob R. Marcus and Stanley F. Chyet, eds., *Historical Essay on the Colony of Surinam, 1788*, trans. Simon Cohen (Cincinnati: American Jewish Archives; New York: Ktav, 1974), 142. The first number comes from a 1762 survey of Jodensavane in Cohen's work. The second number is from Marcus and Chyet's work.

Chapter 13

Diversity and Uniqueness
An Introduction to Sephardic Liturgical Music

Mark Kligman

The diversity and uniqueness of Sephardic liturgical music is exemplified through its broad range of musical styles and its integration into Jewish life. The styles of Sephardic liturgical music evolved through an absorption, adaptation, and reaction to a variety of influences. Like other areas of Jewish culture (language, art, literature, and food), music reflects the way that Sephardic Jews were assimilated into their local culture. This chapter will provide an introduction to Jewish liturgical music in Sephardic communities spanning from America and Europe to North Africa, the Mediterranean, and the Middle East.

History

During the pre- and early Modern period, Jewish life in the Ottoman Empire flourished, and many of the cultural developments from Jewish life in Spain continued. During the sixteenth and seventeenth centuries, or "Golden Age of the Ottoman Empire," territory expanded and economic opportunities were plentiful. The Jews of this region prospered along with all of its other inhabitants.

The end of the seventeenth century brought a decline in the Ottoman Empire's prominence in the world's economy. Consequently, the Jewish community experienced decreasing financial opportunities.[1] An increase of western European financial assistance in the eighteenth century stabilized the region. Western influence continued in the nineteenth century and brought new economic opportunities and renewed cultural aspirations and ideals.

Throughout this period, the Jews in Arab lands were viewed as a distinct group with their own customs and characteristics.[2] For example, the Jewish presence in Aleppo was clearly felt. An eighteenth-century account of Jewish life in Aleppo comments that trade stagnated in the city on Jewish holidays.[3] Throughout most of this period, Jews had autonomy and could worship freely. Their freedom resulted from the *dhimmi* status:

> The Muslim government obliges itself to protect the life and the property of the non-Muslims (*dhimmis*), exempts them from military service, and guarantees them religious freedom, although with certain restrictions. The *dhimmis*, on their part, are obliged to pay the poll tax (*jizya*), not to insult Islam, not to convert Muslims to their religions, not to build new churches or synagogues, and not to betray the Muslim government by conspiring with the enemy, e.g., hiding its spies.[4]

The Jews enjoyed taking part in and contributing to the city's cultural life. These activities included performances by Jewish musicians for Muslims.[5]

> The common cultural patterns included cuisine; the musical system of *maqamat*; the honor-shame code in gender relations; participation in markets; stories and jokes, and popular religious and medical practices....
> ... The patterns of prayer, meditation, and scriptural reading in the houses of worship of the different sects were also distinctive ... and the use of music. For instance, the emotional meaning of a particular *maqam* (melody type) used in local music might be different among Jews among Muslims. *Maʿamul*, a semolina cookie eaten at Purim (a Spring Jewish festival), was an Easter sweet for Christians.[6]

Historian Stanford Shaw divided the population of Jews in the Ottoman Empire into four layers: Romaniote, Sephardic, Mizrahim (Oriental or Eastern Jews), and Europeans. The Romaniote were Greek-speaking Jews surviving persecution of the late Roman and Byzantine times.[7] In the fifteenth century, Sephardic,[8] or Ladino-speaking, Jews were driven from the Iberian Peninsula and lands in which they had immediately taken refuge—Italy and North Africa.[9] Mizrahim, also known as *mustaʾrab* or Arabized Jews, spoke Arabic. Western, central, and northern Europeans fled Christian persecution. Each of the four groups had separate religious customs.

Sephardic Jews emigrated from these locales to Israel and America. The large wave of Jewish immigrants to America, starting in the 1880s, included a few thousand Sephardic Jews.¹⁰ This represented a small fraction compared to the 2.5 million eastern European Jewish immigrants. The current estimate of Sephardic Jews in America, 150,000 to 200,000, suggests that they make up approximately 2.8 percent of the general Jewish population in America.¹¹ Therefore, the Sephardic population is dwarfed in comparison to the Ashkenazic mainstream. The relative dearth of studies of Sephardic immigration and communities likewise limits information to draw upon. Although most Sephardic Jews settled in New York City, they also established communities in Rochester (New York), Atlanta, Birmingham, Indianapolis, Los Angeles, San Francisco, Portland, and Seattle.¹²

Immigrants usually drew themselves together into groups from the same cities and townships of origin. The unified language of Ashkenazic Jews was Yiddish. Sephardic Jews spoke Ladino, Greek, Arabic, and Turkish. Each group exhibited its own unique traits in the institutions it built during the early period of immigration and the goals it sought in America.

Hebrew became the common language in Israel over time. According to Joseph Papo, the Arabic-speaking Syrians in America stressed family unity and a thorough religious education early on. Greek-speaking Sephardic Jews maintained their individualism. The largest of the three groups, the Judeo-Spanish–speaking Jews, "were spurred on by a desire to regain their historic status and assert their equality with Ashkenazi Jewry."¹³ Since Ashkenazic Jews did not accept them, viewing their customs as too different,¹⁴ Sephardic Jews sought members of the same group and language affiliation even more. They had fewer choices of people and organizations with which to associate. In order to meet communal needs such as synagogues, schools, burial organizations, and social interaction, they created societies. There was little effort to have a united Sephardic society. Instead, preference was for solidarity from country or town of origin. Integration into American society eventually developed during the postwar period; wartime service and a general trend of economic affluence and stability steered Sephardic youth into American life.

Historical Music Issues

A lack of musical sources significantly hampered the study of musical history during the period of antiquity. Sources of actual musical notation did not appear until the ninth century. A consideration of music prior to this period came through written accounts, archeological evidence, and iconographic work (artwork such as mosaics that depicted music). Assessing music in the biblical and Temple periods was a specialized task combining musicology, archeology, and biblical scholarship. Joachim Braun's recent study on this subject illustrates the varying degrees of influence of local musical practice on Jews.[15]

Early-twentieth-century musicologists devoted to Jewish music approached Sephardic music with many assumptions. Some felt that the Yemenite community's was the most "authentic" form of Jewish music. It was believed that they had no outside influence and came directly to Yemen after the destruction of the Second Temple. However, recent scholarship does not verify these conclusions. Eric Werner explained in his study of Ashkenazic liturgical music:

> It is because of the devotion of those [German] hazanim [sic] that *minhag ashkenaz*, alone in Jewish tradition, stands as a living, developing, and creative musical structure, in contradistinction to the more or less petrified and stagnant Sephardic and Yemenite traditions. The latter may be of great historical interest, but musically they are far inferior to *minhag ashkenaz*.[16]

This reflected an attitude of the superiority of Western music, and the assumption of the ability to measure worth and value of music. This was most likely based on a lack of knowledge about Sephardic traditions. Scholarship has changed directions, and today Sephardic traditions are a viable topic of study.

A historical view of Jews under Arab and Christian rule in Spain will show the deep connection of Jewish creativity to the surrounding culture. Muslim Spanish scholars followed the ancient Greeks striving to find the spirit of an abstract science of the phenomena of music. A Jewish scholar in tenth-century North Africa, Dunash ibn Tamim, discussed *chokhmat ha-musikah* (knowledge of music) and *chokhmat ha-niggun* (knowledge of melody) taken from similar terms in Arabic sources, such as "*ilm al-musiqi.*"

Further evidence of Muslim influence on Jewish thinkers was seen in Saadiah Gaon's *Emunot ve-De'ot* (933). Following the teachings of Muslim scholar Al-Kindi, Saadiah's last chapter on music described the effect of eight types of musical rhythms on the human temper. It also showed how the two should be mixed in order to lead men to the Golden Mean. Ancient Greek philosophers believed that music provided an ethical influence.¹⁷ In the eleventh through thirteenth centuries, biblical exegesis was significant in influencing Jewish communities in Spain. Music was held in high regard for its strong spiritual power. Developments in poetry and singing reflected the deep interconnection between music and text.

Biblical Cantillation

The melodic practice of reciting the Bible was guided by the *taʾamim* (marking signs). These signs did not appear in the Torah scroll. The *taʾamim* were codified by the family of Ben Asher in Tiberia in the tenth century. These markings, together with the diacritical marks (such as distinguishing a *shin* "שׁ" from a *sin* "שׂ") and vowels, helped the reader prepare to chant the biblical text. The *taʾamim* thus served several functions to aid in the proper pronunciation, syntax, and melodic recitation of the text.¹⁸

Sephardic communities differed significantly in the cantillation of biblical texts. Since there were very few musical renditions of any Sephardic practices in the nineteenth century, the study of Sephardic cantillation has been recent. A. Z. Idelsohn (1882–1938) made significant contributions to this study with his seminal publication, *Thesaurus of Hebrew and Oriental Melodies* (1914–1932). The work documented the cantillation practice of Jews from various locales who immigrated to Israel in the early twentieth century. Born in Europe and trained in Vienna in the *Wissenschaft* tradition, Idelsohn sought to find the "ur-text," or the ancient tradition of cantillation. It was quite enticing for him to look at the plethora of cantillation traditions during his day. He compared the melodic rendering of the *taʾamim* to various traditions and concluded that there were similarities that stemmed from a "Palestinian folk song." He clearly was motivated to find a connection for a common origin of cantillation by the rising tide of Zionism in Israel. Because present-day practice cannot be considered an authoritative proof of an unchanging oral tradition, many scholars disagree with this theory.¹⁹

Music scholars, on the practices of the cantillation of the Bible in the Jewish context today, define eight main musical traditions: those of the Middle East (Iran, Bukhara, Kurdistan, Georgia, and Northern Iraq); Southern Arabian Peninsula (Yemen); Near East (Turkey, Syria, central Iraq, Lebanon, and Egypt); North Africa (Libya, Tunisia, Algeria, and

Morocco); Italy (as practiced in Rome); Sephardi and Portuguese communities of Europe; western European Ashkenazim (German-speaking countries, France, some communities in the Netherlands, and England); and eastern European Ashkenazim (most common Ashkenazic practice, found in America).[20] The two Ashkenazic and the Sephardi and Portuguese traditions were similar in that they used a melodic phrase for each *ta'am* (singular of *ta'amim*). The shape or meaning of the cantillation sign provides an indication for an exact melody. The diversity of the Sephardic practice is evident in the different usage of the *ta'amim*. In the Middle Eastern and Southern Arabian traditions, the melodic rendering is a general formula that applies to the text. Some described this practice as "psalmody," which begins with a rise in the initial intonation of a *pasuk* (sentence of the Bible). The middle portion of the melody stays on a particular note, referred to as a recitation tone, and concludes with a recurring melodic phrase. The *ta'amim* in Middle Eastern and Southern Arabian traditions guide the general shape of the *pasuk*, not a direct melodic phrase for each cantillation sign. The Near Eastern tradition of the Levant is highly ornate with great emphasis applied to some words of the text. The Sephardi and Portuguese practice of cantillation follows the Western tonal system. Melodically, it is clearly different from the Ashkenazic practice. But its function as a mosaic process of combining musical cells is the same. The Near Eastern or Levant practice makes use of the Middle Eastern *makamat* with different books of the Bible cantillated in a different *makam*. The Middle Eastern tradition, as practiced by Iraqi Jews, follows the "psalmody" style with a melodic rise and fall. The musicologist Hanoch Avenary stated the following regarding diversity in cantillation practices: "In many ways, Jewish reading practices of today form a living museum of chanting styles as they were at different stages of their development."[21]

Piyyutim

A significant development in the early history of Jewish music at the end of the first millennium was the development of the *piyyut* (*piyyutim* plural). The original intention of the *piyyut* was to enhance prayers. By the ninth century, prayers were formalized. The *hazzan* recited them out loud, followed by the congregation. As the desire for variety increased, *piyyutim* grew in their influence inside and outside of the synagogue. A *piyyut* was a poetic Hebrew text closely tied to a religious concept and context. These new texts were sung and influenced music in Jewish life.

The writing of *piyyutim* began in the fourth and fifth centuries. The classical period of *piyyutim* occurred during the sixth through the eleventh centuries in Palestine. By the ninth century, it spread to Europe. The most significant developments were in Spain during the tenth century and grew through the fifteenth century with Arab models. Shiloah explained:

> For the next five hundred years [tenth to fifteenth centuries], the *piyyut* blossomed with a direct affinity to the various forms of Arabic poetry. From the standpoint of content and language, the Spanish *piyyut* freed itself of talmudic-midrash content and of the esoteric, allusive language that had previously characterized such works; *piyyutim* were now based primarily on biblical language. From the standpoint of form, one of the major innovations of the Spanish *piyyut* was that it was patterned after strophic and strophic-like poetry.[22]

The clarity of the *piyyutim* during this time made them important models for future generations. The Golden Age of Spain (tenth to twelfth centuries) was the most influential period of *piyyutim* in Jewish history. After the expulsion from Spain, the *piyyutim* spread throughout the Middle East and North Africa.

The context of *piyyut* singing was closely connected to Jewish life. *Piyyutim* were recited inside and outside of the synagogue. Particular Sabbaths were deemed to be "special" because of either the biblical portion read or the time of the year. When the Song of the Sea (Exodus 15:1–19) or the Ten Commandments (Exodus 20:1–14) portions were read, a *piyyut* containing parts of or inspired by this biblical text may have been sung in the synagogue. If a Sabbath fell during the Shelosh Regalim (Three Festivals), a *piyyut* could also be sung for the occasion. Singing at the Sabbath table was another instance. Other contexts included life cycle events: *brit milah*, bar mitzvah, or wedding. Joyous songs were sung to mark these events. In some communities the singing of *piyyutim* was a communal event formalized into a ritual before the Sabbath prayers. In the Moroccan and Syrian communities, this was known as *bakkashot* (supplications). At early hours in the morning, people would gather to sing prior to the morning prayers.

A few hundred years after their inception, *piyyutim* absorbed influences and grew into a poetic art form. The early *piyyut* was organized with an acrostic, often the name of the author, but had no rhyme. After the seventh century, rhyme was added. During this period, authors drew on biblical phrases to create poetry. In Spain, *piyyutim* adopted formal attributes of rhyme, rhythm, symmetry (lines of equal length), and organizational structures.

Arabic poetry was a significant stimulus. Dunash ben-Labrat (b. 920) grew up in Fez and later lived in Cordova, Spain. He was a *hazzan* and *paytan*. Ben-Labrat was influenced by Arabic quantitative meter and introduced it into Hebrew poetry. His well-known *piyyut* "Deror Yikra" served as an example. Meter consisted of the stress of short and long units. A short unit followed by a long unit was called *yated*—such as the word "*gemar*," a short syllable with a vowel, "*ge-*," was combined with a consonant and long vowel, "*-mar.*" A single long syllable was called *tenuʾah*. A single metrical unit consisted of one *yated* unit and two *tenuʾah* units. The metrical unit of "Deror Yikra" was *marnin*, comprised of *yated*, *tenuʾah*, *tenuʾah*. Thus, the metrical flow was: short, long, long, long. This was then applied to a four-syllable unit of text. The first four syllables, "deror yikra," were recited with the pattern: short, long, long, long. The pattern was then repeated with each line of text. In addition to this metrical pattern, the use of an acrostic and rhyme scheme furthered the overall organization of the poetry.

The meter's influence on the music was not always direct. Shiloah provides four renditions of "Deror Yikra" in the Iraqi tradition, displaying a range of interpretations.[23] Often, the rhythm of the music has an organizational structure of its own. Idelsohn commented on the interconnection between poetic meter and music, "While in the case of melodies set to poems of other meters, no relation between the meter of the text and the rhythm of music is traceable."[24]

The Spanish *piyyut* continued to develop during the tenth through twelfth centuries, also known as the Golden Age of Spain. A significant *piyyut* form was the strophic model referred to in Arabic as *muwashshah*. This style consisted of a refrain that was repeated after each verse. Symmetry was a part of the design with equal metrical units. Examples of *piyyutim* in this form were "Tsur Mishelo" and "Ya Ribon Olam." Prolific poets during this time included Shlomo ibn Gabirol (1021–1070), Moshe ibn Ezra (1055–1140), Judah Halevi (1075–1141), and Abraham ibn Ezra (1092–1167). After the fifteenth century, North Africa, Salonika, Rhodes, Egypt, Aleppo, Safed, Yemen, and Kurdistan were all major centers of *piyyut* development. In each of these communities, *piyyutim* were integrated into

Jewish life on religious occasions and life cycle events, creating an emergence in local traditions.

Piyyutim played a significant role in Mizrahi Jewish life as the new melodies were added and incorporated into the synagogue service. The creator of this poetry was known as a *paytan*. This was often the *hazzan*.

> The *paytan* or cantor, those who are responsible for liturgical and paraliturgical singing, are called upon to make these adaptations. In olden times the *paytan* performed a three-fold task: he wrote the text, adapted the words to the melody, and performed the work as part of the prayers or other religious rites. Once a body of *piyyutim* had acquired an accepted place within the regular prayers, fewer and fewer new poetic works were absorbed into the liturgy. This limited the function of the *paytan* to aspects of musical adaptation and performance. At the same time the writing of *piyyutim* continued to flourish outside the framework of prayer and ritual worship, *piyyutim* being sung with the Sabbath Psalms, the lamentations, the penitential prayers and supplications, as well as at paraliturgical events such as circumcisions, weddings and so on.[25]

The three-step process of adaptation consisted of writing a new Hebrew text, setting it to a known song, and making use of that melody in the liturgy. Israel Najara (1550–1620), who lived in Safed, adapted Turkish, Arabic, Spanish, and Greek songs to his newly created Hebrew poetry. In 1587, his popular publication, *Zemirot Israel*, contained 100 songs. Its subsequent editions had 300 songs. Najara hoped that Jews would sing his music rather than "foreign" songs. He saw creating his poems as a sacred task. He indicated in manuscripts the melody of the originating song to be used when singing his text.[26] This was not an unknown practice in Western musicology. The term "contrafactum" refers to the process of taking a melody and adapting it to a new text. The practice goes back hundreds of years and was the means by which new music was constructed in the church. While some looked down upon the process of adaptation because it was not original, Shiloah saw it in *piyyutim*. To him, it was an act of musical composition through which a new creative work could stand on its own merit.[27]

The *piyyut* practice is kept alive in Mizrahi communities. During the second half of the twentieth century, Brooklyn was home to the largest Syrian community. The population ranged between approximately 35,000 and 40,000 people in 1990. The *piyyut* practice for Syrians is known as *pizmon*.²⁸ In a recent study, Kay Kaufman Shelemay looked at the *pizmonim* as a memory device:

> The *pizmon*, provides a cultural space in which individual and collective memories may both be mediate and juxtaposed. . . . In a similar manner, each *pizmon* may be described as a heterotopology, a site for various constructions of present and past, containing simultaneous commemoration of both individuals and collectivities.²⁹

Pizmonim are expressions of a synthesized identity for Syrian Jews who were culturally immersed in an Arab aesthetic milieu.

> The Syrian Jewish memories posited within the pizmonim are further characterized by an essential duality: the song texts recall a world of explicitly Jewish experience, while the melodies evoke extra-Jewish sources and frames of reference. The *pizmonim* therefore constitute a hybrid form, with two expressive channels directly reflecting the bifurcated historical experience of this Judeo-Arab community.³⁰

The Syrian process of *piyyut* adaptation reflects a legacy in which music mirrors a larger cultural trait. The process discussed here reflects the practice of Syrian-born Jews who immigrated to America and lived in Brooklyn. "Hawwid Min Hina" was an Arabic song recorded, and most likely composed, by Zaki Murad (1880–1940) between 1915 and 1920.³¹ The genre of this composition is known as a *taqtuqah*, which typically consists of several verses and a short refrain. The text of a *taqtuqah*, like the music, was simple and straightforward, in colloquial Arabic, on a light-hearted topic, and used a simple rhythmic mode (*wazn*).³² The regularity of this melody was emphasized by the consistent rhythm.

Anne Rasmussen discusses the endurance of the *taqtuqah* genre among Arab-Americans through its simplicity. She contrasts the "easy to sing" nature of this light genre with the so-called "heavy stuff" of other genres.³³ A *taqtuqah* provides a likely source for adapting a melody to a portion of the liturgy that was sung by the congregation.³⁴

"Boʾi be-Rinah," the adapted *pizmon*, was written by Moses Ashear (1877–1940). He was born in Aleppo and, in 1903, became Aleppo's official *hazzan* and reader of the Torah. He immigrated to America in 1912 and served as *hazzan* of the Magen David Congregation in Brooklyn for 28

FIGURE 1
"Hawwid Min Hina" and "Boʾi be-Rinah" Line by Line Transliteration Comparison

line 1	Hawwid min hina:	Hawwid min hi**na**, ta^ɔaala indi**na**
	Boʾi be-rinah:	Boʾi be-rinah yaʾalah adi**nah**
line 2	Hawwid min hina:	Yalla ana winta nhibbi baʾdi**na**
	Boʾi be-rinah:	Le-beiti **atah** ve-imekh eshʾco**nah**
line 3	Hawwid min hina:	Gaana-l fa**rah** zaala-l ta**rah**
	Boʾi be-rinah:	Oiʾvekh ba**rah** yishʾeikh pa**rah**
line 4	Hawwid min hina:	Sadrii-n sha**rah** imta nistila
	Boʾi be-rinah:	Orekh za**rah** eit le-henʾnah

Translation of Texts
(each translated line corresponds to the line of each system in the transcription):

a) "Hawwid Min Hina"
  Stop over, come to us.
  Come on, let us love one another.
  Joy is here, sorrow disappears.
  My heart is enchanted. When shall me meet?

b) "Boʾi be-Rinah"
  Come in Song, gentle graceful woman.
  To my house now and with you I will dwell.
  Your enemy fled your salvation blossomed.
  Your light shined, time to be bestowed to her.

---

years. Ashear wrote hundreds of *pizmonim* and actively encouraged the singing of *pizmonim* through activities such as organizing choirs.[35] "Boʾi be-Rinah" is an example of a typical *pizmon*. It is written for a specific occasion, has a repeating chorus, and is organized with an acrostic and rhyme scheme.

There is a strong textual similarity between "Boʾi Be-Rinah" and its originating Arabic song text "Hawwid Min Hina." Both texts shared the same rhyme scheme (aaba ccca). The text of the Hebrew closely followed the Arabic text as a model; see Figure 1. Located at the end of the first line of text of "Boʾi be-rinah" were the words "yaʾalah indinah." This phrase followed the assonance of its Arabic song model with the words "taʾaala ʾindina" (these words are underlined in Figure 1). The text of "Hawwid Min Hina" began with the unrequited love of a woman to a man who ultimately called on God to unite them. "Boʾi Be-Rinah" started with the expression of love to a woman which allegorically represented the love of man for God.[36] Thus, the Arabic song serves as a model on many levels.

FIGURE 2
"Mahalalakh" Hebrew Text

סִימָן מָרְדְּכַי עַבַּאדִי   **מב**   רֹאשׁ

מְהַלֶּלְךָ וְרֹב גֻּדְלְךָ. אֵין לוֹ תַּכְלִית קֵצֶה וָסוֹף. אֵין גַּם אֶחָד יַעֲרוֹךְ לָךְ. הַלֵּל גָּמוּר עַד לְאֵין סוֹף. וּמִי הָאִישׁ לִבּוֹ **הָלוּךְ**. יַזְכִּיר תְּהִלּוֹת יְיָ:

רְקִיעֵי עֲרָבוֹת מָכוֹן. מְעוֹן זְבוּל גַּם שְׁחָקִים. רָקִיעַ אַחֲרוֹן תִּכּוֹן. נִכְסָפִים וּמִשְׁתּוֹקְקִים. עֲדֵי כָל־אִישׁ הִנּוּ נָכוֹן. יָשִׁיר יִשְׂרָאֵל לַיְיָ:

דּוֹמְמִים כְּרוּבִים אִשִּׁים. חַיּוֹת אוֹפַנִּים חַשְׁמַלִּים. מַלְאֲכֵי־מָרוֹם תַּרְשִׁישִׁים. שַׂרְפֵי קֹדֶשׁ וְאֶרְאֶלִּים. עַד כִּי שׁוֹאֲלִים וְדוֹרְשִׁים. קֹדֶשׁ יִשְׂרָאֵל לַיְיָ:

כּוֹכָבִים שֶׁמֶשׁ יָרֵחַ. וְגַם שְׁאָר כּוֹכְבֵי לֶכֶת. חַיָּתוֹ שָׂדַי עוֹף פּוֹרֵחַ. כָּל־אַחַת שִׁיר הִיא עוֹרֶכֶת. יַחַד כָּל־בָּשָׂר וָרוּחַ. יְהַלְלוּ שֵׁם יְיָ:

כָּל־מַעֲשֶׂיךָ. וְתִבְחַר לְשׁוֹן עֲרוּמִים. חַי חַי כָּמוֹנִי יוֹדְךָ. יְהַלֶּלְךָ כָּל־הַיָּמִים. לִפְנֵי כִסֵּא כְבוֹדְךָ. נָאוָה קֹדֶשׁ בֵּית יְיָ:

הָאֵל יוֹדוּ לִשְׁמוֹ. כִּי צְדָקָה עִמָּם עָשָׂה. וַיִּבְרָא הָאָדָם בְּצַלְמוֹ. לְהוֹדוֹת לוֹ פָּנִים נָשָׂא. וּמִכָּל־מַלְאָךְ הִקְדִּימוֹ. לְזַמֵּר לְשֵׁם יְיָ:

יוֹדוּךָ

עַבְדִּי

תם

Another example of a Syrian *piyyut* was "Mahalalakh." "Mahalalakh," a *bakkasha*, was written by Mordecai Abbadi, a kabbalist who wrote religious poetry.[37] He lived in Aleppo in the nineteenth century and was a rabbi and cantor. There were six verses in this text, see Figure 2, each containing five lines. The arrangement of the verses clearly illustrates the acrostic of the composer's name, "MoRDeCaI Abbadi" (Mem Resh Dalet

FIGURE 2 (cont'd)
"Mahalalakh" / "Your Praise" Translation

(Mem) verse 1:	Your praise and abundant is your greatness. He has no end. There is also no one who will prepare for you. Total praise forever. And who is the man whose heart goes. To mention the praises of God.
(Resh) verse 2:	The Heavens of Aravot Machon. M[hamza]on, Z[hamza]vul, also Sh[hamza]chakim. The last firmament will be put in place. Yearnings and desires. Until Every man, he who is prepared. Israel will sing to God.
(Dalet) verse 3:	Inanimate fiery angles. Animals, wheels, glowing substances (electra). Angels of angels on high. Holy, seraphs and angles. Until questioners and preachers. Israel is holy to God.
(Caf) verse 4:	Stars, sun moon. And also remaining planets. The animals of the field and birds that fly in the sky Each one of them arranges a song. Together every body and soul. Will praise the name of G-d.
(Yud) verse 5:	All Your works will thank you. And you choose crafty language. Living things like me will thank you. They will praise you all the days. Before your glorious throne. Pretty, holy is the house of God.
(Aleph) verse 6:	Servants of the God gives thanks to His name. For He made righteousness with them. He created man in his image. To thank Him carrying his countenance. And from every angel that comes before him. To sing to the name of God.

Caf Yud Ayin—the first five letters were taken from the poet's first name and the last letter from the first letter of his last name). The rhyme pattern for each verse was consonant-vowel-consonant. For example, in the first verse, the "a" rhyme is "*lakh.*" This is similar to the Arabic-influenced poetry in Spain. Additionally, within this genre of poetry, each line contains an equal number of syllables. "Mahalalakh" uses eight syllables per line. The verse rhymes are shown below with lowercase letters indicating the rhyme within each verse, the capital letters representing the same word (the name of God), which is the last word of each verse:[38]

VERSE	RHYME
1. MEM	ababa'C
2. RESH	dededC
3. DALET	fgfgfC
4. KAF	hihih'C
5. YOD	jkjkjC
6. AYIN	lmlmlC

Balance was achieved through the consistent rhyme pattern in every verse, the same final rhyme of each verse, and the use of eight syllables per line.

Some textual lines of this poem were taken from other types of Hebrew literature, evoking known references and images; see translation of "Mahalalakh," Figure 2. Five different names for the seventh level of heaven are listed in verse 2, lines 1 and 2. These names also appear in the Babylonian Talmud, Chagigah 12b: the reference to the seventh heaven drew upon kabbalistic imagery of the heavenly world. Biblical references are found in the following verses: verse 3, line 2 (the illusion of "wheels glowing substances") comes from Ezekiel's dream in Ezekiel 1:27. The opening of verse 5 is taken from Psalms 145:10 (this psalm was recited three times a day as part of the liturgy). Verse 5, line 2 contains an ambiguous reference to Job 15:5. The section in Job mentions his ability to "choose crafty language" to conceal his guilt. In the context of "Mahalalakh," the reference was to God, but it may have additionally stated that man will "choose crafty language" to think and praise God. This demonstrated a common technique of taking the original biblical reference and either changing its meaning or making it ambiguous.

"Mahalalakh," like other *bakkashot*, expresses supplications and conjures images for the exaltation of God. The first verse states an introductory praise of God. The next makes references to God's control of the heavens. The third mentions the angels, followed by a more tangible reference to the planets and animals in the fourth verse. The fifth verse states, "All your works will thank you," with the last verse as the climax, claiming that God's servants will praise and sing God's name. The statement of God's name concludes each verse, serving two purposes: the organized repetition of the end verse rhyme, and the progression in the praise of

God from the heavenly world to the creation of man. Poetic devices and textual elements organize the text.

The musical setting of "Mahalalakh" is ornate to aptly reflect the text; this melody can be found as a setting of the liturgical text "Nishmat Kol Hai" (The Soul of Every Living Thing) discussed below in Figure 3. The creation of a *piyyut* and its application to the liturgy are interconnected. The practice of adapting melodies for *piyyutim* continues into the twentieth century in many communities. It has remained a part of Mizrahi Jewish life today. Noted contributors to modern *piyyutim* were prominent members of their respective communities. Their work displays continuity with the poetic and liturgical traditions of the past. Isaac Algazi (1889–1951) was born in Turkey and immigrated to South America in 1935. He recorded many liturgical melodies in the Turkish style. He also recorded many *piyyutim* and Judeo-Spanish songs, thus encompassing a broad repertoire. Outside of Jewish contexts, he was well respected for his singing of the *ghazal*, a Turkish music genre.[39] In Morocco, Rabbi David Buzaglo (d. 1975) was an expert in the Andalusian tradition. He was credited with keeping the Moroccan *bakkashot*[40] tradition viable in Morocco and Israel, where he immigrated in 1965. He incorporated many contemporary Egyptian melodies into his *piyyutim*. In Israel, concerts of the singing of *piyyutim* are increasing. Since these concerts are not held on Shabbat or a holiday, musical instruments can be added.

Liturgy

Liturgical music serves several functions in Sephardic synagogues. The *hazzan* recites large portions of the prayers with a melodic pattern at a rapid pace. Other portions are highlighted musically. Musical emphasis comes through musical elaboration, as described above in the adaptation of "Nishmat Kol Hai" from "Mahalalakh," and congregational singing.

Comparing various Sephardic practices is instructive. Figure 3 illustrates renditions of three Sephardic traditions. The text, "Nishmat Kol Hai," begins the cantor's prayers for the Sabbath morning service. The text states that all living things will bless God. In this comparative musical example, the Spanish and Portuguese rendition appears on the first line of each system throughout. Likewise, the Turkish is on the second, and the Syrian on the third. The Spanish and Portuguese rendition and the Syrian rendition are the most distinct. The former possesses a consistent rhythm

FIGURE 3
Sephardic Liturgy "Nishmat Kol Hai"

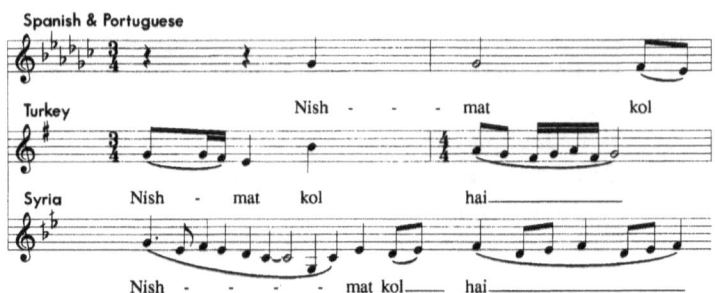

FIGURE 3 (*cont'd*)
Sephardic Liturgy "Nishmat Kol Hai"

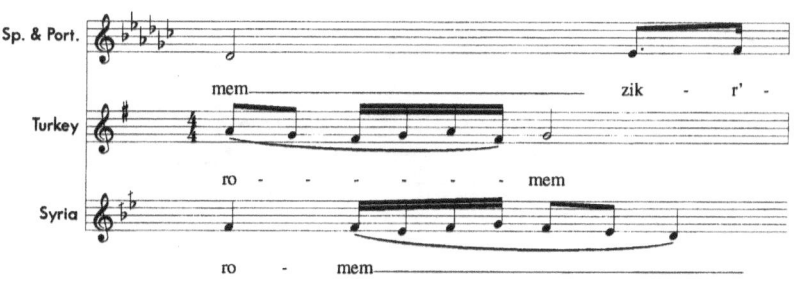

FIGURE 3 (cont'd)
Sephardic Liturgy "Nishmat Kol Hai"

throughout and is not melodically ornate. The latter is rhythmically freer, as indicated in the transcription, with no meter and more notes per word. The Turkish rendition is stylistically between the two, with a consistent rhythm and slight embellishments throughout. All three renditions are similar in that they repeat musical phrases. Interestingly, they are distinct as to when the musical material is repeated. The Spanish and Portuguese rendition begins with a repeated G-flat followed by a descent. This same phrase begins with slight modifications over the words "*v°ruah.*" The Turkish rendition, which begins on a G, descends stepwise quickly to E, and then leaps up to a B. This melody repeats with the word "*t°faer.*" The Syrian rendition began on a G with a dotted quarter note. This melody repeats with the word "*Adoshem.*" Consequently, this or any liturgical text may be rendered differently depending on the community. No single interpretation exists; each expresses a different nuance of the text.

Sephardic liturgical music regularly focuses on congregational participation. They differ as to where this occurs in the liturgy. In Figure 3, only the Spanish and Portuguese tradition sings "Nishmat Kol Hai" congregationally. The Syrian and Turkish recite this text individually by the *hazzan.* Since the Spanish and Portuguese rendition needs to facilitate group singing, the regular rhythm and more simple stepwise musical line allows the congregation to sing together. In the Syrian and even the Moroccan traditions, the *hazzan* begins with a known melody to this liturgical section and then improvises the proceeding portion of the text. Group singing does not appear in all traditions. Rather, different parts of the liturgy are emphasized.

The Kaddish and Kedusha are also emphasized through congregational singing. The highlighting of liturgical passages between these phrases varies according to the community. Choral singing, two or more voices singing to precomposed music, only appears in the Sephardic traditions influenced by Western music in European locales. It is evident in the Spanish and Portuguese tradition, which has a rich heritage of many nineteenth- and twentieth-century liturgical choral compositions.[41] Choral singing is not practiced in Moroccan, *Edot hamizrah,* or Yemenite traditions.

Lively congregational singing is a key aspect of the Sephardic liturgy. While many portions are recited by the *hazzan,* as required by Jewish law, congregational participation is enthusiastic and joyful. Unlike the Ashkenazic practice, which intones the last two to three lines of a liturgical text, known as a *hatima,* Sephardic *hazzanim* recite the entire liturgical text out loud. Congregants are able to join in the recitation; some do so in an undertone. The uniqueness of the Sephardic tradition is not only displayed by its melodies, but also by the liturgical performance practice itself, which combines both active and passive participation from the congregation.

Judeo-Spanish Songs

Sephardic Jews of medieval Spanish ancestry retained many aspects of Ladino culture. Ladino, their Judeo-Spanish written and spoken dialect, represented more than a language. It symbolized the synthesis of Jewish and Spanish culture. The rich traditions of this cultural interconnection were continued from the Golden Age of Spain. However, the amount of preservation versus new influence has varied during the past five hundred years. The Spanish tradition was ongoing for Jews in Morocco, whereas Jews in Turkey and Greece adopted some local Middle Eastern influences. Some historians hold that the venerable musical forms of the Sephardic Jews, namely the ballad and *romancero*, were time-honored traditions, untouched by new cultural influence and, thus, faithfully transmitted. Modern scholars, however, are unable to validate this claim. Nevertheless, Judeo-Spanish music had deep historic roots and, like other forms of Jewish music, was perpetuated and innovatively revitalized by modern performers.

Women have long conserved Judeo-Spanish music. Many of the song texts of the *romancero* and ballad dealt with women's experiences in life-cycle events, passionate or erotic courtly poetry, and epic tales or stories. Dirges related to the death of individuals were known as *endechas*. *Coplas* were short holiday songs. The wedding context has been a particularly rich source of music for Sephardic women. The preparation of the bride for the *mikva* (ritual bath) prior to the wedding, her dowry, and her relationship with her mother-in-law were some subjects of the texts. Some Judeo-Spanish melodies were also incorporated into the liturgy.

Since no standard forms existed, each performer personalized his or her version of Ladino repertoire. Musicologist Israel Katz[42] devotes his scholarly efforts to understanding Judeo-Spanish songs through their past and present manifestations. He sees a distinction between two musical types with respect to the ballad. The western Mediterranean, or Moroccan, Ladino singing style included regular phrases and rhythms with few embellishments. Within this style, many modern performers of Judeo-Spanish music incorporated the Spanish and Arabic musical styles into their song renditions as well. The eastern Mediterranean, or Turkish and Balkan, Judeo-Spanish singing style included more melodic enhancements in a freer, often less regular rhythm. Over time, however, eastern and western styles merged. Katz also postulates that a third style might exist in the ballad style of Greece.

The performance of Judeo-Spanish music grew steadily. Performers drew from a range of sources, which included printed material (such as Isaac Levy's *Chants Judeo-Espagnols,* 1965–1973) and documentation from informants. These melodies were then adapted to a range of musical styles: medieval, Spanish, Arabic, Turkish, and Balkan. Some composers arranged traditional songs into art songs, most notably Alberto Hemsi, Paul Ben Haim, and Yehezkiel Braun. In the latter half of the twentieth century, there was a growing interest in Judeo-Spanish songs. Westernized versions were increasingly found in anthologies of Jewish folk songs. As American Jews became further removed from their eastern European heritage over time, other forms of Jewry were explored. Various ensembles devoted their musical efforts to the Judeo-Spanish repertoire in a wide range of styles.[43]

Israeli Mediterranean Music

The experience of Sephardic Jews during the twentieth century was a process of settling to new locales and reestablishing religious and cultural practices. Music played a significant role in everyday life where aspects of religion were carried over. New forms of music were created, while traditional forms were reinterpreted and adapted into a new context. In the first half of the twentieth century, European and Middle Eastern immigrants to British-mandated Palestine brought with them and perpetuated the culture of their country of origin. There was a desire by these early immigrants to discover or invent a uniquely Jewish music. The music of Yemenite Jews was viewed as ancient, and so it served as a model. Music in synagogues did not use instruments after the destruction of the Temple in the first century because a state of mourning was declared (*Shulhan Arukh, Oreh Hayyim* 338:10; see also Babylonian Talmud Eruvin 104a and Stoah 48a). This practice changed in the Modern period, beginning with the nineteenth-century Reform movement in Germany. Music made for nonsynagogue purposes was not bound by limitations other than the Sabbath restrictions. For Yemenite Jews, the refusal to use musical instruments persisted, except for the rhythmic beating on oilcans and copper trays. These were preferred to the use of drums to accompany dance and singing. One performer of the pre-State period, Bracha Zephira, gained wide popularity through singing Yemenite songs. She collaborated with composers and arrangers, such as Nachum Nardi and Paul Ben Haim, and adapted Yemenite music to folk and artistic styles. Several immigrant composers, such as Paul Ben Haim, Oedoen Partos, and Marc Lavry, developed music in this direction, creating their own Mediterranean style. In the course of this Westernization of Middle Eastern musical features, indigenous Middle Eastern music became marginalized. However, this state of affairs changed dramatically in Israel from the late 1960s through the end of the twentieth century.

In Israel, the European Jews who worked to found the modern State of Israel initially treated Middle Eastern immigrants and their descendants as second-class citizens. The Ashkenazic hegemony often deligitimized Sephardi culture. As efforts to integrate Ashkenazic and Sephardic culture gained priority with Israel's Likud government of the late 1960s through the early 1970s, non-Western cultural expression gained validation. This led to an integrated musical style now known as Musika Yam Tikhonit Yisraelit (Israeli Mediterranean Music). It was first called Musika Mizrahit (Eastern Music) and Muiskat Ha-Tachana Ha-Merkazit (Central Bus Station Music), referring to the location of purchase. The music was pan-ethnic and integrated a variety of styles. Hebrew lyrics commingled with Arabic, Persian, Kurdish, and Turkish texts, while the Eastern European, Greek, Turkish, or Arabic tunes featured local aesthetic markers that drew in Egyptian, Jordanian, Lebanese, Syrian, and Palestinian listeners.[44] A combination of Western and Middle Eastern instruments and musical styles provided a rich source of creative expression. Performers of note included Zohar Argov, Daklon, Ben Mosh, and Haim Moshe. Other artists, such as Ofra Haza, tried to reach broader audiences and have recorded songs in Western languages. The core Musika Yam Tikhonit Yisraelit repertoire used Hebrew for the text and was popular in Israel and throughout the Middle East. Avihu Medina's *Shabbekhi Yerushalayim* took a text from Psalms (Psalms 147:12–13) and created a popular melody with a distinct modern Middle Eastern style, demonstrating continuity with the past.

Conclusion

Diversified styles were found in the music of Sephardic or Middle Eastern Jews. Pre-1948 State of Israel Sephardic music strived to maintain traditions in locales that had been inhabited by Jews for hundreds of years. Today, Sephardic music and its connection to Jewish culture has persisted amid the larger and more Ashkenazic religious authority and institutions in both the Americas and in Israel. This was even after undergoing a significant relocation in the twentieth century. Some of the traditions survived, and others ceased to exist.

Viable contemporary music reflects Jewish culture. It synthesizes influences that are adapted dynamically and grew through the perpetuation of tradition blended with innovative changes. Diversity is found in the range of styles, languages, and contexts of music in living genres of liturgical, paraliturgical, and popular music. Uniqueness describes the specialized contexts of various communities in the uses of *piyyutim, bakkashot,* Judeo-Spanish songs, the adaptation of liturgical music, and the many new concerts and recordings of music. Since Israel's independence, there has been a consolidation of practices as Jews of particular regions joined together. Sephardic music continued as traditions evolved, inspiring both religious and secular musical compositions.

NOTES

1. See Albert Hournai, *A History of the Arab Peoples* (Cambridge: Harvard University Press, 1991), 259; and Norman Stillman, *The Jews of Arab Lands: A History and Source Book* (Philadelphia: Jewish Publication Society, 1979), 90–91.

2. Stillman, *The Jews of Arab Lands,* 4; Abraham Marcus, *Middle East on the Eve of Modernity: Aleppo in the Eighteenth Century* (New York: Columbia University Press, 1989), 39.

3. Alexander Russell, *The Natural History of Aleppo,* 2d ed. (London, 1756), vol. 2, 78.

4. Eliyahu Ashtor, "Dhimma, Dhimmi," in *Encyclopaedia Judaica* (Jerusalem: Keter, 1972), vol. 5, 1604.

5. Marcus, *Middle East on the Eve of Modernity,* 43–44.

6. Walter P. Zenner, *A Global Community: The Jews from Aleppo, Syria* (Detroit: Wayne State University Press, 2000), 36–37.

7. Stanford J. Shaw, *The Jews of the Ottoman Empire and the Turkish Republic* (New York: New York University Press, 1991), 1, 44–45.

8. Sephardic Jews are those whose descent is from the "Mediterranean and western Asia, including their eastern and western diasporas." Daniel J. Elazar, *The Other Jews: The Sephardim Today* (New York: Basic Books, 1989), 14. For purposes of this study I will use the term "Sephardic" to refer to the larger body of non-Ashkenazic Jewry since the Syrian Jews in Brooklyn identify themselves as "Sephardim," most likely they claim a legacy to Spanish Jewry.

9. These Jews never experienced the isolation of a ghetto and were businessmen and leading intellectuals. They mixed with Muslims and Christians as they had previously in Spain. Shaw, *The Jews of the Ottoman Empire*, 45.

10. Joseph M. Papo, "The Sephardim in North America in the Twentieth Century," *Sephardim in the Americas*, special issue of *American Jewish Archives* 4, no. 1 (spring/summer 1992): 270.

11. See ibid., 303; and Elazar, *The Other Jews*, 166.

12. Elazar, *The Other Jews*, 164.

13. Papo, "The Sephardim in North America," 271–72.

14. Ibid., 272–75.

15. Joachim Braun, *Music in Ancient Israel/Palestine: Archaeological, Written, and Comparative Sources* (Grand Rapids, MI: W. B. Eerdmans, 2002).

16. Eric Werner, *A Voice Still Heard . . . : The Sacred Songs of the Ashkenazic Jews* (University Park: Pennsylvania State University Press, 1976), 29.

17. Hanoch Avenary, "Music," in *Encyclopaedia Judaica*, vol. 12, 590–91.

18. For a further discussion of the multifaceted function of the *taʾamim* and an introduction to cantillation see "Cantillation" in Amnon Shiloah, *Jewish Musical Traditions* (Detroit: Wayne State University Press, 1992), 87–109.

19. For Idelsohn's discussion see A. Z. Idelsohn, *Jewish Music in Its Historical Development* (New York: Henry Holt, 1929), 70–71; for a challenge to this ideal of Idelsohn, see Shiloah, *Jewish Musical Tradition*, 108–9.

20. Eliyahu Schleifer, "Jewish Music, Synagogue Music, and Its Development: Biblical Cantillation," in *Grove's Dictionary of Music and Musicians* (London: Macmillan, 2000), 42, 44. See also Avigdor Herzog, "Masoretic Accents," in *Encyclopaedia Judaica*, vol. 11, 1098–1111.

21. Avenary, "Music," 585.

22. Shiloah, *Jewish Musical Traditions*, 111–12.

23. Ibid., 116–17.

24. Idelsohn, *Jewish Music*, 116.

25. Shiloah, *Jewish Musical Traditions*, 122.

26. Edwin Seroussi, "Rabbi Israel Najara: Modeler of Hebrew Sacred Singing after the Expulsion from Spain" (in Hebrew), *Assufot* 4 (1990): 285–310.

27. Shiloah, *Jewish Musical Traditions*, 122.

28. In Modern Hebrew *pizmon* means "chorus" as in the repeated chorus or refrain in a strophic poetic form.

29. Kay Kaufman Shelemay, *Let Jasmine Rain Down: Song and Remembrance* (Chicago: University of Chicago Press, 1998), 10.

30. Ibid., 25.

31. Zaki Murad is known by members of the Syrian community in Brooklyn—of particular interest are his Jewish origins, see Shelemay, *Let Jasmine Rain Down*, 112); see also Anne Rasmussen, "Individuality and Social Change in the Music of Arab-Americans" (Ph.D. dissertation, University of California, Los Angeles, 1991), 216–17. "Hawwid Min Hina" is not a well-known Arabic song. Thus, information on the date of the recording and the song itself is difficult to obtain. The dating of this piece is based on the form of the composition, a *taqtuqah*, and the time period it was most likely written (Virginia Danielson and Hakki Obadia, oral communications).

32. Virginia Danielson, *Shaping Tradition in Arabic Song: The Career and Repertory of Umm Kulthum* (Ph.D. dissertation, University of Illinois, 1991), 355–56); and Lois Ibsen al-Faruqi, *An Annotated Glossary of Arabic Musical Terms* (Westport: Greenwood, 1981), 349.

33. Rasmussen, "Individuality and Social Change," 95.

34. For a further discussion of the Syrian adaptation of *pizmonim* to the liturgy, see chapter 7, "Musical Adaptation Settings of the Liturgical Singing Station," in Mark Kligman, "Modes of Prayer: Arabic *Maqamat* in the Sabbath Morning Liturgical Music of the Syrian Jews in Brooklyn" (Ph.D. dissertation, New York University, 1997), 306–66.

35. Gabriel Shrem, ed., *Shir ush'vaha, hallel v'zimrah*, 7th ed. (New York: Sephardic Heritage Foundation, 1995), 11–13. The first edition was published in 1964.

36. For a further discussion see Kligman, "Modes of Prayer," 138–46, see particularly Examples 4.2c, 143, also 170–75. See also Shelemay, *Let Jasmine Rain Down*, 95.

37. Gershom Scholem, "Kabbalah," in *Encyclopaedia Judaica*, vol. 10, 553.

38. For a more detailed description of "Mahalalakh," see Kligman, "Modes of Prayer," 132–38.

39. Edwin Seroussi, *Mizimrat Qedem: The Life and Music of R. Isaac Algazi from Turkey* (Jerusalem: Renanot Institute for Jewish Music, 1989).

40. Edwin Seroussi, "Politics, Ethnic Identity, and Music in Israel: The Case of the Moroccan *Bakkashot*," *Asian Music* 17 (1985): 32–45; and idem, "The Beginnings of *Bakkashot* Poetry in Jerusalem in the Nineteenth Century" (in Hebrew), *Peʾamim* 56 (1993): 116–20.

41. See Edwin Seroussi, "Schir Hakawod and the Liturgical Music Reforms in the Sephardic Community in Vienna, ca. 1880–1925: A Study of Change in Religious Music" (Ph.D. dissertation, University of California, Los Angeles, 1988); and *Spanish-Portuguese Synagogue Music in Nineteenth-Century Reform Sources from*

Hamburg: Ancient Tradition in the Dawn of Modernity, Yuval Monograph Series, 11 (Jerusalem: Magnes, 1996).

42. Israel J. Katz, "A Judeo-Spanish Romancero," *Ethnomusicology* 12, no. 1 (1968): 72–85.

43. Edwin Seroussi, "New Directions in the Music of the Sephardic Jews," in *Modern Jews and Their Musical Agendas: Studies in Contemporary Jewry: An Annual*, ed. Ezra Mendelsohn, vol. 9 (New York: Oxford University Press, 1993), 61–77; Edwin Seroussi, "Sephardic Music: A Bibliographic Guide with a Checklist of Notated Sources," *Jewish Folk and Ethnology Review*, 15, no. 2 (1993): 56–61; Judith R. Cohen, "Sonography of Judeo-Spanish Song, with Commentary," *Jewish Folklore and Ethnology Review*, 15, no. 2 (1993): 49–55, updates 17, nos. 1–2 (1995): 72–73, 18, nos. 1–2 (1997): 96–100.

44. Jeff Halper, Edwin Seroussi, and Pamela Squires-Kidron, "Musica Mizrakhit: Ethnicity and Class Culture in Israel," *Popular Music* 8, no. 2 (1989): 131–41; Amy Horowitz, "Performance in Disputed Territory: Israeli Mediterranean Music," issue title: *The Performance of Jewish and Arab Music in Israel Today, Musical Performance* 1, no. 3 (1997): 43–53.

Chapter 14

A Double Occlusion
Sephardim and the Holocaust

Henry Abramson

The persecution of Sephardic Jewry has been under a double occlusion. First, although the Holocaust, in general, became the most well-known genocide of the modern era, it has been widely understood to be principally a European phenomenon, particularly eastern European, and therefore the principal victims were Ashkenazic Jews. Sephardim, particularly those populations in northern Africa, have not been considered part of the major narrative and have usually been ignored in popular treatments of Jewish suffering during World War II.[1] Second, while the academic study of the Holocaust has become a major subfield, with numerous institutions devoting considerable resources to the research and teaching of the fate of the Jews under Nazism, only a relatively small number of scholarly works have appeared on the topic of Sephardic experiences of the war. Hidden from both public view and academic attention, the plight of Sephardic Jews during the war has remained understudied and undervalued.

To some degree, this is due to the unique ethnic makeup of the Jewish academic world. North American Jewry is overwhelmingly Ashkenazic, with an estimated 70 percent of contemporary American Jews tracing their lineage to eastern Europe. The *lingua franca* of postwar historical research has certainly been English—a western European language. It is not surprising, therefore, that some of the most significant studies of Sephardim during the Holocaust, few as these studies are, have tended to be published in Hebrew by scholars living in Israel. Most of these, including Irit Abramsky-Bligh's major study of the Jews of Libya and Tunisia, have not yet been translated into English.[2]

The tendency of ethnicity to direct scholarly interests, and the linguistic demands of writing about Sephardic cultures, which many American students of Jewish history lack, have helped account for the otherwise glaring lacuna. The absence of the Sephardic experience of Nazi persecution on the agenda of modern American Jewish historians could not but be reflected in popular culture: "in the collective memory of American Jewry, the *Shoah* has appeared primarily as an Ashkenazi tragedy centering around the decimation of Polish and Soviet Jewry," as Lawrence Baron has argued.[3]

Yet, beyond these obvious technical concerns, more was involved in the double occlusion of the Sephardim and the Holocaust. In a powerful polemic against Ashkenocentrism, unconscious or otherwise, Dr. Seth Ward pointed out several aspects of the phenomenon. One in particular was especially incisive: contemporary American Jewish culture has tended to relegate the Sephardic experience to folkways and traditions rather than history proper: "Music, recipes and ethnography of these communities have had some visibility in North America, but their history has been nearly invisible."[4] For some Jewish academics, the study of the Sephardic experience has remained beyond the pale of normal inquiry, marginalized to a handful of cultural clichés.

This chapter is intended as a small contribution to address the imbalance in contemporary study of the Holocaust in Sephardic lands. Some broad general comments related to the Sephardic experience under Nazi occupation are made.

Contrasting Sephardic Experiences

Ashkenazic experiences of the Holocaust followed a basic pattern: increasing isolation during the thirties with individual acts of violence (*Einzelaktionen*), and concentration into ghettos during the early years of the war. For Jews living east of the border formed by the Soviet-Nazi nonaggression treaty (principally Poland and the Baltic states), the June 1941 invasion of the Soviet Union was accompanied by the mobile killing squads known as *Einsatzgruppen,* who were responsible for approximately 1.5 million deaths. Finally, beginning in the spring of 1942, Jews in the ghettos of Europe were deported to the six major death camps, or *Vernichtungsläger*: Auschwitz, Treblinka, Sobibor, Maidanek, Belzec, and Chelmno. There, a small minority of them were set to slave labor or to be used as medical experiments, and the vast majority ended their lives in gas chambers. Although there were significant differences, not only between the treatment of Jews in eastern and western Europe, but also in the various satellite states under Nazi control, the pattern remained basically the same for Ashkenazic Jews: isolation, ghettoization, deportation, and murder.

Among Sephardic Jews, only the Greek Jews conformed to this basic pattern. Indeed, the Jews of Greece suffered on a scale met by few other prewar communities, and only approximately 10 percent of the population survived the war. Of the large Jewish community of Salonika, the survival rate was less than 4 percent. Greek Jews, however, accounted for only some 75,000 of the nearly 325,000 total Sephardic population in Europe. Approximately a quarter of a million Sephardim lived in North Africa. Nazi control over Jews in Africa was markedly different than that over Jews in Greece. It was not surprising that the persecution in Morocco, Tunisia, Algeria, and Libya was rather unlike that which was experienced by European Jews, whether the Ashkenazim or the Sephardim of Greece.

It was as if the Nazis understood the grammar and syntax of European concerns, and the Jews were part of the vocabulary of every European nation. Nazism was, after all, part of the larger European phenomenon of fascism and integral nationalism, political and social ideologies in which Jews had no place. It was relatively easy for the disaffected intelligentsia of European nations to appreciate the power and promise that Hitler's model offered to their societies, and, despite their ambivalence over German hegemony, fascist movements flourished across the continent, from England to Ukraine. Indeed, when it came to deporting local Jewish populations, the principal difficulty that the Nazis had to surmount was the hesitancy that some of their allies (Italy and Bulgaria, for example) had with persecuting "their own" Jews (i.e., Italian or Bulgarian nationals). The idea of sacrificing Jewish refugees from other countries, on the other hand, was accomplished with relative ease. Such was the impact of Nazi ideology—an idea that could easily be adapted to any European country.

North Africa, however, presented an entirely different set of values and concerns to the Nazi engines of destruction. Unlike European countries, which were concerned ultimately with issues of economic recovery, social integrity, and territorial revisionism, the political environment of Morocco, Algeria, Tunisia, and Libya were overwhelmingly occupied with one major concern: colonialism. Paradigms that held true for modernizing, secularizing Christian countries to the north could not be easily maintained in the premodern Islamic societies, long uncomfortable with

European domination. Nazi Jewish policies, therefore, had to adapt to this radically different environment, in which Christian rulers struggled to maintain control over large, indigenous Muslim populations. Ironically, the local Jewish population was often more broadly similar to their Muslim neighbors than to their far-off coreligionists across the Mediterranean. North African Jewry, living in this context of a colonial society, found itself caught in a dynamic that had more to do with relations between the Christian colonizers and the Muslim majorities than with itself.

Insofar as many of the paradigms common to eastern European integral nationalism were foreign to North Africa and, to a lesser extent, Greece and the Balkan regions, this made for major differences in the implementation of Nazi policies. In general, this meant anti-Semitic measures were used more as a political tool to appease popular dissent rather than as a primary goal of the occupation authority, with significantly different results.[5] Considering Turkey, for example, Esther Benbassa and Aron Rodrigue remarked that the "Jews, together with other non-Muslims, were subject to the Turkicization policies of the state, but they were not singled out as Jews, and an antisemitic popular movement did not develop. However, the Jews suffered from the general suspicion with which all non-Muslim groups were treated, and were subjected to considerable harassment."[6] Generally speaking, the very centrality of anti-Semitism to the political culture of most European nations was not present in Sephardic regions. To be sure, there were anti-Semitic agitations, sometimes instigated by journalists like Cevat Rifat Atilman, who received both inspiration and funding from Nazi Germany, and there were isolated attacks on Jews, particularly in Thrace.[7]

Nevertheless, taken as a whole, anti-Semitic agitation in Sephardic lands during the interwar period was minor and limited to the fringes of popular opinion. Furthermore, unlike anti-Semitic activity in many other European countries, anti-Semitic activity in Sephardic lands lacked official support and was often condemned by the respective governments. This was not to say that the local governments were free from the toxin of anti-Semitism. Algerian authorities, for example, were ordered to prepare weekly reports to monitor anti-Semitic activity, but as Michael Abitbol notes, "even while viewing anti-Semitic agitation as dangerous, particularly when there was a risk of it spreading to native milieus, there were many police officers and inspectors who, in trying to explain this phenomenon, gave vent to their own anti-Jewish convictions."[8]

Finally, one important general observation is in order when comparing the fate of Ashkenazic and Sephardic experiences of the Holocaust. With the exception, once again, of Greece, it must be clearly pointed out that the North African Jews had the great good fortune of coming under Nazi control only relatively late in the war. Moreover, in the case of Algeria and Morocco, the occupation was actually by Vichy France rather than by the Nazis directly. Whereas Vichy France did not waste time in sending Jews from France to the gas chambers, there was far more hesitation to implement these policies in North Africa, where the colonial French had so many other issues to contend with. Tunisia fell under German occupation quite late—November of 1942—and because of the allied invasion, was liberated some six months later.

The experience of Italian and Hungarian Jewry shows that the Nazis were not loath to take matters into their own hands if their allies were slow to support the Final Solution. It is reasonable to assume that, had it not been for the conclusion of the war, the Nazis would have eventually turned their full attention to the large Sephardic population living in North Africa. Nevertheless, due to military developments, the North African experience of the Holocaust, though brutal, was also brief.

Greece: Three Zones

The Holocaust of Greek Jewry began in April 1941, with the Nazi invasion from the north. Greece had valiantly maintained its independence, keeping Italy at bay after hostilities broke out in late 1940. But when Hitler needed to secure Greece in preparation for his massive summer attack on the Soviet Union, the Greek troops were completely overwhelmed. Greece was subsequently divided into German, Italian, and Bulgarian zones. These divisions would ultimately characterize the nature of the Holocaust for Sephardim in this country, as each occupying power had an entirely different attitude with regard to the disposition of their Jewish populations. For Germany, the removal of the Jewish population was clearly one of the most significant policy objectives of the *Reich* as a whole, and the Jews in the German zone were destroyed in very short order, along the typical lines adopted by the Nazis elsewhere.

The Jews in the Bulgarian and Italian zones, on the other hand, benefited, at least partially and temporarily by the phenomenon mentioned earlier, i.e., that many of the satellite states made distinctions between their "own" Jews, that is, Jews who were citizens and generally well acculturated to their host society, a feature that historically characterizes Sephardic Jewry. Some correlations existed between the rate of rescue of Jews in certain countries and their degree of acculturation or assimilation into the surrounding society. This has been measured using markers such as rates of intermarriage, fluency in the vernacular, and religious liberalism.[9]

Although Ashkenazim worked earnestly toward this degree of acculturation through much of the nineteenth century, they contrasted poorly with Sephardic cultures, which had accepted a degree of cosmopolitanism since the era of the Spanish Golden Age. This was a period of time when Hebrew poets were as likely to publish in Arabic as in Hebrew, and statesmen could also compose Talmudic treatises. It was also evident in the eighteenth century in the fact that revolutionary France refused to grant emancipation to the isolationist, Yiddish-speaking Jews of Alsace while offering it to the Francophone Sephardim of Bordeaux and Bayonne. With the major exception of Germany, most of the Nazi-dominated states showed some hesitation at surrendering the Jews that they saw as their "own"—perhaps not beloved members of their society, but a part of society nevertheless. This level of concern, however, was certainly not shown to Jews who came from without.

The Jews in the German zone were placed under Nazi occupation immediately, and the experience of Ashkenazic Jewry was largely duplicated for them. Unfortunately for Greek Jewry, by the time the Nazis occupied the region, their Jewish policies were fairly well articulated, and the Nazis could implement a series of measures that had been proven in many other national environments. Salonika, home to 56,000 Jews, was occupied in early April 1941, and the existing communal council was disbanded in favor of creating a *Judenrat*, or "Jewish Council," the principal organ used by the Nazis to control the Jewish population. The *Judenrat* was an essential tool in the eventual destruction of the Jewish community—through the offices of the *Judenrat*, the Nazis were able to gather vital statistics about the Jews in the region, catalog and confiscate much of their wealth, and organize their movement and eventual deportation to the death camps.

During the first year and a half of the German occupation, Greek Jewry in Salonika witnessed only sporadic persecution. Jewish newspapers were closed, including the last Judeo-Spanish periodical to use "Rashi" script.[10] Major Jewish libraries were sacked, the plunder intended for the planned Nazi museum of Jewish culture, and were never to be seen again. The Jewish community was coerced into turning over its cemetery, which was immediately destroyed (and later became the site of the University of Salonika). During this early period of the war, the deprivations of the winter of 1941–42 were considered far more onerous than the Nazi occupation policies. One of the more significant acts of persecution came in July of 1942, when 9,000 Jewish men between the ages of 18 and 45 were assembled into Liberty Square and forced to perform various types of humiliating calisthenics, and 2,000 of them were later taken into forced labor battalions. These forced labor battalions, as those elsewhere in Europe, were characterized by extreme brutality and cruelty.

A major turning point in the fate of the Jews of Salonika came in the winter of 1942–43. The leadership of the *Judenrat* was revised as the Germans began to plan for the deportation of Salonika's Jews to the newly constructed death camps. The Nuremburg Laws, adopted in Germany before the war, were imposed in February of 1943, placing a series of major restrictions on Jewish activity. Jews were removed to ghettos and forced to wear the yellow star. More seriously, the precise membership of the Jewish community was tallied, to aid the Nazis in their plan to deport them all to Auschwitz-Birkenau. Deportations began in March, and the community was virtually destroyed by May. In August 1974, members of the *Judenrat* and other collaborators were sent on the last train—this time to Bergen-Belsen.

Several major community figures, including a delegation of some 150 lawyers, protested the German treatment of Salonikan Jewry. Several hundred Jews were rescued by moving to Athens, with the collusion of Italian consular officials. The bulk of Salonikan Jewry, however, were destroyed. Out of roughly 48,500 Jews who were deported, over 37,000 were sent immediately to the gas chambers of Birkenau. The majority of the remaining Jews died of causes related to the slave labor conditions of the camp.

The Jews of Sofia, Bulgaria, benefited by being "Bulgarian" Jews. They were held back from the processes of destruction in an attempt to protect a minority population considered, nevertheless, to have significant ties to the majority population. With the occupation of Greece, however, Bulgaria inherited a large population of Greek Jews, who were not beneficiaries of this good will. On the contrary, the sacrifice of these Jews to the Nazi Final Solution was seen by the Bulgarian leadership as a way to appease their German allies—demonstrating their willingness to cooperate in the major Nazi goal of ridding Europe of its long-standing Jewish population. The Jews of Bulgarian-occupied Greece, therefore, were the first to be deported. Over 4,000 Jews were sent to Treblinka via Vienna and murdered upon arrival. A similar fate met the approximately 7,300 Jews of

Bulgarian-occupied Macedonia. Only a handful of Jews escaped, sometimes joining partisan movements in the mountains.

Bulgarian Jews proper, approximately 50,000 by the beginning of the war, were also under threat of ultimate deportation to the death camps, but popular movements led by Bulgarian political activists deferred this calamity for most of the war. German pressure on the Bulgarian government, however, eventually coerced it into rounding up the Jews of Sofia in the summer of 1943 and interning them in 20 camps, impressing several thousand into forced labor. Deportation to the death camps, was successfully averted by the combination of popular opposition and the tide of war, which brought Bulgaria under the Soviet army's control in September 1944. The popular sentiment toward Bulgarian Jews was a remarkable generosity of spirit, but it did not extend to the Greek Jews who were trapped in the Bulgarian zone.

If the Bulgarians were not inclined to deport Jews, the Italians were much less so. Once again, the political agenda that brought Italy and Germany together in a military alliance did not extend to the point where Italians were comfortable implementing German notions of racial purity. On the contrary, not only did Italians in the Greek zone protect the indigenous population, but they also protected Jewish refugees from the German zone who had fled to Athens. This changed dramatically with the fall of Italy to the German forces in September 1943.

With vicious rapidity, the Nazis implemented all the major features associated with German occupation, including the establishment of a *Judenrat* in Athens. In a heroic act, the chief rabbi, Eliahu Barzilai, burned all the communal records and fled, making it difficult for the Nazis to identify the members of the local Jewish community. The Nazis were temporarily denied, but not deterred. In October they demanded that all Jews register, a demand that was met with little response. But repeated orders eventually resulted in the assembly of several hundred Jews, possibly "lulled into a relative sense of security by the SS's lack of further action."[11]

With diabolical cunningness, in March 1944, the Nazis announced that a special shipment of flour was arriving to meet the demands for *matsah* in the upcoming Passover holiday, and many Jews were swayed by this lie to register themselves.[12] Arrests and deportations began in April 1944 and continued through the summer.

Taken as a whole, approximately 87 percent of the roughly 75,000 Jews of Greece were killed in the Holocaust, one of the highest rates of murder in all of Nazi-occupied Europe. Some distinguished their deaths with remarkable acts of resistance, including 135 prisoners in Auschwitz who successfully blew up Crematorium III in October 1944, later to be killed "singing the Greek national anthem."[13]

The experience of the Sephardim of Greece, then, was broadly similar to the way in which Ashkenazic Jewry encountered the Nazi occupation. Indeed, in many ways, it was accelerated by the unique timing of the invasion and the division of the country into three zones. The features of ghettoization, deportation, and gassing were all put into place in very short order, particularly in the case of the Jews in the German zone. Greek Jewry was also emblematic of the ambiguities of the status of a minority ethnicity, in terms of the contrast of the treatment of Bulgaria's Sofia Jewish population and its Greek Jewish population.

Yugoslavia: Serbia and Croatia

Scattered Sephardic populations were found in Croatia, Bosnia and Herzegovina, with a large concentration (approximately 10,000) in Belgrade, which came under German influence in the spring of 1941. The Nuremburg Laws were put into place almost immediately after the German arrival, and Jews were forced to wear the star and surrender their properties and assets under the Aryanization program. Jewish men were forced into labor battalions, and most of them were murdered by the end of the year. In October, the Nazis gathered all the remaining Jews (primarily women and children) into one camp. With refugees, the camp population eventually reached 7,500.

The Sephardim of Serbia became the first Jews in Europe to be gassed to death in experimental gas vans sent to the camp in the spring of 1942. Each van held approximately 100 people and was modified so that the exhaust of the van would be pumped directly into its cargo area where the women and children were held. The vans were then driven through Belgrade to a mass gravesite on the outskirts of the city, where the corpses of the asphyxiated Jews would be buried. These techniques of murder were later modified for use in the death camps.[14]

Croatian Jews, Ashkenazim and Sephardim alike, were subjected to the brutal rule of the Ustasa, a local fascist group that led the Nazi puppet state. Setting up the notorious Jasenovac concentration camp grave of over 20,000 Jews, the Ustasa deported an additional 7,000 Jews to Auschwitz. Many Jews attempted flight to regions held by the Italians, who were less likely to hand over the refugees to the Nazis.

Algeria

Algeria was home to approximately 120,000 Jews on the eve of World War II. Concentrated in three cities: Algiers, Oran, and Constantine, Algerian Jewry made up 1.5 percent of the total population. Unlike neighboring Tunisia and Morocco, Algeria was a French colony that later became part of France proper, which extended full citizenship to Jews. The Jews here were part of a triangular struggle that involved the predominantly Muslim population and European French colonists: Muslims generally resented the favored status granted to Jews as part of the Crémieux Decree of 1870, while the colonial French were heavily influenced by anti-Semitic trends circulating in France. This motivated many Algerian Jews to take advantage of their French citizenship and flee to France, where they faced the difficult situation of being "foreign" Jews, with disastrous consequences.

In June 1940, France surrendered to Germany, and Algeria was considered the responsibility of unoccupied Vichy France. Germans did not act directly in Algeria until they were forced to react to the invasion of the Allies in November 1942. French law was enforced in Algeria as well as in Morocco and Tunisia, despite the political distinctions between the three areas. As Michael Abitbol put it, "the Vichy regime saw in the three countries a single geopolitical entity containing a large Jewish population, sandwiched in between a Muslim majority, whose loyalty to France was doubtful, and a European minority, which had adopted anti-Semitism as its political credo."[15] This meant that anti-Semitism could serve as a very useful tool to placate the restive Muslim population by demonstrating that Jewish privilege was eroded under the new status quo.

Accordingly, in October of 1940, the Crémieux Decree was reversed, and a Nuremburg-like code called the Statut des Juifs was put in its place. Extensive "Aryanization," or the confiscation of Jewish property and assets, was imposed, as well as a numerous clauses that restricted Jewish enrollment in higher education. Going beyond the regulations in France, Algerian Jewish youth were even prevented from attending schools at the elementary and secondary levels. Many Jews were interned in camps at this time. A census of Jews was held in 1941—an ominous harbinger of deportation—and a *Judenrat* was in formation when the Allies interrupted with their invasion of November 1942.

The Jewish reaction to all this, ironically, was to displace blame for these examples of French anti-Semitic persecution onto the Germans, and to remain loyal to France proper, even to the extent of participating in the French underground forces that were otherwise sympathetic to the anti-Semitic elements in Pétain's ideology. Jews actively assisted the Allies, and it was estimated that 315 of the 377 Resistance members who seized Algiers on the night of November 7–8 were, in fact, Jewish.[16] This did not, however, stop the American victors from keeping the Vichy government in place after the defeat of the German forces, thus condoning the Statut des Juifs.[17] Many Jewish prisoners interned under this law actually remained in prison until late 1944. The American failure to remove the anti-Jewish legislation, undoubtedly a political maneuver to maintain stability in the region, was received badly by Algerian Jewry, who felt betrayed after their strong, consistent support for the Allies.

Tunisia and Morocco

Unlike Algerian Jewry, the Jews of Tunisia were not awarded French citizenship under the Crémieux Decree. Some 85,000 Jews lived in Tunisia, more than half of them in the capital city of Tunis. The Muslim population held resentments against the colonial power. When France was defeated by the Germans, a wave of spontaneous anti-Semitic violence erupted in Tunisia, "aimed at the colonial order's weakest link—the Jews."[18] Fortunately, the governor-general of the region was a religious Christian, Vice Admiral Jean-Pierre Estéva. He demurred at implementing the Statut des Juifs until March of 1942. During his term, he also actively assisted the Jewish poor and even visited a synagogue in Djerba. Italian opposition to French authorities' Aryanization of Tunisian Jews with Italian citizenship also preserved the property of Tunisian Jews.

Germans entered the country in early November 1942, in response to Operation Torch, the Allied invasion of North Africa. The military situation and the lack of strong support among local Muslims made it difficult to impose anti-Jewish legislation immediately. The Germans, therefore, had to limit themselves to impressing several thousand Jews into forced labor and deporting only a handful of Jewish leaders to death camps in Europe. The German presence in Tunisia was quite short, however, as the Allies drove them out in May of 1943. As in Algeria, however, the Allies allowed Vichy France to take control of Tunisia, leading to the arrest of several Jews accused of collaborating with Italy. However, they were eventually released, after a few weeks.[19]

The experience of Moroccan Jewry was similar in most respects to that of Tunisian Jewry. Like Tunisia, Morocco was also a protectorate, so Jews there were not granted French citizenship. They were subjected to the stipulations of the Statut des Juifs. Nevertheless, as in Tunisia, the implementation of the Statut was spotty, and, in fact, had comparatively little effect on Moroccan Jewry. Abitbol attributes this to the special nature of Moroccan Jewry: "It is not surprising, then, that the Jews least affected by the Jewish Statute were those—more numerous in Morocco than in Tunisia and Algeria—who had distanced themselves from Western Civilization or had ignored it, in short, those whose way of life and behavior had remained the most traditional."[20] In other words, Moroccan Jews, in many ways a premodern community, were still living in an isolationist manner that made the exclusionist policies of the Statut des Juifs redundant. Like Tunisian Jewry, however, the Jews of Morocco were disappointed that the Allied conquest in November 1942 did not result in a dramatic reversal of the anti-Jewish legislation. Official figures highly prejudiced against the Jews were maintained in positions of authority.

Libya

Libya's experience was unique in that the country was under Italian control until the German takeover in the fall of 1943. Thirty thousand Jews lived in Libya, and, as in Tunisia, half of them lived in the capital city, in this case, Tripoli. Italian policies regarding Jews were generally lenient. However, the Italians were careful not to offend the sensibilities of their German allies and, more importantly perhaps, those of the dominant Muslim population in Libya.

The temporary British invasion of Cyrenaica prompted the Italians to accuse the Jewish population of collaborating with the British, and several hundred Jews were interned in Italian camps. After a second invasion, the Italians stepped up the anti-Jewish persecution, and, in rapid succession, several thousand Jews were interned, new restrictions were placed on Jewish economic activity, and Jews were impressed into forced labor. The Italians were eventually driven out in January of 1943. But the difficulties did not end for Libyan Jewry, as Muslims, incensed by the presence of Jewish units among the British, attacked the Jews on November 5 through 7, 1944, killing 121 Jews.[21]

Conclusion

Why has the Sephardic experience of the Holocaust received so little attention from the scholarly world? Why is the language of the oppressed so often portrayed as a heavily accented Yiddish or German or French, but never Arabic or Greek? This is not an "other" Holocaust. Indeed, while the nature of the Nazi occupation in North Africa was significantly different from that of Europe, the treatment of Sephardic Jews in Greece and Yugoslavia followed precisely the German model of persecution, ghettoization, deportation, and murder. Furthermore, Sephardim were among the first victims of gas technology with the development of the Serbian killing vans. Sephardim also experienced the hatred, not only of Nazis, but also of their enthusiastic supporters, such as the Ustasa. Why then the lacuna in the historical literature? Where was the Sephardic version of *Schindler's List*? The latter was among the more popular of tens of Hollywood films about the Holocaust in Ashkenazic lands.

On the other hand, it is obvious that the Sephardim of North Africa were not subjected to the Final Solution with the same degree of finality as the Jews of Europe were. Factors behind this distinction include the hesitancy of local officials to follow through with the Statut des Juifs, the brief duration of the Nazi occupation after Operation Torch, and the level of modernization of the local Jewish communities. Nevertheless, it was also clear that the Nazi intent was to assemble all the Jews of North Africa eventually for deportation to death camps—the Nazis certainly made no distinctions between Sephardim and Ashkenazim. This, ultimately, is the greatest irony of the occlusion; an occlusion that made the Sephardim invisible to Ashkenazim, but hardly invisible to the Nazis and their willing accomplices.[22] The integration of the Sephardic experience into general Jewish historiography is an issue that should be of paramount concern to the next generation of historians of the Holocaust.

NOTES

1. I am grateful for the comments of my colleagues Aviva Ben-Ur, Marianne Sanua, and Annette Fromm for their comments on an earlier version of this chapter, as well as to Mr. Joel Hager for useful bibliographic suggestions. All errors of fact or interpretation remain my responsibility.

2. Irit Abramsky-Bligh, *Pinkas Hakehilot: Luv, Tunisyah* (Jerusalem: Yad Vashem, 1997).

3. Lawrence Baron, "Experiencing, Explaining, and Exploiting the Holocaust," *Judaism* 50, no. 2 (spring 2001): 160.

4. Seth Ward, "The Holocaust in North Africa," http://www.du.edu/~sward/HoloSephardic.htm, published also in *Intermountain Jewish News*, 20 May 1999.

5. On the centrality of anti-Semitism to Nazi occupation policies in eastern Europe, see Eberhard Jäckel, *Hitler's Weltanschauung: A Blueprint for Power* (Cambridge: Harvard University Press, 1981).

6. Esther Benbassa and Aron Rodrigue, *Sephardic Jewry: A History of the Judeo-Spanish Community, Fourteenth–Twentieth Centuries* (Berkeley: University of California Press, 2000), 161–62.

7. Benbassa and Rodrigue, *Sephardic Jewry*, 162–63.

8. Michael Abitbol, *Jews of North Africa during World War II* (Jerusalem: Yad Ben-Zvi, 1986), 27.

9. See Lawrence Bacon, "The Holocaust and Human Decency: A Review of Research on the Rescue of Jews in Nazi Occupied Europe," *Humboldt Journal of Social Relations* 13, no. 1 (fall/spring 1985–86): 237–51.

10. Michael Molho and Joseph Néhama, *In Memoriam: Hommage aux victimes juives des Nazis en Grèce* (Salonika: N. Nicolaidès, 1948), vol. 1, 31; cited in Benbassa and Rodrigue, *Sephardic Jewry*, 166.

11. Benbassa and Rodrigue, *Sephardic Jewry*, 171.

12. Nikos Stavrolakis, "A Short History of the Jews of Greece," http://www.greecetravel.com/jewishhistory/athens.html, citing a memoir by Errikos Sevillas, *Athens, Auschwitz*, trans. Nikos Stavroulikas (sic) (Athens: Lycabettus, 1983).

13. Steven B. Bowman, "Greece," in *Encyclopedia of the Holocaust*, ed. Yisrael Gutman (New York: Macmillan, 1990), 616.

14. Benbassa and Rodrigue, *Sephardic Jewry*, 165–66.

15. Michael Abitbol, "Algeria," in *Encyclopedia of the Holocaust*, ed. Gutman, 20.

16. Abitbol, "Algeria," 21.

17. See Abitbol, *Jews of North Africa*, 152–65.

18. Michael Abitbol, "Tunisia," in *Encyclopedia of the Holocaust*, ed. Gutman, 1521.

19. For more information on the Holocaust in Tunisia, see Yaron Tsur, "The Jews of Tunisia under the German Occupation: A Divided Community in Time of Crisis," *Contemporary Jewry* 2 (1985): 169–72.

20. Abitbol, *Jews of North Africa*, 68.

21. Michael Abitbol, "Libya," in *Encyclopedia of the Holocaust*, ed. Gutman, 866.

22. This is perhaps an overgeneralization: there is evidence that Nazi officials in Amsterdam held the belief that Sephardic Jews were racially superior to Ashkenazic Jews and therefore should receive preferential treatment. I am grateful to Professor Aviva Ben-Ur for this reference: Salomon Louis Vaz Dias, "Talmoed Tora keneged koelam: Bijdrage tot de geschiedenis der Portugees-Israëlitische Gemeente te Amsterdam in de Tweede wereldoorlog," *Studia Rosenthaliana* 29, no. 1 (1995): 29–70.

Chapter 15

Sephardim and Oriental Jews in Israel
Rethinking the Sociopolitical Paradigm

Zion Zohar

In June 1997, Israel's Labor Party made a historic decision to relocate its convention from its usual venue in the upscale, sophisticated city of Tel Aviv to the rural, underprivileged development town of Netivot. Many of the party delegates naturally assumed that this decision was part of an overall political strategy to seek the support of the Oriental Jews who were the majority of Netivot's residents, and thereby gain greater support from Oriental Jews throughout Israel. Furthermore, since Labor had lost the previous elections to its rival, the Likud Party, primarily due to the votes cast by Oriental Jews, such a gesture made sense to these delegates.

However, as soon as the party leader and candidate for prime minister Ehud Barak delivered his speech, a much more significant motive behind this geographic move became clear. Barak addressed the negative manner in which the absorption of new immigrants from Arab countries had been conducted under previous Labor governments. His unprecedented comments concerning this contentious sociopolitical issue included the following:

> We must admit to ourselves [that] the inner fabric of communal life was torn. Indeed, sometimes even the intimate fabric of family life was torn. Much suffering was inflicted on the immigrants, and this suffering was etched in their hearts as well as in the hearts of their children and grandchildren. There was no malice on the part of those responsible for bringing the immigrants here—on the contrary, there was much goodwill—but pain was inflicted nevertheless. In acknowledgement of this suffering and pain, and out of identification with the sufferers and their descendants, I hereby

ask forgiveness in my own name and in the name of the historical Labor movement.[1]

Anyone familiar with the complexity of the ethnic tension in Israel, which extends from before its establishment as an independent state up to and including our time, is compelled to acknowledge that such an apology is an extraordinary event. Some might say that it took a brave "soldier"[2] to deliver such a controversial and "ethnically loaded" speech. The remarkable nature of this apology is evident from the outraged response to it by veteran members of the Labor Party,[3] as well as a large segment of Israeli society. In retrospect, the apology failed to achieve much effect on its intended subjects, namely the Oriental Jews,[4] who skeptically dismissed it as "election propaganda" and demanded "acts instead of words."[5] Despite that, there were a few voices among the Israeli populace supportive of Barak's apology, such as professor of philosophy Avishai Margalit, who wrote: "Barak expressed regret for the right reason. Labor's sin was the mortal sin of pride; its attitude toward the Oriental immigrants was one of insufferable superiority."[6]

Whether Ehud Barak was indeed making a heartfelt statement of regret for past party behavior or whether he was crassly seeking the political support of a disenchanted segment of the voting public, a number of questions emerge from Barak's apology which need to be examined. Why deliver the speech in the development town of Netivot? What about his words engendered such extreme responses from both Labor opponents and, more surprisingly, Labor supporters? And most notably, what was so important about the subject that the candidate for prime minister found it vital to address the issue during his major speech to the party and the electorate?

To answer these questions thoroughly, some background discussion relating to "the first Aliyah" is necessary. As the first wave of Jewish migration to receive a Zionist-inspired classification, the first Aliyah began in 1882 among residents of eastern Europe, and marked the beginning of an ideological process of settlement in Palestine that would culminate in the middle of the twentieth century. This process was not merely a physical relocation from one country to another. It truly constituted a significant emotional and psychological shift in identity (with stages of crisis, awakening, recovery, and formation)[7] on the part of the early eastern European Zionists and their followers who sought to emigrate. Their goal was to create a new type of Jew who would overcome his or her Diaspora roots.

The Zionists used the slogan "Shlilat Hagalut," meaning "Negation of the Exile," which implied that everything about the exile experience was invalid, necessitating a fresh start in the Land of Israel. Numerous papers, articles, and documents were written about the need to eradicate the persona of the "Yehudi Galuti," the "Exilic Jew," and replace it with a new image.[8] However, Zionist thinkers could not agree what type of identity and nature this so-called New Jew should have.

In pursuit of this "new identity," many European Zionist writers began to denigrate the culture of Europe, which had given birth to the Diaspora mentality, while they simultaneously idealized Eastern or Levantine culture.[9] The Hebrew writer Mordechai Zeev Feierberg painted European society in very gloomy colors, while depicting the East as the new shining culture:

> Europe is sick; everybody senses that its foundations are rotten and its society crumbling. Our destiny lies in the East. I do know that a day shall come when the hundreds of millions of people who live in the East, these dry bones, will come to life, will rise to their feet, a mighty host; then the East will reawake and will rule the world, replacing Western hegemony.[10]

This statement, by a young Russian Jew, the hero of Feierberg's story, envisions change on a global scale. The European West will decline, to be replaced by the up-and-coming power of the East: "Then new vigorous peoples will emerge and will establish the new society."[11] In this utopia, he also finds a place for the Jew who is about to immigrate to Palestine: "and you, my brethren, when you go now eastward, you must always remember that you are Oriental by birth."[12]

A Russian Jew called "Oriental by birth"! And what about "Mother Russia," the enlightened continent of Europe, or the progressive West? To this, our hero gives a striking answer:

> The worst enemy of the Jews is the West and what, therefore, is unnatural is that we, the Hebrew, Oriental people, should put our lot with the nations of the West.... If it is true that the people of Israel have a mission, let them bear it and carry it to the Orient, not merely to Eretz Israel but the whole Orient.[13]

These near-messianic yearnings toward both Eretz Israel and the entire Orient, represented the mindset of a growing number of early European

Zionist thinkers who began to passionately stress the Levantine roots of Judaism.[14] For the first time, the questions surrounding what constituted the "New Jewish identity" were answered by pointing to the image of the Arab peasant. Amnon Rubinstein, in his fascinating analysis of early Zionist attitudes toward Palestinian Arabs, observes: "The Yishuv's [pre-State Jewish community's] early literature is significant.... Many authors filled their writings with empathy and admiration for the native-born, free-spirited, local Arabs. If the Jews sought a release from *galut* [exilic] images and searched for their new, authentic identity, the distant relative rediscovered, the uninhibited Arab, was a figure worthy of emulation."[15]

According to Rubinstein, this positive attitude toward Palestinian Arabs —part of the Orientalist mindset of the early settlers—ran so deep that some even considered the possibility of merging into the Palestinian population through conversion to Islam. Rubenstein records, "This belief was shared by many early settlers, and some went even further and advocated intermarriage with the Arabs as a means of a quick merger."[16]

That conversion to Islam was even entertained as an option was due to a very significant factor in early Zionist thinking—the negative association of Judaism (especially rabbinic Judaism) with the detested Diaspora. To some, becoming a New Jew meant the removal of every last trace of exile, including religious identity. They sought "salvation," by leaving the old exile for the new homeland in Palestine, and by leaving the old self for a new self in a new land.[17] Thus, to many Zionist pioneers, the presence of the Palestinian Arab walking and living on the land seemed to fulfill an authentic, biblical image, uncorrupted by the many centuries Jews had lived in *galut.*

In short, when the early Zionist pioneers began to settle in Palestine, the tendency toward Orientalism seemed prevalent in the land,[18] including some of those in the highest ranks of senior leadership, such as David Ben Gurion and Yitzchak Ben Zvi,[19] to name a few. This affinity for the Arabs continued even when pioneers were subject to banditry and violence by local Arabs, and did not diminish for quite some time.[20] From Ben Gurion's pre–World War I memoirs, it would appear he believed the Arabs would ultimately accept the Zionist efforts with enthusiasm. To him, the Zionists not only had brought prosperity to the region, but even more importantly, were close relatives of the Palestinian Arab peasants, whom he thought were descendents of biblical Jews that had "preferred to deny their religion, rather than to leave the homeland."[21]

In light of the Orientalist leanings expressed so explicitly by some of the early Zionist leaders, it is quite startling to discern the radical shift in their thinking a few decades later, exemplified by Ben Gurion in an interview for the French paper *Le Monde* during which he declared: "We do not want Israelis to become Arabs. We are duty bound to fight against the spirit of the Levant, which corrupts individuals and societies."[22] Far from being biblical "cousins" worthy of emulation, Arabs are depicted clearly as enemies whose ethos "corrupts individuals and societies."

How did this shift[23] in attitude come about? It seems to have occurred mainly after the bloody riots of 1929, in which Palestinian Arab mobs murdered whole families of Jews, many of whom had lived in the same community for generations and had even been neighbors of those who had killed them. Only following this unexpected trauma did Ben Gurion and others begin to wake up and grasp the depth of the hatred Palestinian Arabs held toward the Zionist entity in their midst. Although more than a decade later we still find some sympathetic feelings toward Orientalism,[24] on the whole the 1929 massacres might be seen as the beginning of a gradual decline in the sense of affinity early Zionists professed toward all things "Oriental."

Early Zionism, the Ashkenazi Establishment, and Jewish Orientalism

It is my contention that the transformation made by the early Zionists and their leadership from an early affinity for Orientalism to a sharp rejection of it later on, negatively influenced their views of Oriental Jews as well. As we shall see through the examination of various texts and events, this shift and its profoundly harmful effects would engender far-reaching consequences that shape Israeli society to this day.

Regarding many of the early Zionists, Amnon Rubinstein observed, "In Palestine the young European settlers met with Oriental Jews . . . who came to Eretz Israel upon hearing the call of Zionism. But it was the encounter with the local Arabs which was the most significant and which encouraged the Orientalist tradition among the new pioneers."[25] Ironically, though possessing many of the Oriental characteristics admired in the Arabs, Oriental Jews were deemed too traditionally Jewish, which diminished their status in the eyes of the early European settlers, who perceived religiosity as a remnant of the hated exile.[26]

As with his early view of the Palestinian Arabs, Ben Gurion also depicted Oriental Jewry in biblical terms. He associated them in his writings with the Israelites whom Moses led out of slavery in Egypt to wander in the desert for an entire generation. Similarly, Ben Gurion anticipated that the Oriental Jewish immigrants would be surpassed by their offspring who would not be "afflicted with the slave mentality" of Oriental Arab culture.[27]

Despite the biblical allegory, Ben Gurion's analysis of the first generation of Oriental immigrants and their culture was by no means positive. At about the same time he offered his statement to *Le Monde* rejecting Arab and Levantine influence on Israel, he issued a statement in a similar tone to the American journal *Look* regarding Moroccan Jewry, the largest community of Oriental Jews to come to Israel:

> [Jews] from Morocco have no education. Their customs are those of Arabs. They love their wives, but they beat them. . . . Maybe in the third generation something will appear from the Oriental Jews that is a little different. But I don't see it yet. The Moroccan Jew took a lot from the Moroccan Arabs. The culture of Morocco I would not like to have here. And I don't see what contribution present Persians have to make.[28]

Concerning Oriental Jews in general, Ben Gurion expressed the hope that in future generations their Arab "slave mentality" would be replaced by a "free" Western mindset. However, when particularly speaking about Moroccan Jews, he is not similarly optimistic. In their case, he conveyed his doubt that three generations might not even suffice to socialize Moroccan Jews into European Israeli society. Here, it is important to point out that from the outset of their immigration, Moroccan Jewry became, in effect, a symbol of all the social and cultural "illnesses" of Oriental Jewry as a whole.[29] As a result, more than any other Oriental Jewish group, Moroccans were frequently the objects of the most racist kinds of disparagement from the Israeli European elite, often because of their tenacity to hold on to their own "Arab-influenced" customs and traditional religious heritage.[30] As Avishai Margalit has observed, "for the Labor leaders only Ashkenazi Jews had 'culture'; Oriental Jews had, at best, a 'heritage.'"[31]

There are many reasons underlying the complex and ongoing conflict between Sephardim and Ashkenazim in Israel. The most obvious can certainly be ascribed to cultural and ethnic differences, which cause one group to disparage another it perceives as "different." Another, perhaps less obvious motivation underlying the cultural conflict, grew out of the Israeli government's desire for financial support from Diaspora Jewry. Complaining about the urgent and overwhelming need to feed and educate the ignorant Oriental masses was at that time a popular and successful means of fundraising.[32]

However, based on the analysis presented thus far and expanded upon below, the roots of the conflict would seem to stem principally from the shattering of the almost "messianic," Orientalist-tinged dream held by many early Zionists, and their subsequent radical shift to anti-Orientalism. That difficult transformation, which took place initially regarding the early Zionists' relationship with the Palestinian Arab population, came to apply ultimately to any manifestation of Orientalism in Israel, even by, or perhaps especially by, other Jews.

Until now, scholars of Israeli culture have generally posited that the cultural conflict between Ashkenazi and Sephardi (primarily Oriental) Jews could be attributed chiefly to the concept of the "melting pot."[33] That is to say, all Jewish immigrants who arrived in Israel, particularly after the establishment of the state, were strongly encouraged to "melt down" their own particular exilic identities within the generic social "pot" in order to become "Israeli." Naturally, the notion of what constituted "Israeli" was determined by the beliefs of those who proposed the idea,[34] namely, the very same Zionist leaders who had at first nurtured the idea of an Orientalist utopia and later rejected it. In other words, the "melting pot" idea might have resulted in the creation of a new form of Israeli that was essentially Oriental, if only the early Zionist ideology had continued to embrace Orientalism as it had initially. Thus, contrary to the scholars who see the melting pot idea as the source of the conflict, I believe the melting pot idea, in and of itself, cannot be the primary reason for the cultural conflict between the European and Oriental Jewish communities. Rather, as stated earlier, it was the transformation from pro-Orientalism to anti-Orientalism by the Zionist leadership that stands at the heart of the conflict.

Ariel Hirschfeld, professor of Hebrew literature, sums up the cultural disjunction in a few telling sentences:

> *The Israeli concepts of "the ingathering of the exiles" and "the melting pot" were . . . predicated on the Mizrahi [Oriental] communities breaking with their traditional way of life when they came to Israel. They encountered a more mature Israeli culture and thus were not the object of the love for the archaic East that so moved the early Zionists. (Only the first Yemenite*

immigrants had the "fortune" to be integrated into the Orientalist forefather-imagery.) The yearning anachronistically preserved in the portraits of the Arab village was absent from Israeli culture in the 1950s and 1960s. [Therefore] [t]he particularity and otherness of the Mizrahi Jews elicited scorn and alienation, but nothing more.[35]

We may only speculate what might have been the result if Palestinian Arabs had agreed with the early Zionists' Orientalist dreams.[36] Though many scenarios are possible, perhaps the leadership of Israel would have been more accepting of Oriental culture and thus, of the Oriental Jews who lived it. Rather than viewing them as objects of scorn and derision, Zionist leaders might have embraced Oriental Jews and possibly given them a greater role in shaping the character and policies of the state as a result.

From Anti-Orientalist Sentiments to Policy-Making

In the following pages, I will try to trace the most important and formative events in the modern ethnic and sociopolitical history of Sephardic and Oriental Jewry within Israel through an analysis of statements, like the above-mentioned ones by key policymakers in Israeli society. In addition, I will examine testimonies from Sephardic and Oriental Jews as they comment on historical circumstances.

The Debate over the Question of the Ingathering of the Exiles

In a society as divided as Israel, one is hard-pressed to find a subject about which there is as strong a consensus as there is regarding Operation Kibbutz Galuyyot, literally meaning, "The Ingathering of the Exiles," or the value of absorbing Jewish immigrants. What has been perceived in popular mythology as a consensus, however, was not always so in fact. Just before the nation's establishment, we find voices that doubt both this cherished value and the possibility of realizing it in Israeli society. To some, it was a very dangerous proposition to fill the soon-to-be created state with masses of Jews from cultures that differed so markedly with the one painstakingly crafted by the Ashkenazi Zionist elite. Even after the decision had been made and Operation Kibbutz Galuyyot was in full swing, the doubts concerning its merit did not die; as a matter of fact, with regard to Oriental Jewry, they intensified.

A leading representative of the establishment, Michael Assaf, wrote in the daily newspaper of the country's powerful Histadrut labor union:

> What must therefore be the task of the Ingathering of the Exiles? Not only to bring them [the Oriental Jews] to the soil of Israel, but also to restore to them their first exalted value. . . . And every Jew who is not seized by *the fear of the possibility . . . that we will not be able to prevail and to purify our brethren from the dross of Orientalism* which attached itself to them against their will, will be held accountable for this before the guardian spirit of the nation. There is reason for the most serious anxiety. . . . How to cleanse and purify these brethren—how to lift them up to the Western level of the existing Yishuv.[37]

As is clear from the quotation, the anti-Orientalist mindset ran so deep that Assaf is entirely preoccupied with the task of transforming Oriental Jewry into Europeans.[38] Not only is he unwilling to consider their right to be different, but he also hints of the possibility of not sharing the country with them altogether. All the while, immigration is actually taking place.

A little over three years after the establishment of the State of Israel, we hear yet another voice denying the value of "ingathering the exiles," this time from an entirely unexpected source. The same organization whose main purpose was to carry out Operation Kibbutz Galuyyot, the Jewish Agency, then headed by Berl Locker, passionately rejected the idea that this operation applied also to Oriental Jews. In 1951, Locker declared:

> Has it ever happened in history that a people which had worked very hard for several decades to obtain a place in the family of nations and which had at long last achieved its liberation and independence, then followed this up by making a supreme effort to bring to its country *another people, another race*, which will soon surpass it in numbers and become the ruling element in the State?[39]

The total sense of "otherness" he expresses regarding Oriental Jews, who, it is feared, might become the majority and take over the state is particularly significant. In reading such a remark, one is strongly reminded of the statement in the Bible made by the new pharaoh prior to the enslavement of the Children of Israel: "A new king arose over Egypt, who did not know Joseph. And he said to his people, 'Look, the Israelite people are much too numerous for us. Let us deal shrewdly with them; otherwise in the event of war they may join our enemies in fighting against us and rise from the ground.'"[40] The commentary, found in the English translation of the Jewish Publication Society Bible, understands the phrase "and rise from the ground"[41] to mean "gained ascendancy over the country."[42] In other words, Oriental Jews, like the Israelites in Egypt, posed a threat, perhaps a security risk,[43] to the ruling establishment. To Locker's credit, we must add that he fell short of pharaoh's explicit depiction of the Oriental Jews as enemies.

Such virulently negative perceptions of Oriental Jews were not only restricted to the ruling elite. They tainted a large part of the bureaucracy of the state and thus led to de facto (though generally not de jure) policies of discrimination. The Iraqi community was the first to respond to the discriminatory policies and practices directed against Oriental Jews. Iraqi Jews had arrived in Israel *en masse* by the early 1950s and were 120,000 strong. Among them were the sophisticated elite of Baghdad and Basra, who considered themselves a kind of aristocracy in many ways superior to Ashkenazi Jewry. The historian Howard M. Sachar describes the reactions by Iraqi Jews during this time:

> Angered by the impersonality of government and Jewish agency bureaucrats, the Iraqis became vocal, even strident, in their complaints of ethnic bias. In July 1951, they mounted a large-scale demonstration in Tel Aviv against "race discrimination in the Jewish State"—the first (but by no means the last) display of its kind. They protested their transformation into "second-class" citizens.. . . . By protest and persistence, the Iraqis ultimately succeeded in finding their place in Israel's economy.[44]

This unexpected rebellion by Iraqi Jews had caught the Israeli establishment off guard. In order to reestablish calm in the young state, the authorities were willing to comply with the newcomers' demands, but not without learning a lesson from this episode. Soon after the Iraqi Jewish "uprising," whether as a consequence or just a coincidence, Jewish Agency executives instructed their officers in Casablanca to compel potential Moroccan Jewish immigrants[45] to sign a declaration.[46] Published in French and in Hebrew (see Figure 1), it stated that the signatory agreed he and his family would accept any job assigned to them, in agriculture or any other occupation. Furthermore, the declaration noted that if for some reason

FIGURE 1

DECLARATION	הצהרה
Je soussigné CHETRIT JACOB MEILAH émigrant pour Israël, suivant l'autorisation du Bureau de la Alya de l'Agence Juive à Casablanca, avec ma femme MAZAL et mes enfants MEYER, MOCHE, ARMAND, SIMON, JOSEPH. déclare connaître parfaitement et porter à la connaissance des membres de ma famille qu'à mon arrivée en Israël les organismes chargés de l'absorption des immigrants ne "peront de ma famille et de moi-même qu'à la condition que nous nous consacrions au travail agricole au lieu qui nous sera indiqué ou aux autres travaux de développement qui nous seront fixés par les organismes responsables. Au cas ou je ne remplirais pas la condition ci-dessus, je ne pourrais, en aucun cas, revendiquer l'aide et l'assistance des organismes chargés de l'absorption des immigrants en Israë. Casablanca, le _____ Signature,	אני החתום מטה העולה לישראל עפ"י אישור מחלקת העליה של הסוכנות היהודית בקזבלנקה יחד עם אשתי _____ ובני _____ מצהיר בזה, כי הוסבר לי וקבלתי לתשומת לבי ולידיעת בני ביתי הנלוים אלי, מאחרי בואי לישראל יטפלו המוסדות האחראיים לקליטת עולים בישראל בי ובבני ביתי הנלוים אלי רק בתנאי שאלך לעבודה חקלאית אשר אליה אשלח או לעבודות פתוח אשר תקבענה לי ע"י המוסדות המטפלים בכך. אם לא אקיים את התנאי האמור לא אוכל להיזקק לעזרתו ולטפולו של שום מוסד מהמוסדות המטפלים בקליטת עולים בארץ. קזבלנקה יום _____ חתימה

the undersigned did not fulfill his obligation in this regard, he and his family would be prevented from receiving any assistance from the institutions in charge of immigration. The implications of such a veiled threat were clear, since like most Jews from Arab countries, Moroccan Jews were prohibited from bringing with them any valuables or money (indeed often not more than one suitcase per person). Thus, lack of assistance from the government during the immigration process would mean certain poverty and ruin.

This declaration represented a major setback for the 120,000-strong community of Moroccan immigrants in particular, which was forced by conditions imposed by the Israeli bureaucracy into overwhelmingly menial jobs and low-income fields of employment. This development, in turn, affected their own and their children's economic status in the generations to follow, often leading to a near unbreakable cycle of poverty for many.

Upon their arrival in Israel, Moroccan Jewry was exposed to a new reality in sharp contrast to the portrait that had been painted by the Israeli Aliyah Centers in their native land. Almost nothing they had been told and had expected was fulfilled. In spite of their disappointment, only a small minority of Moroccan Jews left the country.

In Israel, they encountered a new type of Jew to which they were unaccustomed—the "Sabra." A cliche circulated that the native Israeli was called a Sabra after the prickly pear fruit, which is found all over Israel's landscape and is characterized by its thorny outside and sweet, soft core.[47] The Oriental newcomers understood instinctively that life in the new land was not going to be easy at the beginning, just as when eating a Sabra fruit, they expected to be wounded by many thorns before being able to enjoy the sweet and juicy center. At the very least, they had optimism for the future. In time, as life in Israel continued to remain harsh with no hope of improvement on the horizon, the immigrant generation gradually became accustomed to the idea that their dreams might not be realized after all.

The Wadi Salib Uprising

Throughout the 1950s, the economic crisis, in addition to the shortages in employment and housing, precipitated intermittent clashes in Oriental neighborhoods between the immigrants and the police, though it rarely led to social upheaval. One such neighborhood was Wadi Salib, which, following the 1948 War of Independence, had been repopulated by untrained Jewish workers.[48] Virtually all of the 15,000 residents were Oriental Jews, about a third of them Moroccans.

With its overcrowded dwellings of one- and two-bedroom apartments opening into rundown courtyards, Wadi Salib had all the characteristics of a slum; the frustration of its inhabitants was high. On July 9, 1959, clashes between a police officer and a resident erupted following a barroom brawl, and the ensuing confrontation served to symbolize the existence of "two Israels."[49] As the conflict accelerated, police arrived at the scene. Subsequently, a Moroccan Jew was shot and seriously wounded. Although his life was not in danger, as he was taken to the hospital, a rumor rapidly spread that he had died because of "police brutality." The following day, a large number of residents surrounded the Wadi Salib police station in the neighborhood and demanded revenge. The unrest continued periodically throughout the day. Sometime in the evening, around 6:00 P.M., a police force dispersed the crowd, but not before thirteen police officers and two civilians were injured as well as thirty-two people arrested. The next day, stories of the civil uprising appeared on the front pages of virtually every Israeli newspaper.

Following this maelstrom, the government conducted an investigation to ascertain the underlying reasons for what came to be called the Wadi Salib Uprising. Witnesses testified to the bleak, depressing conditions in which they lived, offering numerous accounts of individual and collective discrimination.[50] Yet, when the investigation's report was issued in August 1959, it failed to hold any parties responsible. The events at Wadi Salib would in hindsight be recognized as the proverbial tip of the iceberg, revealing to the public eye the ethnic cleavage that had taken place in the country, and warning the establishment of an open wound that festered at the heart of Israeli society.

The Israeli Black Panthers

After Wadi Salib, the ongoing discrimination against Oriental Jews and the lack of perceptible opportunities to break out of the cycle of poverty accelerated the rage and frustration felt by many in the community. During the 1970s, these emotions eventually gave birth to a new grassroots movement, sardonically called the Black Panthers,[51] which was formed by many of the offspring of Oriental immigrants. In 1971, after a wave of violent demonstrations organized by the Panthers, then Prime Minister Golda Meir recognized the social and ethnic gap in her address to the Israeli parliament. She declared that "she was the last person in the world to shy away from reality and pretend that the communal gap did not exist."[52] However, she refused to connect it in any way to Israeli policies, blaming its existence solely on the world from which Oriental Jewry came:

> Many immigrants from the Islamic countries brought deprivation and discrimination with them in their "baggage" from their countries of origin.... The Jews who came to us from the Islamic countries were of a higher level than the populations from which they came; but it was their fate to live in countries that have not yet developed intellectually, industrially, and culturally, and they were deprived of the opportunity to develop their special characteristics, to express their intellectual capacities, and to acquire the

knowledge and education that were given to those coming from the developed countries of Europe and America.[53]

Meir's speech reflects the stereotypically patronizing and racist attitude of the Ashkenazi establishment in Israel at that time, which extended not only toward Oriental Jews but also toward the Arab and Muslim world in general. A few months following her speech, this kind of thinking almost brought about the country's destruction when the government found itself almost totally unprepared for the 1973 Yom Kippur War, having underestimated the Arab nations' abilities and resolve.

Oriental Jews finally decided that "salvation" would not come from the Labor Party, which had ruled the country continuously over the past three decades. Even at its lowest point, after nearly being defeated in the 1973 war, the leadership of the Labor Party could not find within itself room to create partnerships and share positions of leadership with the same Oriental Jews who had fought, were wounded, and had died in defense of the country.

While many in the country were questioning their support of the Labor Party, some for the very first time, Oriental Jews in particular, were ready for a change. They turned toward the right-wing Likud Party, headed by Menachem Begin, who had sat in "eternal opposition" to Labor Party rule from before the establishment of the state.

The Begin Revolution and Oriental Jews

In the poorer neighborhoods of the urban cities and development towns, young Oriental Jews, disappointed with the Labor Party and its leadership, began to be attracted to Menachem Begin and his party. Although his party displayed no intention of fighting the poverty and discrimination that plagued their community, Begin nevertheless gained the support of Oriental Jews because of the respect he showed them and managed to instill in their hearts.

As Ilan Pappe noted,

> A coalition of dissatisfied Israelis brought Begin to power: Mizrahi Jews suffering from years of discrimination, religious Jews feeling marginalized in the Jewish state, Labourites [longtime Labor Party supporters] shocked by the 1973 Arab surprise attack. . . . The Mizrahi Jews brought Begin to power,

but the disappointed Ashkenazi Jews toppled Labour. They did not vote for Begin, but they did not support Labour.[54]

Indeed, "Begin became the voice—the roar—of all those who felt insulted and rejected by the Labor movement."[55]

In his victory speech, Prime Minister Begin astutely grasped the essence of the ethnic problem and at the same time offered hope and possible solutions. As he passionately roared one word at a time, waving his fist charismatically, he uttered five key words that would sum up what made him so beloved in the Oriental communities: "Ashkenazi? Iraqi? Jews! Brethren! Fighters!"[56]

With that one statement, Begin managed to symbolically break the ethnic wall between Ashkenazi and Oriental Jewries that had grown so large and thick in the preceding 29 years. These five words, perhaps enigmatic and ambiguous to the ear of the outsider, represented everything Sephardi and Oriental Jews had longed to hear. By juxtaposing the words "Ashkenazi" and "Iraqi," Begin eloquently communicated the message that ethnic distinctions would no longer be considered valid under his leadership. Immediately, he enumerated an alternative, new conception of Israeli society that stressed commonalities in order of priority, namely, "Jews! Brethren! Fighters!" First and foremost, all were Jews, sharing a common fate and destiny. Despite the seeming differences, all Jews were essentially brothers; and ultimately, as Jews and brothers, they had and would continue to fight to maintain the state in the face of continued Arab opposition.

This outlook vis-à-vis Oriental Jewry stood in direct contrast to that of the Labor Party. Tel Aviv University Professor Shlomo Ben Ami highlighted the disparity between the Labor and Likud Parties by comparing their two archetypical leaders: "Ben Gurion was a nation builder that wanted to change the character of Jews, and turn them into Israelis. Begin didn't want to change their character; they are Jews, and they should remain Jews."[57]

Begin had managed to do in the Oriental community what no other Israeli political leader had accomplished before—restore its sense of self-respect, pride, equality, and partnership. His attitude implanted in their hearts a deep sense that they had finally, truly, come home, and consequently, they responded with tremendous admiration and love.[58]

The new prime minister's declarations were not empty ones; he truly treated Oriental Jewish politicians as partners in nation-building, integrating their up-and-coming leaders into his party and cabinet (a process that had already started while he sat in opposition). In an interview following the 1977 elections, David Levy, a talented young politician of Moroccan origin tapped for a cabinet post in the new government, underscored the reasons for the Labor Party's defeat:

> We were willing to suffer when we all shared the same fate—living in immigrant transit camps, working in the Gilboa Mountains, picking cotton, laying foundations for buildings.... We accepted it with understanding, if not with love. This is our land! But when the country progresses and leaves some people behind, that shatters the feeling of "one nation and one society," of accepting what we have because we're all in it together.[59]

In the end, the political revolution of 1977 set a precedent that Oriental Jews could not be taken for granted anymore.

The political developments also engendered wider cultural acceptance and greater public legitimacy for the heritage of Oriental Jewry. Since the shift away from Orientalism in the pre-State era, the Israeli establishment had identified almost exclusively with Western, European culture, so much so that to be truly "Israeli" meant "entirely European." Perceived as inferior, Oriental Jewish music, for example, was not allowed on the radio, and the mainstream media ignored singers whose music reflected an Oriental style even if they were singing in Hebrew. It was even worse with Arabic music, which was highly admired by Oriental Jews. Eli Amir, a well-known Iraqi-born author, reflected in an interview: "The tent we lived in . . . we were hungry, the school—I overcame all of them. . . . But taking my self-esteem, my honor. . . . Every time I listen to Umm Kulthum[60] . . . her songs heal my wounds . . . to tell me "this is monotone, Arab music; how can you listen to it? It's primitive music"—it killed me!"[61]

Thus, in addition to the acceptance of particularly Oriental foods, the first signs that Israeli society had begun to integrate Oriental culture into the mainstream took place in the field of music around the late 1970s. In time, Sephardic and Oriental music became more accepted, and Oriental singers gradually gained prominence. Israeli society, at last, started to show some signs of multiculturalism, legitimizing Oriental culture and traditions. Soon celebrations of distinctive Oriental Jewish holidays became a widespread, public phenomenon. Even more recently, the North African holiday of Mimuna,[62] was deemed by the government an optional vacation day for workers interested in observing it.

While grateful to the Likud Party for its initial embrace, Oriental Jews soon realized that the party was not effectively confronting the grave social and ethnic issues afflicting their communities. Instead, it had turned its attention almost exclusively toward promoting the notion of "Greater Israel," which meant maintaining territories captured in 1967 at great monetary and military cost. Many Oriental Jews resented that choice, feeling that this same financial support, which could have helped the development towns in which so many of them resided, was being diverted instead to settlements in the West Bank and Gaza Strip. In addition, many Israelis, Sephardim among them, were disappointed by the outcome of the Lebanon War, and the motives of the Likud leaders who had begun it.[63]

The next cultural shock, to the Labor Party in particular and Israeli society in general, occurred six years after the 1977 elections when Rabbi Ovadiah Yosef founded the Sephardic religious political party, Shas.[64]

The Shas Party—Sephardi Torah Guardians

As soon as Rabbi Ovadia Yosef was removed from his tenure of office as Sephardi Chief Rabbi of Israel (Rishon LeZion) in 1983, due to newly enforced term limitations, he turned his attention toward transforming the Shas Party from a small, localized faction, which had won three seats in the Jerusalem municipal elections of 1983, into a national political phenomenon. Under his leadership, the party won a remarkable four seats in the 1984 national elections.[65] In each subsequent election, Shas enhanced its power, culminating in an astonishing 17 seats out of 120 in the 1999 Israeli parliament, which made it the third largest party in the Israeli political system.[66]

With so many seats accruing to Shas, no major party in Israel, until recently, was able to form a government easily without them. Thus, Shas possessed in effect a tremendous amount of political and financial power. As a result, the party aroused resentment among both religious and secular elements in Israeli society.[67]

In the religious world, the national Zionist camp, represented by Mafdal (the National Religious Party—dominated by Ashkenazi Jews), begrudges Shas for supplanting it as the preeminent religious faction at coalition-making time. Simultaneously, the ultra-Orthodox Ashkenazi parties, for their part, object to Shas's full participation in all strata of the Zionist government, something they themselves refuse to undertake in principle.[68]

Furthermore, they take exception to Shas's unstated but widely known goal of terminating the second-class status of Sephardim in the Ashkenazi-dominated ultra-Orthodox world.[69]

Among secular segments in Israeli society, many Jews fear the ever-increasing political power that has enabled Shas to dictate the religious agenda of the state and has forced the government to pass resolutions and laws that, from the secular point of view, are perceived as a threat to democracy. In addition, their increasing political power has at times allowed Shas to "extort" large financial concessions from the major parties during coalition talks, which has regularly translated into generous financial support from government coffers for Shas institutions (especially its educational system), at the expense (or so it is perceived) of secular institutions and schools. Lately, Rabbi Ovadiah Yosef, Shas's revered spiritual leader, has added even more fuel to the fire by seeming to attack Israel's secular, democratic leadership, as well as non-Jews in general, Arabs in particular, and important elements within the Israeli legal and judicial system. Yosef's condemnations, though usually delivered to his followers in the context of religious sermons, have been published by reporters in the mainstream press, generating enormous turmoil within Israeli society.[70]

Despite its negative image in the eyes of many Israelis, the establishment of Shas is of great significance within the ongoing saga of Oriental Jews in Israel. While it has brought about numerous positive outcomes, for the purpose of our analysis, the main importance of the Shas revolution lies in the fact that it represents yet another level of awakening on the part of a segment within Oriental Jewry, namely, the ultra-Orthodox Sephardim. This group was considered for quite some time to be the more "obedient and submissive" element in Oriental Jewry, since it had been almost completely assimilated into the ultra-Orthodox camp and saw itself as an integral part of it. If not for internal political and ethnic cleavages within the ultra-Orthodox world, which cannot be elaborated upon in this context, the awakening of ultra-Orthodox Sephardim would likely never have happened.

The significance of Shas also lies in the fact that it served as a prelude to the latest link in the chain of Sephardic "uprisings" against discrimination, stretching back all the way to the Iraqi demonstration in July 1951. Though very different from the rebellions that preceded it, new developments, such as the founding of the secular and highly educated Oriental movement known as HaKeshet Ha-Demokratit HaMizrachit, contain many elements resembling the earlier phases of Shas.

HaKeshet Ha-Demokratit HaMizrachit—The Oriental Democratic Rainbow

The Oriental Democratic Rainbow was founded in March 1996 by 40 men and women, the majority of whom are second- and third-generation offspring of Oriental Jewish parents. Nine months later, in December 1996, the Oriental Democratic Rainbow was officially established when its first 100 members constituted the initial board. The organization was inaugurated based upon democratic values, with officers elected by secret ballot, and a commitment to gender equality, such that men and women occupy an equal number of official positions. Among its leaders, one may find academicians, educators, artists, and students, as well as business people and simple workers; as its name attests, it represents the entire rainbow of Israeli society.

According to its mission statement, the movement is apolitical and uninterested in fashioning itself into a political party. Its main purpose appears to be attempting to influence the public agenda and bringing about changes within Israeli society and its institutions. Currently, the movement is struggling for social and cultural pluralism in Israel, particularly emphasizing the need for increased participation by women, minorities, and socially disadvantaged segments of society in all aspects of life.

The Oriental Democratic Rainbow marks a very important step toward the achievement of a more egalitarian society in Israel. Having learned how to navigate the Israeli bureaucracies successfully, they utilize their resources to further the cause of social equality and help break the cycle of poverty and discrimination that still exist in twenty-first-century Israeli society. Already the organization has achieved one remarkable change in the field of land ownership.

In Israel, all land not privately owned is considered government property. Upon the establishment of the state, the government gave communal settlements, known as kibbutzim and moshavim, temporary rights to the land they farmed for a 50-year period. In 1998, those agreements expired, yet the communities appealed to the government for permission to sell off portions of the land and keep the proceeds. Such an arrangement would have allowed a small but well-connected segment of the population to enrich themselves personally by selling land that actually belonged to the entire people of Israel. This request was particularly galling to the Oriental underclass, who were often too poor to purchase land themselves and perceived the kibbutz members as part of the privileged establishment. Thus, the Oriental Democratic Rainbow brought the issue to court and sued the government as well as the official bodies in charge of the lands, demanding the sales be halted until a more fair and balanced division of state resources could be determined. The court accepted their petition and for the first time in the history of modern Israel, the Ashkenazi establishment felt itself on the defensive.

What Happened to Anti-Orientalism?

While things seem to be improving for Oriental Jewry, is it safe to say that anti-Orientalist attitudes have finally disappeared? For some time, following the 1977 political change, it seemed that they were dormant, if not dead, until the 1982 war in Lebanon. A few months after the war started, many began to realize that prejudice was alive and well, especially among the left in the Israeli society. The event that brought it to the fore was the Sabra and Shatilah massacre, in which two villages of Palestinians were murdered by members of the Christian Lebanese militia, while the Israeli army stood by and allowed it to happen. When the tragedy was revealed in the press, the world was stunned and Israeli society was shaken to its core. More than 400,000 Israelis, sickened by the massacre and Israel's role in Lebanon, demonstrated on the streets of Tel Aviv against the war.

Among the many critical articles written by Israelis during and after Lebanon, we find some that blame the war on Oriental Jews who helped to elect Begin and the right-wing government that authorized the war. To a large degree, this criticism of the Oriental community was brought by intellectuals, many of whom were Labor Party activists upset and apprehensive of losing their hegemony in Israeli society. Two articles by leading Israeli intellectuals stand out as illustrations: the first written by Amos Oz, at the height of the Israeli siege of Beirut, and the second by Shlomo Avineri, in the aftermath of the massacre.

Oz, a well-known Israeli novelist and left-wing intellectual, concludes his article in the following manner: "In short, Israel could have become an exemplary state, an open, argumentative, involved society of unique moral standards and future-oriented outlook, a small-scale laboratory for democratic socialists, or—as the old timers like to put it, 'a light unto the nations.'"[71]

However, according to the author, the dream failed because of the "mass immigration of Holocaust survivors, Middle Eastern Jews, and non-Socialist and even anti-Socialist Zionists."[72] He criticizes the Holocaust refugees for bringing with them a craving for "bourgeois coziness and stability," and charges Oriental Jews with being "conservative, Puritan, observant, extremely hierarchical and family-oriented, and, to some extent, chauvinistic, militaristic and xenophobic."[73] For Oz, these are the types of people who brought Begin and his government to power, clearly implying that if only the Labor Party had still been in power, the war in Lebanon could have been prevented.

Shlomo Avineri, a prominent political scientist, follows much the same pattern of thought. He traces the roots of the problems leading to the massacre to the elections of 1977:

> The elections of 1977 that brought Mr. Begin to power were a change from one political culture to another. They showed a shift in the composition of the electorate. With a shift in the number of Sephardi voters. . . . A larger sector of the Israeli population was made up of people from highly traditional societies, much more ethnocentric than the more secularized and liberal European Jews who had dominated Israel's politics for decades. Most of Likud's voters came from the Middle East, while most Labor voters were European Jews or their descendants.[74]

As we can see, Avineri perceives a major difference between the Zionism of the Labor Party and the Zionism of the Likud. For him, the distinction was not only political and ideological, but also and most importantly, cultural. Labor represented the culture of European Jewry and the enlightened Ashkenazim, whereas Likud promoted the culture of "ethnocentric" Oriental Jews. Regarding the massacre, he went on to write:

> The national outcry released a terrible feeling of guilt, yet the demonstrations were mainly limited to that half of Israel's Jewish population that is of European background, liberal, middle-class and well-educated. There is doubt whether what happened really cut into the hard core of Mr. Begin's support among those Israelis who like his tough style, his "goyim-baiting" language and his ethnocentricity.[75]

Clearly for Avineri, Sephardic and Oriental Jews had sinned twice. First, they transgressed by electing Begin and his government and then by absenting themselves from mass demonstrations in Tel Aviv against the war organized by left-wing parties. Thankfully, this accusation was conclusively proven wrong by Daniel Elazar in his excellent book *The Other Jews*.[76]

Epilogue—The Reaction to the Oriental Democratic Rainbow

Thus far, every initiative on the part of Oriental Jewry to improve its status in Israeli society has attracted the criticism of secular left-wing and Labor-oriented Israelis. However, the Oriental Rainbow represents a new kind of Oriental Jewish organization. By adhering to the principle of nonviolence, it has distinguished itself from the Black Panther movement. By refusing to espouse a religious perspective, it departs from the paradigm of Shas. Since it is not right-wing, it cannot be tied to the Likud Party. Its members are, by and large, highly educated, so they cannot be characterized as "primitive and illiterate," and the organization is fully egalitarian so it cannot be labeled "chauvinistic or ethnocentric."

Other than remaining proudly connected to their Oriental roots, members of the Oriental Democratic Rainbow have fulfilled the image of what Ben Gurion had wished the Oriental Jew would become. We can only hope that this organization has finally discovered the secret of how to achieve change within the intricacies of Israeli society and will be successful once and for all in finally legitimizing Orientalism in the Jewish State.

NOTES

I am grateful to Professor Farid Esack, currently at Harvard University, for his detailed comments on this chapter. I only regret that I could not integrate more of his insights into the text due to editorial constraints at this stage. However, in future publications on this issue, I shall endeavor to include them.

1. See Avishai Margalit, *Views in Review: Politics and Culture in the State of the Jews* (New York: Farrar, Straus & Giroux, 1998), 32–33. Margalit also opens his chapter dealing with the "sins" of the Labor Party against the Sephardic and Oriental Jewish immigrants with this very same story, though I give the story a slightly different reading.

2. Barak himself was at that point the immediate past chief of staff of the Israeli Armed Forces and is still the most decorated soldier in the history of the Israeli army.

3. See Margalit, *Views in Review*, 33.

4. Knowing full well the potential power of such a declaration, the Likud Party encouraged Oriental Jews to dismiss the apology as mere political grandstanding.

5. One may find such skeptical reactions even within Barak's own camp. See Shlomo Ben-Ami, of Moroccan origin, in his book *A Place for All* (in Hebrew) (Tel Aviv: Hakibbutz Hameuchad, 1999), 391, who demanded that the government provide the lower strata of Israeli society with housing and higher education rather than offer apologies. He declared:

> No market forces nor communicated media apology rallies to stereotypical towns will solve the problem. The difficult social stratification that I'm talking about is one that will perpetuate itself for eternity also because of the fact that the lower class has no property to leave for their children as an inheritance, contrary to the middle class who provide their children with education and property.

6. See Margalit, *Views in Review*, 33.

7. These stages are not meant to propose a theory, which would require further research and elaboration. Rather, they are preliminary reflections on the historical evolution of Oriental Jewish identity in modern Israel. Some thought about ethnicity and identity from a global perspective may be found in Erik H. Erikson, "Reflections on the American Identity," in *Theories of Ethnicity: A Classical Reader*, ed. Werner Sollors (New York: New York University Press, 1996, 232–65; and George Devereux, "Ethnic Identity: Its Logical Foundations and Dysfunction," in ibid., 385–414.

8. See Eliezer Schweid, "The Rejection of the Diaspora in Zionist Thought: Two Approaches"; Jonathan Frankel, "The 'Yizkor' Book of 1911—A Note on National Myths in the Second Aliya" (particularly 427–28); and the four articles under Section 5, Cultural Questions, all in *Essential Papers on Zionism*, ed. Jehuda Reinharz and Anita Shapira (New York: New York University Press, 1996), 727–821. Also valuable is Amnon Rubenstein, *The Zionist Dream Revisited: From Herzl to Gush Emunim and Back* (New York: Schocken, 1984), particularly chap. 1, "Zionism and the Quest for a New Jewish Identity," and chap. 2, "The Meaning of Normalization," within which are cited numerous sources.

9. The idea of Orientalism is treated thoroughly in the landmark work *Orientalism* by Edward Said (New York: Pantheon, 1978), in which Said addresses issues of power (often by relying on theories proposed by philosopher Michel Foucault) and "othering" in the creation of Orientalism in the West. Many of his points are intriguing and deserve further exploration as they relate to Oriental Jews in Israel. However, critics of his approach are numerous, and works detailing critical perspectives include Philip A. Mellor's "Orientalism, Representation, and Religion: The Reality behind the Myth," *Religion* 34 (2004): 99–112; and Joel Kraemer's "Is the Classical Heritage Western? Some Reflections on Edward Said's Orientalism," *Criterion* 34 (1995): 20–25.

10. Mordechai Zeev Feierberg, "Leʾan?" ("Whither?"), in *Hashiloch* (Tel Aviv,

1899), 62. The text is quoted here from the English translation found in Amnon Rubinstein, *The Zionist Dream Revisited: From Herzl to Gush Emunim and Back* (New York: Schocken, 1984) 51.

11. Rubinstein, *The Zionist Dream Revisited*, 51.
12. Ibid.
13. Ibid.
14. Similar voices were heard from other early Zionists, such as Moses Leib Lilienblum (1843–1910), who wrote:
In the heyday of religion, we were strangers in Europe because of our faith, and now with the ascent of nationalism, we are strangers because of our race. Yes, we are Semites within Aryans, the sons of Shem within the sons of Japhet, a Palestinian tribe from Asia within the lands of Europe. . . . Yes, we are strangers and strangers we shall be forever.

Quoted in Rubinstein, *The Zionist Dream Revisited*, 50.

15. Ibid., 56.
16. Ibid.
17. Ibid., 31.
18. Ibid., 53.
19. David Ben Gurion and Yitzchak Ben Zvi would become, respectively, the first prime minister and the first president of the State of Israel.
20. Rubinstein, *The Zionist Dream Revisited*, 31.
21. David Ben Gurion, "Leverur Matzav Ha'falachim" ("On the State of the Fellahim"), 1917, republished in *Anu Ushcheneinu* (We and Our Neighbors) (Tel Aviv, 1935), 13–25. For the translation in English, see Amnon Rubinstein, *The Zionist Dream Revisited*, 55.
22. Eric Rouleau, *Le Monde*, 9 March 1966.
23. One might argue that what appears to be a "shift" in Ben Gurion's attitude toward Arabs from pro-Orientalism to anti-Orientalism is merely a manifestation of the same basic essentialism and patronizing attitude. I am grateful to Professor Farid Esack, currently at Harvard University, for pointing this out to me.
24. In 1935, Itamar Ben Avi, the son of the Zionist pioneer Eliezer Ben Yehuda, who is credited with almost single-handedly reviving the Hebrew language, wrote very enthusiastically about the Palestinians as being "doubtless remnants of the old Hebrews." Quoted in Rubinstein, *The Zionist Dream Revisited*, 52.
25. Ibid., 53–54.
26. I am thankful to Professor Farid Esack for his insightful comment that often the "otherness" of the other is acceptable, whereas the "otherness" of the insider (who comes from within the same society) is not.
27. Margalit, *Views in Review*, 33–34.
28. David Ben-Gurion, interview by Robert Moskin, *Look*, 5 October 1965.
29. See Ariel Hirschfeld, "Locus and Language," in *Cultures of the Jews: A New History*, ed. David Biale (New York: Schocken, 2002), 1050, where he states: "The

Moroccans have been designated the Mizrahi Jews in the drama that pits East against West in Israeli culture."

30. In a future paper, I plan to explore in detail the unique dilemma of the Sephardic Jewish immigrant, caught between the Scylla of antireligious attitudes espoused by the secular Zionist leadership on the one hand and the Charybdis of anti-Zionist attitudes promoted by many among the ultra-Orthodox Ashkenazi leadership on the other. In between these two polarized ideologies, stood the perplexed Oriental Jew who shared one aspect with each of them and diametrically opposed another aspect. In light of these divergent positions, it was only natural that the newly arrived Oriental Jews, who thought that they had finally come home, became totally disoriented and confused within Israeli's unique social reality.

31. Margalit, *Views in Review*, 33–34.

32. See Daniel J. Elazar, *The Other Jews: The Sephardim Today* (New York: Basic Books, 1989), 9, where he writes: "The original myth of the backwardness of the Sephardim was fueled by the necessity to raise large sums of money abroad to help integrate the newcomers to Israel. It was useful at the time to focus on the truly backward Jews, those from the Atlas Mountains ... to exemplify Israel's need for massive support in order to 'civilize' these new immigrants."

33. See Hirschfeld, "Locus and Language," 1051–52, where he writes:
The idea of the "melting pot" was a poetic fiction. The integration of Mizrahi Jews was in actuality a matter of rupture and eraser, made possible by their suppression from the dominant Western consciousness. Consequently, the first generation of immigrants was utterly destroyed, both as the bearer of a heritage and as a cultural authority for the next generation. Only the children of these immigrants ... could hope to build from the ruins a new cultural presence.

34. See Jane Gerber, *The Jews of Spain: A History of the Sephardic Experience* (New York: Free Press, 1994), 278, where he writes:
The assumption was that a melting pot of all the exile cultures would produce a new Israeli personality completely different from those typifying the different traditions. The principle was to apply to all groups, not just Sephardic Jews. On the other hand, the cultural ideal projected by the European Jews who had formulated the Zionist ethos before the founding of the state was heavily socialist, anti-religious, and reflecting the needs and goals of European Jews. In other words, the Zionism of the founding Labor Party was at odds with some of the most treasured values of the Sephardim.

35. Hirschfeld, "Locus and Language," 1051 (emphasis is mine).

36. By no means do I seek to imply that Palestinian Arabs are to blame for the racism afflicted on Oriental Jews. Rather, both are victims of the racism of the Israeli Ashkenazi elite.

37. See Nissim Rejwan, *Israel's Place in the Middle East: A Pluralist Perspective*

(Gainesville: University Press of Florida, 1998), 143 (emphasis is mine), where he cites Rafael Patai, *Israel between East and West* (New York: Herzl Press, 1953), 311.

38. See Howard M. Sachar, *A History of Israel: From the Rise of Zionism to Our Time* (New York: Alfred A. Knopf, 1996), 423: "The Europeans plainly were obsessed by the danger of levantinization. By their standards, the backward Easterners had to be 'reformed'—'purified of the dross of Orientalism. . . .' The idea of 'reforming the primitives,' of transforming them along the European model, had been the dominant trend of Israel's acculturation effort from the onset of the poststate immigration. . . . The Orientals resented it."

39. Rejwan, *Israel's Place in the Middle East*, 143 (emphasis is mine), where he quotes from *Zion* (Jerusalem: Jewish Agency, August 1951).

40. Exod. 1:8–10. The English translation is taken from *Tanakh: The Holy Scriptures* (Philadelphia, New York, Jerusalem: Jewish Publication Society, 1985), 85.

41. Based on the appearance of the same phrase in Hos. 2:2. See *Tanakh*, 982 n. C.

42. *Tanakh*, 85 n. a-a.

43. See Michael D. Coogan, ed., *The New Oxford Annotated Bible: New Revised Standard Version with the Apocrypha* (New York: Oxford University Press, 2001), 84, commentary to verses 9–10: "The presence of the Israelites on Egypt's frontier is regarded as a security risk."

44. Sachar, *A History of Israel*, 420. The Iraqi Jews' protest was ultimately successful in that only 3 percent of the Iraqi community was shunted to moshavim or development towns (in marked contrast to other Oriental communities.) Moreover, most Iraqi Jews were able to work in the fields and professions they chose, rather than those that had been chosen by the socialist authorities for them. See Sachar's work for a detailed analysis.

45. Most Moroccan Jews immigrated in the mid-1950s and early 1960s.

46. I am indebted to Mimi Dolev for providing me with a copy of this declaration.

47. According to Margalit: "a cliché that gives all clichés a bad name." Margalit, *Views in Review*, 9.

48. Ilan Pappe, *A History of Modern Palestine: One Land, Two Peoples* (Cambridge: Cambridge University Press, 2004), 171.

49. See Sachar, *A History of Israel*, 424: "The Wadi Salib episode had opened a window into the little republic's soul. Almost imperceptibly during the previous decade, two Israels evidently had materialized within one Jewish society."

50. Ibid., 422.

51. After the African American group of the same name.

52. Rejwan, *Israel's Place in the Middle East*, 144.

53. Ibid.

54. Pappe, *A History of Modern Palestine*, 214–15.

55. Margalit, *Views in Review*, 36–37.
56. Menachem Begin, in his victory speech on 17 May 1977, as recorded in the documentary movie *Tkuma*, celebrating the jubilee anniversary of the State of Israel. Jerusalem: Israel Broadcasting Authority, 1998.
57. Shlomo Ben Ami, interview in *Tkuma*.
58. It was common in Israel after Begin's election to see men and women, old and young, approach the newly elected prime minister and shower him with hugs and kisses.
59. David Levy, interview in *Tkuma*.
60. Umm Kulthum is a renowned female singer from Egypt who was admired all over the Arab world and beyond.
61. Eli Amir, interview in *Tkuma*.
62. Moroccan Jews worldwide celebrate Mimuna at the close of the Passover holiday. Mimuna is a celebration of freedom, fertility, and the renewal of spring.
63. See especially Israelis' reaction to the Beirut massacre as described in Elazar, *The Other Jews*, 51–53.
64. "Shas" is an acronym for Sephardi Torah Guardians.
65. Peter Hirschberg, *The World of Shas* (New York: Institute on American Jewish-Israeli Relations of the American Jewish Committee, 1999), 1–3.
66. In the most recent Israeli elections, on 28 January 2003, Rabbi Yosef's party lost a third of its power in the Israeli parliament due to a change in the electoral system from one in which the prime minister is elected directly to one in which the majority party appoints a prime minister from within the party. On the face of it, the Shas party did lose seats. However, in the parliament that preceded the change in the law, Shas earned 10 seats, whereas in this most recent election, it augmented its seats, achieving 11. Thus, if one compares these elections to those that took place prior to the change in the election laws, one might argue that Shas increased its power by one seat. Moreover, what this realignment demonstrates is that the drastic increase in the number of seats Shas received following the electoral change was not indicative of its real percentage of support in Israeli society. Rather, it was an anomaly that solely reflected the change in the election law.
67. The resentment directed toward the party was used very effectively by the new antireligious party called Shinui, which, because of its antireligious sentiments in general and anti-Shas propaganda in particular, gained tremendous power in the most recent Israeli elections (28 January 2003) and has taken the place of Shas as the third largest political party in the current Israeli parliament.
68. Hirschberg, *The World of Shas*, 13. See also a more elaborate deliberation on the issue of the resistance of the ultra-Orthodox Ashkenazi parties to Zionism in Aviezer Ravitzky's *Messianism, Zionism, and Jewish Religious Radicalism* (Chicago: University of Chicago Press, 1996), especially chap. 4, "Exile in the Holy Land: The Dilemma of Haredi Jewry."
69. Hirschberg, *The World of Shas*, 3.

70. See Zion Zohar, "Oriental Jewry Confronts Modernity: The Case of Rabbi Ovadiah Yosef," *Modern Judaism: A Journal of Jewish Ideas and Experience* 24, no. 2 (2004), for a fuller treatment of Rabbi Yosef, his statements as reported by the press and his writings.

71. Amos Oz, "Has Israel Altered Its Vision?" *New York Times Magazine*, 11 July 1982.

72. Ibid.

73. Ibid.

74. Shlomo Avineri, "The Beirut Massacres and the Two Political Cultures of Israel," *International Herald Tribune*, 14 October 1982. Avineri was the former director general of the Ministry of Foreign Affairs under the previous Labor government.

75. Ibid.

76. See Elazar, *The Other Jews*, 51–53.

About the Contributors

Henry Abramson is Associate Professor of Holocaust and Judaic Studies and History at Florida Atlantic University in Boca Raton. He is the author of two books on Jewish history and numerous scholarly articles, and has been the recipient of several prestigious research and teaching awards, including a grant for Holocaust research from the National Endowment for the Humanities. He has twice been a visiting fellow at the United States Holocaust Memorial Museum and recently received the Excellence in the Academy Award from the National Education Association.

David M. Bunis teaches Judezmo linguistics and language at the Center for Jewish Languages and Literatures of the Hebrew University of Jerusalem. He is also an advisor to the National Authority for Ladino Language and Culture, Jerusalem. His publications include *A Lexicon of the Hebrew and Aramaic Elements in Modern Judezmo* and *The Judezmo Language.*

Mark R. Cohen is Professor of Near Eastern Studies at Princeton University. He is the author of more than 80 articles and reviews and several books, including *Jewish Self-Government in Medieval Egypt*, which won the National Jewish Book Award for Jewish history in 1981. Most recently, he has published *Under Crescent and Cross: The Jews in the Middle Ages.* Cohen has lectured widely in the United States, Europe, Japan, Israel, and Egypt, before both scholarly and general audiences, and recently published on Jewish-Muslim relations for popular consumption in important newspapers in Germany and Hungary.

Jonathan P. Decter is Assistant Professor on the Edmond J. Safra Chair in Sephardi Studies at Brandeis University. His works include *Language of Religion, Language of the People* (forthcoming) and *Out of the Garden: Estrangement and Transition in Iberian Jewish Literature* (forthcoming).

Morris M. Faierstein is an independent scholar. His publications include a new Hebrew edition of Rabbi Hayyim Vital's *Sefer Ha-Hezyonot* (forthcoming); *Jewish Mystical Autobiographies*; *Abraham Joshua Heschel: Prophetic Inspiration after the Prophets: Maimonides and Others* (editor); and *All Is in the Hands of Heaven: The Teachings of Rabbi Mordecai Joseph Leiner of Izbica*. He has also published more than thirty articles and reviews in a wide variety of scholarly journals.

Annette B. Fromm is a folklorist and museum specialist and is the Manager of the Deering Estate at Cutler, in Miami, Florida. Dr. Fromm has published articles on Jews in Greece, Sephardic Jews in Florida, Greek folklore, immigrant-ethnic groups in America, multicultural museums, Native Americans in museums, and folk art. She has taught Anthropology and Museum Studies at the University of Tulsa and served as Visiting Associate Professor in the Judaic Studies program at Florida Atlantic University.

Moshe Idel is the academic world's leading authority on Kabbalah and is Max Cooper Professor of Jewish Thought at the Hebrew University. He won the National Book Award in 1988 for his masterpiece, *Kabbalah: New Perspectives*, and has been a Visiting Professor at universities such as Yale, Harvard, Princeton, École de Hautes Études (Paris), UCLA, Dartmouth, Milan, Moscow, Oxford, University of Pennsylvania, and Cluj in Romania. He was awarded the Israel Prize for Jewish Thought in 1999, and in 2001 won the Jerusalem Excellency Prize of the President of Hebrew University.

Isaac Kalimi is currently Distinguished Rosenthal Visiting Professor at Case Western Reserve University (Cleveland), Professor of Hebrew Bible and Ancient Israelite/Jewish History at Spertus Institute of Jewish Studies (Chicago), and Associate Member of the Leiden Institute for the Study of Religions, University of Leiden. He has served as Visiting Professor at various universities, including DePaul University (Chicago), University of Oldenburg (Germany), University of Luzern (Switzerland), and Theological University of Kampen (Holland). Dr. Kalimi is co-editor of many books and is author of, among other works, T*he Reshaping of Ancient Israelite History in Chronicles*.

Mark Kligman is Associate Professor of Jewish Musicology at Hebrew Union College–Jewish Institute of Religion in New York where he teaches in the School of Sacred Music. Dr. Kligman has published several articles on the liturgy of Syrian Jews. His work also extends to historical trends in the liturgical music of Ashkenazic and Sephardic traditions. He was the editor of the Jewish terms in *Worship Music: A Concise Dictionary*. In the spring of 2001, he served as a Research Fellow and Visiting Professor at the Center for Judaic Studies, University of Pennsylvania, where he pursued research on contemporary trends in Jewish music.

Jonathan Schorsch is a historian specializing in the history and culture of the Sephardic Jews in the early modern world. He is the author of *Jews and Blacks in the Early Modern World: A Cultural History*. In addition to essays treating aspects of the same topic, he has published articles on the chuetas of Mallorca, Jewish and Israeli environmental issues, and contemporary Jewish music. He has been a fellow with the Institute for Jewish Studies at Hebrew University, Jerusalem, and the Institute for the Advanced Study of Religion at Yale University, has taught Jewish history at San Francisco State University, and currently teaches the history of the Portuguese Atlantic world at Emory University.

Paméla Dorn Sezgin is Assistant Professor of Anthropology and History at Gainesville College in Watkinsville, Georgia, a unit of the University System of Georgia, and is also in charge of the anthropology program. Her work has been published in several academic journals.

Norman A. Stillman is the Schusterman/Josey Professor of Judaic History at the University of Oklahoma. He is the author of seven books and numerous articles in several languages, including, *The Jews of Arab Lands: A History and Source Book*, *The Jews of Arab Lands in Modern Times*, *The Language and Culture of the Jews of Sefrou*, and *Sephardi Religious Responses to Modernity*. From 1989 to 2000, he was the editor of the AJS Review. Dr. Stillman was the recipient of the Distinguished Humanist Award for the year 2000 from the Melton Center of Ohio State University.

Zion Zohar was born in Casablanca, Morocco, and made aliyah with his family to Israel at the age of three. He is currently the Associate Director of the Institute for Judaic and Near Eastern Studies at Florida International University, where he is also the Chair of the President Navon Program for the Study of Sephardic and Oriental Jewry. He is a recipient of many grants, fellowships, and awards, and has authored numerous articles and book chapters. He is the editor of *Song of My People:*

High Holy Day Liturgy and is the editor of and contributor to *Swords into Plowshares: Peace in the Abrahamic Traditions* (forthcoming).

Zvi Zohar is a senior faculty member at Bar Ilan University, where he teaches at the Faculty of Law and at the Faculty of Jewish Studies and heads the Rappaport Center for Assimilation Research and the Strengthening of Jewish Vitality. He is a Senior Research Fellow at the Shalom Hartman Institute of Advanced Judaic Studies in Jerusalem, where he heads the Alan A. and Loraine Fischer Family Center for Contemporary Halakha. He is also a founding faculty member of Paideia, The European Institute for Jewish Studies in Sweden. He has published over 50 scholarly articles in Hebrew, English, and French, in addition to book-length studies in Hebrew, which include *The Luminous Face of the East: Studies in the Legal and Religious Thought of Sephardic Rabbis of the Middle East* and *A Socio-Cultural Drama in Aleppo in the French Mandatory Period*.

Index

Abarbanel (Abravanel), Don Isaac (Portugal, 1437–1508, Naples), 103, 116n. 6, 242, 255n. 11
Abraham ibn Daud, 33, 39n. 26, 86, 97n. 43
Abravanel, Yehudah (Leone Ebreo), 120, 130, 132
Abulafia, Abraham (kabbalist), 122, 126–28, 130–31, 135n. 26, 139n. 66
Abulafia, Meir (talmudist), 87, 100n. 84
Abulafia, Todros Halevi (poet, Spain, 1247–after 1298), 87, 97n. 44, 126
Adam, 138, 201, 202, 203
Africa, 42, 162, 178, 224, 246, 256, 285; North Africa, 6, 8, 11, 15, 17–18, 22n. 30, 23, 32, 35–36, 38n. 25, 43, 45, 49, 50, 52n. 11, 54n. 23, 55–62, 66, 67, 73n. 15, 79, 83, 105, 131, 140n. 70, 141n. 99, 145, 146, 147, 149, 155, 168, 169, 182, 188, 192n. 21, 194n. 39, 196, 212n. 4, 218, 231, 259, 260, 262, 263, 265, 266, 287, 288, 289, 295, 297, 298nn. 4, 8, 17, 299n. 20, 315
Africans, 18, 240, 242, 245, 248
Al-Andalus. *See* Andalusia; Andalusian
Aleppo, 42, 51n. 5, 104, 183, 218, 260, 268, 270, 281nn. 2, 3, 6
Alexander the Great, 149, 162
AlFasi, R. Isaac (RIF) of Fez (1013–1103), 168, 192n. 21
Algazi, R. Isaac (Turkey, 1889–1951), 273, 283n. 39
Algeria: aliyya from, 181; before and after the Holocaust, 19, 287, 289, 294–96; fleeing from Spanish expulsion to, 35; musical tradition of, 263; in the Ottoman empire, 22n. 27, 149; rabbinic scholars of, 168, 183, 185; waning of Torah in, 180;
Algiers, 168, 178, 294–95
al-Hariri, al-Qasim ibn Ali of Basra (d. 1122), 88, 90, 99n. 66

Al-Harizi, Judah, 12, 84, 90, 91, 98nn. 62, 63, 99n. 66
Ali, Mustafa (16th cent. historian), 150
Alkabetz, Solomon (c. 1505–1584), 154, 197, 206
Alkalai, Judah (Balkan Zionist rabbi), 160
Alliance Israelite Universelle, 50, 61, 73n. 16, 226–230, 234n. 25, 235n. 35
Almohad(s), 32–33, 35, 38n. 25, 39n. 26, 47, 86, 118n. 31, 146
Almoravid(s), 32–33, 39n. 26, 83, 86
Almosnino, Moses (Salonika, c. 1515–1580), 75n. 32, 169, 191n. 6
America: crypto-Jews in North America, 6; European empires in North and South America, 224; Judeo-Arabic in North America, 11, 51; Judezmo in Latin America, 59; Judezmo/Hakitia speakers in North and South America, 62; liturgical music in America, 259, 264; more developed culture of Europe and, 313; place of Sephardic history and culture in American Jewish culture, 286; Sephardic immigration to the Americas, 260–61, 268, 273; twentieth century settlement of Sephardim in North America, 15, 145, 282n. 100
American Jewish Committee, 326
Amoraim (Talmudic masters), 171
Amsterdam: fleeing from Spanish expulsion to, 6, 14; former crypto-Jews in, 75; history of Sephardic Jewish community in, 246–47; Jewish printing houses in, 155; Jewish slaveholders of, 245; messianic frenzy in, 157; Nazi attitudes to Sephardim in, 299; treatment of blacks and mulattos in Sephardic community of, 245–51
Amulet, 223
Ancona, 152

333

Andalusia: cities of, 83; decline in Arabic culture of, 48; defeat of Muslims in, 56; during Muslim persecution, 32, 39n. 26; intelligentia from, 33, 53n. 17, 123; language use in, 77–79, 84, 91, 93n. 2; literary production in, 12, 38n. 17, 77–87, 93, 93n. 2, 96n. 27; Spanish of, 59; symbiosis of Jewish and non-Jewish culture in, 13, 34, 80, 84–85, 99n. 80, 123. *See also* Andalusian

Andalusian: culture, 86, 92, 123; Golden Age, 83, 86, 159; Jewish center for kabbalah, 123; Maimonides as an, 47, 53n. 17; poetry, 53n. 15, 78–88, 96n. 49; refugees, 123, 136; renaissance of 10th and 12th centuries, 120, 128; slavery, 250; tradition in music, 18, 273

antiblack attitudes, 239–40, 245, 253

anti-Jewish legislation, 8, 31, 35, 148, 295–96

anti-Jewish riots, 34, 146

anti-Jewish sentiment, 18, 243, 288

anti-Semitism, 25, 31, 34, 49, 255n. 18, 288, 294–95, 298

Arabic language, 11, 43, 50, 54, 56, 59, 79–80, 101, 115

Arabic poetry, 46, 49, 53–54, 74, 79, 84, 91, 265–66

Arabism, 80

Arabs, 24, 28, 42, 54, 65, 81, 94, 150, 303–5, 307, 317, 323–24

Aristotelianism, 33–34, 121–122, 124, 130

Armenians, 151–52

Aryanization, 293–95

Asher ben Yehiel (rabbi). *See* Rosh

Ashkenaz, 37n. 9, 111, 136n. 29

Ashkenazi, Avraham, 181

Ashkenazi, Bezalel (rabbi), 199, 213n. 18

Ashkenazi, Dan (rabbi), 127, 140n. 72

Ashkenazi, Isaac Luria (AR"I). *See* Luria Ashkenazi, R. Isaac

Ashkenazi, Joseph b. Shalom, 134n. 15

Ashkenazi(c) (Ashkenazim): acculturation compared to Sephardim, 7, 25, 31, 290; Christian persecution of, 24, 25, 31; commentators, 11n. 4; conflict in Israel between Sephardim and, 19, 305, 306, 314, 316–17, 324n. 30; in contrast to Sephardi and Oriental Jews, 4–8, 10, 17, 23, 32; in contrast to Sephardi practices, 8, 39n. 27, 185, 208, 282; establishment in Israel, 19, 37, 304, 305, 307, 313, 319, 324n. 36; great centers of Torah, 169–70; halakhic practices, 7, 32, 37n. 3, 192; and Holocaust, 285–89, 293, 297, 299n. 22; as the Israeli ideal, 19, 22n. 30; and Israeli Labour party, 314, 320; Israeli religious parties and Sephardim, 19, 316, 317; Israeli ultra-Orthodox parties in Israel and Zionism, 324n. 30, 326n. 68; and kabbalah, 122–23, 127, 136n. 29; liturgical music, 154, 262, 264, 277, 281, 282n. 16; Old Yishuv, 184; population in America, 17, 19, 261, 285; rejection of Sephardim, 261, 280; Sephardi cultural dominance over, 21n. 20, 36, 157, 218; Sephardi superiority over, 26, 36–37, 309; Yiddish (culture) and, 42, 55, 261. *See also* Eastern European Jewry

Ashkenocentrism, 286

Asia Minor, 4, 17, 20, 22, 24, 149, 162, 176, 218

assimilation, 7, 22n. 30, 51n. 4, 155, 157, 188, 255n. 18, 290

Athias, David ben Moses, 68

Atlantic slave trade, 239

Auschwitz, 286, 291–94, 298

Averroes (Averroism), 33, 123

Babylonia (Babylonian Jewry), 4–5, 7, 9, 21, 36–37, 51n. 5, 78, 94n. 8, 102, 104–5, 107, 120, 168, 171. *See also* Iraq

Babylonian Talmud, 5, 114, 272

Baghdad, 45, 78, 109–10, 180, 186, 309

Bahir, book of (*Sefer ha-Bahir*), 125, 128–29, 137n. 51, 140n. 80

Balkans, 15, 18, 20n. 12, 22n. 29, 35, 49, 59, 145, 147–49, 151–53, 156, 160–61, 163, 164, 166n. 37, 178, 180, 182, 194n. 37, 218, 222–23, 225, 229–30, 232n. 2, 279, 288

Barbados, 246–48

Barcelona, 35, 73, 75, 124, 126, 130, 139, 146

bar Haim, Eliahu (Turkey, c. 1530–c. 1610), 174

bar Sheshet Perfet, R. Isaac (RIBaSH) (Algiers, 1328–1408), 141n. 95, 168, 191n. 3

Basra (Iraq), 88, 102, 309

Bayazid II (Ottoman Sultan, 1481–1512), 152

Bayonne, 290

Begin, Menachem, 313–14, 319–20, 326n. 54

Beit Yosef, 192n. 14

Belgrade, 66, 69, 75, 293

ben Gershon, Rabbi Levi. *See* Gershonides

Ben-Gurion, David, 303–5, 314, 321, 323nn. 20, 21, 23

Ben Haim, Paul, 279–80

ben Hayyim, Elijah (1530–1610), 170

ben Maimon, Rabbi Moses. *See* Maimonides
ben Nachman, Rabbi Moshe. *See* Nachmanides
ben Yoseph Israeli, R. Yitzhak of Toledo, 170
ben Zemach Duran, R. Shimon (Algiers, 1361–1444), 168, 191n. 3
Biblical exegesis, 12, 18, 42–45, 79, 101–16, 117n. 12, 130, 263
Black Panthers (Israel), 312, 321
blackness, 18, 240–41, 243, 246, 254n. 2
blacks, 18, 239, 240–53, 254nn. 1, 2, 255n. 9
blood libel, 153, 225, 234n. 24
Book of Beliefs and Opinions, The (Emunot veDeot), 52n. 10, 104, 116n. 9, 117n. 23, 118n. 39
Bordeaux, 75, 290
Bosnia, 147, 293
Brazil, 246–49, 255, 257
Bulgaria(n), 22nn. 27, 29, 36, 60, 147, 225, 227, 229, 287, 289, 291–93
Buzaglo, Rabbi David (d. 1975), 273
Byzantine Jews, 36, 148–49, 151, 218, 232n. 3. *See also* Romaniotes (Greek-speaking Jewry)
Byzantium (Byzantine Empire), 23, 27, 29, 78, 131, 147–49, 151, 155–57, 164n. 3, 165n. 7, 168, 260

Cairo (Fostat), 66, 176, 223, 228
Cairo geniza, 26, 29, 38n. 22, 43–44, 51n. 8, 52n. 8, 181
cantillation, 18, 263–64, 282nn. 18, 20
Castilian, 11, 36, 56–62, 67, 72, 86, 91, 127, 137, 162
Catalonia, 121–24, 126, 128–30, 133
Catholic, 7, 8, 23, 24, 32, 33, 34, 35, 89, 135, 146, 152, 193, 239, 250, 253
Catholicism, 8, 34, 35, 91, 99, 146, 243
Cham (biblical character), 242, 247
Christian reconquest of Spain. *See* Reconquista
Christian theology, 123, 211
Christianity, 5, 6, 10, 14, 20, 25, 27, 28, 32, 34, 35, 43, 56, 75, 87, 101, 102, 123, 146, 147, 148, 155, 167, 235, 245
Christians, 9, 14, 24, 25, 26, 27, 28, 29, 31, 32, 33, 36, 38, 44, 48, 59, 77, 78, 86, 93, 101, 136, 145, 146, 147, 150, 154, 155, 156, 157, 160, 162, 186, 221, 225, 234, 243, 244, 245, 246, 251, 255, 260, 282
Constantinople, 147–156, 158, 159, 160, 162, 209, 217

conversion, 5, 10, 14, 24–25, 27, 31–32, 39nn. 26, 28, 91, 110, 158, 167, 177, 209–10, 243, 303
converso(s), 14, 18, 35, 93, 146–47, 155, 199, 211, 220, 222, 239, 242–44, 246, 251, 253, 255n. 14. *See also* crypto-Jews and crypto-Judaism; Marrano(s)
Cordoba, 79, 247
Cordovero, R. Moses of Safed (kabbalist, 1522–1570), 133, 191, 197–99, 213n. 12, 214n. 35
courtier, 26, 33–35, 46, 79
Cracow, 170
Crescas, Hasdai (Spain, 1340–c. 1410), 91, 120–21, 130, 141n. 94
Crete, 4, 151
Croatia, 19, 293
Crusades, 5, 28, 31–32
crypto-Jews and crypto-Judaism, 6, 10, 14, 24, 75n. 30, 245
curse, 223, 240–42, 254n. 2
custom(s) (*minhag*), 7–8, 36, 38n. 16, 61, 64, 105, 138n. 59, 148, 150, 153, 158, 161, 163, 168–69, 174–75, 179, 181, 183, 205, 207, 214n. 40, 215n. 54, 218–20, 224, 233n. 16, 252, 260–61, 305

Damascus, 69, 172, 225
deLeon, R. Moshe (b.1240), 126, 137n. 41
dhimmi, 28–29, 150, 218, 225, 260
Diaspora, Sephardic, 4, 12, 15, 16, 17, 24, 41, 49, 51n. 5, 57, 74n. 23, 93, 138n. 54, 168, 177, 180, 196, 256, 282n. 8
Diaspora mentality, 301, 302, 303, 322n. 8
Dominicans, 14
Donme (Doenmeh), 157, 158, 159, 161, 162, 163, 165, 210, 215n. 58
Dreyfus affair, 228
Dunash ibn Labrat (Spain, b. 920), 46, 79, 94n. 12, 266
Dunash ibn Tamim, (N. Africa, c. 960) 45, 262
Duties of the Heart, The (Hovot haLevavot), 46

Eastern European Jewry, 5, 28, 36, 40, 231, 261, 264, 279–80, 285, 288, 301
Edirne, 66, 148, 151–52, 228
edot ha-mizrach (Oriental Jews), 36
education, 11, 44, 48, 50, 60–61, 115, 160, 180, 192, 199, 208, 216, 222, 226–29, 261, 294, 305, 313, 317, 322
Egypt, 4, 9, 20–22, 32–35, 39, 45–47, 50, 54, 91, 102–4, 120, 124, 146, 149, 176, 181–82, 198, 218,

336 *Index*

Egypt *(continued)*
  230, 234, 242, 255, 263, 266, 305, 308–9, 325–26
emancipation, 15, 17, 25, 38n. 12, 188, 230, 290
emigration, 4, 11, 15, 17, 57–58, 136n. 35, 162, 229, 235
England, 15, 23, 35, 42, 51, 52, 59, 75, 93, 109, 113, 115, 134, 137, 145, 149, 220, 224, 257, 264, 287
Enlightenment, 26, 61, 68, 121
eschatological, 127, 172
esoteric, 16, 121, 123, 126, 128, 136n. 29, 141n. 89, 199, 208, 211, 265
Ethiopians, 240, 247, 251
Europe, 5, 11, 15, 17, 23, 25–26, 28–30, 38, 42, 45–46, 49–50, 55, 58, 60–62, 66, 68, 71, 91, 124, 132, 137, 141, 145, 148–49, 151, 153, 155, 157, 159–61, 169–70, 174, 178–82, 218, 222, 224–25, 228, 230–31, 243, 245–46, 253, 259, 263–65, 285–87, 291, 293, 296–98, 301–2, 313, 323
European Jewish communities, 113, 115, 155
evil, 116
exile and the exiles, 4, 8, 11, 14–16, 20n. 15, 21, 24–26, 32, 35–36, 41, 54n. 24, 58, 63, 66, 71, 80, 83, 104, 123, 125n. 54, 138, 143, 145–47, 149, 153, 155, 157, 163–64, 167–68, 170, 196, 202, 204–6, 220, 243, 247, 254, 302–8, 324–26
expulsion, 3, 5, 7, 11, 14–16, 20n. 9, 21n. 25, 25, 29, 31, 36, 57–67, 71, 73n. 8, 92, 93, 116n. 6, 120, 131–32, 141n. 99 142n. 106, 143, 145–47, 152–53, 167, 170, 196, 203, 212n. 2, 243, 245, 265, 282n. 26

Ferdinand, King, 14, 24, 142, 146, 152
Fez, 67, 168, 191, 266
Final Solution, 289, 291, 297
folk literature, poetry, and tales, 11, 49, 54n. 21, 57, 68, 73, 163, 231n. 1, 234n. 23
folk religion, 222–23, 233
folk songs, 263, 279–80
folktales, 58–59, 64, 74n. 20, 98n. 55, 99n. 80, 100n. 88, 163, 178, 231n. 1, 233n. 15, 284
France, 5, 11–15, 23, 32–35, 37, 42, 50, 55, 59, 64, 67, 101, 109, 111, 113, 115, 123, 126, 145–46, 149, 151, 167, 169, 192, 224, 226, 228, 232, 264, 289, 290, 294–96
French language, 41, 50, 54n. 23, 59–62, 69–70, 73n. 10, 154, 161, 222, 226, 228, 230, 309

Gaonic period, 171
Gaza Strip, 316

Germany, 5, 7, 23, 25, 34, 35, 36, 55, 119, 165, 169, 192, 214, 280, 288, 289, 290, 291, 292, 294
Gerondi, R. Nissim (Spain, 1310–1375), 141n. 95, 192n. 19
Gerondi, R. Yonah, 126
Geronese school, 126
Gershonides (Rabbi Levi ben Gershon, RaLBaG) of Bagnolle (1288–1344), 103
Gikatilla, R. Joseph of Segovia (b. 1248), 124, 126, 135n. 26
Gnosticism, 121
God, 7, 27, 28, 38, 47, 53, 66, 80–81, 85, 91, 95, 104, 109, 112–14, 123–25, 135, 137, 171–72, 174–75, 184, 187, 189, 190, 193, 195, 198, 201, 208, 241, 246–47, 250, 257, 269–73
Golden Age of Spain, 3, 6–7, 9, 11, 13, 25, 29–30, 83, 86, 96n. 28, 159, 265–66, 278, 290
Golden Age of the Ottoman Empire, 259
Granada, 24, 26, 31, 83, 257
Greco-Turkish war, 210
Greece, 4, 19–22, 36, 64, 91, 147–51, 160–62, 165, 176, 194, 196, 218, 278–79, 287–98
Greek Jewry, 154, 160–61, 216–22, 229, 235n. 31, 260–61, 287, 289–93
Greek language, 41, 43, 56, 60–68, 161–62, 216, 221–22, 261, 280, 297
Greek philosophy, 101, 105, 122, 262. *See also* philosophy and philosophers
Greek-speaking Jews. *See* Romaniotes (Greek-speaking Jewry)
Greek War of Independence, 160
Guide of the Perplexed, The (*Moreh Nevukhim*), 47, 53n. 17, 90, 98n. 64, 104, 117n. 11, 121–23, 126, 128, 130, 135, 135n. 25, 136n. 33, 139n. 66

Hakitia, 11, 58, 60, 62, 64, 66, 71, 72, 73
Halachic studies, 105
halakha (Jewish law), 7, 15–16, 108, 126–27, 130, 138n. 57, 154, 167–91, 192n. 23, 193n. 26, 194n. 1, 195n. 1, 197, 200, 208, 217, 239, 243, 249, 253
Ham (biblical character), 240, 241, 242, 254
Hamburg, 284
HaLevi, Hayyim David (1924–1998), 185, 187–88, 195n. 55
HaLevi, Judah (1075–1141), 9, 46, 52n. 14, 79, 83, 84, 92–93, 96n. 27, 118n. 39, 121, 123, 187, 241, 266
Ha-Nagid, Shmuel. *See* Ibn Nagrela, Shmuel
harem, 97n. 50, 154, 220

Hasidic movement, 126, 179, 190
Haskala movement, 50
Hayyim, R. Joseph of Iraq, 186
Hazan, R. Israel Moshe of Egypt (1808–1863), 181, 195n. 60
hazzan (cantor), 264, 266–68, 273, 277
Hebrew grammar and lexicography, 10, 42–43, 45–46, 60, 69, 79, 108, 113, 115
Hebrew language, 7, 8, 10, 12, 26–27, 34, 36–37, 40–42, 44–46, 49–50, 54n. 22, 55–63, 66, 68–70, 77–78, 86, 90–91, 101, 105–6, 108, 111, 115, 146, 153, 170, 177, 180, 221–22, 226–28, 261, 302, 309, 323
Hebrew poetry, 12, 26, 34, 38n. 17, 42, 46–47, 53n. 22, 78–85, 87–95, 265–67, 272, 290
Hellenistic thinking, 122
Hellenization, 161
heresy, 34, 146, 179, 215n. 65
Hermeticism, 127
Hispania, 24
Hispanic culture, 11, 15, 57, 59, 61, 73n. 28, 97n. 42, 145–63, 164n. 2, 165n. 30,
Hispano-Romance, 56, 77, 85, 92
Holland, 6, 14, 15, 59, 145. *See also* Amsterdam
Holocaust (*Shoah*), 15, 17, 19, 22, 25, 145, 285, 286, 289, 292, 297, 298, 299, 320
Hungary, 149, 151

Iamphet, 247
Iberia, 12, 39n. 32, 46–47, 56, 77, 92, 102, 116n. 6, 243–46
Iberian: colonies, 250–53; Jewish culture, 15, 18, 36, 47, 57–58, 84, 145, 164, 254, 255n. 18; Jewry, 9, 48, 56, 58, 71, 155, 163, 217–18, 232n. 2, 247
Iberian peninsula, 6, 8–9, 14–15, 24, 77, 88, 96n. 35, 145–46, 164, 242–43, 260
Ibn Ezra, Moses (Spain, ca. 1055–after 1135), 46, 52n. 12, 79–80, 82–84, 87, 95n. 18, 266
Ibn Ezra, R. Abraham (Spain, 1089–1164), 13, 45–46, 83–84, 96n. 28, 101, 108–15, 117n. 17, 118nn. 31, 32, 121, 123, 127, 241, 266
Ibn Gabirol, Solomon (ca. 1027–57), 9, 12, 46, 77, 81, 83, 85, 86, 93n. 1, 95, 110
Ibn Nagrela, Shmuel (Ha-Nagid) (993–1056), 9, 26, 38n. 17, 46, 81–83, 95n. 22
Ibn Shaprut, Hasdai (905–75), 9, 20n. 15, 46
Ibn Tibbon, Judah, 116n. 10, 123
Ibn Tibbon, Samuel, 98n. 64, 123, 130
Ibn Yahya, Tam (d. 1542), 170

India, 5, 10, 20, 42, 43, 51, 180, 228
Indians, 244, 247, 250, 257
Ingathering of the Exiles, 306–8
Inquisition, 14, 21, 22, 35, 132, 146, 153, 155, 157, 250, 257n. 51
Iran (Persia), 23, 27, 29, 36, 41, 55, 88, 102, 105, 180, 228, 263, 280, 305
Iraq, 4, 20, 36, 42, 45, 49–50, 51n. 5, 54n. 24, 79, 91, 102, 149, 180–183, 186, 194, 230, 263–64, 266, 309, 314–15, 317, 325n. 44
Isaac the Blind (Isaac Sagi Nahor), 121, 125, 126, 129
Isabella, Queen, 14, 24, 146
Ishmael, 28, 77, 94, 117, 177
Islam, 4–6, 9, 20, 23, 25, 27–33, 37–39, 42–44, 51, 54, 56, 81, 94, 101, 106, 110, 117, 134, 146, 150, 154, 158, 162, 165, 177, 209, 260, 303
Islamic civilization, 31, 44, 47
Islamic culture, 44, 120
Islamic law, 26, 29, 30, 150, 155
Islamic legal system, 218
Islamic world, 13, 23, 29, 30, 44, 48, 90
Israel: Ashkenazi influence in, 19, 300–327; author Amos Oz, 319–20; "Black Panthers" in, 312; center of Torah in, 168, 170, 172, 174, 176, 178, 181, 183, 185–86; community in the Land of, 5; concept of the "melting pot," 306, 324nn. 33, 34; concept of returning to, 160, 184, 302, 304; concept of "two Israels," 311; connection of Spanish Jewry to, 141n. 98; ethnic tension in, 301, 304–5, 309, 311–12, 316, 318–19; exile from the Land of, 4, 23, 80, 123; history of, 117n. 12, 119nn. 44, 45, 256n. 28, 305, 307; Iraqi Jews in, 309; Israeli identity and the Israeli ideal, 19, 304, 306, 311, 314–15; Jewish literature written in, 106; Judeo-Arabic culture in, 11, 40–41, 50, 218, 231; Judezmo in, 70–72, 75n. 37; kabbalah and, 131–32, 203, 205; Likud and Labor parties in, 300, 313–16, 319–21; modern Sephardic and Oriental aliyah to/settlement in, 15, 19, 50, 145, 180–81, 185, 230, 235n. 35, 260, 263, 305, 308–9, 311, 320; Moroccan Jews in, 311; "Old Israel" vs. "New Israel," 27–28, 38n. 18; Oriental Democratic Rainbow in, 318, 321; the People of (Israelites or Jews), 80, 94n. 9, 107, 118n. 39, 123, 173, 184, 188, 248, 302, 308–9; poetry about, 38n. 17, 53n. 22, 80–81, 83, 95n. 18; religious customs of, 181, 183, 214n. 40, 281; religious/secular

Israel *(continued)*
tensions in, 316–17; *semikha* (rabbinic ordination) only in, 171–72; Sephardic and Oriental population of, 17, 50, 320; Sephardic identity in, 36, 305, 314–15; Sephardic music and, 64, 271, 273, 279–81, 282n. 15, 282n. 40, 284n. 44, 315; Sephardic/Mizrachi life in State of, 4, 17, 19, 23, 54n. 24, 279–281, 300–327; Sephardic/Mizrahi studies for Jews in, 3; Shas party in, 316–17; significance of treatment of non-Ashkenazi immigrants in, 280, 300–327; sovereignty of, 190; views of Arabs and Arab culture in, 305–7; Wadi Salib uprising in, 311–12; Zionism and Zionist ideology in, 195n. 52, 302, 306–7, 316. *See also* Begin, Menachem; Ben-Gurion, David
Israel, Moshe and Eliyahu (Rhodes), 178
Israeli, Isaac (philosopher), 45, 52n. 11
Israeli culture and society, 17, 19, 36, 45, 50, 52, 54, 141, 170, 195, 284, 300–326
Istanbul, 59, 66, 68, 70–71, 75, 153, 165, 169, 176, 178, 181, 220–34, 255
Italy, 6, 11, 17, 22–23, 35, 55, 58–59, 64, 67, 91, 102–3, 109, 113, 115, 120, 131–32, 142, 146, 152, 154, 169–70, 177, 180, 182, 194, 196, 213, 220, 222, 246, 256, 260, 264, 287, 289, 292, 296
Izmir, 66, 67, 69–70, 147–48, 157, 159, 176, 178, 180, 208

Jahiliya period, 80
Jerba (Tunisia), 180, 182–83, 295
Jerusalem, 20, 24, 26, 32, 37–40, 51–54, 64, 66, 70–76, 81, 93–99, 102, 116–19, 131, 134–42, 146–47, 155, 172, 176, 181–86, 191–95, 205, 212–15, 228, 232–33, 254–55, 258, 281–84, 298, 316, 325–26
Jewish Agency, 308, 309, 325
Jewish communities, 4, 8, 17–18, 20, 32, 36, 42, 102, 109, 113, 115, 118, 131, 146, 151, 155, 160, 163–64, 180, 184, 209, 212, 218, 220, 225, 230, 263, 297, 306
Jewish law. *See halakha* (Jewish law)
Jewish mysticism, 13, 121, 126, 128, 129, 130, 140. *See also* Kabbalah
Jewish nationalism, 80, 160, 230
Jewish philosophy, 13, 120, 121, 123, 125, 129, 130, 131, 133, 134
Jewish settlements, 148, 153
Jewish theology, 45, 123

Jewish women, 16, 154, 216, 217, 220, 221, 222, 223, 227, 228, 229, 230, 232
Judeo-Arabic culture, 10–12, 40–54, 55–59, 71, 74n. 28, 78, 83, 86, 90, 93n. 4
Judeo-Spanish culture, 11, 16, 55–72, 163–64, 217–18, 230–31, 278–81, 298n. 6
Judeo-Spanish language, 11–12, 92–93, 154–55, 161–62, 221–22, 227–30, 261. *See also* Judezmo; Ladino
Judezmo, 11, 58–76, 162
Judezmo literature, 66, 69, 74
Judezmo newspapers, 69–70, 75, 228–31, 290

Kabbalah: Aleppo rabbis and, 183; arrival of Jewish Philosophy and Kabbalah in Spain, 120–22; Hayyim Joseph David Azulai (HIDA, c. 1724–1806) and Eliyyahu of Vilna (the GRA, c. 1720–1797), 178; beginning of, in North Africa, 140n. 70; centerness of, 129–31; as a distinctive Sephardic spiritual creativity under Christiandom, 13–14; "... and Elites in Thirteenth-Century Spain," 139n. 61; encounters between diverse forms of, 140n. 74; first appearance of Spanish, 34; "... Halakhah and Spiritual Leadership," 138n. 57; influence of Maimonides on, 135nn. 21, 23, 136n. 35, 137nn. 38, 43; literary genres and intellectual disparity of, 128–29; Lurianic, 134n. 16; "The Magical and Neo-platonic Interpretations ... ," 136n. 26, 142n. 102; *Messianic Idea*, 22n. 25; Messianic Mythology in Thirteenth Century, 140n. 75; move eastward of Spanish, 131–33; "The Mystical Intention in ... ," 136n. 29; *Origins of the Kabbalah*, 134n. 10; postexpulsion Lurianic, 21n. 25; "Prayer in Provencal ... ," 140n. 83; ... *Provençal, The Emergence of*, 138n. 54; ReMAh and, 170; Rosenzweig and, 134n. 14; Renaissances and, 133n. 3; Safed, and the Sephardic heritage, 196–212; scholarship, beginnings in, 134n. 11; Shabbetai Zvi, 157–58; shifts from philosophy to, 139n. 62; sixteenth-century, sociological approach to, 142n. 103; "Some Forms of Order in," 136n. 28; struggle over the status of, 142n. 56; Spanish, and two West European Renascences, 122–28; as umbrella term for different schools, 133n. 5; Moshe Zacuto (c. 1620–1697) and, 176–77
kadi courts, 216

Kahal, 169, 184–85
Karaites, 13, 21, 45, 101–2, 106–8, 111, 115–16, 151, 157, 161
Karo, Joseph (1488–1575), 8, 154, 170, 172–75, 186, 190, 197, 205, 213n. 8,
Khazar kingdom, 20
Kimchi family from Narbonne, 103
Kimchi, R. David (Radak, 1160–1235), 103
Kimchi, R. Joseph (ca. 1105–70), 103
Kimchi, R. Moshe (died ca. 1190), 103, 113
Kush, 241, 246
Kuzari, 46, 92, 118n. 39, 134n. 17
Kyra, Esther, 154, 165n. 24, 220–21

Ladino, 10–11, 36, 41, 49–50, 54, 58, 60, 65–75, 92, 100, 162, 211, 221–22, 233, 260–61, 278. *See also* Judeo-Spanish culture; Judeo-Spanish language; Judezmo
Latin, 23, 28–29, 33, 38, 44–46, 53, 56–59, 66, 86, 91, 99, 123, 125, 127, 170
Lebanon, 20, 50, 218, 263, 316, 319, 320
Lebanon War, 316
Levantine, 22n. 27, 58, 61, 67, 218, 225, 232n. 2, 264, 302–5
Levantinization, 325n. 38
Libya, 4, 19, 22, 50, 218, 242, 263, 285, 287, 296, 299
Lisbon, 169, 244, 255–56
Lithuania, 5, 169
liturgical music and rite (liturgy), 8, 18, 21, 25, 42, 47–48, 56, 78–79, 93, 94n. 12, 106, 108, 115, 177–78, 205–6, 208, 259–81
Livorno, 67, 157, 179, 195
London, 37, 52–53, 75, 98, 109, 133, 139, 142, 164, 213, 232, 234, 254–57, 281–82
Louis XV, 223
Lublin, 170, 193
Luria Ashkenazi, R. Isaac (AR"I, 1534–1572, Safed), 197–207, 213nn. 15, 17
Luria, Shlomo (MaHaRShaL, 1510–1574), 193n. 26
Lurianic Kabbalah, 21n. 25, 134n. 16, 199–204, 211–12, 214

magic, 51, 127, 130, 132, 139, 142, 199, 223
Maimonidean controversy, 124
Maimonidean philosophy, 124, 131
Maimonides, Abraham (Egypt; 1186–1237), 47, 53n. 17
Maimonides (R. Moshe ben Maimon, Rambam, Spain, 1135–1204, Egypt), 9, 11, 33–34, 39n. 31, 47, 53n. 17, 90, 98n. 64, 104, 108, 117n. 11, 118n. 28, 121–27, 130, 133, 135–37, 146, 170–74, 178, 192n. 21, 241, 250, 253–54
Maimonides synagogue, 223
Mappah (gloss to Shulhan Arukh), 170
maqama(t), 12, 88–91, 97n. 49, 99n. 78, 260, 283n. 34
Marrano(s), 6, 14, 35–36, 152–53. *See also* converso(s); crypto-Jews and crypto-Judaism
martyrdom, 25, 32–33, 35, 37n. 9, 39n. 27
medicine, 9, 26, 33, 45, 146, 148, 153–54, 169, 176, 255n. 9
Medina, 27, 169, 191, 280
Mediterranean, 4, 10–11, 15, 23, 37–39, 58, 61–65, 69, 71, 75, 139, 145, 148–51, 154, 162, 164, 168, 176, 180, 200, 218, 220, 223, 233, 239, 253, 259, 278, 279, 280, 284, 288
Mehmet II, Ottoman Sultan, 149–51, 154
Mendes Nasi, Dona Gracia, 154, 169, 220, 232n. 9
Merkavah, 135
messiah, 27, 67, 104, 133n. 4, 157–61, 171, 174, 177, 194n. 35, 199, 208–10, 213n. 22, 215n. 56, 253. *See also* Sabbatai Sevi (Zevi)
Messianic age or times, 16, 170, 171, 174, 186, 196, 203, 209
messianism, 22n. 25, 39n. 27, 132, 135n. 21, 140n. 75, 158, 170, 199, 204, 208, 212n. 6, 302, 306, 326n. 68
Mimuna, 315, 326n. 61
Mizrahi, R. Eliyahu (c. 1450–1526), 169–70, 191n. 7
Mizrahi Jewry (*mizrahim*), 3–4, 15, 36, 41–42, 260, 267, 277, 306–7, 313, 324n. 29. *See also* Oriental Jews
modernity, 181, 182, 281n. 2, 284n. 41, 327n. 70
modernization, 49, 60–61, 64, 73n. 15, 76n. 41, 161, 180, 224, 287, 297
Mohammed (Mahamad), 248, 249, 250
Molkho, Joseph (Salonika, 18th cent.), 175
Moors, 56, 242, 244, 257
Morocco, 11, 14, 19, 22, 35–36, 39–40, 49–54, 58, 62, 127, 131, 146, 163, 168, 178, 181, 183, 185, 218, 228, 264, 273, 278, 287, 289, 294–96, 305
mulattos, 245, 247–48, 252–57
music, 17, 18, 56, 60, 62, 64, 74, 164, 217, 231, 259–284, 286, 315
Musika Mizrahit (Eastern Music), 280, 284n. 44, 315

Musika Yam Tikhonit Yisraelit (Israeli Mediterranean Music), 280
Muslim conquest, 5, 6, 57
Muslim rule, 5, 6, 9, 12, 26, 32, 156, 217
Muslim women, 223, 229
Muslims, 8, 14, 24, 27–33, 48, 56, 59, 77–78, 84, 93, 136, 137, 145–46, 152, 154, 156, 158, 160, 162, 218–21, 225, 243, 260, 282, 294, 295, 297
muwashshah, 93, 96–97
mysticism, 13–14, 21n. 25, 56, 69, 121–22, 126–30, 134n. 16, 135, 137n. 51, 138, 139, 140n. 74, 141, 158, 167, 180, 213n. 11

Nachmanides (Rabbi Moshe ben Nachman, RaMBaN) of Gerona (1194–1274 Acre), 87, 103, 114, 124–26, 128–29, 138n. 57, 141n. 89
Nagid, Shmuel ha-. *See* Ibn Nagrela, Shmuel
Nasi, Dona Gracia Mendes. *See* Mendes Nasi, Dona Gracia
Nasi, Joseph (Duke of Naxos), 153, 220
Nathan of Gaza, 137, 208, 209
Navarre, 109, 147
Nazism, 70, 162, 228, 285–99
Neoplatonic, 45–46, 81, 129, 132, 136, 142
Neoplatonism, 95, 121, 130, 133, 135
Netherlands, 38–39, 51–52, 97, 117, 119, 136, 140, 224, 232, 256, 258, 264
Noah (biblical character), 240–46, 254
Nuremburg Laws, 291, 293

Obadiah (biblical book), 23–24, 37, 147
Operation Torch, 295, 297
oriental culture, 17, 19, 60, 101, 115, 263, 305, 307
Oriental Democratic Rainbow, 318–19, 321
Oriental Jews, 4–7, 17, 19, 20n. 7, 21n. 20, 41, 182, 260, 300–327
orientalism, 36, 303–4, 306, 308, 315, 319, 321–25
Orientalist, 303–4, 306–8, 319
Ottoman, 6, 10–11, 14–20, 35–36, 39, 54, 58–62, 66–69, 75–76, 131, 142, 145–74, 183, 191, 196, 209, 216–43, 255, 259–60, 281–82
Ovadia Yosef (rabbi). *See* Yosef, R. Ovadiah

Palestine, 19–20, 32–37, 78, 104, 141, 149, 160, 162, 184, 218, 226, 230, 265, 279, 282, 301–4, 325
Passover, 63, 66, 141, 186, 204–5, 208–9, 292, 326
Persia. *See* Iran
philology, 94n. 13, 101, 115, 118n. 41, 139n. 68
philosophy and philosophers, 7, 9, 10, 13, 24, 26, 32–34, 42, 44–47, 56, 67–68, 77–81, 83, 86, 90, 95n. 19, 101–10, 115–16, 120–42, 163, 170, 176, 240, 262, 302n. 9
physicians. *See* medicine
poetry, 37, 47, 53, 78–79, 87, 94–97, 283
Poland, 5, 23, 169, 170, 286
Portugal, 6, 35, 48, 103, 147, 163–64, 168–69, 220, 224, 239, 242–46, 251, 255–56
prayer, 74, 136–37, 140, 203, 215, 283
prophecy, 116, 135
Provence, 12, 34, 42, 86, 90, 98, 101, 103, 109, 121–24, 128, 136–37, 147
Purim, 63, 227, 260

Queen Isabella and King Ferdinand. *See* Ferdinand, King; Isabella, Queen

Rambam. *See* Maimonides
Rashi, (R. Shelomo Yitzhaki), 110–12, 114, 169, 241, 290
Recife (Brazil), 255
Reconquista, 11–12, 24, 32–34, 56, 86
Reform movement, 280
Renaissance era, 103
responsa, 37, 193–95
Rhodes, 36, 148, 178, 231n. 1, 233n. 19, 266
Rif. *See* AlFasi, R. Isaac (RIF) of Fez
Romance languages, 11, 57–58
Romaniot language, 57, 72n. 4
Romaniotes (Greek-speaking Jewry), 36, 155, 157, 161, 169, 218, 232, 260–61
Rome, 5, 24, 27, 102, 134, 264
Rosh (Rabbi Asher ben Yehiel, Germany, 1250–1327, Spain), 20n. 14, 119, 173, 174, 192nn. 21, 23
Rumania, 147
Russia, 17, 36, 149, 159, 302

Saadia Gaon, Rav (882–942), 13, 45, 52n. 11, 78, 94n. 8, 101–15, 116n. 9, 262
Sabbatai Sevi (Zevi), 67, 194n. 35, 208–11, 215
Sabbatean activities and movement, 137n. 46, 177, 208, 210, 211, 212, 214n. 33
Sabbath, 63, 154, 157, 197, 199–200, 203, 205–6, 214n. 43, 251, 253, 265, 267, 273, 280, 283
sabra (Israeli) image, 22n. 30, 311
Sabra and Shatilah massacre, 319
Safed, 16, 21, 131–32, 147–52, 154, 170, 172, 174, 176, 192, 196–200, 204–8, 212–15, 266–67
Safed Kabbalah, 196, 208

Salonika (Thessaloniki), 66, 68, 70, 73–74, 147–55, 158–62, 165–66, 169, 175–76, 191, 193, 210, 228–29, 266, 287, 290–91, 298
Sanhedrin (high court), 171
Sefarad, 53, 72, 94, 95, 96, 97, 100, 124, 212
Sefer Yetzira (*The Book of Creation*), 45, 126
Sem (biblical character), 247
semikha (rabbinical ordination), 170–74
Sephardic and Ashkenazi Jewry, distinctions between, 5–10, 16–17, 23–24, 27–31, 37n. 3, 40, 43, 55–56
Sephardic and Mizrahi/Oriental Jewry, distinctions between, 5–6, 9, 23–24, 36, 48, 55–56
Sephardic biblical commentary (exegesis), 12–13, 42, 45, 68, 79, 101–16
Sephardic community, in Ottoman Empire, 15–18, 35–36, 39n. 33, 58–59, 66–70, 131
Sephardic culture: achievements of, 9, 13, 26, 46; in Christian Spain, 33–34, 39n. 32, 56, 86–93, 120; flowering of, 6–7, 9, 25, 29, 31, 46, 58, 77, 79, 120; and identity in Israel, 19; impact of modernity on, 17, 48–50, 61, 64, 68, 73n. 15, 76n. 41; influence of the Alliance Israelite Universelle on, 61, 73n. 16; influence of Arab Muslim culture on, 13–14, 25–28, 30–31, 33, 35, 44, 56, 77, 79–80, 88, 101, 120, 123, 136n. 35; influence in Morocco, 36, 58, 141n. 99; influence in Ottoman territories, 36, 48, 58–59, 66–67, 142n. 100; material culture of, 56–57, 60–61, 73n. 13; openness to secular subjects, 7, 12, 14, 44, 61–62, 80; origins of, 3, 5–6, 9–10, 23–37, 56, 72n. 5; roots in medieval Arab culture, 10, 12, 18, 33–34; revival of, 15; tolerance within, 6–7, 16, 25; women and 16–17, 145, 168, 180, 181, 226, 280, 286, 290. *See also* Judeo-Arabic culture; Judeo-Spanish culture
Sephardic dispersion and Diaspora, 4, 7, 11, 14–16, 21n. 25, 24, 32, 35, 48–50, 56–58, 61, 67, 71, 117n. 31, 120, 131–32, 142n. 106
Sephardic *halakha* (law): attitude towards martyrdom, 32; development of, 15, 42, 56; influenced by Islamic jurisprudence, 26; rulings of Rabbi Joseph Caro, 8
Sephardic heritage, 9, 19, 56, 72n. 6, 212n. 2
Sephardic Jewry (Sephardim): acculturation of, 12, 25–26, 29–31, 44, 61–62, 93, 136n. 35; assimilation by, 7, 15, 70; attitudes towards race and blacks, 17–18; definition of Sephardic and Mizrahi Jewry, 4–6, 9–10;

23–24, 36; diminished prominence of, 17, 48, 120; distinctiveness of, 6–7, 9, 18, 24, 55–56, 71, 77, 79; economic life of, 28–30, 35, 48, 69; edict of expulsion from Spain, 14, 24, 35–36, 57, 71, 132; effects of WWII and Holocaust on, 11, 15, 17, 19, 69; historical influence of, 9–10; messianic speculations within, 16, 39n. 27, 132; nationalism of, 12, 46, 64, 79; rulings of Rabbi Joseph Caro and, 8; self-identity, 17–18, 26; status as *dhimmi*, 28–30
Sephardic kabbalah and mysticism, 13, 16, 21n. 25, 34, 47, 56, 69, 120–32, 133n. 9, 134n. 10, 135n. 23
Sephardic literature, 12, 34, 42, 46, 50, 57, 63, 69, 74n. 23, 77–93, 104, 122, 132, 246
Sephardic music and liturgy, 8, 17–18, 36, 42, 45, 47–48, 56, 60, 63, 73n. 26, 78, 93, 106
Sephardic philosophy, 9, 13, 26, 33, 45–46, 56, 81, 86, 101, 103–7, 110, 115, 120–32
Sephardic physicians and scientists, 33, 45, 47, 110
Sephardic poetry and song, 9, 12–13, 26–27, 34, 42, 46–47, 49, 56–57, 60, 63–64, 67, 78–90, 94nn. 5, 12, 13, 95n. 25, 96nn. 30, 37, 97n. 47, 108–10, 113. *See also maqama(t)*
Sephardic political leadership, 9, 19, 25–26, 33–34, 36, 46, 116n. 6
Sephardic pride, 9–10, 17–18, 26, 47, 53n. 17; "myth of Sephardic supremacy," 10, 26, 36–37, 38n. 14
Sephardic proverbs, sayings, and folktales, 64–65, 68, 74nn. 20, 21, 88, 92, 100n. 88
Sephardic rabbinic leadership: involvement with kabbalah, 16; knowledge of secular subjects, 7, 45–46; of Mizrahi Jewry also, 21n. 20, 48; scholarship of, 14, 16, 45–46, 67–68, 78, 103, 107–8
Sephardic Talmudic study, 34, 46, 167
Sephardic tradition, 176, 262, 273, 277, 278
Sephardic translators and translation, 13, 33, 86, 90, 92, 105–6, 108, 116n. 10, 123, 126
Sephardic/Mizrahi customs, 8
Sephardic/Mizrahi demography, 17, 71
Sephardic/Mizrahi history: apostasy and crypto-Judaism in, 10, 14, 32, 35; "myth of the interfaith utopia," 26, 31–32, 37; overview, 8–10, 21nn. 16, 24, 22n. 29, 23–25, 32–36, 72n. 6; persecutions, 14, 25–26, 30–32, 34–35; the Shoah in, 19; three major parts, 3–4

342 Index

Sephardic/Mizrahi languages, 40–41, 55, 61–69, 72n. 6, 73n. 15, 77, 92; Hakitia, 11, 58, 60, 62, 64, 66, 71, 72, 73; Hebrew, 12, 27, 36, 40, 42, 45–46, 48–50, 63, 77–80, 86–87, 93, 94n. 13, 105, 108, 113; Judeo-Arabic, 10, 26, 40–51, 53n. 17, 55–57, 77–88, 104; Judeo-Spanish (Judezmo), 11, 36, 56–71, 74n. 23, 76n. 42, 85, 91–92, 100n. 87. *See also* Hakitia; Hebrew language; Judeo-Arabic culture; Judeo-Spanish culture; Judezmo
Sephardic/Mizrahi life in the State of Israel, 4, 17, 19, 75n. 37
Sephardic/Mizrahi studies, significance of the field, 3, 73n. 6
Serbia, 19, 293
Seville, 100, 146, 250
Shas Party in Israel, 316
Shekhinah, 202–6
Sheshet, R. Yitzhak. *See* bar Sheshet Perfet, R. Isaac
Shulhan Arukh (Code of Jewish Law), 8, 154, 170–80, 183, 187, 190, 192n. 14, 193n. 26, 279
Sicily, 151–52, 169
slaves, 247, 253, 255, 257
Slavic, 55, 60, 73
Soviet Jewry, 286
Soviet Union, 36, 286, 289
Spain, 3, 20nn. 14, 15, 21nn. 17, 24, 25, 37nn. 5, 6, 8, 39nn. 30, 32; after the exile from, 36; Abravanel and the Expulsion of the Jews from, 116n. 6; anti-Jewish sentiment, 243; Arabic-Jewish language from India to, 42; arrival of Jewish mysticism and Kabbalah to, 128–29; Bahya Ibn Paquda in, 46; Bible exegesis, 101–2; Catholic/Christian and Muslim, 32–35; Christian, Jewish poetry in, 87; conversion and exile from, 146–47, 196; culture of Sephardic Jews out of, 71; emigration from, 15; expulsion from 6, 14; Hispano-Romance, 77; Ibero-Romance in, 63, 65, 66; ibn Ezra left, 118n. 31; influence on other Jewries, 10; interactions of Jews, Christians, and Muslims, 145–46; Jewish Castilian, 72n. 5; Jewish history and culture in, 7–16; "... Jewish Life in Islamic ... ," 53n. 16; Jewish philosophy and Kabbalah in, 120–21, 123, 133n. 1, 136n. 35, 137n. 42, 139n. 61, 140n. 75, 142n. 106; Kabbalah during the Jewish expulsion from, 131; Judeo dialects, 91–93; Judeo-Spanish culture in, 56–59; linguistic link with the Jews of Babylonia, 9; Lurianic Kabbalah and the expulsion from, 203; Muslim, Hebrew poetry in, 53n. 15, 78, 94nn. 5, 9, 12, 95n. 25, 97n. 47; the "myth of Sephardic superiority," 37; origin of Sephardic Jewry in, 23–26; Ottoman empire and the expelled Jews from, 152–64, 164n. 1, 170; relationship between the Spanish and the Italian Kabbalah, 131–32; seeds of the destruction of the Jewish community in, 13; Sephardic Liturgical Music in, 259, 262–63, 265–66, 271, 278, 282nn. 9, 26; Sephardim and blacks, 257nn. 45, 46; shift of the Jewish centers from, 167–69, 191n. 1, 192nn. 19, 21; sixteenth-century spiritual revolution in Safed and the descendants from, 16; translating Arabic texts into Latin in, 86; woman in the Ottoman Empire upon leaving, 217–24
Spanish and Portuguese Jewry, 170
Spanish language, 155, 163, 217, 221, 227
Spinoza, Baruch (Benedict), 130
St. Augustine, 27
Synod of Dordt, 249
Syria, 4, 20, 35–36, 51, 104, 149, 182–83, 209, 218, 255, 263, 281

Taitatzak, Joseph (c. 1480–c. 1540), 169
Talmud, 5, 7–8, 21, 42, 46, 78, 112, 114, 117, 119, 137, 167, 176, 192–94, 208, 228, 272, 279
Tannaitic times, 170
Tanzimat Reforms, 219, 225
Taqqanot, 74n. 27, 168
Tetragrammaton, 208
Thessaloniki. *See* Salonika (Thessaloniki)
tikkun (repair), 201
Tosafot, 167, 173, 192, 193n. 26
Trani, Joseph, 176
translation, 74, 97–99, 140, 213, 269, 271
Tunisia, 19, 22, 45, 50, 180, 218, 263, 285, 287, 289, 294–96, 298
Turkey, 4, 22, 35, 36, 49, 64, 70–71, 91, 131, 151, 152, 174, 178, 180, 182, 191, 194, 196, 209, 223, 230–35, 263, 273, 278, 283, 288
Turkish, 18, 60–65, 69–70, 73, 149, 153–54, 158, 161–62, 172, 176, 210, 218, 221, 222, 227–34, 261, 267, 273, 277, 279, 280–81

Ustasa (fascists of Croatia), 293–94, 297

Venice, 67, 131, 157, 170
Vichy regime, 289, 294–96
Vital, Hayyim, 198–201, 205, 213n. 20

Wadi Salib (uprising) in Israel, 311, 312, 325
West Bank, 316
West India Company, 247
women, 16–17, 26, 38n. 17, 49, 53, 54n. 21, 63, 89, 92, 96n. 35, 154, 184–85, 190, 195n. 54, 216–35, 248, 252, 278, 293, 318

Yemen and Yemenite Jewry, 20, 36, 42, 49, 91, 105–6, 118n. 28, 262–63, 266, 277, 279–80, 306
Yeshiva, 61, 104–5, 117, 169–70, 172, 176, 178–79, 183, 189, 250–51

Yiddish, 10–11, 26, 40–42, 49–55, 58, 67, 74–75, 211, 261, 290, 297
Yishuv, 75, 184–85, 303, 308
Yitzhaki, R. Shelomo. *See* Rashi
Yom Kippur, 205, 210, 313
Yom Kippur War, 313
Yosef, R. Ovadiah (b. 1924), 16, 183–86, 195, 316–17, 327n. 70
Young Turk Revolution, 225
Yugoslavia, 19, 22, 36, 73, 293, 297

Zionism and Zionists, 36–37, 46, 49, 70, 184, 195, 263, 301–7, 320–26
Zohar, The Book of the (Book of Splendor), 15, 34, 69, 121, 127, 131, 137, 140, 167, 194–200, 204–7, 214, 280
Zoroastrians, 44

www.ingramcontent.com/pod-product-compliance
Lightning Source LLC
Chambersburg PA
CBHW032026290426
44110CB00012B/683